french
classical

by Byron Jacobs

EVERYMAN CHESS

Published by Everyman Publishers plc, London

First published in 2001 by Everyman Publishers plc, formerly Cadogan Books plc, Gloucester Mansions, 140A Shaftesbury Avenue, London WC2H 8HD

British Library Cataloguing-in-Publication Data
A catalogue record for this book is available from the British Library.

ISBN 1 85744 232 6

Distributed in North America by The Globe Pequot Press, P.O Box 480, 246 Goose Lane, Guilford, CT 06437-0480.

All other sales enquiries should be directed to Everyman Chess, Gloucester Mansions, 140A Shaftesbury Avenue, London WC2H 8HD
tel: 020 7539 7600 fax: 020 7379 4060
email: dan@everyman.uk.com
website: www.everyman.uk.com

The Everyman Chess Opening Guides were designed and developed by First Rank Publishing.

EVERYMAN CHESS SERIES (formerly Cadogan Chess)
Chief advisor: Garry Kasparov
Commissioning editor: Byron Jacobs

Typeset and edited by First Rank Publishing, Brighton.
Production by Book Production Services.
Printed and bound in Great Britain by The Cromwell Press Ltd., Trowbridge, Wiltshire.

CONTENTS

1 e4 e6 2 d4 d5 3 ♘c3 ♞f6

BIBLIOGRAPHY

Books

Baker, C. *A Startling Chess Opening Repertoire* (Cadogan 1998)
Gufeld,E. & Stetsko, O. *The Classical French* (Batsford 1999)
Harding, T.D. *The Classical French* (Batsford 1991)
Krnic, Z. et al. *Encyclopaedia of Chess Openings Volume C, 4th edition* (Sahovski Informator 2000)
Nunn, J., Burgess, G., Emms, J. & Gallagher, J. *Nunn's Chess Openings* (Everyman/Gambit 1999)
Watson, J. *Play the French* (Cadogan 1996)

Periodicals

British Chess Magazine
Chess Informant
Correspondence Chess (BCCA)
New in Chess Yearbooks

Databases

ChessBase Mega Database 2001
Chess Informant
Mega Corr (ed. Harding, T.D.)

INTRODUCTION

It is well known that in chess different openings can wander in and out of fashion, the style often being set by the world champion and other players at the top of the chess tree. A case in point is the King's Indian Defence. While the great strategist Anatoly Karpov was world champion in the late 1970s and early 1980s, this slightly risky opening was a rare guest at the highest levels. However, then along came Garry Kasparov who, with his ferocious attacking play, demonstrated that the King's Indian was a perfectly viable defence for Black. Suddenly this opening was all the rage and everyone was playing it. Then, in the late 1990s Kasparov lost interest, switching to other defences against 1 d4, and suddenly enthusiasm for the King's Indian waned again.

The French Classical (1 e4 e6 2 d4 d5 3 ♘c3 ♘f6) has not always been at the forefront of theoretical debate, but is currently extremely popular. For example, at the recent Astana tournament in Kazakhstan, featuring Kasparov, Kramnik, Shirov, Gelfand and Morozevich, the French Classical was seen in three of the 30 games played. Another recent world class gathering was seen at the tournament in Leon, where players are allowed access to computer software and databases during play. In that event, where the competitors were Anand, Shirov, Topalov and Leko, the French Classical accounted for three out of just 14 games.

One of the reasons that this line is suddenly being seen so much more often is that I sense that many top grandmasters are becoming slightly bored with playing the Sicilian. The Sicilian has for a long time been regarded as the 'correct' reply to 1 e4, creating dynamic positions where Black has a sound structure. The problem is that, if White so wishes, play can easily become ferociously complex. Thus a number of top players are starting to use the French more and more as a means of obtaining unbalanced positions but avoiding the horrendous complications that are often a hallmark of the Sicilian Defence.

The French Classical fits in well with this modern desire to create dynamic counterchances as Black but to start off from a sound base. For a long time the Classical was possibly seen as a poor relation of the Winawer variation (1 e4 e6 2 d4 d5 3 ♘c3 ♗b4), where Black invariably doubles White's c-pawns, but at the cost of the bishop pair and with a resultant weakening of the dark squares. Black certainly gets counterplay in the Winawer but he has to reconcile himself to taking on a number of weaknesses in order to do so. The Classical variation is an altogether more solid choice.

I hope that an examination of the games in this book will prove useful even for players who do not expect to play these lines that often. The reason is that most of the games here see the creation of a central situation where White has pawns on d4 and e5 facing black pawns on d5 and e6. Such closed centres can arise from numerous different openings, such as Sicilians, Caro-Kanns and even Pirc and Modern Defences. The plans and strategies that are employed in the games in this book may well prove helpful in obtaining an understanding of certain positions that can arise in those openings.

I would like to thank Jonathan Tait as well as grandmasters Nigel Davies and Glenn Flear, all of whom have made excellent contributions to the material here.

Byron Jacobs,
Sussex,
July 2001

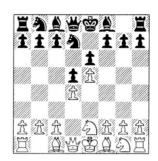

CHAPTER ONE

Modern Main Line
with 4 e5 ♘fd7 5 ♘ce2

1 e4 e6 2 d4 d5 3 ♘c3 ♘f6 4 e5 ♘fd7 5 ♘ce2

In subsequent chapters we will see how White is happy to play the position by allowing an exchange of pawns on d4 in situations where he is obliged to recapture with a piece. By playing 5 ♘ce2, White adopts a different tack. He decides that, at whatever cost, he is determined to maintain central pawns on d4 and e5, thus 5 ♘ce2 prepares to play c2-c3 and White will (usually) meet ...f7-f6 with f2-f4. The plan is to take time in the early part of the game to stifle Black's attempts at counterplay and then exploit the powerful centre and extra space at a later date.

Nevertheless, 5 ♘ce2 has very obvious drawbacks and is not the kind of move you would recommend to a beginner. Let's examine its merits objectively: White has only one piece developed and decides to move it again; the knight was perfectly well placed on c3 – it is clearly less happy on e2 where it obstructs White's development by completely blocking in the f1-bishop and also hampers the queen and king's knight.

However, it is important to bear in mind that the position is blocked and, of course, a loss of time is much less serious in a closed position. Furthermore, White's strong

centre is persuasive compensation for the shortcomings of the move 5 ♘ce2. In the French Black is often reliant on the breaks ...c7-c5 and ...f7-f6 to prise open the white centre and generate counterplay. Here, although these moves may be useful for Black in terms of file opening, neither will actually directly undermine White's centre. In fact, White's pawns on d4 and e5 can often prove so suffocating for Black that he feels obliged to resort to hefty material sacrifices such as ...♘dxe5 to blow the position open. The resulting positions are very double-edged. When it goes wrong for White he can find himself minus two pawns, way behind in development with no centre and his king wandering around in the middle of the board. In such circumstances a mere piece can seem paltry compensation. For those of a nervous disposition, it is also possible for Black to play more circumspectly and look for counterplay with queenside pawn advances.

I have given substantial coverage to this variation, since over the past couple of years it has been subject to extensive tests at the highest level. It is a particular favourite of Viswanathan Anand, who seems to win every single game he plays with it. His favourite opponent is Alexei Shirov, whom he has played three times in this line. The fiery ex-Latvian tries a different defensive set-up in every game, but just gets blown away time after time.

In Games 1-6 we see Black adopting a straightforward queenside counterattacking plan with 5...c5 6 c3 ♘c6 7 f4 ♕b6, whereas in Games 7-9 Black prefers pawn play with 7...b5. Game 10 sees White declining to form the large pawn centre, preferring instead 7 ♘f3. Finally, in Games 11-13 Black delays the development of his queen's knight in favour of the immediate central attack 6...cxd4 7 cxd4 f6.

Note that the variation seen in Games 1-6 (5...c5 6 c3 ♘c6 7 f4 ♕b6), and also others in this chapter, can arise from the following line in the Tarrasch Defence: 1 e4 e6 2 d4 d5 3 ♘d2 ♘f6 4 e5 ♘fd7 5 c3 c5 6 f4 ♘c6 7 ♘df3 ♕b6. Here if White plays ♘e2, either immediately or in the near future, a direct transposition is possible (although, curiously, the knights have reversed themselves – it is now the king's knight which is on e2 and the queen's knight on f3). However, in the Tarrasch route, the white knight is not yet committed to e2 and White often exploits this fact to play ♗d3, or to delay the placing of the kingside minor pieces altogether in favour of moves such as h2-h4, g2-g3 or even ♔f2.

Game 1
Anand-Shirov
FIDE Knockout, Tehran 2000

---

1 e4 e6 2 d4 d5 3 ♘c3 ♘f6 4 e5 ♘fd7 5 ♘ce2 c5 6 f4 ♘c6 7 c3 ♕b6 8 ♘f3 f6

For 8...♗e7 see Games 4 and 5, while 8...a5 is the subject of Game 6.

9 a3

An important little move which prevents the highly annoying ...♗b4+ and also creates the possibility of b2-b4, gaining space on the queenside. The inferior 9 g3 is the subject of Game 3.

9...♗e7

Black's alternatives here are considered in the next main game.

10 h4

A remarkable move, calmly preparing to develop the king's rook whilst still behind in development. However, this move does also clamp down on the kingside and thus inhibits the advance ...g7-g5 which is often useful for Black in undermining the white centre. As we shall see in the next main game, White also has a couple of other moves here.

10...0-0 11 ♖h3

'Knights before bishops' is a well-known piece of advice for those starting out in the game. 'Rooks before bishops' is another concept altogether.

11...a5 12 b3

Preventing Black's ...a5-a4, which he could follow up with ...♘a5 securing a powerful clamp on the queenside.

12...♕c7

12...♕d8 is seen in the next game.

13 ♘eg1

This bizarre-looking move leads to a strange position where White has moved seven of his pawns and only developed two pieces. Meanwhile Black has mobilised most of his forces and seems well prepared for action in the centre. However, it is not all doom and gloom for White: he has a very strong centre and good attacking chances on the kingside. Left to his own devices he will complete his development when he will have a promising kingside initiative. Shirov therefore opts for a sacrifice of a piece in an attempt to maximise the advantages of his position. Note that White's text move is the best as 13 ♘g3? gets blown away by 13...cxd4 14 cxd4 fxe5 15 fxe5 ♘dxe5! and White is in big trouble, mainly due to the hanging rook on a1.

13...a4 14 b4 fxe5

A more circumspect approach is 14...cxd4 15 cxd4 f5 16 ♗b2 (this is a little slow; the immediate 16 ♘g5, possibly intending ♗d3 and g2-g4, looks more to the point) 16...♘b6 17 ♘g5 ♗xg5 18 hxg5 ♕f7 19 ♖c1 ♗d7 20 ♖cc3 g6 21 ♖h6 ♖ac8 22 ♖c5 ♘a7 23 ♖a5 ♖a8 24 ♖c5 ♖ac8 25 ♖a5 ♖a8 26 ♖c5 ♖ac8 ½-½ Kuczynski-Zaragatski, German League 2001.

15 fxe5 ♘dxe5

Black launches in with a typical piece sacrifice for such positions.

16 dxe5 ♘xe5 17 ♘xe5 ♕xe5+ 18 ♕e2 ♗xh4+ 19 ♔d1

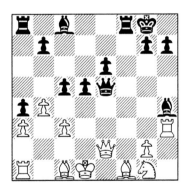

Not 19 ♖xh4 ♕xc3+.

19...♕f6??

This move is based on a horrible miscalculation after which Black is lost. Much better was 19...♕xe2+ 20 ♗xe2 ♗f2 leading to an interesting endgame with balanced chances.

20 ♘f3 ♕xc3 21 ♗b2 ♕b3+ 22 ♔c1

If Black could now simply retreat his bishop he would have nothing to complain about. However, White not only attacks the bishop on h4 but is also threatening ♘d2, trapping the black queen. Black has no decent way to deal with these two threats and must resign himself to jettisoning a further piece.

22...e5

If 22...♗f6 23 ♗xf6 ♖xf6 24 ♘d2 and the queen goes.

23 ♖xh4 ♗f5 24 ♕d1 e4 25 ♕xb3 axb3 26 ♘d2 e3 27 ♘f3 ♖ae8 28 ♔d1 c4

Black's horde of passed pawns look impressive, but White has two extra pieces and good control of the dark squares.

29 ♗e2 ♗e4 30 ♔c1 ♖e6 31 ♗c3 ♖g6 32 ♖h2 ♗d3 33 ♗xd3 cxd3 34 ♔b2 d2 35 ♔xb3 ♖g3 36 ♔b2 g5 37 ♔c2 ♖c8 38 ♔d3 g4 39 ♗e5 ♖c1 40 ♖h1 ♖xg2 41 ♘h4 1-0

> ## Game 2
> ## Sakaev-Bareev
> *Elista 1998*

1 e4 e6 2 d4 d5 3 ♘c3 ♘f6 4 e5 ♘fd7 5 ♘ce2 c5 6 c3 ♘c6 7 f4 ♕b6 8 ♘f3 f6 9 a3 ♗e7

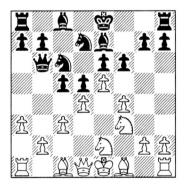

Immediate queenside action with 9...a5 is also possible: 10 g4 (White may be better advised to settle for the more restrained 10 g3, e.g. 10...♗e7 11 ♗h3 f5 12 g4 0-0 13 0-0

a4 14 ♔h1 ♚h8 15 ♖g1 cxd4 16 cxd4 ♕d8
17 ♕e1 ♘b6 18 gxf5 exf5 19 ♗e3 with
good play in Mateo-Prakken, Ubeda 2000)
10...♗e7 11 ♗g2 0-0 12 ♕d3 (this is too
slow) 12...cxd4 13 cxd4 fxe5 14 fxe5 ♖xf3!
(a highly thematic sacrifice which leads to
the rapid dismantling of the white centre)
15 ♗xf3 ♘dxe5 16 dxe5 ♘xe5 17 ♕e3 (one
point of Black's play is 17 ♕c3 d4! 18 ♘xd4
♕xd4 19 ♕xd4 ♘xf3+ 20 ♔f2 ♘xd4 with a
winning position) 17...♕xe3 18 ♗xe3
♘xf3+ 19 ♔f2 ♘e5 20 ♗d4 ♘xg4+ 21 ♔g3
♘h6 22 ♗e5 ♘f7 23 ♗c7 e5 with a
fabulous position for Black who won
quickly in Sendur-Kaidanov, Istanbul 2000.

10 h4

Others:

a) 10 f5!? is a typically random
Morozevich move which led to wild play in
Morozevich-Gleizerov, Alushta 1993, viz.
10...cxd4 11 fxe6 ♘dxe5 12 ♘fxd4 ♗c5 13
♘f4 ♘xd4 (instead of this, 13...♗xd4 14
cxd4 ♕xd4 looks pretty solid for Black; it is
difficult to see how White can justify his
play in this position) 14 cxd4 ♗xd4 15
♕a4+ ♘c6 16 ♗d3 g5 17 ♘h5 ♔d8 18 h4
♗xe6 19 hxg5 fxg5 20 ♗xg5+ ♔d7 21 ♘f6+
and White went on to win.

b) 10 b4 cxb4 11 cxb4 a5 12 b5!? (White
gives up a pawn in return for several tempi)
12...♕xb5 13 ♘c3 ♕b6 14 ♖b1 ♕d8 15
♗d3 f5 16 h3 h5 17 ♖g1 h4 18 ♔f1 ♘f8 19
♕c2 with reasonable play for the pawn in
Lanka-Glek, Zillertal 1993.

10...0-0 11 ♖h3 a5 12 b3 ♕d8 13 ♘g3

An alternative idea to placing the knight
on g1 as in the previous game. From g3 the
knight can often hop to the h5-square.

13...h6

Others possibilities here are:

a) 13...♘b6 14 ♗d3 f5 15 ♗c2 ♗d7 16
♗e3 cxd4 17 cxd4 a4 18 b4 ♘a7 19 ♘h5
♗e8 20 ♘g5 ♕c8 21 ♖c1 ♘c4 with a tense
position in Smirin-Psakhis, Las Vegas 1999.

b) 13...cxd4 14 cxd4 ♘b6 15 ♗d3 f5 16
♘e2 (White temporarily abandons his

pretensions towards a kingside attack and
relocates his forces on the queenside) 16...a4
17 b4 ♗d7 18 ♘c3 ♘a7 19 ♗b2 ♕e8 20
♖c1 ♖c8 21 ♘d2 with a balanced position
in Brodsky-Dgebuadze, Wijk aan Zee 2001.

**14 ♗e3 f5 15 ♗d3 cxd4 16 cxd4 ♘b6
17 ♘h5**

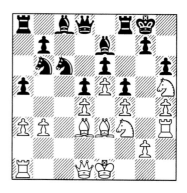

17...♕e8

A remarkable variation given by Finkel is
17...a4 18 ♖g3 ♗xh4? (18...♖f7!?) 19 ♘xh4
♕xh4 20 ♗f2! ♔h8 21 ♖xg7 ♕h1+ 22 ♗f1
axb3 23 ♖g3! and White wins. It can be
surprisingly easy for White to whip up an
attack on the kingside despite Black having
blocked the position with ...f7-f5.

18 ♘h2 g6 19 ♘f6+

White is obliged to sacrifice a pawn as 19
♘g3 h5 spells the end of his initiative on
the kingside.

**19...♗xf6 20 exf6 ♘d7 21 h5 ♘xf6 22
hxg6 ♕xg6 23 g4**

White heads for an endgame where he
maintains good chances, despite his pawn
minus, as his pieces are so active.

**23...♘xg4 24 ♘xg4 ♕xg4 25 ♕xg4+
fxg4 26 ♖xh6 ♘e7 27 ♔d2 ♖f7 28 ♗f2
♖g7 29 ♖ah1 g3 30 ♖h8+ ♔f7 31 ♗e1
g2 32 ♖g1 b6 33 ♗h4 ♗b7 34 ♖xa8
♗xa8 35 ♗g5 ♘f5**

This is a mistake. After 35...♘c6! 36 ♔e3
e5 37 dxe5 ♘xe5 38 ♗e2 d4+ 39 ♔xd4
♘f3+ 40 ♗xf3 ♗xf3 the position is
completely equal.

36 ♗xf5 exf5 37 ♖xg2 ♔e6 38 ♖h2

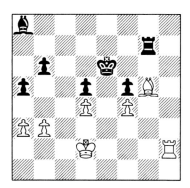

38...♔d7

Now Black has some problems to solve as his pieces are passive and his pawns are weak. Bareev sensibly decides to jettison a pawn to activate his forces, after which he has little trouble maintaining the balance.
39 ♖h6 ♗c6 40 ♖f6 ♖h7 41 ♖xf5 ♖h2+ 42 ♔e1 a4

Sacrificing a further pawn to build a fortress.
43 bxa4 ♗xa4 44 ♖xd5+ ♔c6 45 ♖e5 ♗b3 46 f5 ♖h5 47 f6 ♖h7 48 ♔f2 ♖d7

Black now has a rock solid structure and White cannot make any progress.
49 ♖e3 ♗f7 50 ♖c3+ ♔d5 51 ♔e3 ♖a7 52 ♗f4 ♔e6 53 ♗e5 ♔f5 54 ♔d2 ♖a4 55 ♖f3+ ♔e6 56 ♖b3 ♔f5 57 ♖f3+ ♔e6 58 ♖c3 ♔f5 59 ♖h3 b5 60 ♖h7 ♔e6 61 ♖h3 ♔f5 62 ♖f3+ ♔e4 63 ♖g3 ♔f5 64 ♔c2 b4 65 axb4 ♖xb4 66 ♖g7 ♖b7 67 ♔d3 ♖b3+ 68 ♔d2 ♖b2+ 69 ♔e3 ♖b3+ 70 ♔f2 ♔e6 71 ♖h7 ♖a3 72 ♖h8 ♔f5 73 ♖d8 ♖a7 74 ♔g3 ♗e6 75 ♖e8 ♗f7 76 ♖b8 ♖d7 77 ♖b1 ♖d8 78 ♖b7 ♖f8 79 ♔f2 ♔g6 80 ♔e3 ♖h8 81 ♖b1 ♖h3+ 82 ♔f4 ♖h4+ 83 ♔g3 ♖e4 84 ♖g1 ♔f5 85 ♖h1 ♖e3+ 86 ♔f2 ♖xe5 87 dxe5 ♔xe5 88 ♔e3 ♔xf6 89 ♔f4 ♔g7 90 ♔g5 ♗g8 91 ♖b1 ♗d5 92 ♖b5 ♗c4 93 ♖b7+ ♔h8 94 ♔f6 ♔g8 95 ♖d7 ♗b3 96 ♖d2 ♗c4 97 ♖f2 ♗d5 98 ♖c2 ♗e4 99 ♖c5 ♗d3 100 ♖a5 ♗c2 101 ♖a8+ ♔h7

102 ♖h8+ ½-½

Game 3
Dolmatov-Bareev
Elista 1997

1 e4 e6 2 d4 d5 3 ♘c3 ♘f6 4 e5 ♘fd7 5 f4 c5 6 ♘f3 ♘c6 7 ♘e2 ♕b6 8 c3 f6 9 g3?!

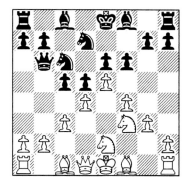

This move just does not seem to work. The problem is not particularly that White is wasting important development time with pawn moves (he frequently does that in this variation) but that this move creates weakness along the f-file. This drawback will become abundantly clear in the subsequent play.
9...cxd4 10 cxd4

Although supporting the centre like this is thematic, it doesn't work out well for White as the black initiative is just too strong. White would do better to change plans and try 10 ♘exd4 fxe5 11 fxe5, although it will only be equal, e.g. 11...♘xd4 (not 11...♘dxe5 12 ♘xe5 ♘xe5 13 ♕h5+ ♘g6 14 ♗d3) 12 cxd4 ♗b4+ 13 ♔f2 0-0 14 ♔g2 ♗e7 15 ♗d3 ♖f7 16 h4 ♘f8 17 ♘g5 ♗xg5 18 hxg5 g6 with a balanced position in Psakhis-Dizdar, Zagreb 1993.
10...fxe5 11 fxe5 ♗b4+ 12 ♘c3 0-0 13 ♗f4 ♗e7 14 ♕d2

This is clearly refuted by Black but the position is already difficult. Other examples:

a) 14 ♘a4 ♛a5+ 15 ♘c3 ♛b6 16 ♘a4. This is not the most ambitious way to handle the position, but in Jaracz-Gleizerov, Katowice 1991, Black declined White's tacit peace offer and went on to win after 16...♛d8 17 ♗d3 ♘b6 18 0-0 ♘xa4 19 ♛xa4 ♗d7 20 ♛c2 h6 21 ♛d2 ♗e8 22 h3 ♗b4 23 ♛h2 ♘e7 24 a3 ♗a5 25 ♗e3 ♗g6 26 ♗xg6 ♘xg6 27 ♖ac1 ♗b6.

b) 14 ♗h3 ♛xb2 15 ♛c1 ♛xc1+ 16 ♖xc1 ♘b6 17 ♘b5 ♘d8 18 ♘c7 ♖b8 19 0-0 (White is trying to generate an initiative in the endgame but his forces are easily repulsed) 19...h6 20 ♗d2 ♘c4 21 ♗c3 b5 22 ♘h4 ♖xf1+ 23 ♗xf1 ♖b7 and Black soon won in Anand-Sisniega, Philadelphia 1987.

14...g5!

A thematic blow which seriously undermines White's centre. The weaknesses along the f-file are now seriously apparent.

15 ♘xg5 ♗xg5 16 ♗xg5 ♘xd4

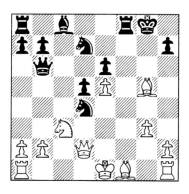

17 ♗g2

Remarkably, this position had already occurred nearly 100 years previously. In Alapin-Maroczy, Vienna 1908, White tried his luck in the endgame after 17 0-0-0 ♘f3 18 ♗e3 ♘xd2 19 ♗xb6 axb6 20 ♖xd2 ♘xe5 21 ♗h3 ♘c6 22 b3, but that proved to be pretty hopeless too.

17...♘xe5 18 0-0-0 ♖f2!

A triumphant and thematic invasion along the f-file.

19 ♛xf2 ♘b3+ 20 axb3 ♛xf2 21 ♖d2 ♛f5 22 ♗h6 ♘d3+ 23 ♔b1 ♘f2+ 0-1

Game 4
Anand-Shirov
Frankfurt 2000

1 e4 e6 2 d4 d5 3 ♘c3 ♘f6 4 e5 ♘fd7 5 ♘ce2 c5 6 c3 ♘c6 7 f4 ♛b6 8 ♘f3 ♗e7 9 a3

For 9 g3 see Game 5.

9...0-0 10 h4

Again White adopts the familiar plan of h2-h4 and ♖h3.

10...f6 11 ♖h3 ♘a5

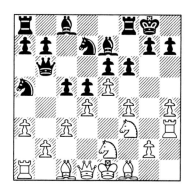

Black wants to gain squares for his pieces on the queenside, but this move takes the pressure off d4 completely.

12 b4 cxb4 13 axb4 ♘c4 14 ♘g3 a5

This looks promising for Black, but the pin along the a-file means that he will have to waste more time before developing a serious initiative on the queenside.

15 ♗d3 f5

If Black tries to open the centre he falls foul to a typical combination: 15...fxe5 16 ♗xh7+ ♔xh7 17 ♘g5+ ♗xg5 (if 17...♔g8 18 ♛h5 ♘f6 19 ♛g6 and Black is helpless against ♘h5) 18 hxg5+ ♔g8 19 ♛h5 and wins.

16 ♘g5 ♖d8

If 16...♗xg5 17 hxg5 ♖d8 intending to meet 18 ♛h5 with 18...♘f8, White can play

18 ♘h5 maintaining a strong attack. White has possibilities such as g2-g4, prising open the kingside or maybe even ♘f6+.

17 ♕h5 ♗xg5

Now, as we saw previously 18 hxg5 is reasonably well countered by 18...♘f8 but White has a better recapture...

18 ♕xg5 ♖f8

The black rook has to come scurrying back to deal with the threat of ♘h5.

19 ♘h5 ♖f7 20 ♖g3 g6

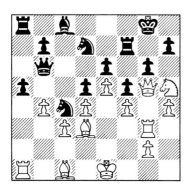

21 ♗xc4!

Now to add to Black's woes the white dark-squared bishop enters the game.

21...dxc4 22 b5 ♕xb5 23 ♗a3 b6 24 ♕h6 ♗b7 25 ♖xg6+ hxg6 26 ♕xg6+ ♔h8 27 ♕xf7 ♖g8 28 ♗f8! 1-0

28 ♘f6 was also sufficient, but this is a very elegant conclusion. After 28...♘xf8 29 ♘f6 forces checkmate.

Game 5
Lalic-Speelman
Hastings 2000

---

1 e4 e6 2 d4 d5 3 ♘c3 ♘f6 4 e5 ♘fd7 5 ♘ce2 c5 6 c3 ♘c6 7 f4 ♕b6 8 ♘f3 ♗e7 9 g3

This move has been the popular interpretation of how White should handle this position for many years but, in view of the recent games with h2-h4 and ♖h3, it now looks a little slow.

9...a5 10 h4

Instead 10 ♗h3 ♕a6 11 0-0 ♘b6 12 dxc5 ♗xc5+ 13 ♘ed4 ♗d7 14 ♖f2 g6 15 a4 ♘c8 16 ♗e3 ♕b6 17 ♗f1 ♘8e7 18 ♗d3 ♘xd4 19 ♗xd4 h5 led to a draw in the game Plaskett-Karolyi, Graz 1978.

10...a4 11 ♗h3

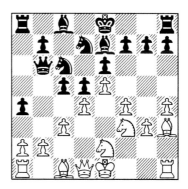

11...♘db8!?

Speelman, as is often the case, finds a new plan in the opening. Rather than trying to blunt White's kingside aspirations with a combination of ...f7-f6 and/or ...f7-f5, he allows White a free hand in that sector in the interests of developing his own play on the other wing. As you might assume, this is a double-edged strategy.

12 h5 cxd4 13 cxd4 ♗d7 14 0-0 ♘a5 15 ♘c3 ♘c4 16 f5 ♘xb2 17 ♕e2 a3

Black creates a secure, albeit unusual, outpost for his knight on b2. It may have been possible to bring the knight back into the action with 17...♘c4, but a continuation such as 18 f6 gxf6 19 exf6 ♗xf6 20 ♘xd5 ♗xd4+ 21 ♔h2 ♕c5 22 ♘xd4 ♕xd5 23 ♘f5 gives White tremendous play for his material.

18 f6 gxf6 19 exf6 ♗d6 20 ♗h6?

This amounts to a critical loss of a tempo after which Black activates his entire position. White had to try 20 ♘xd5 ♕b5 21 ♘f4 ♗xf4 22 ♕xb5 ♗xb5 23 ♗xf4 ♗xf1 24 ♖xf1 when his bishop pair, lead in development and the generally disorganised nature of the black position give him excellent play for the exchange.

20...♘c6

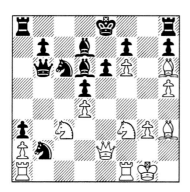

Now the pressure against d4 swings the game Black's way.

21 ♔h1?

White caves in completely. Finkel offers the variation 21 ♘xd5 ♘xd4! 22 ♘xb6 ♘xe2+ 23 ♔f2 ♗c5+ 24 ♗e3 ♗xb6 25 ♗xb6 ♘c3 but Black has all the chances.

21...♘xd4 22 ♕e3 ♗c5 23 ♗g7 ♘f5 24 ♕g5 h6 25 ♘xd5 hxg5 26 ♘xb6 ♖xh5

Earlier in the game it would have been hard to anticipate that Black's rook would play a key role by becoming active along the h-file.

27 ♘xa8 ♖xh3+ 28 ♔g2 ♖xg3+ 29 ♔h2 ♗d6 0-1

Game 6
Arakhamia-Volkov
Isle of Man 2000

---

1 e4 e6 2 d4 d5 3 ♘c3 ♘f6 4 e5 ♘fd7 5 ♘ce2 c5 6 c3 ♘c6 7 f4 ♕b6 8 ♘f3 a5

In this game we see Black again declining to advance his own f-pawn and relying on his own queenside play to balance the chances. This method of handling the position has been seen often in the games of the young Russian Grandmaster, Alexander Volkov.

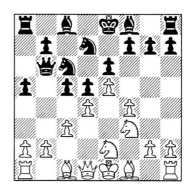

9 a3

Volkov provides all the other practical experiences for Black in this position:

a) 9 g3 has led to a couple of quick draws, viz. 9...a4 10 ♗h3 cxd4 11 cxd4 a3 12 b3 ♗b4+ 13 ♔f2 ♘db8 and now:

a1) 14 ♗e3 ♗d7 15 g4 h5 16 gxh5 ♖xh5 17 ♗f1 ♘e7 18 ♘g3 ♖h8 19 ♖c1 ♘bc6 20 h4 0-0-0 21 ♗d3 ♔b8 22 ♗b1 ½-½ Khalifman-Volkov, St Petersburg 1999.

a2) 14 ♔g2 ♘a6 15 ♗e3 ♗d7 16 ♖c1 ♗e7 17 ♘c3 ♘ab4 18 ♕d2 ♕a5 19 ♘a4 b6 ½-½ Ulibin-Volkov, Krasnodar 1998.

b) 9 a4!? is a rarely seen idea but is well worth a look. White gives away the b4-square but he usually has to make some sort of concession on the queenside in these variations anyway. By advancing the a-pawn he at least gains some space on the queen's wing and prevents Black having matters entirely his own way there. Another Volkov game saw 9...♗e7 10 g3 (obviously the familiar idea of h2-h4 and ♖h3 also comes into consideration) 10...0-0 11 ♗h3 cxd4 12 cxd4 f6!? (this sacrifice is another of the devices at Black's disposal for generating counterplay in these positions) 13 ♗xe6+ ♔h8 14 exf6 (a computer would be highly tempted to go 'all in' here with 14 ♗xd5 fxe5 15 fxe5, when it is not easy to see how Black can develop sufficient play to justify his two-pawn deficit) 14...♗b4+ 15 ♘c3 ♘xf6 16 ♗xc8 ♖e8+ 17 ♔f2 ♗xc3 18 bxc3

♖axc8 (Gorin-Volkov, Bydgoszcz 2000). Black's lead in development and the weakness of White's light squares offer him reasonable play for the pawn.

9...a4 10 h4 ♖a7

A very provocative move that encourages White into an immediate demonstration of force. The point of 10...♖a7 is that Black would like to develop his queenside play with ...♘a5 but, if played at once, this move drops a pawn after 10...♘a5 11 ♕xa4. Volkov therefore protects his rook so that after, say, 11 ♖h3 ♘a5, 12 ♕xa4? becomes impossible due to 12...♘b3. He may also have been thinking that this rook might come in handy one day for defending along the seventh rank.

11 f5 exf5 12 ♘f4 cxd4 13 cxd4 ♕a5+ 14 ♗d2 ♕d8 15 ♗d3

15 ♘xd5 is well met by 15...♘dxe5.

15...♘b6 16 ♕c2 g6 17 h5 g5 18 ♘e2 f4 19 ♗xh7 ♘c4 20 ♗f5?

This lands White in trouble. The more restrained 20 ♗d3 was called for when the position is unclear.

20...g4 21 ♘g5!?

21 ♘fg1 ♘xd2 22 ♔xd2 (22 ♗xc8 ♘b3 23 ♗xb7 ♕a5+ is strong) 22...f3 was rather unpalatable for White, so she decides to mix things up.

21...♕xg5 22 ♗xc8

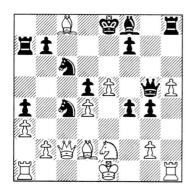

22...♘xd2?

White's imaginative play pays off as this

move allows the white queen to invade the black position and generate sufficient play to force a draw. There was nothing wrong with the simple 22...♖xh5 23 ♖xh5 ♕xh5 and White is in a bad way. One satisfying feature of the black position here is that the rook on a7 performs a crucial role in defending the b7-pawn!

23 ♗xb7

Volkov must have underestimated this move.

23...♘e7

After 23...♖xb7 24 ♕xc6+ Black should acquiesce in a draw by perpetual check with 24...♖d7 25 ♕c8+ ♖d8 26 ♕c6+ ♖d7.

24 ♕c7 ♖xb7

Forced as the threat of ♕b8+ had to be dealt with somehow.

25 ♕xb7 ♘c4 26 ♕a8+

A sneaky way to force a draw here is 26 ♘xf4 ♕xf4 27 ♕b8+ ♘c8. The point of White's play is that (27...♔d7 drops the queen after 28 e6+) 28 ♕xc8+ ♔e7 29 ♕c7+ ♔e6 30 ♕c8+ with a perpetual.

26...♔d7 27 ♕xa4+ ♔e6 28 ♕a6+ ♔f5 29 ♘g3+

This move is good enough to hold the balance, but unfortunately for White she follows it up incorrectly. It was also possible to play the position in a slightly calmer way with 29 b3 ♘e3 30 ♕d3+ ♔e6 31 g3 when matters remain completely obscure although White is probably not worse.

29...fxg3 30 0-0+

Someone who gets excited about such things may want to scan a large database to discover if this is the latest example of castling with check in a tournament game.

30...♔e4 31 ♖ae1+?

A further example to add to the case histories of 'the wrong rook'. After 31 ♖fe1+ ♘e3 32 ♖ad1 Black has nothing better than 32...♔f5 33 ♕d3+ ♔e6 34 ♖xe3 ♕xh5 35 ♕a6+ with another perpetual check.

31...♘e3

Now unfortunately, White's initiative is at an end.

32 ♕e2 ♖xh5 33 ♕c2+ ♔xd4 34 ♕c3+ ♔e4 35 ♕c2+ ♔xe5 36 ♕c7+ ♔e6 37 ♕xg3 ♗h6 38 ♕c7 f5 39 ♕b6+ ♔f7 40 ♖f2 g3 0-1

Game 7
Anand-Shirov
Leon 2000

This game was played under the curious conditions that both players had access to computer software and databases during play.

1 e4 e6 2 d4 d5 3 ♘c3 ♘f6 4 e5 ♘fd7 5 ♘ce2 c5 6 c3 ♘c6 7 f4 b5

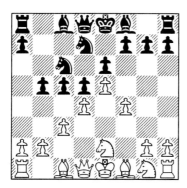

Black decides to take the initiative on the queenside with pawn rather than piece play. Since lines are now clearly going to opened quickly on the queenside it would be overly ambitious of White to attempt to carry out an attacking plan on the kingside with moves we have seen before such as h2-h4 and ♖h3. Anand therefore joins in with the battle on the queenside and proves that White is well placed to meet Black's advances there.

8 a3

A useful move which, as well as inhibiting ...b5-b4, prevents a potentially annoying ...♗b4+. 8 ♘f3 is seen in Game 9.

8...cxd4

For 8...c4 see the next game.

9 ♘xd4 ♘xd4 10 cxd4 b4 11 a4

11 ♕a4 seems less testing for Black, e.g. 11...a5 (11...♕b6 led to an edge for White after 12 ♘f3 bxa3 13 bxa3 ♖b8 14 ♗d3 ♕b3 15 ♕xb3 ♖xb3 16 ♔e2 ♗e7 17 ♗d2 in A.Sokolov-Glek, Moscow 1992) 12 ♘f3 ♕b6 13 ♗b5 ♖b8 14 ♗c6 ♗e7 15 ♗d2 ♕d8 16 axb4 ♗xb4 17 ♗xb4 ♖xb4 18 ♕xa5 ♕xa5 19 ♖xa5 ♖xb2 20 ♗xd7+ ♔xd7 21 0-0 ♗b7 and the endgame was equal in Lanka-Lempert, Hyeres 1992.

11...♕a5

Shirov has himself experienced the white side of this variation: 11...♘b6 12 ♘f3 ♗e7 13 b3 a5 14 ♗b5+ ♘d7 15 0-0 ♗a6 16 ♗xa6 ♖xa6 17 ♕d3 ♖c6 18 ♗d2 0-0 19 ♖ac1 ♘b8 20 f5 and White had a promising position although Black held on to the draw in Shirov-Korchnoi, Lucerne 1993.

12 ♗d2 ♗e7 13 ♘f3 0-0?!

After this Black ends up losing a tempo whilst carrying out the ....♗a6 manoeuvre. It was therefore better to play 13...♗a6 immediately.

14 ♗b5!

The pressure on the knight on d7 is a nuisance for Black as if 14...a6?! 15 ♗d3 and Black is no longer able to exchange the light-squared bishops. White will have a free hand on the kingside.

14...♘b6 15 b3

White avoids castling as he already has his eye on the coming endgame.

15...♗a6 16 ♗xa6 ♕xa6 17 a5 ♘d7

Black has achieved his desired bishop exchange but it has cost him more time than it needed to. White has used this extra time to expose the advanced black b-pawn.

18 ♕e2 ♘b8

After 18...♕xe2+ 19 ♔xe2 ♖ac8 20 ♖hc1 White will continue with ♘e1-d3 when defence of the b-pawn could prove problematic for Black.

19 ♔f2 ♕xe2+ 20 ♔xe2 ♘c6 21 ♖hc1 ♖fc8

Black has obtained greater protection for his b-pawn but now his knight will be subject to an uncomfortable pin.

22 ♖a2 ♖c7 23 ♖ac2 ♖ac8 24 a6

This is a key moment for Black who has to decide whether to prevent White's coming f4-f5 advance by playing the move himself.

24...♔f8

24...f5 is certainly possible. After 25 exf6 gxf6 26 g4 White maintains an edge.

25 g4 ♔e8 26 f5 ♔d7 27 ♗f4 g5?

Shirov loses patience and creates a horrible weakness in his kingside. Also bad was 27...♘a5 28 ♖xc7+ ♖xc7 29 ♖xc7+ ♔xc7 30 f6 ♗f8 31 ♘g5 but Black could have continued to resist with 27...g6.

28 ♗e3 h6 29 f6 ♗f8 30 ♔d3

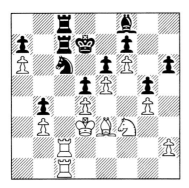

30...♘a5?!

After this White wins easily. Shirov could have forced his opponent to conclude the game accurately by playing 30...♖b8 31 ♖a1! (but not 31 ♘xg5? hxg5 32 ♗xg5 ♖b6 33 h4 ♖xa6 34 h5 ♖a3 35 ♖b2 ♘a5 36 ♖xc7+ ♔xc7 37 ♔c2 ♖a1 38 ♗c1 ♘c6 and Black wins) 31...♖b6 32 ♘xg5 hxg5 33 ♗xg5 ♘b8 34 ♖xc7+ ♔xc7 35 h4 ♘xa6 36 ♗d2 when Black has no counterplay and the h-pawn will inevitably roll up the board (variations given by Finkel).

31 ♖xc7+ ♖xc7 32 ♖xc7+ ♔xc7 33 ♘xg5! hxg5 34 ♗xg5 ♘xb3 35 h4 ♘a1 36 ♗c1 ♘b3 37 ♗e3 ♘a5 38 g5 ♘c4

39 ♗c1 1-0

Game 8
Anand-Morozevich
Frankfurt 2000

---

1 e4 e6 2 d4 d5 3 ♘c3 ♘f6 4 e5 ♘fd7 5 ♘ce2 c5 6 c3 ♘c6 7 f4 b5 8 a3 c4?!

Morozevich is a fantastically talented player who often comes up with highly original ideas in the opening. However, closing the centre this early is rarely a good idea for Black in the French and so it proves in this game.

9 ♘f3 ♘b6 10 g4

White gets on with it. It will be a very long time before Black can generate serious play on the other wing.

10...f5 11 gxf5 exf5 12 ♗g2

This is not the most energetic continuation. White should probably prefer 12 h4 ♗e7 13 h5. It is a curious feature of these variations that White often does not need to worry overly about completing development but can successfully pursue his initiative with his pieces all posted on the back rank.

12...♗e7 13 0-0 h6 14 ♖f2 ♗e6 15 ♗f1 g5

Morozevich is not a player who likes to sit still, but this is going too far. Although White's king will now be stripped of pawn protection, he has a huge preponderance of pieces nearby and Black has little opportunity to create trouble there. Meanwhile, Black's advanced pawns will now become a source of weakness.

16 fxg5 hxg5 17 h4!

A bold decision, but a correct one.

17...g4

This leads to a hardening of the arteries in Black's position. A better chance was 17...gxh4 18 ♘f4 when play might go 18...♕d7 19 ♗h3 0-0-0 20 ♘xe6 ♕xe6 21 ♘g5 ♕g8 22 ♖xf5 ♔b8 23 ♔h2 and White is on top.

18 ♘g5 ♗c8 19 ♖h2 a5 20 ♘g3 ♖a6 21 ♗e3 ♘a4

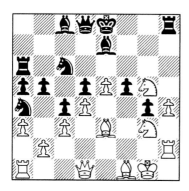

22 ♕c2

White remorselessly targets the weakling on f5.

22...♖f8 23 ♖f2 ♕d7 24 e6 1-0

Game 9
Finkel-Meessen
Budapest 1996

---

1 e4 e6 2 d4 d5 3 ♘c3 ♘f6 4 e5 ♘fd7 5 ♘ce2 c5 6 c3 ♘c6 7 f4 b5 8 ♘f3 b4

Black takes immediate advantage of White's omission of 8 a3.

9 f5

White presses on but Black is quite well placed to meet this. Probably better is 9 g4 bxc3 10 bxc3 ♕a5 11 ♔f2 ♗a6 12 ♗d2 ♘b6 with an unclear position in Mortensen-Schussler, Vejstrup 1989.

9...exf5

A very solid alternative for Black is 9...bxc3 10 fxe6 fxe6 11 bxc3 cxd4 12 cxd4 ♗b4+ 13 ♗d2 0-0 14 ♗xb4 ♘xb4 15 ♕d2 ♕a5 16 ♔f2 ♘b6 and a draw was agreed in Sax-Korchnoi, Wijk aan Zee 1991.

10 ♘f4 cxd4

10...bxc3 is playable but risky for Black, e.g. 11 bxc3 cxd4 12 ♗b5 ♕a5 13 ♘xd5 ♘e7 and now 14 ♕b3 has been seen in two games: 14... a6 15 ♘g5 axb5 16 ♘c7+ ♔d8 17 ♘xa8 ♘xe5 18 ♗f4 (or 18 0-0 h6 19

♘xf7+ ♘xf7 20 ♕xf7 ♕xa8 21 ♖d1 ♘d5 and Black was well on top in A.Hernandez-J.Sequera, Valencia 2000) 18...♘d3+ 19 ♔d2 ♘xf4 20 ♘xf7+ ♔e8 21 ♘xh8 ♕xa8 22 ♖ae1 ♕xg2+ 23 ♔c1 ♕d5 and Black won easily in Lagua-Orlov, Chicago 1991. However, 14 ♕xd4 appears to be much more dangerous for Black, e.g. 14...♘xd5 15 ♕xd5 ♕xc3+ 16 ♔d1 ♕xa1 17 ♘g5 and White will regain the rook with a strong attack.

11 cxd4 ♘b6 12 ♗b5 ♗d7 13 e6!?

White pummels his way forward.

13...fxe6 14 ♘xe6 ♕c8

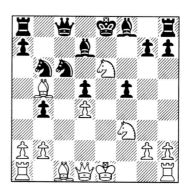

This is preferable to 14...♕e7? 15 0-0 when the knight on e6 is still immune and White has a very powerful initiative.

15 ♘c5?!

This is over-ambitious. The best plan was the simple 15 ♘xf8 ♔xf8 16 0-0 with decent compensation for the pawn.

15...♘xd4 16 ♘xd7 ♘xb5 17 ♕e2+

Again a better plan was 17 ♘xf8 ♔xf8 18 0-0, although now White is two pawns down which will be hard for him to justify.

17...♔xd7 18 ♕xb5+ ♔c7 19 ♗e3 ♕e8

Now Black is just winning, although he makes a complete hash of the ending with two extra pawns and nearly ends up worse.

20 ♕e2 ♘c4 21 ♗d4 ♗d6 22 b3 ♕xe2+ 23 ♔xe2 ♖he8+ 24 ♔d3 ♘e5+ 25 ♘xe5 ♗xe5 26 ♖ac1+ ♔b7 27 ♖c5 ♗xd4 28 ♔xd4 ♖e4+ 29 ♔d3 ♖ae8 30 ♖xd5

♖e3+ 31 ♔c4 ♖3e4+ 32 ♔b5 a6+ 33 ♔a5 ♖8e5 34 ♖hd1 ♖xd5+ 35 ♖xd5 ♖e2 36 ♖d7+ ♔c6 37 ♖xg7 ♖xa2+ 38 ♔xb4 a5+ 39 ♔c4 ♖e2 40 ♖g5 ♖e1

I suspect that the score of the game may not be entirely accurate here as this leaves the f-pawn en prise and White inexplicably fails to take it.

41 ♔d3 ♖g1 42 ♖xf5 ♖xg2 43 ♖h5 ♖a2 44 ♔c3 a4 45 b4 ♖f2 46 ♖xh7 ½-½

Game 10
Hort-Knaak
Dresden 1995

---

1 e4 e6 2 d4 d5 3 ♘c3 ♘f6 4 e5 ♘fd7 5 ♘ce2 c5 6 c3 ♘c6 7 ♘f3

White declines to set up the large centre with 7 f4, relying instead on pure piece play. However, the evidence is that this approach should not be unduly worrying for Black.

7...cxd4 8 cxd4 f6

Black gets the thematic break in before White has a chance to hold it up with ♘f4 (eyeing the e6-square).

9 ♘f4

9 exf6 ♘xf6 10 ♘c3 transposes directly into Nijboer-Glek (see Game 13), which is unexciting for White.

9...♕e7

Another perfectly acceptable continuation for Black is 9...♗b4+ 10 ♗d2 ♕e7 11 ♗xb4 ♕xb4+ 12 ♕d2 ♕e7 (the endgame after 12...♕e7 13 exf6+ gxf6 14 ♕xb4+ ♘xb4 15 ♔d2 ♘b6 16 a3 ♘c6 17 ♗b5 ♗d7 18 ♗xc6 ♗xc6 19 ♖he1 ♗d7 20 b3 ♔d6 as in Shirov-Ivanchuk, Tilburg 1993, is fine for Black.) 13 exf6 ♘xf6 14 ♗d3 ♘e4 15 ♕e3 ♕b4+ 16 ♔f1 0-0 17 ♖e1 ♕xb2 18 ♗xe4 dxe4 19 ♕xe4 ♕xa2 with an unclear position in Velimirovic-Moskalenko, Belgrade 1988.

10 exf6 ♕xf6

Or 10...♘xf6 11 ♘d3 ♕c7 12 g3 ♗d6 13 ♗g2 0-0 14 0-0 ♗d7 15 ♗f4 (White has gained control of the dark squares, but

Black still has an active position and good counterplay) 15...♗e8 16 ♘c5 ♘d8 17 ♗e5 ♗h5 18 ♖c1 ♕e7 19 ♕a4 ♗xc5 20 dxc5 ♘e4 with a balanced position in Jerez-Jimenez, Albacete 2000.

11 a3 ♗d6 12 ♘h5 ♕e7 13 ♘g3 0-0 14 ♗g5 ♘f6

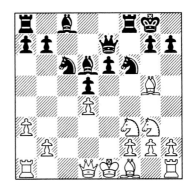

Equal.

15 ♗e2 h6

Black had a good opportunity here for the thematic advance 15...e5, e.g. 16 dxe5 ♘xe5 17 ♘xe5 ♗xe5 18 ♕d2 and now 18...♗e6 is a simple continuation or Black can be more ambitious with 18...h6 19 ♗e3 d4 20 ♗xd4 ♖d8 21 ♗c5 ♕c7 with good play for the pawn (21...♖xd2 22 ♗xe7 ♖xb2 is also fine).

16 ♗d2 ♗d7 17 0-0 a6

This move serves little purpose. More natural is 16...♗e8 to relocate the bishop on a better diagonal.

18 ♗d3 ♘g4

Black is playing as if he stands better and should be looking to take the initiative. In fact the position is about equal and so again the simple 17...♗e8 is called for. Black tries to get something going on the kingside but merely ends up getting his pieces in a tangle.

19 ♗c3 ♕f6

This move cuts off the retreat square for the g4-knight but Black is trusting that the tactics will favour him. However, this turns out to be a forlorn hope. Admittedly White

cannot immediately exploit the position of the knight as 20 h3 ♘xf2 21 ♔xf2 ♕h4 is good for Black... but there is no hurry.
20 ♗c2 ♘e7 21 ♕d3 g6 22 a4 ♖f7

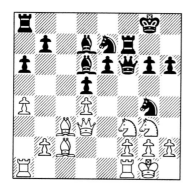

23 ♕e2!

White has the e5-square well under control and the position of the knight on g4 is looking increasingly shaky.
23...h5 24 ♗d2 ♗f4

This loses but 24...e5? 25 ♘g5 ♖ff8 26 f3 ♘h6 27 ♘5e4 was also winning for White.
25 h3 ♖h7 26 ♗xf4 ♕xf4 27 hxg4 h4 28 ♕e5 1-0

Game 11
J.Polgar-G.Hernandez
Merida 2000

---

1 e4 e6 2 d4 d5 3 ♘c3 ♘f6 4 e5 ♘fd7 5 ♘ce2 c5 6 c3 cxd4 7 cxd4 f6 8 f4

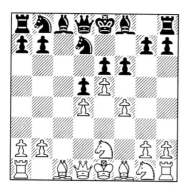

Again White is banking on the strong centre but, in this particular position, this involves paying a heavy price in terms of king safety. More circumspect moves are 8 ♘f4 (Game 12) and 8 exf6 (Game 13).
8...fxe5

8...♗b4+ is possible, but if Black is going to play like this, it makes sense to flick in the pawn exchange first as then White cannot respond with the natural ♗d2 – see the note to White's tenth. Play could continue 9 ♗d2 ♕b6 10 ♗xb4 ♕xb4+ 11 ♕d2 ♘c6 12 ♘f3 fxe5 13 fxe5 ♕xd2+ 14 ♔xd2 ♘b6 15 ♘c3 a6 16 ♗d3 ♗d7 17 ♖af1 with an edge for White in Kozlov-Matveeva, Moscow 1999.

9 fxe5

The alternative 9 dxe5 has been played a few times. However, it is hard to believe that White, with such constipated development, can allow his opponent a central passed pawn, use of the c5-square and g1-a7 diagonal, and still keep an advantage. Practice has seen:

a) 9...♘c6 10 ♘f3 ♗b4+ 11 ♘c3 ♘c5 12 ♗e3 ♕a5 13 ♕c2 0-0 was Shirov-Ivanchuk, Tilburg 1993. Now White erred with 14 ♖c1 and after 14...d4 Black was better. However, even after the preferable 14 a3, White's position is unexciting.

b) 9...♕b6 10 ♘c3 ♘c6 11 ♘f3 ♗b4 12 ♗d2 ♘c5 13 a3 ♗xc3 14 ♗xc3 0-0 15 g3 ♗d7 and again Black was very comfortable in Bologan-Short, Beijing 2000.

c) 9...♗c5 10 ♘f3 ♘c6 11 ♘c3 ♕b6 (Black has a powerful concentration of force along the g1-a7 diagonal but it proves impossible to keep his queen and bishop stationed here and he ends up losing time when they are driven back; thus one of the plans seen in either Shirov-Ivanchuk or Bologan-Short seems preferable) 12 ♗d3 ♗e7 13 ♘a4 ♕a5+ 14 ♗d2 ♘b4 15 ♗e2 ♘c5 16 ♘xc5 ♕xc5 17 ♖c1 ♕b6 18 ♕b3 a5 19 ♗e3 ♕d8 20 a3 a4 21 ♕d1 ♘c6 22 ♗d3 and White was firmly in control of the position in Voitsekhovsky-Alavkin, Bor 2000.

9...♗b4+

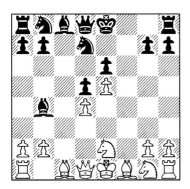

10 ♔f2

Unfortunately White must make this awkward move as 10 ♗d2 ♕h4+ is very good for Black, as indeed is 10 ♘c3 ♕h4+.

10...0-0+ 11 ♘f3 ♘c6

This is a typical position for these variations where White attempts to maintain a strong centre at all costs. If White can unravel her pieces, she will have a great position. Black therefore invariably gambits a large amount of material, usually a piece or so, to exploit his lead in development and get at the white king. To a large degree, positional considerations now go out the window and the position becomes purely tactical.

12 a3 ♘dxe5

Here we go! The more restrained 12...♗a5 is also possible when play might continue 13 h4 (a useful move, as Black can often hurl ...g7-g5 in White's direction) 13...♕e7 14 ♘g3 ♗c7 15 ♔h3 ♕f7 16 ♘f4 ♘f6 17 ♗d3 ♘e4 18 ♖f1 and White stands well.

13 axb4 ♕h4+ 14 ♔g1?!

In her understandable haste to get her king out of the firing line, Polgar jettisons slightly too much material. A better plan was 14 ♘g3 ♘xd4 15 ♗e2 ♘xe2 16 ♕xe2 ♕d4+ 17 ♔f1 ♗d7 18 ♗e3 with an unclear

position.

14...♘xf3+ 15 gxf3 ♖xf3 16 ♘g3 ♘xd4

With three pawns for the piece and a reasonable attack, Black now stands quite well.

17 ♗g2

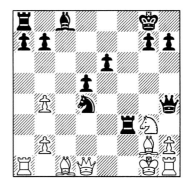

Lateral defence with 17 ♖a3 was a plausible alternative.

17...♖f7?

Black misses a very good chance here. With 17...♘e2+ 18 ♕xe2 ♕d4+ 19 ♗e3 ♖xe3 20 ♕f2 ♖d3 he would inevitably gain a fourth pawn for the piece and obtain a clear advantage.

18 ♗e3

Following Black's oversight Polgar is over the worst and now has all the chances.

18...♘f5 19 ♘xf5 ♖xf5 20 b5!

This pawn now transforms from a sickly weakness to a powerful thorn in Black's flesh on the queenside.

20...♗d7 21 b6 a6 22 ♕d4

White's bishop pair will be a potent force in the endgame.

22...♕h5 23 h3 ♗c6 24 ♔h2 e5 25 ♕g4 ♖d8 26 ♕xh5 ♖xh5 27 ♖hf1 g6 28 ♗f3

Suddenly White's whole position has come to life. This bishop will transfer to e6 when the pressure on Black's position will quickly become intolerable.

28...♖f5 29 ♗g4 ♖xf1 30 ♖xf1 ♔g7 31 ♗e6 ♗e8 32 ♗c5 1-0

Game 12
Anand-Bareev
Shenyang 2000

1 e4 e6 2 d4 d5 3 ♘c3 ♘f6 4 e5 ♘fd7 5 ♘ce2 c5 6 c3 cxd4 7 cxd4 f6 8 ♘f4 ♗b4+

This is the only sensible way for Black to play as White's last move threatened the e6-pawn.

9 ♗d2 ♕b6

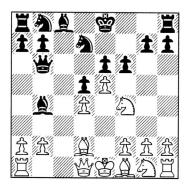

The routine 9...♗xd2+ 10 ♕xd2 ♕e7 11 exf6 ♘xf6 12 ♗d3 ♘c6 13 ♘ge2 0-0 14 0-0 ♗d7 15 a3 ♕d6 16 ♖ad1 ♖f7 17 ♗b1 ♖e8 18 f3 ♖fe7 19 ♘d3 gave White a pleasant edge in Sax-Glek, Germany 1993. Even if Black plays the freeing advance ...e6-e5, this will only serve to leave him with a weak d-pawn.

10 ♗xb4

Others:

a) 10 exf6 ♘xf6 11 ♕a4+ ♘c6 12 ♗xb4 ♕xb4+ 13 ♕xb4 ♘xb4 got White nowhere in Vukovic-Piskov, Igalo 1994, viz. 14 ♗d3 0-0 15 a3 ♘h5! (this clever move maintains Black's slight initiative) 16 axb4 ♘xf4 17 ♗f1 e5 18 dxe5 ♖e8 19 ♔d2 ♖xe5 20 g3 ♘e6 21 ♗d3 ♘g5 and Black had an edge although his opponent hung on to draw.

b) 10 ♖c1 0-0 11 ♗xb4 ♕xb4+ 12 ♕d2 ♕e7 13 exf6 ♘xf6 14 ♘d3 ♘c6 15 ♘f3 (White has nailed down the e5-square but at

the cost of exposing the e4-square – Black now hastens to exploit this) 15...♘e4 16 ♕e3 ♕d8 17 ♗e2 ♕a5+ 18 b4 ♘xb4 19 0-0 (White has good compensation for the pawn as Black's queenside is gummed up and his bishop is so bad) 19...♘c6 20 ♖c2 ♘d6 21 ♘de5 ♘f5 22 ♕g5 ♘xe5 23 dxe5 ♗d7 with unclear play in Dvoirys-Nielsen, New York 2000.

10...♕xb4+ 11 ♕d2 ♕xd2+ 12 ♔xd2 ♔e7 13 exf6+ gxf6 14 ♖e1 ♘b6 15 ♘f3

Anand finds a much better plan than did Bezgodov in the following game: 15 ♗d3 ♘c6 16 ♘f3 ♔d6 17 ♘h5 ♖f8 18 ♗xh7 (White has gained a pawn but at the cost of severe disruption to his pieces, and he is unable to retain his booty for long) 18...e5 19 ♘g3 e4 20 ♘h4 ♘xd4 21 f3 ♖h8 22 ♘hf5+ ♗xf5 23 ♘xf5+ ♔e5 24 ♘xd4 ♔xd4 25 ♗f5 ♘c4+ 26 ♔e2 ♖ag8 27 ♖d1+ ♔e5 28 g4 ♖h3 and Black soon won in Bezgodov-Sakaev, Moscow 1999.

15...♘c6 16 ♗b5 ♗d7 17 ♗xc6 bxc6 18 ♖e2 ♖ae8 19 ♖he1 ♔f7 20 ♔c1 ♘c4 21 ♘d2 ♘xd2 22 ♔xd2

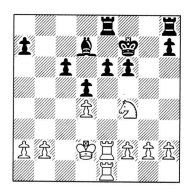

Anand has managed to keep control over the position and Black has an unpleasant defensive task ahead.

22...c5

This is a clever idea, but Anand spots a flaw in Bareev's plan.

23 dxc5 e5 24 ♘xd5

It looks as if this drops material and,

indeed, it does. However, Anand has appreciated that he can limit his losses to the exchange and in return he gains two pawns and a powerful pawn roller on the queenside.

24...♗b5

The dual threats of ...♗xe2 and ...♖d8 win material, but Anand has everything under control.

25 ♔c3 ♗xe2 26 ♖xe2 ♖c8 27 ♔c4 ♔e6 28 b4 ♖hd8 29 ♖d2 ♖d7 30 f4

It goes against the grain to present Black with a passed pawn but Anand has calculated that he can quickly undermine it.

30...e4 31 ♖d4 f5 32 g4 ♖g7 33 ♘e3

White's forces co-ordinate beautifully.

33...fxg4 34 ♖d6+ ♔f7 35 ♘f5

Regaining the exchange. It is all over.

35...e3 36 ♘xg7 ♖e8 37 ♘xe8 e2 38 ♖f6+ 1-0

If 38...♔e7 39 ♖f5 and the career of the new black queen will be short indeed.

> ### Game 13
> ### **Nijboer-Glek**
> *Wijk aan Zee 1999*

---

1 e4 e6 2 d4 d5 3 ♘c3 ♘f6 4 e5 ♘fd7 5 ♘ce2 c5 6 c3 cxd4 7 cxd4 f6 8 exf6 ♘xf6 9 ♘f3 ♘c6 10 ♘c3 ♗d6 11 ♗d3

This is a very natural developing move for White but it doesn't place his opponent under any great pressure. Other tries here are:

a) 11 ♗b5 attempts to increase White's control over e5. Practice has seen 11...0-0 12 0-0 ♕c7 13 h3 ♗d7 14 ♖e1 (14 ♗e3 a6 15 ♗xc6 ♗xc6 16 ♖e1 ♖ae8 17 a3 ♘d7 18 ♖c1 ♕b8 19 ♖c2 ♖f5 20 ♗c1 e5 and Black had an active game in Kuzmin-Lempert, Alushta 1994) 14...♖ae8 15 ♗e3 a6 16 ♗f1 ♕b8 17 a3 ♖e7 18 b4 ♗e8 19 b5 axb5 20 ♘xb5 ♗f4 21 ♗xf4 ♕xf4 22 ♕c1 ♘e4 was fine for Black in Lau-Gleizerov, Dresden 1994.

b) 11 ♗e2 0-0 12 0-0 h6 13 h3 (White's

play in this game is highly – probably overly – cautious and this encourages Black into an ambitious demonstration on the kingside) 13...♗d7 14 ♗e3 ♕e7 15 ♖e1 g5 (this is an interesting plan – Black is not concerned about freeing his game with the standard ...e6-e5 but is happy to hold the centre and play on the kingside) 16 ♘h2 ♕g7 17 ♖c1 ♖f7 18 ♘f1 ♘e7 19 ♘b5 ♗xb5 20 ♗xb5 ♘f5 21 ♗d3 g4 22 ♗xf5 exf5 23 hxg4 fxg4 24 ♘g3 ♕g6 and Black had a very pleasant position and went on to win with a kingside attack in Hort-Knaak, Germany 1996.

c) 11 g3!? is White's most imaginative try in this position. Placing the bishop on g2 shores up the kingside and makes it slightly more difficult for Black to achieve the advance ...e6-e5, as this piece would then be pressing strongly against the isolated d-pawn. One possibility is 11...♗d7 12 ♗g2 0-0 13 0-0 ♖c8 14 ♖e1 ♕b6 15 ♘a4 ♕c7 16 ♗e3 b5 17 ♘c3 a6 18 ♖c1 ♕b8 19 ♗g5 and White had a modest initiative in Kuzmin-Cederqvist, Yerevan 1997.

11...0-0 12 ♗g5 ♕e8

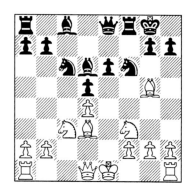

13 ♕d2?!

This already looks like a step in the wrong direction. The queen achieves very little on this square and actually becomes a target for moves such as ...♘f6-e4. Furthermore, moving away from d1 also encourages Black to look for opportunities to sacrifice the exchange with ...♖f8xf3 at some point.

13...♘h5 14 ♘e2

The impression is that White is already fighting a rearguard action. Here 14 0-0 is better than the text, but Black still has a pleasant game after 14...h6 15 ♗e3 ♘f4.

14...e5!

This thrust is lent extra energy by the fact that the white king is still languishing in the centre.

15 ♘xe5

This is unpalatable but forced as after 15 dxe5? ♗b4 16 ♘c3 ♖xf3! 17 gxf3 d4 White gets torn apart, e.g. 18 f4 dxc3 19 bxc3 ♘xe5! 20 fxe5 ♕xe5+ and the white position has collapsed.

15...♘xd4 16 ♘xd4 ♕xe5+ 17 ♗e3 ♘f4

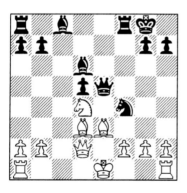

18 ♗f1

An awful move to have to make but now at least White plans to consolidate and get organised with g2-g3 and ♗f1-g2.

18...♗g4?!

This is a superficially attractive move but it plans a sacrifice which turns out to be only good enough for a draw. Thus the calmer 18...♗d7 may be better. Play might continue 19 g3 ♕e4 20 f3 ♕e7 and life looks difficult for White as 21 gxf4 runs into 21...♗b4.

19 h3 ♗h5 20 g3 ♖ae8

This sacrifice was the idea behind 18...♗g4. Black wants the bishop on the d1-

h5 diagonal to prevent ♖d1.

21 gxf4 ♖xf4

White's position looks desperate but Nijboer defends coolly.

22 ♗e2

White must get his pieces out. 22 ♘e2 again allows 22...♗b4 and Black is winning.

22...♖xd4 23 ♕xd4!

White defends carefully. 23 ♗xd4 looks as if it will probably lead to the same position but in fact Black has the sneaky 23...♕e4! which enables him to capture on e2 with the bishop and keep the queens on. Nevertheless, even here White has further resources which keep him in the game, e.g. 24 ♖g1 ♗xe2 25 ♕e3 (even 25 ♖xg7+, which looks hopeless after 25...♔f8, still gives White chances – 26 ♕e3 ♗h5 27 ♔f1! ♕h1+ 28 ♔g1) 25...♗b4+ 26 ♘c3 (26 ♔xe2 ♕c2+ 27 ♔f3 ♖xe3+ 28 fxe3 ♕f5+ is good for Black) 26...♗xc3+ 27 bxc3 ♕a4 appears to be all over, but now White launches a counterattack aiming for perpetual check with 28 ♖xg7+! ♔xg7 29 ♕g5+ and Black's only way to try to avoid this is 29...♔f7 30 ♕f5+ ♔e7 31 ♔xe2 and White is still in the game.

23...♕xd4 24 ♗xd4 ♖xe2+ 25 ♔f1

Black has a pawn and an active position for the exchange but it is not enough to push for the advantage.

25...♖e4 26 ♗xa7 ♗e2+ 27 ♔g2 ♖e6 28 f4!

This is another good defensive move. White jettisons a pawn to free up space for his king. Now White gets his pieces out and the position quickly fizzles out into a draw.

28...♗xf4 29 ♖he1 ♗d2 30 ♔f2

Guaranteeing the draw.

30...♗xe1+ 31 ♖xe1 ♖a6 32 ♗d4 ♗h5 33 ♖e7 ♔f8 34 ♖xb7 ♖xa2 35 ♗xg7+ ♔e8 36 ♔e3 ♖a4 37 ♗d4 ♗g6 38 b4 ♖a3+ 39 ♔f4 ♖xh3 40 ♔e5 ½-½

This was a gritty defensive performance from White but hardly a good advert for his choice of opening variation.

Summary

The main lines in this chapter, as seen in Games 1-5, look quite promising for White as long as he keeps a close eye on potential Black sacrifices on e5 and is careful not to waste time with g2-g3. The best plan for Black may be Volkov's idea of 8...a5 (Game 6). The theory is not well developed here and there is certainly much scope for original play.

7...b5 (Games 7-9) is best met by 8 a3 and a direct challenge to Black's queenside ambitions.

The early exchange with 6...cxd4 7 cxd4 f6 (Games 11-13) may turn out to be Black's most reliable method of meeting 5 ♘ce2. White has the choice between the thematic but risky 8 f4 (Game 11) and the more solid 8 ♘f4 (Game 12). With the latter move White abandons his ideas to maintain the d4/e5 structure but hopes to gain a small edge anyway. 8 exf6 (Game 13) appears unlikely to cause Black any trouble.

1 e4 e6 2 d4 d5 3 ♘c3 ♘f6 4 e5 ♘fd7 5 ♘ce2 c5 6 c3

6...♘c6
> 6...cxd4 7 cxd4 f6
>> 8 f4 – *Game 11*; 8 ♘f4 – *Game 12*; 8 exf6 – *Game 13*

7 f4
> 7 ♘f3 – *Game 10*

7...♛b6
> 7...b5 *(D)*
>> 8 a3
>>> 8...cxd4 – *Game 7* ; 8...c4 – *Game 8*
>> 8 ♘f3 – *Game 9*

8 ♘f3 f6
> 8...♗e7 *(D)*
>> 9 a3 – *Game 4*; 9 g3 – *Game 5*
> 8...a5 – *Game 6*

9 a3
> 9 g3 – *Game 3*

9...♗e7 10 h4 0-0 11 ♖h3 a5 12 b3 *(D)* ♛c7
> 12...♛d8 – *Game 2*

13 ♘eg1 – *Game 1*

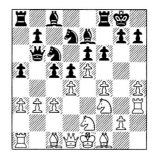

7...b5   *8...♗e7*   *12 b3*

CHAPTER TWO

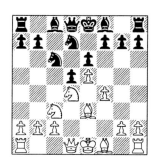

Old Main Line with 7...cxd4 8 ♘xd4

1 e4 e6 2 d4 d5 3 ♘c3 ♘f6 4 e5 ♘fd7 5 f4 c5 6 ♘f3 ♘c6 7 ♗e3 cxd4 8 ♘xd4

In this chapter we consider the position that arises after Black opts for the immediate exchange of pawns in the centre with 7...cxd4. Black opens the c-file at once and will soon castle his king to safety (or what he hopes will be safety) on the kingside. The battle lines are then drawn with White usually castling on the queenside.

There are a number of games which see a classic situation with competing attacks on opposite wings: White charges forwards on the kingside, often using the lever f4-f5, while Black pursues an initiative on the other wing. However, practical experience seems to indicate that Black should be perfectly happy when such a scenario arises. The white knight on c3 acts as a target for the pawn advances, while the open c-file also helps Black to get at the white king. Even when the white attack prises open the black king – after, for example, f4-f5-f6, forcing ... g7xf6 – the black king proves to be hard to get at.

In fact, many games nowadays see White adopting a more restrained strategy. He does not try to force the pace on the kingside but is content to take the view that

he has a long-term space advantage and can concentrate on trying to nullify Black's queenside play. To this end we often see plans such as ♔b1, ♖c1 and c2-c3.

The latest word in these lines for White is a semi-waiting strategy with an early g2-g3. White may still end up with his king on the queenside but keeps open the option of a quieter plan with 0-0 and perhaps ♗h3.

The main line sequence with 8...♗c5 9 ♕d2 0-0 is considered in detail in Games 14-20. However, Black has two other main ways to approach this position. He can head for a very dull, slightly worse endgame with 9...♗xd4 10 ♗xd4 ♘xd4 11 ♕xd4 ♕b6, which is seen in Game 21, or he can grab a hot, but not necessarily poisoned, pawn with 8...♕b6 9 ♕d2 ♕xb2 (Games 22-23).

Game 14
Kasparov-Short
Amsterdam 1994

---

1 e4 e6 2 d4 d5 3 ♘c3 ♘f6 4 e5 ♘fd7 5 f4 c5 6 ♘f3 ♘c6 7 ♗e3 cxd4 8 ♘xd4 ♗c5 9 ♕d2 0-0 10 0-0-0

Kasparov recent try, 10 g3, is the subject of Game 20.

10...a6 11 h4

11 g3, the Kasparov try deferred, is seen

in Game 19.

11...♘xd4

It is also possible to take the view that the knight on c6 will prove to be the more useful minor piece and play 11...♗xd4, which we consider in Game 18.

12 ♗xd4 b5 13 ♖h3

A multi-purpose move. The rook can either be used for attacking purposes on g3 or, as is more often the case, help to play c2-c3 and challenge Black along the c-file. 13 h5 is seen in Game 17.

13...b4 14 ♘a4

A natural attempt to hold Black up on the queenside, but this piece can become rather exposed. 14 ♘e2 is the subject of Game 16.

14...♗xd4 15 ♕xd4

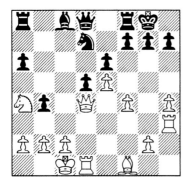

15...f6

At the time this was a new move. Black's plan is, not unusually for the French, to seek to undermine the white centre. What Short probably did not anticipate was that Kasparov would be quite happy to let him do this! For 15...a5 see Game 15.

16 ♕xb4

A slightly surprising move. One might expect White to concentrate on maintaining his centre. Instead he allows it to be demolished but in return generates active piece play, particularly along the dark squares.

16...fxe5 17 ♕d6

This leads to great complications. A simpler course was available: 17 fxe5 ♘xe5 18 ♖e3 ♘f7 19 g3 with approximate equality. However, Thorhallsson-Limp, Istanbul 2000, finished swiftly from this position viz. 19...♘d6 20 ♗h3 ♘f5 21 ♖f3 ♘d6 22 ♖xf8+ ♕xf8 23 ♘b6 ♖b8 24 ♕c5 ♘e4 25 ♕c7 ♕d6 26 ♕xd6 ♘xd6 27 ♘xc8 ♘xc8 28 ♗xe6+ 1-0.

17...♕f6

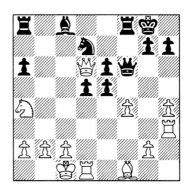

18 f5!?

A typically violent Kasparov thrust, the main point of which is revealed after 18...♕xf5 19 ♖f3 ♕g4 20 ♖xf8+ ♘xf8 21 ♘b6 and White wins.

18...♕h6+ 19 ♔b1 ♖xf5

After this Black is in trouble as he is struggling to get his queenside pieces into the game and his back rank is rather exposed. A better try for Black is 19...♘f6 with the following possibilities:

a) 20 ♕c7 is uninspiring: 20...exf5 21 ♘b6 f4 22 ♘xc8 ♖axc8 23 ♕xe5 and now in Van Blitterswijk-Stellwagen, Holland 2000, Black found the highly practical pawn sacrifice 23...♘g4!? and after 24 ♕xd5+ ♔h8 25 ♖c1 ♘e3 26 ♕a5 ♕g6 27 h5 ♕e4 28 ♗d3 ♕xg2 29 ♖hh1 ♕d5 he had regained his pawn and went on to win. Quieter methods were also possible as after 23...♕g6 Black should have little to complain about.

b) 20 fxe6 is given an '!' by Knaak but he

has made a mistake in his analysis. After 20...♘e4 21 ♕xd5 ♘d2+ 22 ♖xd2 (Knaak spots 22 ♔a1? ♗xe6!) he gives 22...♖xf1+, missing the superior 22...♗xe6! which is very good for Black.

c) 20 ♘b6 ♘e4 21 ♕c7 ♖f7 22 ♕d8+ ♖f8 23 ♕c7 ♖f7 24 ♕xe5 ♖xf5 25 ♕d4 ♘d2+ 26 ♖xd2 ♕xd2 27 ♕xd2 ♖xf1+ 28 ♕c1 ♖xc1+ 29 ♔xc1 ♖b8 30 ♖b3 a5 31 ♔d2 and White held an edge in Van der Weide-Stellwagen, Wijk aan Zee 2000.

20 ♖f3 ♖xf3 21 gxf3 ♕f6 22 ♗h3 ♔f7

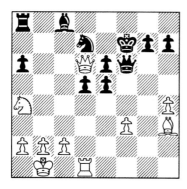

23 c4

Kasparov plays this game with his usual immense energy. However, his play is also very logical. White is forcing open lines before his opponent has a chance to complete his development.

23...dxc4

If Black tries to keep the position closed (or at least not wide open) with 23...d4 then White forces further line opening with 24 f4! exf4 25 ♖xd4 and wins.

24 ♘c3 ♕e7 25 ♕c6 ♖b8 26 ♘e4

Now White's pieces co-ordinate perfectly and the game is up for Black. One particularly attractive finish, given by Ftacnik is 26...♘f8 27 ♘d6+ ♔g8 28 ♘xc8 ♕b4 and what appears to be a promising counterattack is brutally extinguished by 29 ♕xe6+! ♘xe6 (29...♔h8 30 ♕xe5 is easy) 30 ♗xe6+ ♔f8 31 ♖d8 checkmate.

26...♘b6 27 ♘g5+ ♔g8 28 ♕e4 g6 29

♕xe5 ♖b7 30 ♖d6 c3 31 ♗xe6+ ♗xe6 **32 ♖xe6 1-0**

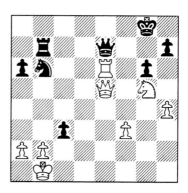

Short resigned due to 32...♘c4 33 ♕xc3! (not 33 ♖xe7 ♖xb2+ 34 ♔a1 ♘xe5 35 ♖xe5 ♖h2 when Black can struggle on) 33...♘a3+ 34 ♔c1 ♕f8 35 ♕xa3 and wins.

Game 15
Sedlak-Antic
Subotica 2000

---

1 e4 e6 2 d4 d5 3 ♘c3 ♘f6 4 e5 ♘fd7 5 f4 c5 6 ♘f3 ♘c6 7 ♗e3 cxd4 8 ♘xd4 ♗c5 9 ♕d2 0-0 10 0-0-0 ♘xd4 11 ♗xd4 a6 12 h4 b5 13 ♖h3 b4 14 ♘a4 ♗xd4 15 ♕xd4 a5

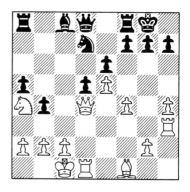

One of the drawbacks of Black's plan with ...f7-f6 as seen in the previous game is that Kasparov's energetic response enabled his knight on a4 to play an active role in proceedings. Here Black's play is far simpler, concentrating on completing his queenside development and hoping to show up the seamy side of the positioning of the knight on a4. It may appear dangerous to allow White a free hand on the kingside, but Black's position has no weaknesses and it takes a while for White to generate any serious threats there.

16 ♗b5

Others possibilities are:

a) 16 ♔b1 ♕c7 17 ♗b5 ♕b7 18 ♗e2 ♕c6 19 b3 ♗a6 20 c4 (this is a common theme; White exploits the pin along the d-file to prevent his pawn on c2 from becoming a liability) 20...♖ac8 21 ♔a1 ♗xc4!? (an imaginative piece sacrifice from Korchnoi) 22 ♗xc4 dxc4 23 ♕xd7 ♕xg2 24 ♖hh1 c3 25 ♖hg1 (25 ♕e7? loses beautifully after 25...c2 26 ♖c1 ♕xh1! 27 ♖xh1 c1♕+ 28 ♖xc1 ♖xc1+ 29 ♔b2 ♖fc8 and the white king is caught in a mating net. Even 30 ♘c5 ♖1xc5 does not help.) 25...♕h2 26 ♕d3 g6 27 ♕g3 ♕e2 28 ♖de1 ♕d2 29 ♖d1 ♕e2 30 ♖de1 ♕d2 31 ♖d1 ½-½ Glek-Korchnoi, Willingen 1999.

b) 16 c4 was seen in Nijboer-Korchnoi, Arnhem 1999. Play continued: 16...bxc3 17 ♖xc3 ♕xh4 (a typically bold pawn grab from Korchnoi) 18 g3 ♕d8 19 ♔b1 ♗a6 20 ♗xa6 ♖xa6 21 ♖h1 ♖a8 22 g4 with good compensation for the pawn, as White has a free hand on the kingside and Black's counterplay on the opposite wing is nowhere to be seen.

16...♖b8 17 ♗d3

Or:

a) 17 c4 bxc3 18 ♘xc3 ♕b6 19 ♕xb6 ♖xb6 20 b3 f6 21 exf6 ♘xf6 22 a4 ♘g4 23 ♖d4 ♘h6 24 ♔b2 ♘f5 25 ♖d1 with a balanced endgame in Yurtaev-Goloshchapov, Calcutta 2000.

b) 17 ♗xd7?! (such a simple plan seems unlikely to cause Black any problems) 17...♗xd7 18 ♘c5 ♖c8 19 ♖d2 ♕c7 20 ♘xd7 ♕xd7 (positions such as these are

usually good for Black who has the open c-file on which to operate and a weak pawn on c2 to target, while White finds it hard to get anywhere on the kingside) 21 h5 ♕b5 22 ♖f3 a4 23 h6 ♖c4 24 ♕f2 ♖fc8 25 f5 b3 26 fxe6 fxe6 27 axb3 axb3 28 c3 0-1 Wells-Glek, Vienna 1998. Queen to the a-file is quickly decisive.

17...♕c7

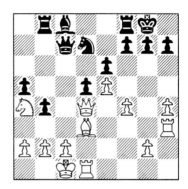

Black puts pressure on the e-pawn to hold up White's f4-f5 advance. After 17...♗b7 White took his chances at once in Fedorov-Korchnoi, Batumi 1999 with 18 f5 and after 18...♕c7 19 ♖e1 exf5 20 ♗xf5 ♗c6 21 ♘c5 ♘xc5 22 ♕xc5 ♖fe8 23 ♖he3 ♕b6 24 ♕xb6 ♖xb6 25 e6 g6 26 exf7+ ♔xf7 27 ♗e6+ ♔g7 28 ♗g4 ♖bb8 29 ♔d2 he had a useful endgame advantage.

18 ♖e1

18 h5 ♕c6 19 b3 ♗a6 20 f5 ♖bc8 21 ♖d2 ♗xd3 22 ♖hxd3 ♕c7 23 ♖e2 ♖fe8?! was seen in Berndt-Furlan, Bled 2000. Black is playing to pressurise the e5-pawn but his plan has a rather large tactical drawback. Much better was 23...h6 24 f6 gxf6 25 exf6 ♔h7 with play as in the main game. Black's kingside has been broken up but it is still remarkably difficult for White to make any progress in that sector – mainly because of the useless knight on a4. After 23... ♖fe8?! play continued 24 ♖g3 exf5? (this is a disaster; it was still possible to mount a defence with 24...♔h8 25 ♕g4 ♖g8 26 fxe6

♘xe5 27 ♕f5 ♘c6 with unclear play) 25 e6 (whoops!) 1-0.

18...♕c6 19 b3 ♗a6 20 ♗xa6 ♕xa6

21 h5

Or 21 ♖g3 ♖bc8 22 f5 ♕c6 (not 22...exf5? 23 e6 winning) 23 ♖e2 ♔h8 24 h5 ♖g8 25 ♖f3 f6!? 26 exf6 e5 27 fxg7+ ♖xg7 28 ♕d2 ♘f6 and Black had reasonable play for her sacrificed pawn in Arakhamia-Grant - Matveeva, Kishinev 1995.

21...♖fc8 22 f5 ♕c6 23 ♖e2 ♘c5 24 f6

Here White should have been less ambitious and taken the opportunity to exchange knights. Instead he hopes to generate play on the kingside, but Black's defensive resources are considerable.

24...♘e4

One of White's major problems from here on is in the huge disparity in strength between the knights. Black's is wonderfully placed on e4 whilst White's is a feeble spectator on a4. White would like to arrange an exchange sacrifice on e4 but the pressure along the c-file makes it impossible for him to achieve this in an advantageous manner.

25 fxg7 h6!

An excellent defensive move, keeping control over the dark squares. Instead 25...♔xg7 26 h6+ would have given White all sorts of chances.

26 ♖f3 ♖b7 27 ♕e3 ♔xg7 28 ♖f4

Black's knight on e4 is so strong that White has to perform all sorts of convoluted manoeuvres to activate his major pieces on the kingside.

28...♖bc7 29 ♖g4+ ♔h7 30 ♕d3 ♖g8

One of White's attacking units is exchanged off. Endgames will always favour Black because of the numerous white pawn weaknesses.

31 ♖xg8 ♔xg8 32 ♖e3

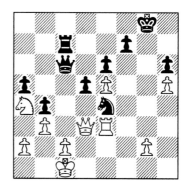

32...♖c8!

This is a very clever move played not to defend the back rank but to create space for the manoeuvre ...♕c7-e7-g5 clamping down on the dark squares.

33 ♖e2 ♕c7 34 ♕d4 ♕e7 35 ♕e3 ♔g7

35...♕g5 was also possible, but Black's king is in no particular danger and there is no hurry to force the queen exchange.

36 ♕f4 ♖c6 37 ♔b2 f5!

Well timed!

38 ♕e3

The endgame after 38 exf6+ ♕xf6+ 39 ♕xf6+ ♔xf6 is hopeless for White as the black king comes to g5 and White is still playing without the knight.

38...♔h7 39 ♖e1 ♕g7

Hitting the pawns at e5 and g2.

40 ♕d4 ♕xg2 0-1

Game 16
J.Polgar-Shirov
Prague 1999

---

1 e4 e6 2 d4 d5 3 ♘c3 ♘f6 4 e5 ♘fd7

5 f4 c5 6 ♘f3 ♘c6 7 ♗e3 cxd4 8 ♘xd4 ♗c5 9 ♕d2 0-0 10 0-0-0 a6 11 h4 ♘xd4 12 ♗xd4 b5 13 ♖h3 b4 14 ♘e2

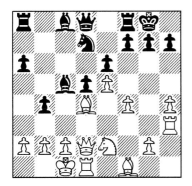

As we saw in previous games, White can easily find the knight horribly stuck out of play on a4 and so it is a logical attempt to improve by playing to e2 instead, where it also aims at the strong d4-square. However, this plan also has its disadvantages, not least of which is that the f-bishop is temporarily impeded. Furthermore, although the knight could prove out of play on a4 it did at least help to counter Black's queenside play with ..a6-a5-a4-a3.

14...a5 15 ♕e3

White forces his opponent into an immediate decision by pressurising the bishop on c5. However, various other moves have been tried here:

a) 15 g4 ♗a6 16 g5 (this is a very committal way for White to play) 16...♗xe2 17 ♗xe2 ♕c7 18 ♔b1 ♖fc8 19 ♖c1 a4 20 h5 a3 21 b3 ♗xd4 22 ♕xd4 ♕c5 23 ♕d2 ♖a7 24 g6 (this breakthrough looks impressive but in fact, as we see so often in this line, Black can still defend the kingside without too much trouble) 24...fxg6 25 hxg6 hxg6 26 ♗g4 ♘f8 27 ♖ch1 ♖ac7 28 ♗d1 ♔f7 29 ♖d3 ♕e7 30 ♕g2 ♖c3 and Black was fine in Brustman-Zielinska, Suwalki 1999.

b) 15 h5 ♗a6 16 h6 g6 17 ♖f3 ♖c8 18 ♔b1 ♕b6 19 c3 ♖c7 20 g4 ♖fc8 21 f5 (here

we have another familiar theme for this variation: White achieves the optically desirable f4-f5 push but finds that this has only served to weaken the e-pawn) 21...bxc3 22 ♗xc3 ♗b4 23 fxg6 fxg6 and Black's queenside play, combined with the weakness of the white e-pawn, gave him a fine game in Rahal-A.Martinez, Barbera 1999.

c) 15 ♖g3 ♕xh4 (why not?) 16 ♕e3 ♗a6 17 f5 ♖fc8 18 f6 ♗f8 19 ♘f4 ♗xf1 20 ♖xf1 ♖c4 21 ♕f2 ♔h8 22 c3 bxc3 23 bxc3 ♖b8 with an extra pawn for Black and a decent initiative on the queenside in Bryson-Orr, Edinburgh 1999.

15...♕c7 16 ♗xc5 ♘xc5

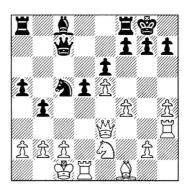

17 ♘d4

So, White has got her knight round to the attractive d4-square and effected the positionally desirable exchange of dark-squared bishops. However, this has all taken much time and Black is ready to launch forwards on the queenside. He also has a good square for his own knight on e4.

17...a4 18 ♔b1?

This is a serious mistake after which White is struggling. Black's threat of ...a4-a3 must be prevented and the only way to do this is with the bizarre-looking 18 a3! It looks suicidal to open lines on the queenside but in fact White can keep the position under control and hold the balance. A possible variation, given by Finkel, is 18...bxa3 19 ♕xa3 ♕b6 20 h5

♗a6 21 ♗xa6 ♖xa6 22 h6 g6 23 g4 ♘e4 24 ♖f3 with an unclear position.

18...a3 19 b3 ♗a6 20 ♗xa6 ♖xa6

With ...♘c5-e4-c3 in the offing it is clear that Black already stands very well.

21 ♕e1 ♖b6

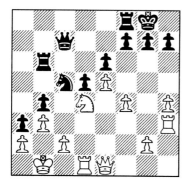

22 c3

White tries to compete on the queenside but now it is too late as Black is so well mobilised there and has already created serious weaknesses around the white king.

22...♕b7 23 ♖c1 ♘e4 24 cxb4 ♖xb4 25 ♖d3 ♖c4!

A clever move from Shirov which ensures him domination of the c-file.

26 ♖xc4

It is difficult to suggest how White might defend. For example, if 26 ♖dd1 ♖fc8 27 ♔a1 ♕b6 and White is collapsing.

26...dxc4 27 ♖d1 ♘c5 28 ♕c3 ♕xg2 29 b4 ♘d3 30 ♕xa3 ♖a8 31 ♖xd3 cxd3

31...♖xa3 32 ♖xa3 ♕g1+ 33 ♔c2 ♕f2+ 34 ♔b1 ♕e1+ 35 ♔c2 ♕e4+ also wins.

32 ♕xd3 ♕xa2+ 33 ♔c1 ♕a1+ 34 ♔d2 ♖d8 35 ♔e3 ♕e1+ 0-1

A gory example of how this variation can go horribly wrong for White.

> ## Game 17
> ### Topalov-Morozevich
> *Sarajevo 1999*

1 e4 e6 2 d4 d5 3 ♘c3 ♘f6 4 e5 ♘fd7

5 f4 c5 6 ♘f3 ♘c6 7 ♗e3 cxd4 8 ♘xd4 ♗c5 9 ♕d2 0-0 10 0-0-0 a6 11 h4 ♘xd4 12 ♗xd4 b5 13 h5 b4 14 ♘e2

Here White has the usual choice between trying to block Black's queenside play or simply getting on with it himself on the opposite wing. Here are some examples of the blockading strategy following 14 ♘a4: 14...♗xd4 15 ♕xd4 ♕a5 (15...a5 16 ♗b5 ♖b8 17 ♗d3 ♗b7 18 h6 g6 19 f5!? was the violent continuation of Nunn-Lputian, Manila 1992; Black declined to capture the white pawn and played safe with 19...♗c6 when, following 20 fxe6 ♕g5+ 21 ♔b1 ♕xe5 22 ♕xe5 ♘xe5 23 ♘c5 fxe6 24 ♖he1 ♘xd3 25 cxd3, White had a small edge in the endgame) 16 b3 ♗b7 17 f5 (White goes for it; a more restrained, and probably preferable approach is 17 ♔b1 ♗c6 18 ♘b2) 17...♗c6 18 f6 gxf6 19 exf6 ♔h8 20 ♗d3 (White's initiative on the kingside looks terrifying but, as we have seen in previous examples, Black has good defensive resources and his counterplay on the queenside comes very quickly) 20...♗xa4 21 ♕f4 ♖g8 22 bxa4 ♕xa4 23 ♔b1 ♘c5 24 g3 ♖ac8 and Black was well on top and went on to win in Gallagher-Barsov, Bern 1994.

14...a5

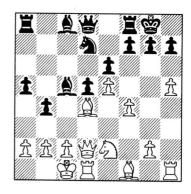

15 ♕e3

Other possibilities are:

a) 15 ♗xc5 ♘xc5 16 ♕e3 ♕b6 17 f5

(White takes advantage of the lack of protection of d5 to make this thematic push, but Black is well mobilised and in a good position to meet it) 17...a4 18 ♔b1 b3 19 cxb3 axb3 20 a3 exf5 21 ♖xd5 ♖a5 22 ᐃf4 h6? (this is too slow and, according to Knaak, Black could have obtained a good position with 22...♗b7! – one point being that 23 ♖d6 ♗e4+ 24 ♗d3 ♕b7 25 ♗xe4 ᐃxe4 26 ♖b6 ᐃd2+ 27 ♔a1 ♕a7 is very awkward for White) 23 ♗d3 (now White is on top) 23...♗e6 24 ♖d6 ♕b7 25 ♖c1 ♖c8 26 ♕d4 ᐃxd3 27 ♖xc8+ ♗xc8 28 ᐃg6! ♔h7 (28...fxg6 29 hxg6 wins) 29 ᐃf8+ ♔g8 30 ♖d8 g5 31 ♕d6 1-0 Smirin-Lputian, Rostov 1993.

b) 15 f5?! ♗xd4 16 ᐃxd4 ᐃxe5 looks speculative to say the least; Zakic-Dizdar, Cetinje 1990, continued 17 h6 g6 18 fxg6 fxg6 19 ♗b5 ♕d6 20 ♖he1 ᐃf7 21 ♕e3 e5 22 ᐃc6 d4 23 ♕g3 ♗d7 24 ᐃxd4 ♗xb5 25 ᐃxb5 ♕c5 26 a4 bxa3 27 ᐃxa3 ♖ab8 with an excellent position for Black.

c) The unsubtle 15 g4 ♗a6 16 g5 ♕c7 17 g6 was adopted in Wiersma-Luther, Leeuwarden 1992. Play continued 17...a4 18 h6 fxg6 19 hxg7 ♖f7 20 f5 ♗xe2 21 fxg6 ♖xg7 22 gxh7+ ♔h8 23 ♗xe2 (although White has stripped the pawn cover away from the black king it turns out that his own king is the more vulnerable) 23...b3 24 axb3 axb3 25 ♕c3 ♗b4!

15...♕c7 16 ♔b1 ♗a6

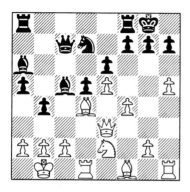

17 ♗xc5

17 h6 g6 18 g4 a4 19 ♗xc5 ᐃxc5 20 ᐃg3 ♖fc8 (this looks suspiciously like a waste of time; why not just get on with it with 20...b3?) 21 ♗xa6 ♖xa6 22 ♖c1 a3 23 b3 ᐃd7 with an approximately equal position in Kotter-Kaid, Germany 1999.

17...ᐃxc5 18 ᐃg3

It is important for White to cover the e4-square. 18 ᐃd4 a4 19 ♗xa6 ♖xa6 20 f5 ᐃe4 21 ♕f4 a3 leads to one of those positions where Black is invariably much quicker than his opponent. However, White's play does not make a positive impression. Most of his effort appears to be in frantic attempts to contain his opponent rather than further his own ambitions.

18...♖fc8 19 ♖c1 a4 20 ♗xa6 ♖xa6 21 ♖hd1 a3 22 b3 ♖c6

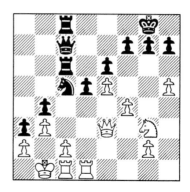

Black has a good position with the usual white weaknesses to aim at and the usual good squares for his own pieces.

23 ♕d4 ᐃa6 24 ♖d2 ♕e7!

Black observes that his opponent's kingside pawn advances have also created weaknesses.

25 ♕d3 ♕h4 26 ♕f3 ♖c3 27 ♖d3 h6!

Black is in no hurry and tidies up his own position. One point is that 28 ♖h1, apparently expelling the black queen, runs into the brutal 28...♖xc2!

28 f5 28...♕g5

White's last served only to give away

another dark square on the kingside.
29 ♕f1 ♖xd3 30 ♕xd3 ♘c5 31 ♕f3 ♘d7 0-1

Resignation may seem surprising but White cannot defend his e-pawn and his position will soon cave in.

Game 18
Apicella-Bricard
Besancon 1999

---

1 e4 e6 2 d4 d5 3 ♘c3 ♘f6 4 e5 ♘fd7 5 f4 c5 6 ♘f3 ♘c6 7 ♗e3 cxd4 8 ♘xd4 ♗c5 9 ♕d2 0-0 10 0-0-0 a6 11 h4 ♗xd4

Black decides that the knight on c6 will prove to be a more useful piece in the ensuing play than the bishop on c5. Obviously Black may soon capture again on d4 in which case play is likely to transpose into positions considered earlier. However, in practice, he tends not to do this. This line seems to make it a little easier for White to organise a solid defensive set-up on the queenside and this is probably why it is not seen as often as 11...♘xd4.

12 ♗xd4 b5 13 h5 b4 14 ♘e2

As usual 14 ♘a4 is an alternative here and may be stronger, e.g. 14...♕c7 15 ♔b1 a5 16 ♗f2 ♗a6 17 ♗xa6 ♖xa6 18 ♘c5 ♘xc5 19 ♗xc5 ♖c8 20 ♗d6 ♕d7 21 g4 and White stood a little better in Larsen-Gausel, Aars 1995.

14...a5

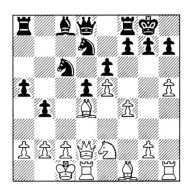

15 ♔b1

White has also tried:

a) 15 ♗e3 a4 16 ♘d4 ♘xd4 17 ♗xd4 b3 gave Black little cause for complaint in Apicella-Vallin, Vichy 2000. Play continued 18 cxb3 axb3 19 a3 ♗a6 20 ♗xa6 ♖xa6 21 ♔b1 ♘b6 22 ♗xb6 (a slight condemnation of White's play – he has been to some trouble to preserve the dark-squared bishop but now ends up exchanging it off anyway) 22...♕xb6 23 h6 g6 24 ♖c1 ♖a4 25 ♖h3 ♖c4 with equality.

b) 15 g4 a4 16 ♔b1 b3 17 cxb3 axb3 18 a3 ♗a6 19 h6 g6 20 ♖h3 ♕b8 21 ♖c3 ♗c4 22 ♘c1 ♘a5 23 ♕f2 with a small plus for White, as Black was not really getting anywhere on the queenside in Hickl-Franke, Luxembourg 1988.

15...a4 16 ♘c1 ♗a6 17 g4 ♕c7 18 ♖h2 ♖fc8 19 ♗xa6 ♖xa6 20 h6 g6 21 ♖e1

White is building up slowly, concentrating first on hoping to deprive Black of his queenside play before pursuing his own ambitions on the other wing. However, Black's reply is strong so maybe 21 ♗e3 was better.

21...b3!?

A typical pawn sacrifice to open lines on the queen's wing. At the very least this is a good practical move.

22 cxb3 axb3 23 ♘xb3 ♖ca8 24 ♘c1 ♘xd4 25 ♕xd4 ♖a4 26 ♕d2 ♘c5

With his knight about to parachute into e4 it is clear that Black's idea has been a great success.

27 ♖he2 ♘e4 28 ♕d3 ♕a5 29 ♖xe4 dxe4 30 ♖xe4

30...♖xa2

This looks very promising for Black, but in fact White can probably hang on after this. Better therefore was the simple 30...♖xe4 31 ♕xe4 ♖c8

31 ♘xa2 ♕xa2+ 32 ♔c2 ♖c8+ 33 ♔d1 ♕a1+ 34 ♔e2 ♕xb2+ 35 ♔f1 g5?!

Now, with a series of accurate moves, White equalises the position. In his notes Finkel gives 35...♕c1+ 36 ♔g2 ♖c2+ 37 ♖e2 ♖xe2+ 38 ♕xe2 ♕xf4 39 ♕d1 as leading to a draw. However, after 39...♕xh6 40 ♕d8+ ♕f8 (Finkel gives only 40...♔g7 which does indeed lead to an immediate draw after 41 g5) 41 ♕f6 h6, although Black is tied down he is two pawns ahead and must have reasonable winning chances.

36 ♖e2 ♕c1+ 37 ♔g2 gxf4 38 ♖d2

Suddenly White has generated his own threats thanks to Black's weak back rank.

38...f3+ 39 ♔f2 ♕c7 40 ♔xf3 ♖f8 41 ♕d4 ♕b7+ 42 ♔g3 ♕e7 43 ♖f2 ♕g5 44 ♕f4 ♕xf4+ 45 ♖xf4 ♖a8 46 ♖b4 f6?

Black, presumably frustrated at his inability to land a killing blow, becomes flustered and goes into self-destruct mode. He could still have drawn easily enough with 46...♔f8 47 ♔f4 ♖a7 48 ♔g5 ♔e7 49

♖b8 ♖c7 50 ♖h8 ♖c5.

47 exf6 ♔f7 48 g5

Now White is winning.

48...♔g6 49 ♖b5 ♖a7 50 ♖c5 ♖b7 51 ♖a5 ♖b3+ 52 ♔f4 ♖b4+ 53 ♔e3 ♖b8 54 ♔d4 ♖b7 55 ♔c5 ♖d7 56 ♔c6 ♖d8 57 ♖b5 ♖d1 58 ♖b8 ♖d5 59 ♖g8+ ♔f7 60 ♖g7+ ♔f8 61 ♖xh7 ♖xg5 62 ♖g7 1-0

1 e4 e6 2 d4 d5 3 ♘c3 ♘f6 4 e5 ♘fd7 5 f4 c5 6 ♘f3 ♘c6 7 ♗e3 cxd4 8 ♘xd4 ♗c5 9 ♕d2 0-0 10 0-0-0 a6 11 g3

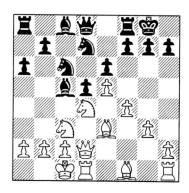

This is a decent alternative to the attempt to activate the king's rook with 11 h4, as seen in previous games. To a certain extent White is playing a waiting game with this move, intending to see how Black deploys his forces before committing his own pieces. Another move along similar lines is 11 ♕f2, as seen in Pedzich-Aaberg, Copenhagen 1991, which continued 11...♘xd4 12 ♗xd4 ♕c7 13 ♗d3 ♗xd4 14 ♕xd4 b5 15 ♖he1 ♕b6 16 ♕xb6 ♘xb6 17 ♘e2 b4 18 ♘d4 a5 19 b3 and White had a small edge in the endgame.

11...♕c7

11...♗xd4 12 ♗xd4 b5 has also been tried, when in Zolnierowicz-Dizdar, Baku

1988, White played the strange 13 h4. If you want to play like this you might as well get on with it on move 11. It certainly did not work out well for White: 13...b4 14 ♘e2 a5 15 g4 ♕c7 16 ♔b1 ♗a6 17 ♘g3 ♖fc8 18 ♖h2 a4 (Black's attack is a whole rank further advanced than White's) 19 ♘h5 b3 20 cxb3 axb3 21 a3 ♘xd4 22 ♕xd4 ♗xf1 23 ♖xf1 ♘b6 and Black soon crashed through on the queenside. The rest of the game is instructive: 24 ♖e2 ♘c4 25 f5 ♖a4 26 ♕d3 ♕a7 27 ♖c1 ♖a8 28 ♕c3 ♖xa3 29 bxa3 ♘xa3+ 30 ♔b2 ♘c4+ 31 ♔b1 b2 32 ♖xb2 ♘a3+ 0-1.

12 ♔b1

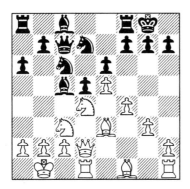

12 ♗h3 demonstrates a further point of the move 11 g3 – the white bishop can be developed actively on the h3-c8 diagonal where it may prove useful for the f4-f5 advance or possibly for a potential sacrifice on e6. Note also that Black's advance ...f7-f6 is impeded by this plan. Another encounter between the two combatants featured in our main game saw 12...♘xd4 13 ♗xd4 b5 14 ♖he1 ♖e8 (with f4-f5 on the cards Black feels obliged to make this not terribly useful move) 15 ♔b1 ♗b7 16 a3 ♗f8 17 f5 ♗c6 18 fxe6 fxe6 19 ♘e2 ♘c5 20 ♘f4 ♕d7 21 ♕e2 ♘b7 22 ♕g4 ♘d8 23 ♗f1 (White has ganged up effectively on the e-pawn and driven Black back but it is difficult for him to now annexe this pawn because the forcing line

23 ♗b6 ♘f7 24 ♘xe6 ♘h6 25 ♘xf8 ♕xg4 26 ♗xg4 ♘xg4 is fine for Black, as the white knight is isolated on f8) 23...b4 24 ♗d3 ♗b5 25 axb4 ♗xd3 26 ♖xd3 ♗xb4 27 ♘h5 ♔h8 28 ♖f1 ♖f8 29 ♖xf8+ ♗xf8 30 ♗c5!? ♘c6 (the crafty point of White's move is that 30...♗xc5 is met by 31 ♖xd5! ♕e7 32 ♖xc5 and White is on top – however, by declining the sacrifice Black is able to hold the balance) 31 ♖xd5 ♕xd5 32 ♗xf8 ♕h1+ 33 ♔a2 ♕d5+ 34 ♔b1 ♕h1+ ½-½ Enders-Knaak, Germany 1994. Both sides must settle for perpetual check.

12...♘xd4 13 ♗xd4 b5 14 ♗g2 ♗b7 15 ♖he1 ♗xd4 16 ♕xd4

White's set-up is solid but rather unambitious.

16...♖fc8 17 ♖c1 ♕a5 18 ♕d2

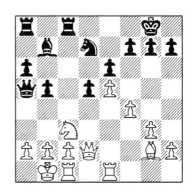

18...d4!?

This move initiates great complications. Black will lose the exchange but in return will seriously inconvenience the white king. At the very least, this is an excellent practical decision, especially as the alternative 18...♘b6 19 ♘e4 allows White to steer the game towards a dreary position, albeit one in which Black has no difficulties whatsoever.

19 ♗xb7

Another way to win the exchange was 19 ♕xd4 ♗xg2 20 ♕xd7 ♖xc3 21 bxc3 ♗d5 22 ♖cd1 ♕xa2+ 23 ♔c1 but then the huge black bishop on d5 does not look any worse than one of the white rooks.

19...dxc3 20 ♕d6 ♘c5

20...♖c4!? 21 b3! ♖c5 22 ♕a1 ♕a3 23 ♖b1 b4 24 ♕xc5 ♘xc5 25 ♗xa8 leads to a strange position which is difficult to judge.

21 ♗xc8 ♖xc8 22 ♖e3 b4 23 ♖d1 cxb2

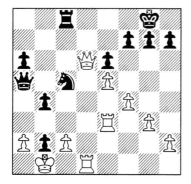

24 f5!

This is an excellent move from White. It is imperative for him to try to regain the initiative as quickly as possible. Chances are balanced.

24...h6?

However, this is too slow and now White has a chance to get on top. Black had a chance to force a remarkable draw with 24...exf5 25 e6 ♘xe6! 26 ♖xe6 b3!! 27 cxb3 ♖c1+ 28 ♖xc1 bxc1♕+ 29 ♔xc1 fxe6 30 ♕xe6+ ♔f8 and the position has fizzled out.

25 fxe6 ♘xe6 26 ♖f1?

White in turn errs. Much better was 26 ♖d5 ♕a4 27 ♖b3 when Black's queenside play is under control and White holds the advantage.

26...♕a4 27 ♖b3 ♕b5 28 ♕d3 ♕b7 29 ♕f3 ♕c7 30 ♖xb2 a5

The position may objectively be balanced and, although a computer would probably prefer to play White with the extra material, such a position is horrible to defend, especially in time trouble.

31 a3 ♘d4 32 ♕d3 ♕xe5 33 axb4 axb4 34 ♖xb4 ♘xc2 35 ♕a6 ♕c3 36 ♖b2 ♘b4 37 ♕d6?

After this White cannot cope with Black's threats. He had to try 37 ♕xc8+ ♕xc8 38 ♖xb4 when the game should end in a draw.

37...♘d3 38 ♖b8 ♕c2+ 39 ♔a1 ♕a4+ 40 ♔b1 ♕c2+ 41 ♔a1

41...♔h7!

Presumably having negotiated the time trouble Black now finds a killing quiet move. This frees his rook to join in the attack after which White has no chance to resist. Of course now 42 ♖xc8 is met by 42...♕b2 mate.

42 ♕b6 ♖c4 0-1

Notes to this game are based on variations given by Knaak in *ChessBase Magazine*.

Game 20
Kasparov-Bareev
Novgorod 1997

1 e4 e6 2 d4 d5 3 ♘c3 ♘f6 4 e5 ♘fd7 5 f4 c5 6 ♘f3 ♘c6 7 ♗e3 cxd4 8 ♘xd4 ♗c5 9 ♕d2 ♗xd4 10 ♗xd4 ♘xd4 11 ♕xd4 ♕b6

This used to be quite a popular line for Black at a high level, where gaining a half point is often the limit of the ambition of the player with the black pieces. White keeps a tiny edge and, of course, Black should be able to draw, but it is not an exciting way to spend an afternoon. The main lines offer Black equally good chances and with interesting positions to boot and this dreary line has therefore fallen out of favour recently, which is no bad thing.

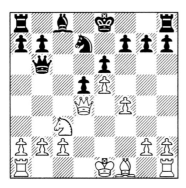

12 ♕xb6

This is probably White's best. Others:

a) 12 ♕d2 ♘c5 (it is difficult to see why Black does not want to capture on b2 but having played 11...♕b6 Black is peaceably inclined) 13 0-0-0 ♗d7 14 ♕d4 a6 15 h4 0-0-0 16 ♖h3 ♗c6 17 ♘e2 ♔b8 18 ♖c3 ♘a4 19 ♕xb6 ♘xb6 (so White ends up with his tiny endgame edge anyway) 20 ♘d4 ♗d7 21 b3 ♘c8 22 h5 ♘e7 23 g4 ♖df8 24 g5 h6 (this is instructive play from Black – he hits back on the kingside before White has a chance to ferry his forces across and create a serious clamp) 25 ♖h3 g6 26 hxg6 ♘xg6 27 ♖xh6 ♘xf4 28 ♗d3 ♖hg8 29 ♖g1 ♖g7 30 ♔d2 ♖fg8 31 ♗h7 ♖h8 32 ♔e3 ♖hxh7 33 ♖xh7 ♖xh7 34 ♔xf4 ♖h4+ 35 ♔g4 ♖h1 36 ♘f3 ♖c1 37 ♖g2 ♔c7 38 a4 ♔d8 39 ♖h2 ♗e8 40 ♔e3 ½-½ Kasparov-Timman, Horgen 1995. A draw with Black against Kasparov is rarely a bad result.

b) After 12 ♘b5 ♕xd4 13 ♘xd4 White's knight is beautifully posted on d4, carefully blocking the black d-pawn and well situated to aid with the advance f4-f5. The only problem is that Black can kick it away pretty quickly with the following manoeuvre, after which the position is a bit dead. This is why 12 ♕xb6 is the preferred method of

handling this position: 13...♔e7 14 0-0-0 ♘b8 15 ♗d3 ♘c6 (the white knight is now driven away from its fine outpost and the position is utterly level) 16 ♘f3 ½-½ Khalifman-Dreev, Novosibirsk 1995.

12...♘xb6

13 a4

Or 13 0-0-0 ♗d7 14 ♗d3 h5 15 ♘e2 ♔e7 16 ♘d4 g6 17 g3 ♗c6 18 ♖de1 ♘d7 19 c3 ♖ag8 20 ♖hf1 g5 (White's play has been passive and Black grabs the initiative) 21 f5 g4 22 ♖e2 h4 23 b4 (this creates weaknesses in the queenside; if White were to sit still he should not be in any great danger) 23...hxg3 24 hxg3 ♗a4 25 ♔b2 ♖h3 26 ♖g1 ♖gh8 27 ♔a3 ♖c8 28 ♔b2 a6 29 ♖gg2 ♗d1 30 ♖e3 ♘b6 31 ♖f2 ♖h1 32 fxe6 fxe6 33 ♖f1 ♘a4+ 34 ♔c1 ♖xc3+ 0-1 Nunn-Korchnoi, Lucerne 1985.

13...♔e7

It is also possible to prevent the advance of the a-pawn at the expense of giving away the b5-square, e.g. 13...a5 14 ♔d2 (14 ♘b5 ♔e7 15 b3 f6 16 exf6+ gxf6 17 ♔d2 ♗d7 18 ♖e1 ♗xb5 19 ♗xb5 ♘c8 20 c4 dxc4 21 ♗xc4 ♖d8+ 22 ♔c3 ♖d6 left Black slightly behind in development, but this did not prove serious in Kir.Georgiev-M.Gurevich, Manila 1990: 23 ♖d1 ♖c6 24 ♔b2 ♘d6 25 ♗d3 ♖g8 26 g3 h5 27 ♖hg1 ♖c5 28 ♗e2 and the game was soon drawn) 14...♗d7 15 b3 ♔e7 16 ♖e1 ♖ag7 17 h4 h6 18 ♗d3 g5 (Korchnoi's patent plan of challenging on the kingside before White gets a grip again proves its value) 19 hxg5 hxg5 20 g3 ♗c6 21 ♖xh8 ♖xh8 22 ♘e2 ♘d7 23 ♘d4 ♖h3 24 ♖g1 gxf4 25 gxf4 ♖h4 26 ♔e3 ♖h3+ 27 ♔f2 ♘c5 28 ♖g3 ♖xg3 29 ♔xg3 ♘xd3 30 cxd3 f6 31 ♔f3 fxe5 32 fxe5 ♗d7 33 ♔e3 ♔f7 34 ♔f4 ½-½ Short-Korchnoi, Groningen 1997.

14 a5 ♘d7 15 ♔d2 g5 16 g3 gxf4 17 gxf4 f6

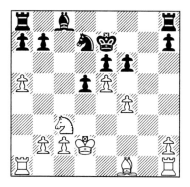

Bareev is living dangerously here. Although an endgame has been reached, it is still risky to neglect development whilst opening up the centre in front of your king. Nevertheless, it is not at all obvious if there is anything wrong with Bareev's idea.

18 ♖g1

The start of a typically violent plan from Kasparov. However, more reserved play got White nowhere in Short-Timman, Novgorod 1995: 18 exf6+ ♘xf6 19 ♗d3 ♗d7 20 ♘e2 ♖hg8 21 ♖hg1 ♔d6 22 c3 and a draw was agreed.

18...fxe5 19 ♗h3 exf4 20 ♖ae1 ♘f8

After his brave play in accepting Kasparov earlier pawn sacrifices, Bareev loses his nerve and returns the material, reconciling himself to a slightly worse endgame. However, if he had held his nerve, it is not entirely clear how Kasparov could justify his two-pawn deficit. The critical move is 20...♘f6 and after 21 ♖g7+ (21 ♖gf1 ♖f8 22 ♖xf4 ♘e4+ is definitely

good for Black) 21...♔f8 (Black can also consider 21...♔d6 22 ♖f7 ♘e8 23 ♘b5+ ♔c5) 22 ♖c7 ♘e8 and the white rook is expelled.

21 ♘xd5+ ♔d6 22 ♘xf4 e5

Bareev may have been relying on this move to equalise the position. It looks as if White may have nothing better than 23 ♗xc8 ♖xc8 when Black would have little to fear. However, Kasparov finds a typically energetic move to keep the initiative.

23 ♖g3!

This activates the rook and creates enough momentum to keep Black under pressure.

23...♗xh3

The point of Kasparov's play is that 23...exf4 runs into 24 ♖d3+ ♔c7 25 ♖e7+ ♔b8 26 ♖e8 ♘g6 27 ♖xh8 ♘xh8 28 ♖d8 and White wins.

24 ♖d3+ ♔c6 25 ♖c3+ ♔d6 26 ♘xh3 ♖g8 27 ♖d3+ ♔e6 28 ♘f4+ ♔f5 29 ♘d5 ♖g2+ 30 ♔c1 ♖f2 31 ♖b3

The b-pawn is also a weakness in the black camp.

31...♖b8 32 a6 b5 33 ♘e7+ ♔f6 34 ♘c6 ♖b6 35 ♘xe5 h5 36 ♘d3 ♖xh2 37 ♘b4 ♔g5 38 ♖f3 ♘g6 39 ♖f7 ♖h4 40 c3

Bareev has fought very well but is now obliged to give up the exchange to prevent White from obtaining a decisive passed a-pawn.

40...♖xb4 41 cxb4 ♖xa6 42 ♖g1+ ♔h6 43 ♔d2 ♖d6+ 44 ♔e3 a6 45 ♔e4 ♘h8 46 ♖a7 ♘g6 47 ♖a1 ♖d2 48 ♖7xa6 ♖xb2 49 ♔f5 ♖f2+ 50 ♔e6 ♖f4 51 ♖b1 h4 52 ♖b6 h3 53 ♖xb5 h2 54 ♖h1 ♖h4 55 ♔d6 ♘f4 56 ♖f5 ♘h5 57 ♖f2 ♖xb4 58 ♖fxh2 ♖b5

Whatever the theoretical status of this endgame it must be very difficult to defend in practice.

59 ♖a2 ♔g6 60 ♖a6 ♘f4 61 ♔e7+ ♔g5 62 ♖g1+ ♔h4 63 ♖a4 ♖f5 64 ♖g8 ♔h3 65 ♖a3+ ♔h2 66 ♖a2+ ♔h3 67 ♖d2

♖e5+ 68 ♔f6 ♖e3 69 ♔f5 ♘e2 70 ♖b2 ♔h2 71 ♖g7 ♖e8 72 ♖g6 ♖e3 73 ♖e6 1-0

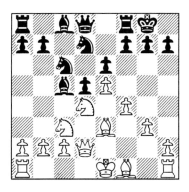

Game 21
Kasparov-Shirov
Astana 2001

1 e4 e6 2 d4 d5 3 ♘c3 ♘f6 4 e5 ♘fd7 5 f4 c5 6 ♘f3 ♘c6 7 ♗e3 cxd4 8 ♘xd4 ♗c5 9 ♕d2 0-0 10 g3

White tries a plan similar to that seen in the previous game. However, as Kasparov points out, playing g2-g3 here maintains the option of castling kingside.

10...♕e7

This is not a terribly good square for the black queen in terms of attacking on the queenside. However, the flip side is that the possibility of ... f7-f6 is created. Other treatments for Black are:

a) 10...♘xd4 11 ♗xd4 a6 12 ♗g2 b5 13 ♘e2 a5 14 a3 ♗xd4 15 ♘xd4 ♕b6 16 0-0 (the advantage of not committing the king too early) 16...♘c5 17 g4 ♗b7 18 ♖ad1 b4 19 f5 exf5 20 gxf5 ♖ae8 21 axb4 axb4 22 ♕f4 and White had a good position in Gofshtein-M.Gurevich, Noyon 2001.

b) 10...♗xd4 11 ♗xd4 ♘xd4 12 ♕xd4 ♘b8 was seen in Anand-Shirov, Leon 2001, played just a couple of weeks after the Kasparov-Shirov game. Play continued 13 0-0-0 ♘c6 14 ♕f2 ♗d7 15 ♔b1 ♕a5 16

♗d3 ♖fc8 17 ♕e1 ♘b4 18 a3 ♘xd3 19 ♖xd3 ♖c4 20 ♕d2 ♖ac8 21 ♘e2 ♕xd2 22 ♖xd2 ♖e4 23 ♘c3 ♖ec4 24 ♖e1 and White had a tiny edge in the endgame but Shirov hung on to draw.

11 0-0-0

Having extracted the small concession of ...♕e7, Kasparov decides to return to normal play.

11...♘b6 12 ♘b3 ♗xe3 13 ♕xe3 ♗d7 14 ♔b1 ♖fc8 15 g4 ♘b4 16 ♘d4 ♖c5

Black has other possibilities to develop his attack. One idea is 16...♕c5 17 ♗d3 ♗a4 which is highly unclear.

17 a3 ♘c6 18 ♘cb5?!

Kasparov missed a good opportunity here. The move 18 ♘b3 forces Black to sacrifice a pawn with 18...d4 19 ♘xd4 ♘xd4 20 ♖xd4 ♖ac8. At first sight this does not look like the kind of gambit one wants to accept, but here White has the strong move 21 ♖d6. By preventing the black queen from coming into play, White makes it difficult for his opponent to justify his gambit.

18...♘xd4 19 ♘xd4 ♖ac8 20 ♗d3 ♘c4 21 ♕h3

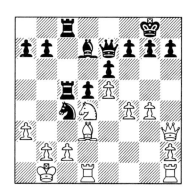

21...h6

This looks suicidal but Shirov has prepared an amazing counterattacking idea. Furthermore, the more natural 21...g6 leaves White with a pleasant choice between the simple 22 ♗xc4 dxc4 23 ♕c3 with a small but persistent edge and the more complex 22 ♘f3, intending to come to g5.

22 g5 ♘xa3+! 23 bxa3 ♖c3 24 gxh6 g6

This is the critical position of the game. White is a piece ahead and Black has no immediate threats. Furthermore, the black king is also not entirely happy. Nevertheless, despite all that, it is not clear that White can win this position.

25 ♕g2

Some variations given by Kasparov demonstrate how tricky this position is:

a) 25 ♔c1 ♖8c4 26 ♔d2 to escape from the danger zone with the king looks logical but after 26...♖xa3 27 ♘f3 ♕c5 the black major pieces are running riot.

b) 25 ♕g3 ♖xa3 26 ♘b3 ♗a4 27 h7+ ♔g7 28 ♕g5 ♕xg5 29 fxg5 ♗xb3 30 ♔b2 ♗xc2 31 ♔xa3 ♗xd1 32 ♖xd1 is a long forcing variation which leads to an endgame where White may be slightly better but it is unlikely to be enough to win.

25...♖xa3 26 ♘b3 ♕b4 27 ♗xg6

White must act at once. If he delays with 27 ♖hg1 ♖c3 28 ♗xg6 then Black has the sneaky move 28...♔h8! preparing a powerful sacrifice on b3.

27...♖xb3+ 28 cxb3 ♕xb3+ 29 ♕b2 ♕xb2+ 30 ♔xb2 fxg6 31 h4 ♔h7 32 h5 ♔xh6 33 hxg6+ ♔xg6 34 ♖hg1+

34...♔f5??

A hideous blunder from Shirov which at once brings his individual score against

Kasparov in tournament games to a thoroughly dismal 0-13. After 34...♔f7 Kasparov admitted that White had very little chance to win the game.

35 ♖d4 1-0

Suddenly ♖g5 will be mate.

Game 22
De Firmian-Hübner
Polanica Zdroj 1995

---

1 e4 e6 2 d4 d5 3 ♘c3 ♘f6 4 e5 ♘fd7 5 f4 c5 6 ♘f3 ♘c6 7 ♗e3 cxd4 8 ♘xd4 ♕b6 9 ♕d2 ♕xb2 10 ♖b1 ♕a3 11 ♗b5 ♘xd4 12 ♗xd4 ♗b4 13 ♖b3

The alternative to this is to castle at once. However, White invariably plays ♖b3 at some point in this line and he doesn't often go anywhere with the king other than on the kingside, so the two lines can easily transpose. After 13 0-0 play continues 13...a6 14 ♖b3 ♕a5 15 ♖fb1 and now:

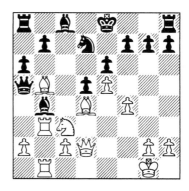

a) 15...♗e7 is possible but, bearing in mind that a white rook will soon be landing on b7, the bishop can become a target here, e.g. 16 ♗xd7+ ♗xd7 17 ♖xb7 ♖c8 18 ♕e3 ♖c4 19 f5 exf5 (19...♖xd4 runs into 20 ♖b8+) 20 ♖xd7! ♔xd7 21 ♖b7+ ♔e8 22 e6 (and not 22 ♖b8+ ♔d7 23 ♖xh8 when 23...♖xd4 is fine for Black) 22...♕a3 (this loses; Black had to play 22...♕d8 when 23 exf7+ ♔xf7 24 ♘xd5 ♖e8 25 ♕e5 ♖xd4 26 ♕xd4 keeps White's advantage to a minimum) 23 ♖b8+ ♗d8 24 ♕g5 ♕d6 25 exf7+ ♔d7 26 ♕xf5+ ♔c6 27 ♕c8+ 1-0 Soffer-Blauert, Budapest 1998.

b) 15...♗a3 16 ♗xd7+ ♗xd7 17 ♘e4 (17 ♗b6, trying to trap the black queen, fails to 17...♗c5+, but White can prepare this threat with 17 ♔h1 when 17...♗c5 18 ♖xb7 ♖c8 19 ♗xc5 ♖xc5 20 ♖1b3 ♗c8 21 ♖7b4 ♕c7 22 h3 0-0 was about equal in Ernst-Manninen, Reykjavik 1995; while 17 ♕e3 resulted in complex play leading to a draw in Santo Roman-Züger, Moscow Olympiad 1994: 17...♖c8 18 ♖xb7 ♖c4 19 f5 ♗c8 20 fxe6 fxe6 21 ♖xg7 ♖xd4 22 ♕g5 ♕xc3 23 ♕h5+ ♔d8 24 ♕g5+ ♔e8 25 ♕h5+ ½-½) 17...♕xd2 18 ♘xd2 ♗e7 19 ♖xb7. Structurally White stands worse but the activity of his pieces is reasonable compensation. Chances are balanced, e.g.

b1) 19...♗b5 20 c4 dxc4 21 a4 ♗xa4 22 ♘xc4 ♗b5 23 ♘d6+ ♗xd6 24 exd6 0-0-0? (this is asking far too much of the black position, especially as 24...0-0 should be fine for Black – in the worse case scenario he would have to give up a rook for the white bishop and d-pawn, but even then he would have excellent chances to hold the game) 25 ♖a7 ♖xd6 26 ♗e5 1-0 Luther-Züger, Altensteig 1995. Now Black loses the exchange in terrible circumstances.

b2) 19...♗c6 20 ♖c7 ♗b5 21 c4 ♗d8 22 ♖c5 dxc4 23 ♘xc4 0-0 24 ♗e3 ♗e7 25 ♘d6 ♖fd8 26 ♖d1 ♗xd6 27 exd6 ♖ac8 28 ♖xc8 ♖xc8 29 ♗b6 ♗d7 30 ♗c7 ♔f8 with an equal position in Kir.Georgiev-Züger, Altensteig 1995.

13...♕a5 14 a3

14 0-0 0-0 15 ♕e3 (or 15 ♕f2!? f6 16 ♗xd7 ♗xd7 17 exf6 gxf6 18 ♖fb1 ♗d6 19 ♕g3+ with a good attack in Kruppa-Nikolenko, Budapest Open 1990) 15...♘b6 16 ♔h1 ♖d8 17 f5 exf5 18 e6 ♗xe6 19 ♕g5? (Black can defend after this, so White had to play 19 ♗xg7 ♔xg7 20 ♕g5+ ♔f8 21 ♕h6+ when the game will be a draw unless Black is willing to risk 21...♔e7 22 ♕h4+,

after which White regains the piece and has a strong attack for the two pawns) 19...♗f8 (now Black has numerous extra pawns for insufficient compensation) 20 ♘xd5 (this doesn't work but it is difficult to find a good plan when you are three pawns down for nothing) 20...♘xd5 21 ♗xg7 ♗xg7 22 ♖g3 ♔f8 23 ♕xg7+ ♔e7 24 a4 ♔g8 25 ♕h6 ♕b4 26 c4 ♘f6 27 ♕f4 ♕d6 28 ♕e3 ♖xg3 29 hxg3 ♘e4 0-1 Sedlak-Marjanovic, Subotica 2000.

14...♗e7 15 f5

In a later game De Firmian preferred a more restrained build-up which also served him well: 15 ♕e3 0-0 16 0-0 ♕c7 17 f5 ♗c5 18 ♗xd7 ♗xd4 19 ♕xd4 ♗xd7 20 f6 ♖fc8 21 ♕g4 g6 22 ♕g5 ♕c5+ 23 ♔h1 b6 24 ♘e2 ♕f8 25 ♘d4, when in De Firmian-Kaidanov, Lexington 1995, White had excellent compensation for the pawn thanks to his well posted knight on d4 and the serious dark-square weaknesses around the black king.

15...exf5

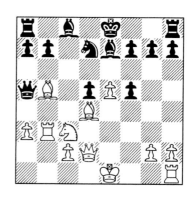

15...b6 is a calm response. Mencinger-Rogulj, Bled 1992, continued 16 0-0 ♗a6 17 ♗xa6 ♕xa6 18 ♘b5 0-0-0!? 19 fxe6 ♘c5 20 ♖xf7 (20 ♕c3 should keep White on top; now the tables turn) 20...♘xb3 21 ♕e2 ♔b8 22 cxb3 ♖he8 23 a4 ♕c8 24 h3 ♕xe6 25 ♖xg7 ♖g8 26 ♖xh7 ♖c8 27 a5 ♖c1+ 28 ♔h2 ♕g6 29 ♖xe7 ♕g3 checkmate.

16 ♘xd5

If White wishes to keep the queens on, he must play rather speculatively, e.g. 16 e6 fxe6 17 ♗xg7 ♖g8 18 ♕h6 ♔f7 19 ♗xd7 ♗xd7 20 ♗e5 d4 (20...♖ac8!?) 21 ♕xh7+ ♔f8 22 ♗f4 ♖xg2 23 ♗h6+ ♔e8 24 ♕h8+ ♔f7 25 ♕h7+ and the players agreed a draw in Van der Wiel-Ree, Holland 1986. Black could try for a win with 25...♔f6, but 26 h4 is a dangerous reply. After 26...dxc3 27 ♗g5+ ♔e5 28 ♕xe7 the position is highly unclear.

16...♗h4+ 17 ♔d1

17 ♔e2 would transpose to the next note after 17... ♕xd2+ 18 ♔xd2.

17...♕d8

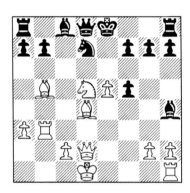

Keeping the queens on is a brave decision which, in this particular case, turns out to be rather foolhardy. Exchanging queens leaves a balanced endgame where, as usual, White's active pieces compensate for the pawn. Examples of play: 17... ♕xd2+ 18 ♔xd2 ♗d8 19 ♖g3 (19 ♖c3 is much less relevant, e.g. 19...a6 20 ♗d3 ♘f8 21 ♗b6 ♗e6 22 ♘c7+ ♗xc7 23 ♗xc7 g6 24 g4 ♗d5 25 ♖g1 f4 when Black stood well and went on to win in Sahu-Singh, Calcutta 1996) 19...a6 20 ♗xd7+ ♗xd7 21 ♖xg7 ♗e6 (the position is equal) 22 ♘f4 (or 22 ♘f6+ ♔f8 23 ♖g3 ♖c8 24 ♖f1 ♖c4 25 ♖f4 ♗xf6 26 exf6 ♖g8 27 ♖g7 ♖xg7 28 fxg7+ ♔g8 ½-½ Apel-Blauert, Germany 1997) 22...♗e7 23 g4 fxg4 24 ♘xe6 fxe6 25 ♖f1 ♖d8 26 ♔e3 ♖d7 27 a4 ♖c7 28 ♔d3 ♗d8 29 ♖xc7 ♗xc7

30 ♖b1 b5 31 axb5 axb5 32 ♖xb5 ♔d7 and White had a tiny edge in Nijboer-Kuijf, Wijk aan Zee 1996.

18 ♘f6+!

This results in a devastating opening of lines after which the black king cannot survive.

18...gxf6 19 exf6 0-0

This gets mated by force. However, the position was already hopeless, e.g. 19...h6 20 ♕b4 (20 ♕e3+ ♔f8 21 ♕e7+ ♕xe7 22 fxe7+ ♔xe7 23 ♗xh8 wins the exchange but 20 ♕b4 is much stronger) 20...♗xf6 21 ♖e3+ ♗e7 22 ♖xe7+ ♕xe7 23 ♖e1 and the game is up.

20 ♖g3+! ♔h8 21 ♕h6

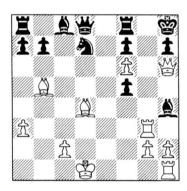

21...♖g8

If 21...♗xf6 the brutal 22 ♖g7 forces mate next move but White might prefer the flashy 22 ♕g7+, achieving the same end, albeit by taking one move more.

22 ♖g7 ♘f8 1-0

Not waiting for 23 ♖xg8+ and mate next move.

Game 23
Fedorov-Volkov
St Petersburg 1997

---

1 e4 e6 2 d4 d5 3 ♘c3 ♘f6 4 e5 ♘fd7 5 f4 c5 6 ♘f3 ♘c6 7 ♗e3 cxd4 8 ♘xd4 ♕b6 9 ♕d2

This is certainly the critical test of Black's

idea as the alternatives do not seem to promise much:

a) 9 a3 and now:

a1) 9...♘xd4 10 ♗xd4 ♗c5 11 ♘a4 ♕a5+ 12 b4 ♕xa4 13 bxc5 b6 14 cxb6 axb6 leaves the white position looking a bit of a mess. Kobalija-Bareev, Moscow 1999, continued 15 ♗e2 ♗a6 16 ♗xa6 ♕xa6 17 ♕d3 ♕xd3 18 cxd3 ♖a4 19 ♗e3 ♔d8 20 ♔d2 ♔c7 21 ♖hc1+ ♔b7 22 ♖cb1 ♖ha8 23 ♖b3 d4 and Black went on to win.

a2) 9...♗c5 and now:

a21) 10 ♘cb5 ♘xd4 11 ♗xd4 0-0 12 ♗xc5 (after 12 ♗d3 ♗xd4 13 ♘xd4 ♕xb2 14 ♘b5 ♘xe5 15 fxe5 ♗d7 16 ♖b1 ♕xe5+ 17 ♕e2 ♕xe2+ 18 ♗xe2 a6 19 ♘c3 ♗c6 Black's pawns proved more valuable than the piece in Dueball-Smejkal, Raach 1969) 12...♘xc5 13 ♕d4 ♗d7 14 ♘d6 f6 15 ♗e2 fxe5 16 fxe5 with an equal position in Macieja-Gradalski, Suwalki 1999.

a22) 10 ♘a4 ♕a5+ 11 c3 ♗xd4 12 ♗xd4 ♘xd4 13 ♕xd4 b6 (13...♘b8 14 ♘c5 b6 15 ♘b3 ♘c6 16 ♘xa5 ♘xd4 17 0-0-0 bxa5 18 ♖xd4 ♗d7 19 ♗e2 left White with a typical and useful endgame advantage in Videki-Guliev, Szekszard 1994) 14 ♕b4 ♕xb4 (or 14...♗b7 15 ♗b5 ♖c8 16 ♕xa5 bxa5 17 ♗xd7+ ♔xd7 18 0-0-0 ♖c4 19 ♖d4 ♖hc8 20 ♔b1 ♔e7 21 b3 ♖4c7 22 ♔b2 ♗a6 23 b4 ♗c4 24 ♘c5 again with a small edge for White in Kveinys-Züger, Yerevan 1996) 15 axb4 ♔e7 (alternatively 15...0-0 16 ♗b5 f6 17 exf6 and now in Sax-Klinger, Szirak 1985, Black committed a horrible blunder with 17...♖xf6?? and after 18 ♗xd7 ♗xd7 19 ♘xb6 ♖d8 20 ♖xa7 ♗e8 21 0-0 he could go home; however, 17...gxf6 instead looks quite reasonable) 16 ♗b5 ♗b7 17 0-0 (or 17 ♔d2 ♖hc8 18 ♖he1 ♖c7 19 ♗xd7 ♔xd7 20 b3 ♖ac8 21 ♖e3 ♔e7 22 ♖g3 ♔f8 23 ♘b2 ♗c6 24 ♘d3 ♗b5 25 ♘e1 a5 26 bxa5 ♖a7 27 a6 ♖xa6 28 ♖xa6 ♗xa6 29 ♘c2 and White had a small plus in Balinov-Vigh, Poland 1997) 17...♖hd8 18 ♔f2 f6 (this is the right idea; once Black makes this break

he should have no problems) 19 ♗xd7 ♖xd7 20 ♔e3 ♖f8 21 b3 ♗c6 22 ♘b2 ♗b5 23 ♖f3 ♔d8 24 ♖d1 ♔e7 25 ♖a1 ♖c7 26 ♔d4 with equality in Nunn-Ehlvest, Reykjavik 1988.

b) 9 ♘cb5 is pretty much scuppered by the reply 9...a6 10 ♘f5 ♗c5 11 ♗xc5? (after this White has a very bad position; best is 11 ♘bd6+ ♔f8 12 ♕h5 ♘d8 13 ♘xg7! ♗xe3 14 ♘xe6+! fxe6! 15 ♕h6+ ♔g8 16 ♕g5+ ♔f8 and White gets a perpetual check – this is best play for both sides but does not constitute a good reason to play 9 ♘cb5) 11...♘xc5 12 ♘bd6+ ♔f8 13 ♕h5 ♘d8 14 ♘xg7 (White's problem is that his queenside is falling apart, e.g. 14 ♘xc8 ♕b4+ 15 c3 ♕xb2) 14...♕b4+ 15 c3 ♕xb2 16 ♖d1 ♕xc3+ 17 ♖d2 h6 18 ♘ge8 ♘e4 0-1 Hübner-Korchnoi, San Francisco 1995.

c) 9 ♗e2 ♗c5 10 ♘a4 ♕a5+ 11 c3 ♗xd4 12 ♗xd4 ♘xd4 13 ♕xd4 b6 14 0-0 ♘c5 (after 14...♗a6 15 ♗xa6 ♕xa6 16 f5 0-0 17 b3 b5 18 ♘c5 ♘xc5 19 ♕xc5 ♖fc8 20 ♕b4 ♕b6+ 21 ♔h1 a5 Black was fine in Sherzer-Almasi, Hungary 1995) 15 ♗d1 ♗a6 16 ♖e1 ♕b5 17 ♘xc5 bxc5 18 ♕f2 ♕b6 19 f5 0-0-0 (White's play has been so convoluted that Black easily gets away with this) 20 ♗e2 ♗xe2 21 ♖xe2 ♔b8 22 ♖d1 ♖d7 23 ♕g3 g6 24 fxe6 fxe6 25 ♖f2 ♖dd8 26 h3 ♕a6 ½-½ Olenin-Itkis, Alushta 2000.

9...♕xb2 10 ♖b1 ♕a3 11 ♗b5 ♘db8

A rather retrograde move but it does at least go some way towards untangling the black queenside. Highly dangerous is 11...♘xd4 12 ♗xd4 a6 13 ♗xd7+ ♗xd7 14 ♖b3 ♕e7 15 ♖xb7 which leaves Black way behind in development. This proved to be too much of a handicap in Golubev-Zakharov, Moscow 1995: 15...♕d8 16 0-0 ♕c8 17 ♖b3 ♗c5 18 f5 exf5 19 ♘xd5 0-0 20 ♘f6+! ♔h8 21 ♖h3 ♗xd4+ 22 ♔h1 1-0.

12 ♗xc6+

A violent alternative is 12 f5!? ♗b4 13 ♖b3 ♕a5 14 0-0 exf5 15 ♖fb1 f4! (a good move which throws White off balance and allows Black to simplify the position) 16 ♖xb4 fxe3 17 ♕xe3 0-0 18 ♗xc6 ♘xc6 19 ♖b5 ♕a6 20 ♖xd5 ½-½ Dolmatov-Volkov, Kstovo 1997.

12...bxc6 13 0-0 a6

In an earlier game between the same two players Black had tried 13...♗c5 14 ♖b3 ♕a5 15 ♖fb1 ♗b6 16 ♕c1!? (White is using his initiative to create play on the queenside as well as the kingside) 16...♗xd4 17 ♗xd4 ♘d7 18 f5 exf5 19 e6 fxe6 20 ♕g5 ♕d8 21 ♕xg7 ♖f8 22 ♘e2 with highly unclear play in Fedorov-Volkov, Omsk 1996.

14 ♖b3

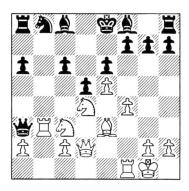

14...♕a5

Black must be very careful here. For example, the plausible 14...♕e7? loses at once to the reply 15 ♘a4 c5 16 ♘xc5! ♕xc5 17 ♖c3.

15 ♖xb8 ♖xb8 16 ♘xc6 ♕c7 17 ♘xb8 ♕xb8 18 f5

Instead 18 ♖b1 ♕c7 19 f5 ♕xe5 20 fxe6 fxe6 21 ♗d4 ♕c7 22 ♕e3 ♗e7 23 ♗xg7 ♗c5 24 ♗d4 ♗xd4 25 ♕xd4 ½-½ was Chandler-Klinger, Vienna 1986.

18...♕xe5 19 ♗d4 ♕c7 20 ♕e3 ♕c4 21 ♘e2 h5!?

Black hits upon the plan of developing the rook via h6. The position favours White as it is difficult to see how his opponent can

co-ordinate with such a vulnerable king.

22 ♘f4 ♖h6 23 c3 h4 24 h3 a5 25 a4 ♗a6 26 ♖e1 ♗c8 27 ♖f1 ♗a6 28 ♖b1 ♗c8 29 ♕e5 ♖f6 30 ♖e1 ♗e7 31 fxe6 fxe6 32 ♕h5+ ♔d7 33 ♗xf6 ♗xf6 34 ♘xe6

White has won the exchange but the bishops on the open board will be hard to cope with.

34...♔d6 35 ♘d4 ♗d7

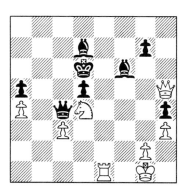

36 ♕f3

Here White misses a remarkable manoeuvre. With 36 ♕h8! planning ♕b8, he could have placed intolerable pressure on the black king.

36...♗xa4 37 ♕f4+ ♔d7 38 ♕g4+ ♔c7 39 ♕f4+ ♔d7 40 ♖b1 ♗c6 41 ♕f5+ ♔c7 42 ♕f4+ ♔d7 43 ♖b8

White seems to be making decisive inroads into the black position, but now Volkov finds a cold-blooded defence.

43...♕xc3! 44 ♕f5+ ♔d6 45 ♕e6+ ♔c7 46 ♘b5+ ♗xb5 47 ♖c8+ ♔b7 48 ♖xc3 ♗xc3 49 ♕xd5+ ♔b6

White has won the black queen but the bishops and a-pawn render any winning attempts impossible.

50 ♕d8+ ♔c5 51 ♔f2 ♔b4 52 ♕xh4+ ♗c4 53 ♕e7+ ♔b3 54 ♕b7+ ♔a2 55 ♕c7 ½-½

Summary

The main lines, as seen in Games 14-18, are holding up well for Black. When one considers the structure, this is not entirely surprising. White has the usual space advantage and attacking chances on the kingside, but his opponent has a quick queenside counterattack and an open c-file to press against the white king. Indeed, when the game turns into a race, Black invariably gets the better of it. The best way for White to play seems to be with a plan of challenging on the queenside and hoping to steer for a slightly better endgame. However, the quieter plans with either 11 g3 or 10 g3 (Games 19 and 20 respectively) have received recent experimentation at a high level and may be the way for White to go.

The endgame variation of Game 21 has fallen out of favour – hardly surprising when Black has good counterplay in the main lines while here he has to resign himself to a turgid endgame. The pawn grab with 8...♛b6 (Games 22 and 23) certainly seems to be playable but it is not a choice for those of a nervous disposition.

1 e4 e6 2 d4 d5 3 ♘c3 ♘f6 4 e5 ♘fd7 5 f4 c5 6 ♘f3 ♘c6 7 ♗e3 cxd4 8 ♘xd4

8...♗c5
    8...♛b6 9 ♛d2 ♛xb2 10 ♖b1 ♛a3 11 ♗b5 *(D)*
        11...♘xd4 – *Game 22*; 11...♘db8 – *Game 23*
9 ♛d2 0-0
    9....♗xd4 10 ♗xd4 ♘xd4 11 ♛xd4 ♛b6 – *Game 21*
10 0-0-0
    10 g3 – *Game 20*
10...a6 *(D)* **11 h4**
    11 g3 – *Game 19*
11...♘xd4
    11...♗xd4 12 ♘xd4 b5 – *Game 18*
12 ♗xd4 b5 13 ♖h3
    13 h5 – *Game 17*
13...b4 14 ♘a4
    14 ♘e2 – *Game 16*
14...♗xd4 15 ♛xd4 *(D)* **f6**
    15...a5 – *Game 15*
16 ♛xb4 – *Game 14*

11 ♗b5

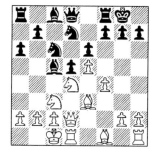

10...a6

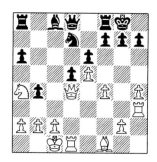

15 ♛xd4

CHAPTER THREE

Old Main Line with 7...a6

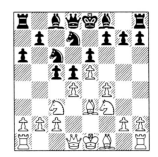

1 e4 e6 2 d4 d5 3 ♘c3 ♘f6 4 e5 ♘fd7 5 f4 c5 6 ♘f3 ♘c6 7 ♗e3 a6

The major difference between the play in the games in this chapter and the previous one is that here White invariably castles on the kingside. This sets the scene for a more docile encounter where the blunt strategy of attacking on opposite wings is replaced by a more positional struggle. At some point White tends to make the capture d4xc5 which is usually met by ...♗xc5 and the exchange of dark-squared bishops. Black has reasonably easy play on the queenside, as his knights and pawns become active there, but must be careful not to wind up in an endgame where he is stuck with the archetypal bad light-squared bishop.

White has two main ways to handle the position. He can gear up for a big push on the kingside or he can be more circumspect and try to restrain Black's play whilst maintaining the positional advantages of his game such as the dark square control (especially the key d4-square) and extra space.

The main line with 8 ♕d2 b5 9 dxc5 ♗xc5 10 ♗xc5 ♘xc5 11 ♕f2 is examined in Games 24-26. Game 27 sees 9...b4, while alternative tries for White on move 9 are seen in Games 28 and 29. Finally, Murey's

patent 8 a3 is the subject of Game 30.

Game 24
Anand-Bareev
Dortmund 1992

1 e4 e6 2 d4 d5 3 ♘c3 ♘f6 4 e5 ♘fd7 5 f4 c5 6 ♘f3 ♘c6 7 ♗e3

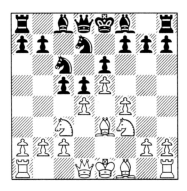

7...a6

Preparing a general pawn advance on the queenside. Not wishing to 'castle into it', White's king will generally seek a safe haven on the other wing.

8 ♕d2 b5 9 dxc5 ♗xc5 10 ♗xc5 ♘xc5 11 ♕f2 ♕b6 12 ♗d3

The ambitious tactical thrust 12 b4 is the subject of Game 26.

12...♖b8

Aiming for active piece play and defending his own queen. Instead the experimental 12...♗b7?! 13 0-0 0-0-0 is probably not too bad if Black then meets 14 a3 with 14...♕c7, when Khalifman feels that with 15 b4 White is only slightly better (space advantage and better minor pieces). However, after 14...b4 15 axb4 ♕xb4 16 ♘e2 White was able to develop a strong attack against the black king in Khalifman-Speelman, Munich 1992. 12...b4 is seen in Game 25.

13 0-0

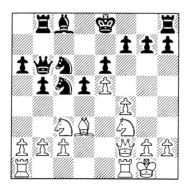

13...♘b4

Black could also consider the immediate 13...♘a4 when after 14 ♘xa4 bxa4 15 ♕xb6 ♖xb6 16 b3 he is able to rapidly activate his forces, e.g. 16...♗d7 17 ♔f2 ♔e7 18 ♔e3 h6 19 h4 ♖c8 20 h5 ♘b4 21 ♘d4 ♗b5 with reasonable play in Maciejewski-Gleizerov, Lubniewice 1993.

14 ♖fd1 0-0?!

This move is the source of Black's later woes. The king is lacking in support from his minor pieces, so nowadays everyone plays 14...♘a4! exchanging queens. As we saw in the previous note the doubled a-pawns are not really a weakness as White will probably have to play b2-b3 at some point, exchanging one off. The typical result is that Black has an isolated a-pawn, but has counter-pressure against the b- and c-pawn

couplet. After 15 ♘xa4 bxa4 (or 15...♕xf2+ 16 ♔xf2 bxa4 17 b3 ♔e7 18 ♘d4 ♗d7 19 ♗f1 ♖hc8 20 ♖d2 a5 21 c4 axb3 22 axb3 a4 23 cxd5 ♘xd5 24 bxa4 ♘c3 25 ♔f3 ♘xa4 Arakhamia-Kiriakov, Port Erin 2000, and Black had equalised) 16 b3 (after 16 ♕xb6 ♖xb6 17 b3 axb3 18 axb3 ♔e7 19 ♔f2 ♗d7 20 ♘d4 h6 21 ♔e3 f6 22 c3 ♘xd3 23 ♔xd3 g5 Black had sufficient counter-chances in Khalifman-Bareev, Moscow 1992) 16...axb3 (Black could also consider 16...♗d7!? maintaining the tension) 17 axb3 0-0 18 ♕xb6 ♖xb6 19 ♘d4 f6 (not allowing White's king early access to the centre) 20 g3 fxe5 21 fxe5 ♗d7, as in Kuczynski-Dolmatov, Polanica Zdroj 1991, White retains the better minor piece and thus he can probably claim a nominal edge.

15 ♘e2 ♗d7 16 ♘ed4 ♘bxd3

Not really the move that Black wants to play but after 16...a5 Anand analyses 17 ♗xh7+ ♔xh7 18 ♕h4+ ♔g8 19 ♘g5 ♖fc8 and now simply 20 ♔h1! (taking the king off the sensitive a7-g1 diagonal) leaving White with a strong attack.

17 cxd3 ♘a4 18 b4!

A strong move that fixes the b-pawn to b5. Now White has a classic 'good knight against bad bishop'.

18...a5 19 a3 ♖fc8 20 ♖dc1 axb4 21 axb4 ♖xc1+ 22 ♖xc1 ♖c8 23 ♖xc8+ ♗xc8 24 ♕c2

By controlling the c-file White obliges his opponent to protect several points of entry. It's also difficult to get the a4-knight back into play.

24...♗d7 25 ♔f2 ♔f8 26 g4

With everything under control White builds up his space advantage.

26...♔e8 27 ♔e3 f6

Played in order to obtain some breathing space, but nevertheless the big squeeze continues.

28 h4 ♕b8 29 ♕c1 ♔f8 30 ♔e2 ♔f7 31 ♕e3 ♕f8

Hoping to distract his opponent by

hitting the b4-pawn, but White's initiative is overwhelming.

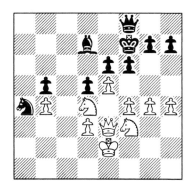

32 f5! ₩e8 33 g5! exf5 34 gxf6 gxf6 35 ₩h6 fxe5 36 ₩xh7+ ⌘f6 37 ₩h6+ ⌘f7 38 ♘g5+ ⌘e7 39 ₩g7+ ⌘d6 40 ♘f7+ ⌘c7 41 ♘xe5

White's king-hunt has not yet won any material but the result is not in doubt. The passed h-pawn is a strong asset and Black's pieces are too badly placed to prevent the loss of a couple of pawns.

41...♘b6 42 ♘xb5+ ⌘b8 43 ♘d4 ₩h5+ 44 ♘df3 ♗e8 45 ⌘f2 f4 46 ₩e7 ♘c8 47 ₩f6 ⌘b7 48 ₩xf4 ₩h8 49 ♘g5 ₩h6 50 ⌘g3 ♘d6 51 ₩f3 ♗c6 52 ♘gf7 ♘xf7 53 ₩xf7+ ⌘b6 54 ₩f4 ₩e6 55 h5 ♗b7 56 ₩f6! 1-0

A neat way to extinguish any resistance. If 56...₩xf6 then White has 57 ♘d7+ and ♘xf6 followed by queening the h-pawn.

Game 25
Lutz-Zifroni
Tel Aviv 1999

---

1 e4 e6 2 d4 d5 3 ♘c3 ♘f6 4 e5 ♘fd7 5 f4 c5 6 ♘f3 ♘c6 7 ♗e3 a6 8 ₩d2 b5 9 dxc5 ♗xc5 10 ♗xc5 ♘xc5 11 ₩f2 ₩b6 12 ♗d3 b4

Continuing the queenside advance and preparing to place the bishop on the a6-f1 diagonal.

13 ♘e2 a5 14 0-0

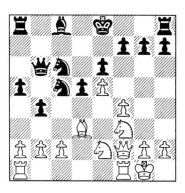

14...♗a6

The standard move. In Romero Holmes-Schwartzman, Wijk aan Zee 1995, Black experimented with 14...♖b8 15 ⌘h1 ♘xd3 16 cxd3 ₩xf2 17 ♖xf2 ♗a6 18 ♖d1 ⌘e7 19 ♘ed4 ♘xd4 20 ♘xd4 ♖bc8 21 g3 and White had an edge.

15 ⌘h1

The most popular. Others:

a) After 15 ♖fd1 0-0 16 ♘ed4 ♖fc8 17 ♘b3 ♘a4 18 ₩xb6 ♘xb6 19 ♘bd4 ♘a4 20 ♖db1 ♘c5 21 ♗xa6 ♖xa6 22 a3 ♘e4 Black had adequate counter-chances in Kuczynski-Glek, Bundesliga 1995.

b) Naturally White can keep the annoying black knight from the a4-square with 15 ♖ad1 ♘a4 16 ₩xb6 ♘xb6 17 b3, but after 17...⌘e7 18 ♘ed4 ♘xd4 19 ♘xd4 ♖hc8 20 ♗xa6 ♖xa6 21 a3 bxa3 22 ♖a1 ♘d7 23 ♖xa3 ♘b8 24 ♖f2 ♘c6, as in Kuczynski-Djurhuus, Manila Olympiad 1992, White's initiative had been neutralised. The ending is not really particularly promising for White after his opponent has been able to exchange off his light-squared bishop.

c) Sharper is the pawn sacrifice 15 f5!?, but after 15...♗xd3 16 cxd3 exf5 17 ♘f4 ♘e7, as Nunn points out, it's not clear that White has enough compensation.

15...♘e7

With Black having made space gains on the queenside, he now prudently restrains White's intended f5-advance. 15...♗xd3 16 cxd3 ♕b5 is met by the aggressive 17 f5 leading to complications, e.g. 17...♘xd3 18 ♕h4 ♘dxe5 19 ♘xe5 ♘xe5 20 ♘d4 ♕b8 21 fxe6 0-0 with unclear play in Morgado-Carlsson, correspondence 1996.

16 b3

The critical move cutting out Black's annoying ...♘a4. White has three main options: a) 16 ♖ad1 ♘a4 17 ♕xb6 ♘xb6 18 ♘ed4?! (18 b3 as in Kuczynski-Djurhuus above is nothing special for White) 18...♘a4 19 ♖b1 ♘c5! 20 ♖fd1 0-0 21 ♔g1 a4 22 ♔f2 ♖fb8 when Black's well-placed pieces and advanced pawns offered him the better options in Vehi-Glek, Biel 1997.

b) 16 ♖fd1 h6 17 ♘g3 g6 18 ♘e2 h5?! (18...♘a4 looks safer) 19 ♘ed4 ♘a4 20 ♖ab1 ♗xd3 21 cxd3 ♖c8 22 ♖d2 ♖c7 23 ♖e1 ♔d7 24 ♕h4 ♖hc8 25 b3 ♘c3 26 ♕f6 gave White some pressure in Rowson-Barsov, York 1999.

c) 16 ♘g3 ♘a4 (this seems adequate but 16...g6!? is an interesting try, cutting out f4-f5 but loosening the dark squares; Lutz-Glek, German Bundesliga 1995, was unclear after 17 ♘e2 ♖b8 18 ♗xa6 ♘xa6 19 ♘ed4 ♘c5 20 ♕h4 ♘e4 21 ♖ad1) 17 ♕xb6 ♘xb6 18 ♘d4 g6 19 ♗xa6 ♖xa6 20 a3 bxa3 21 ♖xa3 ♔d7 22 ♖fa1 a4 23 ♘ge2 ♖c8 with equal chances in Votava-Glek, Germany 1997.

16...h6

An essential preparatory move for kingside castling.

17 ♖ad1 ♖c8

The provocative 17...0-0!? was tried in the encounter Skripchenko-Lautier - Piskov, Recklinghausen 1996, which continued 18 g4 ♖fb8 19 ♘fd4 ♘e4 20 ♕e3 ♘c6 21 ♖g1 ♗xd3 22 ♖xd3 ♖c8 23 ♖g2 ♖c7 24 h4 and White was intent on smashing open the kingside. However, this only led to perpetual check in the game and it's not clear if the attack is all that strong.

18 ♘g3 g6

The standard reaction to the threat of f4-

f5. Now White switches to the plan of invading on f6.

19 ♘e2 ♕b7 20 ♘fd4

The primitive 20 ♕h4 ♘xd3 21 cxd3 ♖c2 22 ♘ed4 ♖xa2 23 ♕f6 looks good for Black after 23...♖h7.

20...♘e4

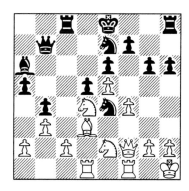

This well-posted knight seems to give Black a satisfactory position. If White captures on e4 then his central control is weakened, e.g. 21 ♗xe4?! dxe4 22 ♖fe1 (not 22 ♖d2? as 22...♘d5 wins material) 22...♘d5 23 ♘g3 e3 and Black has good play.

21 ♕h4 ♕b6 22 ♗xa6 ♕xa6 23 g4?

Too risky. Perhaps it was time for 23 ♘g3.

23...h5!

With ideas such as 24...g5 25 fxg5 ♘g6 in the air.

24 f5 g5! 25 ♕h3 ♖xc2!

A dramatic exchange sacrifice to kill off the attack.

26 fxe6 fxe6 27 ♘xc2 ♕xe2 28 ♕g2

28...hxg4!

Another blow for White. Black obtains a second pawn and further important squares for his pieces.

29 ♕xe2 ♘g3+ 30 ♔g2 ♘xe2 31 ♘d4 ♘f4+ 32 ♔g1 ♖h3 33 ♖d2 ♘eg6 34 ♖e1 ♔d7

The white rooks are powerless to stop the e-pawn being picked off.

35 ♖c2 ♘d3 36 ♖f1 ♘dxe5 37 ♖f6 ♘f4
38 ♖f8 ♖d3 39 ♘e2 ♘f3+ 40 ♔f2
♘h3+ 0-1

White loses at least a rook.

Game 26
Feletar-Kovacevic
Pula 2000

---

1 e4 e6 2 d4 d5 3 ♘c3 ♘f6 4 e5 ♘fd7
5 f4 c5 6 ♘f3 ♘c6 7 ♗e3 a6 8 ♕d2 b5
9 dxc5 ♗xc5 10 ♗xc5 ♘xc5 11 ♕f2
♕b6 12 b4!?

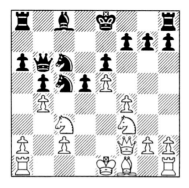

Aiming for tactical play before Black
becomes better organised.

12...♘xb4

If this proves to be too risky then Black
could consider retreating his attacked knight
with 12...♘d7 13 ♖b1 ♕xf2+ 14 ♔xf2 ♘b6
15 ♗d3 ♗d7 when a premature draw was
agreed in Tissir-Komarov, Tanta 2001.
Black has been pushed back and his pawns
are fixed on light-squares, but he can seek
counterplay by using a4, c4 and c3 – squares
that have been weakened by the aggressive
advance 12 b4. This position requires
further tests before one can make a final
judgement on 12 b4.

A more risky alternative to 13 ♖b1 is 13
a4?! and after 13...♘xb4 14 axb5:

a) 14...♕xf2+ 15 ♔xf2 ♘xc2 16 ♖a5 0-0
17 ♗d3 d4? (17...♘b4! 18 ♗e2 ♘c5 looks
playable) 18 ♗e4! dxc3 19 ♗xa8 ♘b4 20

♖a3 c2 21 ♘d4 axb5 22 ♗e4 ♘c5 23 ♗xc2
♖d8 24 ♖a8 and having won the exchange
White was better in Sherzer-Glek, Budapest
1998.

b) 14...♕c7! 15 ♔d2 ♘c5 16 ♕d4 a5 17
♖a3 0-0 18 ♗d3 ♗b7 19 ♖c1 ♖fc8, as in
Tissir-Vysochin, Cappelle la Grande 2001.
With White tied down to holding onto the
queenside, Black had a pleasant game.

13 ♖b1 ♘c6

A combative alternative is 13...d4!? 14
♘xd4 ♕a5! with interesting complications
(after 14...♘e4 15 ♘xe4 ♕xd4 16 ♘d6+
♔f8 17 ♕d2! ♕xd2+ 18 ♔xd2 ♘d5 19 g3
White has the better endgame). If 15
♘dxb5 then 15...♘e4 16 ♕f3 ♘d5 17
♕xe4 axb5 18 ♖b3 ♗d7 looks fine for
Black. Clearly there is room for further
investigation here, but at first sight 13...d4
looks promising.

14 ♗xb5 ♗d7

14...axb5?! is dubious: 15 ♖xb5 ♘d3+ 16
cxd3 ♕xf2+ 17 ♔xf2 d4 18 ♘e2 0-0
(18...♖xa2? leads to all sorts of problems
after 19 ♖c1 ♔d7 20 ♖b6) 19 ♖c1 ♘e7 20
♖b2 and White had maintained an extra
pawn in Zelcic-B.Kovacevic, Pula 2000.

15 0-0 ♕a7 16 ♗xc6 ♗xc6 17 ♘d4!

An improvement on 17 f5 exf5 18 ♘d4
♘a4!, as in Wiersma-Radjabov, Groningen
1999, which led to easy equality. By playing
17 ♘d4 first, White aims to gain a tempo
for the attack.

17...♖c8?

A poor move that clearly underestimates
White's attacking potential. Instead
17...♘a4! is playable. Then 18 ♘xa4 (if 18
♘ce2 then 18...♗d7 takes the sting out of
White's f5-break; White should probably try
18 ♘xc6! ♕xf2+ 19 ♖xf2 ♘xc3 20 ♖b7
with the slightly better prospects in the
ending) 18...♗xa4 19 ♖b4 (19 f5 only leads
to equal chances after 19...exf5 20 ♖b4 ♗d7
21 ♘xf5 ♕xf2+ 22 ♖xf2 ♗xf5 23 ♖xf5 0-0)
19...♗d7 20 ♖fb1 is not really anything as
Black can continue 20...0-0! 21 ♖b7?! ♖fb8!

with equal play.
18 f5 exf5 19 ②xf5 0-0

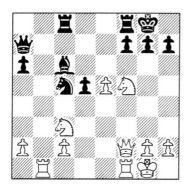

20 ③b4!

The storm clouds gather around the black monarch.

20...f6 21 ③g4 g6?

A blunder. Feletar intended to meet 21...③c7 with 22 ②xg7! ③xg7 23 ③xg7+ ③xg7 24 exf6+ with a persistent attack. White can proceed slowly as his opponent cannot put up much of a defence, e.g. 24...③f7 25 ③h1 h6 26 ③f5 ③b7 27 ②e2 ③e8 28 f7+ ③d8 29 ③f6+ and although Black has a piece more White's f-pawn gives him the better prospects.

22 exf6 ③c7 23 f7+ ③fxf7 24 ②h6+ ③f8 25 ②xf7 ③xf7 26 ③f4 1-0

Game 27
Magem-Vaisser
Escaldes 1998

---

1 e4 e6 2 d4 d5 3 ②c3 ②f6 4 e5 ②fd7 5 f4 c5 6 ②f3 ②c6 7 ③e3 a6 8 ③d2 b5 9 dxc5 b4

Obliging White to make an immediate decision about the future of his knight.

10 ②a4

The most popular. The alternatives are not thought to be dangerous for Black:

a) 10 ②d1 ②xc5 11 ③d3 ③b7 12 0-0 d4 13 ③f2 ③e7 14 b3 f6! 15 exf6 gxf6 16 ②b2 (Kamsky-Lautier, New York 1991) is fine

for Black after Kamsky's 16...③c7! 17 ②c4 (17 ②xd4? gives Black a strong initiative after 17...②xd4 18 ③xd4 0-0-0) 17...0-0-0 with an unclear position.

b) 10 ②e2 ②xc5 11 ②g3 ③e7 12 ③f2 ③a5 13 ③e2 h5 (13...b3+!? 14 ③d2 ②b4 15 0-0 bxa2 is murky) 14 h4 g6 15 0-0, as in Yudasin-Machulsky, Haifa 1989, and now according to M.Gurevich Black can equalise with 15...②a4 16 ③ab1 ③c5.

10...③a5 11 ②b6 ②xb6

Not entirely forced. Black has also tried the dubious looking 11...③b8?! In Ziatdinov-Miljanic, Niksic 1991, Black obtained good play for his pawn after 12 ②xd7 ③xd7 13 ③d3 ③xc5!? 14 ③xc5 ③xc5 15 ③xa6 0-0 16 ③f2?! (White is probably better after 16 ③f1! f6 17 ③d3! ③f7 18 ③f2 ③xf2+ 19 ③xf2, but after 19...g5 Black made it messy in Arakhamia-M.Horvath, Lenk 1991) 16...③xf2+ 17 ③xf2 f6 18 ③he1?! (I prefer 18 ③g3) 18...g5 19 exf6 gxf4 20 ②e5 ②xe5 21 ③xe5 ③xf6 and he even went on to win.

12 cxb6 ③c5

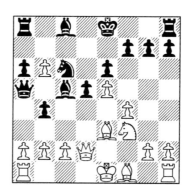

13 ③xc5

13 ③f2? fails tactically to 13...b3+ 14 c3 ③xa2!

13...③xc5 14 0-0-0

14 ③f2 ③xf2+ 15 ③xf2 ③b8 16 ③e3 ③xb6 17 ②d4 ③d7 18 ③d3 ③e7 19 ③hf1 ②xd4 20 ③xd4 ③c8 21 ③f2 h5 didn't yield anything for White in Fedorowicz-Vaisser,

New York 1998.

14...♕xb6 15 h4

White could also consider pressing in the centre. A game M.Hansen-Krause, OLNN 1992, continued 15 ♗d3 a5 16 ♔b1 a4 17 b3 ♗a6 18 f5 ♗xd3 19 ♕xd3 ♕c5 20 ♖he1 with a complex struggle ahead.

15...h5

Stopping the h-pawn before it gets too far. Instead 15...♗b7 16 ♖h3 0-0-0?! 17 ♘d4 ♔c7 18 c3 ♘xd4 19 ♕xd4 ♕xd4 20 ♖xd4 bxc3 21 ♖xc3+ ♔d7 22 ♖b4 gave White a strong initiative in Ziatdinov-Glek, Kusadasi 1990. Black shouldn't be in too much of a hurry to castle in this line.

16 ♖h3 a5 17 ♔b1

After 17 f5!? Magem gives 17...exf5 18 ♕g5 ♗e6 19 ♕xg7 0-0-0 as Black's best line, with good counter-chances for the second player.

17...♗a6

Risky. It was safer to solidify the kingside first with 17...g6.

18 ♗xa6 ♕xa6 19 f5!?

Sharp, but it's not clear that White's initiative gives him anything concrete.

19...exf5 20 ♕g5

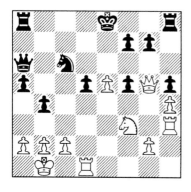

20...♘e7!

Magem rejects the alternatives. After 20...0-0 White's attack with 21 ♖g3 g6 22 e6 is crushing. 20...g6 on the other hand is best met by 21 ♕f6! (clearer than 21 e6) 21...♖f8 22 ♘g5 ♘e7 23 ♘h7 and Black loses

material.

21 e6?!

21 ♕xg7 was objectively stronger, leading to an unclear position after 21...♖g8 22 ♕h7 ♖xg2.

21...♕xe6

21...fxe6? allows 22 ♘d4 ♔f7 23 ♖e3 ♖h6 24 ♖de1 and White piles on the pressure.

22 ♕xg7 ♖g8 23 ♕d4 ♖xg2 24 ♖e1 ♖e2 25 ♖hh1 ♖c8 26 ♕d1 ♖xe1?

The opening of the e-file gives a strong initiative for White. Magem points out that after 26...♖e4! 27 ♘g5 ♕e5 28 ♘xe4 fxe4 Black has plenty of compensation for the exchange; two pawns, the centre and shelter for his king on d7. Furthermore, White's rooks are ineffective.

27 ♖xe1 ♕d6 28 ♘e5 ♕c5?

An oversight but if Black defends the h-pawn with 28...♕h6 then White switches to the queenside with 29 ♕e2 ♖c7 30 ♕b5+.

29 c4!

A shock. White threatens 30 ♕a4+ and the black position crumbles.

29...b3 30 ♕xh5 ♔d8 31 ♕xf7 ♕b4 32 ♘d3 bxa2+ 33 ♔a1 ♕d6 34 c5 ♕d7 35 ♘e5 ♕e8 36 ♕e6 1-0

Game 28
Chuprov-Gleizerov
St Petersburg 1994

---

1 e4 e6 2 d4 d5 3 ♘c3 ♘f6 4 e5 ♘fd7 5 f4 c5 6 ♘f3 ♘c6 7 ♗e3 a6 8 ♕d2 b5 9 ♗d3

White doesn't have to capture on c5. He can instead just try and complete his development. Another way of doing this is 9 ♕f2 – see Game 29.

9...b4 10 ♘d1 ♕b6

Black can also gain time and space with 10...c4. This plan of blocking up the centre is considered to be acceptable for Black and leads to unclear play in each of the following examples: 11 ♗e2 h5 (or 11...♘b6

12 0-0 &e7 13 &f2 g6 14 ♘e3 a5 15 &g3 &d7, as in Stripunsky-Dreev, Rostov 1993) 12 0-0 &e7 (alternatively 12...g6 13 &f2 &e7 14 ♘e3 &b7 15 c3 ♛a5 16 &h4 bxc3 17 bxc3 &xh4 18 ♘xh4 ♘e7, as in Shaposhnikov-Smikovski, St Petersburg 1997) 13 a3 ♖b8 14 axb4 &xb4 15 c3 &e7 16 ♘g5 ♘f8 17 ♛c2 ♛b6, as in Shirov-Glek, Bundesliga 1996. Here Glek suggests 17...&xg5 18 fxg5 ♘e7 as equally unclear.

11 ♛f2

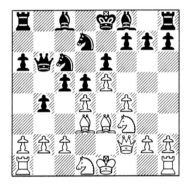

11...cxd4

Perhaps the most logical plan is to exchange the light-squared bishops with 11...a5! 12 0-0 &a6 13 &xa6 ♖xa6 14 c3 &e7. In Shaposhnikov-Volkov, Samara 2000, White tried to react aggressively with 15 f5?! exf5 16 &f4 cxd4 17 cxd4 0-0 but this wasn't convincing.

12 ♘xd4 &c5

Black could try 12...♘xd4 13 &xd4 &c5 14 &xc5 ♘xc5. However, in the game Shaposhnikov-Meshkov, St Petersburg 1999, he quickly got into difficulties: 15 ♘e3 0-0?! (why not 15...a5 followed by ...&a6 and only castling later?) 16 0-0-0!? a5 17 ♔b1 &a6 18 ♘g4! &xd3?! 19 ♖xd3 ♘d7 20 ♘f6+! (Black clearly overlooked this move) 20...♔h8? (20...gxf6 is a better defence, e.g. 21 ♛h4 ♖fc8 22 ♛h6 ♖c3! 23 exf6 ♘xf6 with chances to hold) 21 ♛h4 ♘xf6 22 exf6 e5 23 fxe5 ♛e6 24 ♖f1 ♛xe5 25 ♖h3 ♛e4 26 fxg7+ 1-0.

13 ♘f3!

Preferable to 13 ♘xc6?! ♛xc6 14 0-0 &b7 15 ♛g3 f5! 16 &xc5 (16 ♛xg7? is just asking for trouble on the g-file after 16...0-0-0) 16...♘xc5 17 a3 ♘e4 18 &xe4 fxe4 19 axb4 d4 when Black had good play in Novik-Gleizerov, Moscow 1992.

13...&b7 14 0-0 f5 15 exf6

The opening of the centre helps White obtain some targets for his pieces.

15...gxf6 16 ♖e1 d4 17 &d2 ♘e7 18 ♛e2 ♘f8 19 ♘f2

Probing away at the centre and forcing concessions.

19...f5

To stop the knight coming to e4, but it weakens other squares...

20 ♘g5 ♖g8 21 ♛h5+ ♖g6

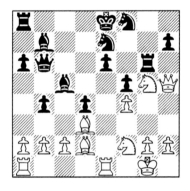

22 a3!

Creating play on the queenside, where Black is more or less obliged to seek shelter for his king.

22...bxa3

If 22...b3 23 cxb3 ♛xb3 White switches to the c-file with. 24 ♖ac1 then after the further 24...♛xb2? White obtains a winning attack with 25 ♘xe6 ♘xe6 26 ♖xe6 ♔d8 27 &a5+.

23 bxa3 0-0-0 24 ♔h1 h6 25 ♘f3 ♘d7 26 ♛h3 ♘f6 27 ♖ab1 ♛c6 28 ♖xb7!

An excellent exchange sacrifice. By eliminating this bishop, Black's counter-pressure on g2 is reduced. With the harmony lost in his opponent's position the white pieces suddenly flood into Black's weaknesses.

28...♕xb7 29 ♘h4 ♘g4

Or 29...♖g7 30 ♖xe6 with several threats.

30 ♘xg4 fxg4 31 ♕g3 ♖g7

Knaak prefers 31...♖f6 but admits that Black still has a difficult defensive task after 32 ♕xg4 ♕c6 33 ♗a5 ♖d7 34 ♘f3.

32 ♖xe6 ♖d6 33 ♕e1 ♕b6?

Missing the point. Instead the only chance was to try 33...♔d7! when after 34 ♖xd6+ ♗xd6 35 f5 Black has problems but is still alive.

34 ♖xe7 ♖xe7 35 ♕xe7 ♖e6 36 ♕xe6+ 1-0

Game 29
Shaposhnikov-Alavkin
Samara 2000

---

1 e4 e6 2 d4 d5 3 ♘c3 ♘f6 4 e5 ♘fd7 5 f4 c5 6 ♘f3 ♘c6 7 ♗e3 a6 8 ♕d2 b5 9 ♕f2 ♕b6 10 ♗d3 cxd4

Otherwise, possible is 10...♖b8 intending to meet 11 0-0 with 11...cxd4 12 ♘xd4 ♘xd4 13 ♗xd4 ♕xd4!? (a clever idea but White retains the slightly better ending) 14 ♕xd4 ♗c5 15 ♘e2 f6 (15...b4!? aiming to put the queenside pawns on dark squares) 16 ♖f2 ♗xd4 17 ♘xd4 fxe5 18 ♘c6 ♖b7 19 ♘xe5 ♘xe5 20 fxe5 ♖f7 21 a4!, as in Marjanovic-Itkis, Bucharest 1999. White clearly had the better minor piece and went on to win.

Another recent try is 10...♗b7 11 0-0 c4 12 ♗e2 f5 13 exf6 ♘xf6 14 ♘g5 ♘e7 15 a4 Sharapov-Vysochin, Polanica Zdroj 2000, and now after 15...h6! Black should be okay.

11 ♘xd4 ♗c5

A solid alternative is 11...♘xd4 12 ♗xd4 ♗c5 13 ♘e2 ♗xd4 14 ♘xd4 ♘c5 where White has yet to prove an advantage, e.g. 15 0-0 0-0 16 b4 ♘e4 17 ♗xe4 dxe4 18 ♘b3 ♕xf2+ 19 ♔xf2 ♗b7 and with the bishop coming to d5 he had no problems in

Kruppa-Savchenko, Minsk 1996.

12 ♘ce2 b4

The immediate 12...f6 is also reasonable: 13 exf6 ♘xf6 14 h3 0-0 15 0-0-0 e5 16 fxe5 ♘e4 with sharp play in Macieja-Schmidt, Legnica 1994.

13 0-0 f6

Creating tension in the centre. The other plan of exchanging off the light-squared bishops has recently been popular: 13...a5 14 c3 ♗a6 15 ♗xa6 ♖xa6 16 ♖ac1 0-0 17 ♖fd1 (17 cxb4 ♘xb4 18 ♖xc5!? led to a lively exchanges followed by a drawish ending in Miladinovic-Kosic, Niksic 1997: 18...♘xc5 19 ♘b3 ♘bd3 20 ♗xc5 ♘xf2 21 ♗xb6 ♖xb6 22 ♔xf2 a4 23 ♘c5 ♖xb2 24 ♘xa4 ♖xa2 25 ♘ac3 ♖a3 26 ♔e3 and a draw was agreed) 17...bxc3 18 bxc3 f6 gave Black adequate counter-chances in Mitkov-Kastanieda, Istanbul Olympiad 2000.

14 ♔h1 0-0

Taking the e-pawn is risky, e.g. 14...fxe5 15 fxe5 ♘dxe5 16 ♕g3 ♖a7 17 ♘xc6 ♘xc6 18 ♗xc5 ♕xc5 19 ♗xh7 and Black doesn't even possess an extra pawn to compensate for having the inferior king.

15 exf6

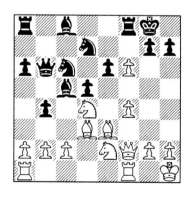

15...♖xf6

Finkel judges the position after 15...♘xf6 16 ♘xc6 ♗xe3 17 ♕g3 to be slightly better for White, but after 17...♗b7 18 ♘e5 ♖ad8 Black is ready for anything.

16 ♘xc6 ♗xe3 17 ♕g3 ♗b7

17...♗c5 18 ♘e5 ♕c7! is a reasonable alternative.

18 ♘e5 ♘xe5 19 fxe5 ♗f2!

Better than 19...♖xf1+ 20 ♖xf1 which would give White the initiative due to his control of the f-file and superior presence on the kingside. After 19...♖f2 Finkel suggests 20 ♕h3 h6 21 ♖xf2 ♗xf2 22 ♘f4 maintaining the pressure.

20 ♕g4 ♖h6 21 ♘f4 ♖f8 22 ♘h5

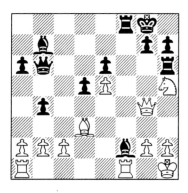

22...♖f7?

Much better was 22...♕c7 which stops 23 ♘f6+?? in view of 23...♖fxf6 24 exf6 ♕xh2 checkmate.

23 ♘f6+ ♔h8 24 ♘xh7 ♕e3

24...♖xh7 allows the decisive fork 25 ♕g6.

25 ♖ae1

More precise was 25 ♘g5! ♖f4 26 ♖ae1!

25...♕f4

25...♕xe1 26 ♖xe1 ♗xe1 fails to 27 ♘g5 ♖e7 28 ♘f3 when Black loses one of his bishops as 28...♗f2 29 ♕xb4 ♖f7 30 ♘g5 is resignable.

26 ♕xf4 ♖xf4 27 ♘g5 d4?

Losing on the spot. Instead 27...♔g8 continues the fight, but a clear pawn down. Then after 28 ♖e2 ♗g3 29 ♖xf4 ♗xf4 30 ♘f3 White consolidates but would have technical difficulties to convert the material advantage.

28 ♖e2 1-0

After 28 ♖e2 ♗g3 (28...♖xh2+ 29 ♔xh2

♖h4+ fails to 30 ♘h3) 29 ♘f7+ White wins the exchange.

Game 30
Lalic-Korchnoi
Calcutta 2000

1 e4 e6 2 d4 d5 3 ♘c3 ♘f6 4 e5 ♘fd7 5 f4 c5 6 ♘f3 ♘c6 7 ♗e3 a6 8 a3

An idea championed by Yacob Murey. White competes for control of the dark squares on the queenside. However, this represents a tempo not spent on kingside development. Black does best to keep some tension in the centre and prepare for a timely ...f7-f6.

8...cxd4

Others:

a) 8...c4?! takes the tension away from the centre and therefore enables White to build pressure on the other wing with 9 ♘e2 h5 10 ♘g5 ♘e7 11 ♗f2 ♕a5+. Now in Murey-Korchnoi, Beersheva 1984, White exchanged queens with 12 ♕d2 and Black had few problems. Better is 12 c3 followed by a general advance on the kingside. Play could be as in a well-known line in the Advanced variation.

b) 8...♗e7? either loses time or cedes space, e.g. 9 dxc5 ♘xc5 10 b4 ♘d7 11 ♗d3 ♕c7 12 ♘e2 ♘b6 13 0-0 ♗d7 14 ♕e1 ♘a4 15 ♕g3 g6 16 ♘g5 ♘d8 17 ♘d4 and Black had a passive game in Korchnoi-Keller, Switzerland 1984.

9 ♘xd4 ♗c5 10 g3

Or:

a) 10 b4?! seems to lead to self-weakening if Black reacts quickly with ...f7-f6, e.g. 10...♗xd4 11 ♗xd4 0-0 12 g3 b5 13 ♗e2 ♗b7 14 0-0 ♖c8 15 ♖f3 f6 16 exf6 ♘xd4 17 ♕xd4 ♕xf6 with advantage to Black in Murey-Moskalenko, Paris 1992.

b) 10 ♕d2 is perhaps the most solid, but in this case is White's a2-a3 move just a waste of time? For example, 10...♘xd4 11 ♗xd4 ♗xd4 (11...b5 is more positive) 12

♕xd4 ♕b6 13 0-0-0 ♕xd4 14 ♖xd4 b6 15 g3 ♗b7 16 ♗g2 ♖c8 17 ♖hd1 ♖c7 18 ♘e2 h5 and Black had a comfortable game in Murey-Komarov, Montauban 2000.

10...♕b6 11 ♘a4 ♕a5+ 12 ♘c3

12 c3 is less cowardly but after 12...♗xd4 13 ♗xd4 ♘xd4 14 ♕xd4 ♕c7! (14...b6!? intending ...♗b7-c6 is also interesting) 15 b4 b6 Black has a fine game as he will obtain play on the c-file.

12...♕b6 13 ♘a4 ♕a5+ 14 ♘c3 ♕c7!?

Playing for more than a draw.

15 ♘ce2 0-0!

15...h5 has also been played, but I prefer Korchnoi's move which ensures a safe king.

16 ♗g2 ♘xd4 17 ♘xd4

The alternative is 17 ♗xd4 when 17...f6?! 18 exf6 ♘xf6 19 0-0 ♗d7 is playable for Black, but because of his hold on the centre, White can claim a shade of an edge. Instead of 17...f6, then 17...a5!, intending ...b7-b6 and ...♗a6 is recommended.

17...♘b6 18 b3 f6 19 exf6

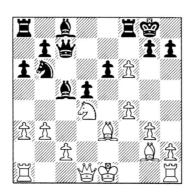

19...e5!

Black takes the initiative. White's slow play has left his king dangerously exposed.

20 fxe5 ♕xe5 21 ♕d2 ♖xf6 22 ♖f1

White could have sought safety with 22 0-0-0 despite the fact that it loses a pawn.

22...♗f5?!

More to the point was 22...♗g4! keeping

the white king in the centre.

23 a4

Very slow. Instead 23 0-0-0 ♗xa3+ 24 ♔b1 is more practical, when after 24...♖c8 25 ♗f4 ♖xc2 26 ♗xe5 ♖xd2+ 27 ♘xf5 ♖xd1+ 28 ♖xd1 ♖xf5 29 ♗d4 White should hold the ending despite the two-pawn advantage. In view of this variation Korchnoi suggests 24...♗e4 maintaining the better game.

23...♖c8 24 c3?!

The last chance for White to castle. Now Black is able to force an ending with two pieces for a rook.

24...♖e8 25 ♖f3

25 ♔e2 holds for the moment, but after 25...♗g4+ 26 ♔d3 ♗xd4 27 cxd4 ♗f5+ 28 ♔e2 ♕e7 Black has too many threats.

25...♗g4

Black now forces an ending with two minor pieces for the rook.

26 ♖xf6 ♗xd4 27 cxd4 ♕xe3+ 28 ♕xe3 ♖xe3+ 29 ♔f2 ♖e2+ 30 ♔f1 gxf6 31 h3 ♖xg2 32 ♔xg2 ♗d7 33 ♖c1 ♗c6 34 ♔f3 ♘d7 35 g4 ♘f8 36 h4 ♘e6

Black's plan is to avoid any rook invasions and hit away at the white weak points.

37 ♔e3 ♔g7 38 ♖f1 ♗d7 39 ♖f2 ♔g6 40 ♖f1 ♘d8 41 ♖g1 h6 42 ♔f4 ♘c6 43 ♖d1?

Losing quickly. Korchnoi instead suggests the line 43 ♔e3 ♘a5 44 ♖c1 ♗xg4 45 ♖c7 ♗d1 when White sheds a pawn or two but achieves some activity for his rook, and therefore some hope for the cause. However, Black should objectively still be able to win.

43...h5 44 gxh5+ ♔xh5 45 ♖g1

45 ♔g3 loses the h-pawn after 45...♘e7.

45...♘xd4 46 ♖d1 ♘e2+ 47 ♔e3 d4+! 0-1

After 47...d4+ 48 ♔xe2 (or 48 ♔f2 ♗g4) 48...♗g4+ Black wins comfortably.

Summary

The move 7...a6 generally seems to be a little less incisive for Black than the plan of capturing on d4 and continuing ...♝c5, as seen in the previous chapter. The problem with allowing White to capture on c5 is that this results in an exchange of dark-squared bishops which obviously favours White. Also the queens often end up opposing each other along the g1-a7 diagonal and this can easily lead to a queen exchange, again the simplification favouring White.

White seems to do best to stick to the main lines of this variation as seen in Games 31 and 32, where he is guaranteed a small edge. Having said that, this variation is quite solid for Black and could be a good choice against a white opponent hell-bent on attack.

1 e4 e6 2 d4 d5 3 ♘c3 ♘f6 4 e5 ♘fd7 5 f4 c5 6 ♘f3 ♘c6 7 ♗e3 a6 *(D)*

8 ♕d2
> 8 a3 – *Game 37*

8...b5 *(D)* **9 dxc5**
> 9 ♗d3 – *Game 35*; 9 ♕f2 – *Game 36*

9...♗xc5
> 9...b4 – *Game 34*

10 ♗xc5 ♘xc5 11 ♕f2 ♕b6 *(D)* **12 ♗d3**
> 12 b4 – *Game 33*

12...♖b8
> 12...b4 – *Game 32*

13 0-0 – *Game 31*

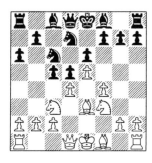

7...a6　　　　　　8...b5　　　　　　11...♕b6

CHAPTER FOUR

Old Main Line:
Other Variations after 6 ♘f3

**1 e4 e6 2 d4 d5 3 ♘c3 ♘f6 4 e5 ♘fd7
5 f4 c5 6 ♘f3**

This chapter deals with variations after 6 ♘f3 where Black avoids heading straight for the positions from Chapters 2 and 3. This generally means that Black has some exotic piece development in mind and in this chapter we frequently see moves such as ...c5-c4, an early ...a7-a6, an early ...♛b6, or – particularly if Morozevich is playing Black – the black minor pieces ending up anywhere and everywhere.

Game 31 deals with the piece sacrifice which occurs after 6...♘c6 7 ♗e3 ♛b6 8 ♘a4 ♛a5+ 9 c3 cxd4 10 b4 ♘xb4. This was frequently seen in the 1980s, but its popularity has waned since then. It is also possible for Black to play without gambitting a piece with 9...c4 (Game 32).

Instead of 7... ♛b6, 7...♗e7 is the subject of Game 33 and the offbeat 7... b6 of Game 34. Finally, the plan of delaying ...♘c6 with 6...a6 is seen in Games 35-37.

Game 31
Chandler-M.Gurevich
Leningrad 1987

**1 e4 e6 2 d4 d5 3 ♘c3 ♘f6 4 e5 ♘fd7
5 f4 c5 6 ♘f3 ♘c6 7 ♗e3 ♛b6 8 ♘a4**

♛a5+ 9 c3 cxd4!?

For 9...c4 see Game 32.

10 b4 ♘xb4

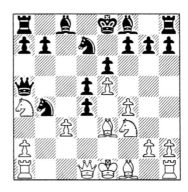

This piece sacrifice variation has been thoroughly investigated over the years. The main conclusion is that although Black has practical chances, there remains a suspicion that he doesn't quite get enough compensation. If instead Black chickens out with 10...♛c7 then White keeps his opening advantage due to a firm grip on key dark squares such as d4 and c5. Here is an example: 11 ♘xd4 ♘xd4 12 ♗xd4 ♘b8 13 a3 ♘c6 14 ♗e3 ♗e7 15 ♗d3 0-0 16 0-0 ♗d7 17 ♖f3 g6 18 ♘c5 a5, as in Suetin-Liberzon, USSR Championship 1960, when by 19 ♘b3 axb4 20 cxb4! Suetin claims a clear advantage for White.

11 cxb4 ♗xb4+ 12 ♗d2 ♗xd2+ 13 ♘xd2 b6

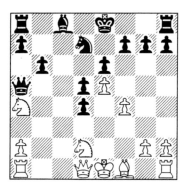

Black can also try 13...g5!? to break up the white centre. Although it hasn't done particularly well in practice, this could be his best option, e.g. 14 ♖b1 (14 ♘b2 gxf4 15 ♘d3 b6 16 ♔f2 ♗a6 17 ♘f3 ♖c8 led to a complicated struggle in Anand-Dreev, Madras 1991) and now:

a) 14...a6 is considered inferior, e.g. 15 ♗d3 gxf4 16 0-0 b5 (16...♘xe5 is met by 17 ♘b6 with a bind) 17 ♘b2 ♘xe5 18 ♖xf4 ♘g6 19 ♗xg6 hxg6 20 ♘f3 ♕b6 21 ♘d3 0-0 22 ♘fe5 ♖a7 23 ♕f3 ♕d6 24 ♖f6 ♖c7 25 ♖f1 and in Kalegin-Chigvintsev, Russia 1992, Black resigned as he is powerless to stop the threats of ♘xf7 and ♘xg6.

b) 14...gxf4 15 ♗b5 ♖b8 (best is 15...♔f8! 16 ♕e2 d3! with unclear complications) 16 ♘c5 ♕c3 17 ♘d3 a6 18 ♖c1 ♕a3 19 ♕b3 ♕a5 20 ♗xd7+ ♗xd7 21 ♘xf4 and White won quickly in Short-Timman, Amsterdam 1994, as his extra piece is far more use than Black's three pawns.

14 ♗d3!

White has tried several other moves but the text is now considered to be the strongest. Alternatives are:

a) 14 ♕b3 ♗a6 15 ♗xa6 ♕xa6 16 ♘b2, as in Timman-Yusupov, Bugojno 1986, is not very clear as after 16...♕a5!, intending

...♘c5, Black has reasonable play.

b) 14 ♔f2 0-0 15 ♘f3 ♘c5 16 ♘b2 ♘e4+ was murky in Tseshkovsky-Dolmatov, USSR Championship 1986.

c) 14 ♕c2 led to balanced chances after 14...♗b7 15 ♕c7 ♗a6 16 ♗xa6 ♕xa6 17 ♕c6 ♖c8 18 ♘c5 ♖xc6 19 ♘xa6 g5! in another Timman-Yusupov encounter, this time from Tilburg 1986.

d) 14 h4 0-0 15 ♖h3 f6! 16 ♖b1 ♗a6 17 ♗xa6 ♕xa6 18 ♖b4 fxe5 19 fxe5 ♘xe5 20 ♖xd4 ♖f6 21 ♘c3 ♖af8 22 ♕e2 ♕xe2+ 23 ♘xe2 ♘c6 was fine for Black in Yurtaev-Vaisser, Frunze 1987, but he could have played for even more with 20...♖c8! when Vaisser then prefers Black.

14...♗a6 15 ♘b2 ♘c5

15...♗xd3?! allows White to get organised rather easily: 16 ♘xd3 ♘c5 17 ♘f2! ♘a4 18 0-0 ♘c3 19 ♕g4 0-0 20 ♘f3 ♖ac8 21 ♕h4 ♕a4 22 ♘g4 and White had a strong attack in Timman-Korchnoi, Brussels 1987.

16 ♗xa6 ♕xa6 17 ♕e2

Ghinda suggests 17 a4!? in order to deny Black the a3-square.

17...♕a3

17...d3?! 18 ♕e3 ♕a3 19 ♕d4 is considered by theory to be a clear advantage to White, but after 19...0-0 20 0-0 ♖ac8 21 ♘d1 ♖fd8 22 ♘f2 ♘e4 23 ♘fxe4 dxe4 24 ♕e3 ♖c2 25 ♘xe4 ♕b2 Black was able to hold in Psakhis-Dizdar, Portoroz 1987.

18 ♕b5+ ♔e7 19 0-0 ♕e3+ 20 ♖f2 ♖hc8 21 ♖d1

White could also try 21 ♘f1! ♕c3 22 ♖f3 d3 23 ♖d1 ♕d4+ 24 ♔h1 ♘e4 25 ♘xd3 ♖c2 26 ♘e3 and despite the fact that Black has active-looking pieces, White was well in control in Nunn-Zysk, Germany 1988.

21...g6 22 ♘f1 ♕a3 23 ♖xd4 ♕xa2 24 ♘g3!?

Up to here everything had been seen before! Chandler was probably aware of the game Van der Sterren-Gurevich, Tallinn 1987, which continued 24 ♘a4 ♕a1 25

♖fd2 ♘d7 26 ♕b4+ ♔e8 27 ♖d1 ♖c1 with an unclear struggle.

24...♕b3 25 ♕e2

Black has three passed pawns and no problems in any simplified position. White's chances lie in a middlegame with the possibilities of getting at Black's king.

25...♘d7 26 ♖d1 ♖c3 27 ♘d3 ♖ac8 28 ♖ff1

28...a5?

Pinning the knight by 28...♕c4 is given by Chandler as unclear.

29 f5!

White goes on the offensive to smash open Black's king

29...gxf5 30 ♘f4 ♖8c5 31 ♕h5! ♘xe5 32 ♕g5+ ♔d7 33 ♘xf5! ♘c6

After 33...exf5 34 ♕xf5+ ♔d6 35 ♕f6+ White picks up the black knight.

34 ♘xe6!

A crushing blow.

34...♔xe6

34...fxe6 allows an even swifter mate: 35 ♕g7+ ♔d8 36 ♘d4 ♘xd4 37 ♖f8.

35 ♖de1+ ♔d7 36 ♖e7+! ♔c8 37 ♕g8+ 1-0

Game 32
Short-Psakhis
Moscow Olympiad 1994

1 e4 e6 2 d4 d5 3 ♘c3 ♘f6 4 e5 ♘fd7 5 f4 c5 6 ♘f3 ♘c6 7 ♗e3 ♕b6 8 ♘a4

♕a5+ 9 c3 c4

Closing the centre and threatening to embarrass the white knight. White has to react immediately.

10 b4 ♕c7

Alternatives:

a) Playing the closed position is surest. Instead 10...cxb3?! 11 axb3 leaves White with the better pawn structure and his centre intact. If then 11...b5? White can safely play 12 ♘c5 as 12...♕xc3+ 13 ♗d2 ♕b2 14 ♘d3 costs Black his queen.

b) The speculative 10...♘xb4!? 11 cxb4 ♗xb4+ 12 ♔f2 b5 (Sek-Nizialek, Porabka 1987) is hard to refute, but I suspect that it's not quite sound: 13 ♘c5! ♗xc5 14 dxc5 ♗b7 15 ♕d4 b4 (15...♖c8 16 c6 ♗xc6 17 ♕xa7 ♕xa7 18 ♗xa7 only gives Black two pawns in the ending) 16 ♗e2 ♗c6!? (again 16...♖c8 17 c6 ♗xc6 18 ♕xa7 must be preferable for White) and it's not clear how White can use his extra piece, although he has many options and he must be better. Perhaps 17 ♘d2 0-0 18 ♗f3 ♗b5 19 ♖hb1 is a good start.

11 ♗e2

11 g3 ♗e7 12 ♗h3! restrains Black's use of the f-pawn. Then 12...b5 13 ♘c5 a5 14 a3 axb4 15 axb4 ♖xa1 16 ♕xa1 ♘xc5 17 dxc5 0-0 18 ♘d4 gave White a pleasant edge in Svidler-Bareev, Russian Championship 1997.

11...♗e7 12 a3

If White wishes to discourage ...f7-f5 then he can try 12 g4!? This was reasonably successful in Kamsky-Bareev, Madrid 1994: 12...b5 13 ♘c5 a5 14 a3 0-0 15 0-0 axb4 16 axb4 ♖xa1 17 ♕xa1 ♘xc5 18 dxc5 f6 19 exf6 ♗xf6 20 g5 ♗d8 21 ♕c1 ♕b8 22 ♕d2 ♗c7 23 ♘d4 ♘xd4 24 ♕xd4 with a bind. To mix it, Black then sacrificed a pawn with 24...♗b7 25 ♕d2 d4!? but it shouldn't really have been enough.

12...f5

12...a5!? 13 0-0 f5 14 h3 ♘d8 15 g4 ♘f8 16 ♕c2 ♘g6, as in Ernst-Ulibin, Stockholm

1998, is a more flexible way of playing the position. The added tension on the queenside makes it more difficult for White to build pressure on the other wing.

13 ♖g1!

An improvement on 13 ♘c5?! ♘f8! leaving the knight on c5 looking a bit silly. After the further 14 ♕a4 b6 15 ♘a6 ♕d7 Black had no particular worries in Short-Bareev, Novgorod 1994. White has some choice as to how to manoeuvre his pieces. Anand has even suggested the manoeuvre 13 ♘b2 followed by a3-a4, ♕c2, ♘b2-d1-f2 but this seems long-winded.

13...♘f8 14 g4 fxg4

In an analogous position Ulibin just put his knight on g6 allowing White to capture on f5. Here, with his king still in the centre, White is better placed to counter this plan with 14...♘g6 15 gxf5 exf5 16 ♔d2 ♘d8 17 ♕e1 ♘e6 18 ♕g3 and pushing the h-pawn to h5. White will be able to slowly build pressure on the g-file and against d5 and f5, whereas Black has no counterplay.

15 ♖xg4 g6 16 ♗f2

This 'bad' bishop will eventually come to h4 to exchange itself for a black minor piece. First of all White consolidates the other wing.

16...b6 17 ♘b2 ♗d7 18 a4 a6 19 ♕b1 ♕b7 20 ♘d1 b5

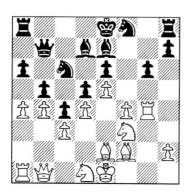

21 axb5

Opening the a-file because pressure

solely on the kingside will be insufficient to win.

21...axb5?!

Short considers 21...♕xb5 22 ♘e3 a5 to be more dynamic for Black.

22 ♘e3 ♖xa1 23 ♕xa1 ♗d8 24 ♔d2 ♘e7 25 ♗h4 ♘f5 26 ♗xd8 ♔xd8 27 ♖g1 ♖g8 28 ♗d1 ♖g7 29 ♗c2

White now threatens to capture on f5 with the bishop gaining the 'knight pair' in a closed manoeuvring game. The further exchange of a pair of knights would leave Black with his 'bad bishop' and holes on the dark squares.

29...♘xe3 30 ♔xe3 ♗e8 31 ♕e1 ♕e7 32 ♕g3 ♔c8 33 ♖a1 ♗c6 34 ♕h3 ♔b7 35 ♕h6 ♖g8 36 h4

White prepares the additional threat of h4-h5.

36...♗e8 37 ♖g1 ♕g7 38 ♕g5 h5

Stopping White's h-pawn, but this is a concession as the g-pawn becomes chronically weak.

39 ♕d8 ♕d7 40 ♕a5 ♕c7 41 ♕xc7+ ♔xc7 42 f5!

Generating a protected passed pawn.

42...exf5 43 ♗xf5 ♗f7 44 ♗h3 ♗e6 45 ♘g5 ♗xh3 46 ♘xh3 ♘e6 47 ♖f1

47 ♘f4 would allow counterplay after 47...♘xf4 48 ♔xf4 ♖f8+ 49 ♔g5 ♖f3. Short prefers to prepare ♘f4 under more favourable circumstances

47...♖a8 48 ♖f2 ♔c6 49 ♖f6 ♔d7 50 ♘f4

White could also have played 50 ♖xg6 as 50...♖a3 can be met strongly by 51 ♘f4 ♖xc3+ 52 ♔d2 ♘xf4 53 ♖d6+.

50...♘xf4 51 ♔xf4 ♔e7 52 ♖xg6 ♖f8+ 53 ♔e3 ♖f1 54 ♖d6 ♖h1 55 ♖xd5 ♖xh4 56 ♖xb5 ♖h3+ 57 ♔e4 1-0

Game 33
Ivanchuk-Morozevich
Amsterdam 1996

---

1 e4 e6 2 d4 d5 3 ♘c3 ♘f6 4 e5 ♘fd7

5 f4 c5 6 ♘f3 ♘c6 7 ♗e3 ♗e7 8 dxc5

Nowadays this is considered to be best as naturally if Black recaptures with the bishop he loses a tempo on other variations. White can also develop naturally: 8 ♕d2 0-0 9 ♗e2 cxd4 10 ♘xd4 ♘xd4 11 ♗xd4 ♘b8 12 0-0 ♘c6 13 ♗f2 ♗d7 14 ♘b5 a6 15 ♘d4, as in Timman-Hort, Linares 1983, when Black does best to play 15...♘xd4 16 ♗xd4 ♕c7 with a quick ....♗c5. Despite having the superior minor piece White then couldn't claim to have much advantage.

8...♘xc5

The most natural but not the only way of handling the position:

a) 8...0-0!? has been played more recently by Morozevich. It could transpose back to normal lines after 9 ♗e2 ♘xc5, but Black retains the option of ...♗xc5 depending on White's approach: 9 ♕d2 ♘xc5 10 ♗e2 b6 11 0-0 ♗a6 12 ♘d4 ♕d7 13 ♗xa6 ♘xa6 14 ♘xc6 ♕xc6 15 f5!? exf5 16 ♘xd5 ♗c5 17 ♖ad1 ♖ad8 18 c4 ♗xe3+ 19 ♕xe3 ♕xc4 20 ♘e7+ ♔h8 21 ♘xf5 ♖xd1 22 ♖xd1 ♘c5, as in Shaposhnikov-Morozevich, St Petersburg 1997, was not better for White.

b) 8...♗xc5!? happily loses a tempo, but despite this fact, after 9 ♕d2 0-0 10 0-0-0 ♕b6 11 ♗g1 ♗xg1 12 ♖xg1 ♘c5 13 ♗d3 ♘b4 14 ♔b1 ♗d7 Black was okay in Ivanchuk-Korchnoi, Roquebrune 1992.

9 ♗e2 0-0 10 0-0 ♗d7

10...f6?! is premature as after 11 exf6 ♖xf6 12 ♕d2 b6 13 ♘d4 ♗b7 14 ♘xc6 ♗xc6 15 ♗d4 ♖f8 16 ♗g4 White obtained good pressure on the central pawns in Groszpeter-Meszaros, Vienna 1996. Morozevich doesn't believe that 10...b6 solves all Black's problems either. He continues his analysis with 11 ♕e1 ♗a6 12 ♗xa6 ♘xa6 13 ♖d1 ♘c5 14 f5 giving White a nice edge.

11 a3 ♗e8 12 ♕e1 ♖c8

Morozevich suggests 12...f6 intending ....♗g6 as a better way of continuing Black's development.

13 ♖d1 ♕c7 14 b4

Black's unadventurous and passive scheme allows his opponent to gain space.

14...♘d7 15 ♘b5 ♕b8 16 ♗d3 f6

Too late!

17 ♕h4 f5 18 ♕h3 ♘b6 19 ♗xb6!

Killing off attempted counterplay with ...♘c4 and gaining time to prise open the g-file.

19...axb6 20 g4 g6 21 gxf5 exf5

If 21...gxf5 then 22 ♔h1 followed by doubling on the g-file would give White a strong attack.

22 ♖f2 ♘d8 23 ♘bd4 ♔h8 24 ♖g2 ♖c3

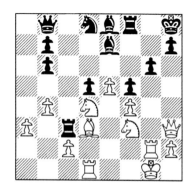

25 ♘h4

White's pieces are all poised to pounce something has to give.

25...♘c6 26 ♘e6 ♖g8 27 ♘xf5 ♕c8

27...gxf5 leads to a rapid mate after 28 ♖xg8+ ♔xg8 29 ♕h6.

28 ♖g3! h5

28...♕xe6 is met by 29 ♕xh7+!

29 ♘h6 ♖g7 30 ♗f5 ♖xg3+ 31 ♕xg3 ♕b8 32 ♖xd5 ♖h7 33 ♗xg6 ♖xh6 34 ♗f7 1-0

A delightful attacking game punishing an over-passive approach.

Game 34

Ovetchkin-Morozevich

Moscow 1998

1 e4 e6 2 d4 d5 3 ♘c3 ♘f6 4 e5 ♘fd7

5 f4 c5 6 ♘f3 ♘c6 7 ♗e3 b6?!

Another experimental idea is 7...♖b8!? 8 ♕d2 c4 9 f5 ♗e7! (better than 9...b5?! 10 fxe6 fxe6 11 ♘g5 b4 12 ♘d1 ♘b6 13 ♗e2 ♘e7, as in Hellers-Ivanchuk, Tilburg 1993, when instead of 14 g4!? White can cheekily get away with 14 ♕xb4! ♘f5 15 ♕d2) 10 fxe6 fxe6 11 ♘e2 with an unclear position according to Ivanchuk.

8 ♗e2

8 ♗b5 ♗b7 9 0-0 ♗e7 (9...g6 is more solid) 10 f5 0-0 11 f6! gxf6 12 ♗h6 fxe5 13 ♕e1! gave White a strong attack in Gipslis-Shereshevsky, USSR 1981.

8...♗e7 9 0-0 0-0 10 ♕d2 ♘db8 11 ♖ad1 ♔h8 12 ♔h1 ♗a6!?

Consistent but arguably a little slow. The other possibility was 12...cxd4 13 ♘xd4 ♘xd4 14 ♗xd4 ♘c6, which despite being unappetising at least diminishes the power of White's f4-f5 break.

13 f5 ♗xe2 14 ♘xe2 exf5 15 c3?!

As Ovetchkin mentions, more to the point is 15 c4! cxd4 16 ♘exd4 dxc4 17 ♕c2 trying to exploit the lead in development. Then 17...♕d5 18 ♘xf5 ♕e6 19 ♘xe7 ♕xe7 20 ♕xc4 is better for White.

15...cxd4?!

With such lagging development, it was more prudent for Black to block the centre with 15...c4.

16 ♘exd4 ♕d7 17 ♕d3 g6 18 c4 ♖d8 19 ♘b5!? d4

If 19...dxc4 then Ovetchkin gives 20 ♕c2 with many threats, but then after 20...♘b4!? things are far from clear, e.g. 21 ♖xd7 ♘xc2 22 ♖xe7 ♘xe3 23 ♖e1 ♘c6 with complications.

20 ♘fxd4 a6

20...♘xe5 is far too risky as 21 ♕e2 ♕b7 22 ♗f4 ♘g4 23 ♘c7 wins at least the exchange.

21 ♘c3 ♕b7

Taking the e-pawn is quickly punished; e.g. 21...♘xe5 22 ♕e2 ♕b7 23 ♘d5! ♗f8 (23...♘xc4? loses to 24 ♘xe7 ♕xe7 25

♕xc4 ♕xe3 26 ♘xf5) 24 ♗g5 ♖e8 25 ♘f6 and Black has to abandon the exchange.

22 ♘d5 b5

23 ♘xf5!

With Black's queenside still half-asleep his king is too exposed to survive.

23...bxc4 24 ♕e4 gxf5 25 ♖xf5 ♗f8 26 ♖df1 1-0

Game 35
Anand-Bareev
Linares 1993

---

1 e4 e6 2 d4 d5 3 ♘c3 ♘f6 4 e5 ♘fd7 5 f4 c5 6 ♘f3 a6

Black hopes to profit by delaying development of the queen's knight.

7 ♗e3 b5

This rapid pawn expansion can easily transpose to the previous chapter if Black opts for an early ...♘c6. Playing on the queenside with 7...♕b6 is seen in Games 36 and 37.

8 ♕d2

There are a couple of notable alternatives but these are not convincing:

a) 8 g3!? is an unusual try, but in M.Kuijf-M.Gurevich, Germany 1996, White never did develop his bishop to g2 or h3: 8...♗e7 9 ♘e2 ♘c6 10 c3 0-0 11 h4 b4! (opening lines and making it difficult for White to press on the kingside) 12 cxb4 ♘xb4 13 ♘c3 cxd4 14 ♘xd4 ♗b7 15 a3 ♘c6 16

♗d3 ♘xd4 17 ♗xd4 ♘c5 18 ♗c2 ♘e4 19 ♕f3 ♖c8. The move 8 g3 has hardly been a raging success as Black has obtained good play and at least equality.

b) 8 dxc5 ♘xc5 9 ♗d3 ♗e7 10 0-0 ♘c6 11 ♘d4 ♘xd4 12 ♗xd4 b4 13 ♘e2 0-0 14 g4 ♘e4 15 ♘g3 ♗b7 16 ♕e1 ♖c8 17 ♖d1 ♕c7, as in Nijboer-M.Kuijf, Netherlands 1995, and again the centrally posted knight on e4 frustrates hopes for a white attack.

8...♗e7

An earlier try was 8...♗b7. After 9 ♗d3 b4 10 ♘d1 ♘c6 11 0-0 cxd4 12 ♘xd4 ♗e7 13 ♖f3! 0-0?! (rather castling into it; instead Kamsky suggests 13...g6 14 ♘f2 ♕c7 keeping open the option of ...0-0-0) 14 ♖h3 g6 15 ♘f2 ♘c5 16 ♘g4 ♘e4 17 ♗xe4 dxe4 18 ♘xc6 ♗xc6 19 ♗d4 the storm clouds were developing around Black's king in Kamsky-Ivanchuk, Tilburg 1992.

9 ♗d3 g6 10 0-0 ♗b7 11 ♘d1!

With the positional threat of solidifying the centre with 12 c3.

11...cxd4 12 ♘xd4 ♘c5 13 b4

Forcing Black's hand and fixing the opposing b-pawn on a light square.

13...♘a4

Anand prefers White slightly after both 13...♘e4 14 ♕e1 and 13...♘xd3 14 cxd3 ♘c6 15 a3 a5 16 ♖b1.

14 c3 ♘b6 15 ♗f2 ♕c7 16 ♘b2 ♘c4 17 ♕e2 ♘c6?

A crucial moment because after this the white initiative is perhaps impossible to resist. Instead with 17...♘a3 (blocking the a-pawn advance) 18 ♖ac1 ♘d7 19 ♘b3 ♘b6 20 ♘a5 ♘bc4 Black has a firm grip on some crucial squares making it difficult for his opponent to make progress.

18 a4! ♘xd4 19 ♗xd4 ♗c6 20 axb5 axb5 21 ♖xa8+ ♗xa8 22 ♘xc4 bxc4

22...dxc4 23 ♗e4 0-0 24 ♖a1 is catastrophic for Black who cannot prevent the rook's entry onto the seventh rank.

23 ♗c2 ♗c6 24 ♕e3 0-0 25 f5! exf5 26 ♗xf5! ♕d8

26...gxf5? is simply a blunder as 27 ♕g3+ ♔h8 28 e6+ wins Black's queen.

27 ♗g4 ♗g5 28 ♕e2

Things are getting desperate for Black, for instance the main threat is 29 e6.

28...h5 29 ♗xh5! gxh5 30 ♕xh5 ♗e8 31 ♖f6! 1-0

If 31...♗c1 then 32 e6 mates quickly.

Game 36
Lutz-Morozevich
Elista Olympiad 1998

1 e4 e6 2 d4 d5 3 ♘c3 ♘f6 4 e5 ♘fd7 5 f4 c5 6 ♘f3 a6 7 ♗e3 ♕b6 8 ♘a4

8 a3 is the subject of Game 37.

8...♕a5+

Others:

a) An interesting alternative is 8...♕c6 when after 9 ♘xc5 ♘xc5 10 dxc5 ♗xc5 11 ♕d2 the rather slow 11...♕b6?! (more dynamic instead is 11...♗d7 when 12 0-0-0 ♗xe3 13 ♕xe3 ♕a4 14 ♔b1 ♘c6 15 ♗d3 0-0-0! 16 c3 d4! proved to very unclear in Luther-Piskov, Erfurt 1993) seems to lead to a pleasant edge for White: 12 ♗xc5 ♕xc5 13 0-0-0 ♘c6 14 ♔b1 ♗d7 15 g3 ♖c8 16 h4 ♕b4 17 ♕f2 (White retains the queens as his plan of a general kingside pawn push is then more effective) 17...♘a5 18 ♘d4 0-0 19 h5 b5 20 ♕e3 ♕e7 21 ♗d3 ♘c4 22 ♗xc4 dxc4 23 c3 b4 24 g4 and possession of the superior minor piece will ensure that

White's attack will prove the most dangerous in Ulibin-Alavkin, Russia 1997.

b) 8...♕c7 is similar: 9 dxc5 ♘xc5 10 ♘xc5 ♗xc5 11 ♕d2 ♗d7 12 0-0-0 ♗b5 13 ♗xc5 ♕xc5 14 f5! exf5 15 ♘d4 ♗d7, as in Riemersma-Barsov, Vlissingen 1996, and now White can keep an edge with the straightforward 16 ♘b3! ♕c7 17 ♕xd5.

9 c3 cxd4 10 b4 ♕c7 11 ♕xd4 ♘c6

11...a5!? makes sense as after 12 b5 b6 Black has a useful square on c5 for a knight. After 13 ♗e2 ♘c5 14 0-0 ♘bd7 15 ♖ac1 ♗b7 16 ♔h1 ♗e7 Black had a fine position in Jonasson-Thorhallsson, Icelandic Championship 1996.

12 ♕d2 b5!?

Another plan based on cracking open the queenside seems reasonable: 12...♗e7 13 ♗e2 b5 14 ♘b2 a5!? 15 0-0!? (15 ♗xb5 axb4 16 ♗xc6 ♕xc6 17 cxb4 is well met by 17...♕b5!) 15...axb4 16 ♖fc1?! (16 ♗xb5 is safer) 16...♕b7 17 cxb4 ♗xb4 18 ♕c2, as in Vratonjic-Drasko, Yugoslavia 1993, 18...♗a3 19 ♖ab1 ♘b4 with complications that seem suspicious for White.

13 ♘b2

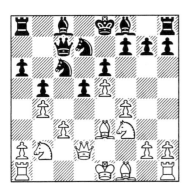

13...f6!?

Aiming to undermine the centre before White can get fully developed.

14 exf6?!

14 a4 is critical, e.g. 14...bxa4 (not 14...♖b8?! 15 axb5 axb5 16 ♘d4! ♘xd4 17 ♗xd4 fxe5 18 fxe5 ♗e7 19 ♖a7 with a clear advantage to White, who has bolstered her centre and maintained a bind in Skripchenko-Matveeva, Belgrade 1996) 15 ♖xa4 ♗b7 (15...fxe5 16 b5 ♘cb8 17 fxe5 ♘xe5 18 ♘xe5 ♕xe5 19 ♗e2 gives White good piece play for the pawn) 16 exf6 ♘xf6 17 ♘g5 ♕d7 18 ♗d3 ♗d6 19 0-0 0-0 20 f5 left White with an initiative in Luther-Topakian, Austria 2000.

14...♘xf6 15 ♗d3 ♗d6 16 0-0 0-0 17 a4 ♖b8 18 axb5 axb5 19 ♘d4?!

Morozevich instead recommends 19 ♖ae1 ♗d7 20 ♘d1, just mobilising his decentralised pieces, with an unclear game.

19...♘xd4 20 ♗xd4 ♘e4! 21 ♗xe4 dxe4

The clear-out in the centre has left White weakened on the light squares.

22 ♗e3?

Surely the best move is 22 g3! which has been played in a more recent game, i.e. 22...♗b7 23 ♕e3 ♗d5? (better is the immediate 23...e5! 24 fxe5 ♗xe5 25 ♗xe5 ♕xe5 26 ♖xf8+ ♖xf8 27 ♖f1 ♖xf1+ 28 ♔xf1 ♕d5 and Black shouldn't be worse as the white knight is badly placed) 24 ♖a7 ♖b7 25 ♖xb7 ♗xb7 26 ♘d1 ♗d5? (26...e5!) 27 ♘f2 e5 28 fxe5 ♗xe5 29 ♗xe5 (29 ♕g5! is strong) 29...♕xe5 30 ♘g4 ♖xf1+ 31 ♔xf1 ♕f5+ 32 ♘f2 and with his knight in play White was able to press for the win in Van der Weide-Jagodzinski, Senden 1999.

22...♗b7 23 c4 g5! 24 cxb5?

24 g3 trying to hold onto f4 is better.

24...gxf4 25 b6 fxe3!

Sacrificing the exchange for two massive pawns in the centre. There is no defence.

26 bxc7 ♖xf1+ 27 ♖xf1 exd2 28 cxb8♕+ ♗xb8 29 ♘d1 ♗a7+ 30 ♖f2 ♗a6 0-1

Game 37
Klimov-Kruppa
St Petersburg 2000

1 e4 e6 2 d4 d5 3 ♘c3 ♘f6 4 e5 ♘fd7

---

5 f4 c5 6 ♘f3 a6 7 ♗e3 ♕b6

8 a3!

8 ♖b1 is less effective, e.g. 8...♘c6 9 ♕d2 ♕a7!? (preparing to increase pressure on the a7-g1 diagonal with ...♗c5, without allowing ♘a4 hitting both bishop and queen) 10 ♗e2 (or 10 ♘d1 cxd4 11 ♘xd4 ♘xd4 12 ♗xd4 ♗c5 13 c3 f6, as in Reefat-Shulman, Dhaka 1999) 10...cxd4 11 ♘xd4 ♗c5 12 ♖d1 0-0 13 0-0 b5 14 ♖f3 ♗b7 gave Black comfortable development in Szelag-Radjabov, Lithoro 1999.

8...♘c6

8...♕xb2?? loses to 9 ♘a4. A move order trick to avoid the text move is 8...cxd4!? 9 ♘xd4 ♘c6 10 ♗e2 ♗c5 which transposes to 8...♘c6 9 ♗e2 cxd4 10 ♘xd4 ♗c5, e.g. 11 ♘a4 ♕a5+ 12 c3 ♗xd4 13 ♗xd4 ♘xd4 14 ♕xd4 0-0 (14...b6 15 ♗d1! ♕b5 16 b4 a5 17 ♘b2 ♕c6 18 ♗f3 axb4 19 cxb4 b5 20 ♔f2 ♕b6 21 ♔e3 ♕b8 22 ♖hc1 0-0 left White with a persistent edge in Topalov-Korchnoi, Dos Hermanas 1999) 15 0-0 ♕c7 16 b4 b6 17 ♘b2 ♗b7 with equal chances in Berg-Radjabov, Aviles 2000.

9 dxc5

The latest fashion. 9 ♘a4 is less precise here: 9...♕a5+ 10 c3 c4 11 b4 cxb3 12 ♕xb3 b5 13 ♘b2 b4! 14 cxb4 ♗xb4+ 15 ♔f2 ♖b8 gave adequate play for Black in Apicella-M.Gurevich, Cappelle la Grande 1999.

9...♗xc5 10 ♘a4 ♕a5+ 11 b4 ♕xa4 12 bxc5 0-0

12...f6!? is interesting and could be best. After 13 c4?! (13 exf6 ♘xf6 14 ♗d3 is better) 13...♕a5+ 14 ♕d2 ♕xd2+ 15 ♔xd2 fxe5 16 cxd5 exd5 17 fxe5 0-0 18 ♗e2 ♘dxe5 19 ♘xe5 ♘xe5 20 ♖ab1 White had more or less enough play for the pawn to hold the game in Berndt-Soln, Bled 2000.

13 c4! ♕a5+ 14 ♕d2 ♕xd2+ 15 ♔xd2 d4!?

Otherwise White improves his pawn structure and Black will have problems with his lack of space.

16 ♘xd4 ♘a5 17 ♔c2

Or 17 c6!? bxc6 18 ♖b1 offers White an edge as he has the more active king and the bishop pair as well as a space advantage.

17...♘xc5 18 ♘c6 ♘xc6 19 ♗xc5 ♖d8 20 ♗b6 ♖f8 21 ♗c5 ♖d8 22 ♗e2 ♗d7

Kruppa and Komarov suggest 22...b5! as an interesting try for freedom, although after 23 cxb5 axb5 24 ♖hd1 (24 ♗xb5? fails to 24...♖d5) 24...♗b7 25 ♔b2 the bishop pair and loose b-pawn still offer White the better chances.

23 ♗b6 ♖e8 24 ♖ad1 ♘b8 25 ♔b3 ♗c6 26 ♗f3!

Exchanging an important defensive piece in order to gain access to the seventh rank. A slight weakness on the kingside is a small price to pay for such a rich prize.

26...♗xf3 27 gxf3 h5 28 ♖d6 ♘c6 29 ♖d7 ♘e7 30 ♖hd1 ♘g6 31 ♖1d4 ♖eb8 32 c5 ♘h4 33 ♖d3 ♘g2 34 ♖3d4 ♘e3

Losing a pawn and the game. Better is 34...♘h4, but White can progress with 35 ♗c7 ♖c8 36 ♖b4 ♖a7 37 ♔c3 ♘xf3 38 ♖b2 ♘h4 39 ♗b6 with excellent chances.

35 ♗c7 ♖c8 36 ♗d6 ♘f5 37 ♖c4 ♖c6 38 ♖xb7 ♖ac8 39 ♖b6 ♔h7 40 ♖xc6 ♖xc6 41 ♖b4 ♔g6 42 ♖b6 ♖c8 43 ♔c4 ♘h4 44 c6 ♘xf3 45 c7 ♘xh2 46 ♖b8 ♖xc7+ 47 ♗xc7 h4 48 ♖b3 ♘g4 49 ♖h3 ♔h5 50 ♗d8 f6 51 exf6 gxf6 52 a4 ♘f2 53 ♖f3 ♘e4 54 ♔d4 ♘g3 55 ♗xf6 ♔g4 56 ♖f2 h3 57 ♔e5 ♘h5 58 ♔xe6 ♔g3 59 ♖a2 h2 60 ♖a1 1-0

Summary

The piece sacrifice in Game 31 has not been refuted but is no longer popular. The main reason is probably that if White has a reasonably grasp of the theory it will be an uphill struggle for Black to draw. The plans of development with 7...♗e7 and 7...b6 are a little too slow for Black and are not to be recommended, especially as White gets a good game just by playing natural moves in reply. The best of the offbeat tries here is 6...a6 followed by ...♕b6. This plan leads to unusual positions where a well prepared Black can set awkward problems for his opponent.

1 e4 e6 2 d4 d5 3 ♘c3 ♘f6 4 e5 ♘fd7 5 f4 c5 6 ♘f3

6...♘c6

    6...a6 7 ♗e3 *(D)*
        7...b5 – *Game 35*
        7...♕b6
            8 ♘a4 – *Game 36*
            8 a3 – *Game 37*

7 ♗e3 ♕b6 *(D)*
    7...♗e7 – *Game 33*; 7...b6 – *Game 34*

8 ♘a4 ♕a5+ 9 c3 *(D)* **cxd4**
    9...c4 – *Game 32*

10 b4 – *Game 31*

      7 ♗e3   7...♕b6   9 c3

CHAPTER FIVE

The Burn Variation:
4 ♗g5 dxe4 5 ♘xe4 ♗e7

1 e4 e6 2 d4 d5 3 ♘c3 ♘f6 4 ♗g5 dxe4 5 ♘xe4 ♗e7

By simplifying the position with 4...dxe4, known as the Burn variation, Black gives up the 'traditional' French Defence plan of encouraging e4-e5 and then undermining White's centre with ...c7-c5. Whilst this gives him fewer prospects of a violent counterattack on the queenside, he also avoids the dangers to his kingside caused by White's cramping pawn on e5.

The resultant pawn structure is known as a 'little centre'. White has a half-open e-file and will often place a knight on the outpost on e5. Black, on the other hand, has the d5-square and will usually try to liquidate White's d4 pawn with ...c7-c5 at some point. Very occasionally he will be able to free his game with ...e6-e5.

By comparison with the Rubinstein variation (3...dxe4) the presence of White's bishop on g5 is of doubtful value. Either it will be exchanged on f6 (giving Black the bishop pair) or White will have to spend time retreating or defending it.

All in all the Burn variation is Black's most solid and durable fourth move alternative which nevertheless maintains good counterattacking chances. For these reasons it is a favourite with many leading players: Alexander Khalifman, Nigel Short, Mikhail Gurevich, Alexander Chernin and Evgenny Bareev are amongst its leading exponents.

Games 38-43 see Black breaking the pin immediately with 5...♗e7, while in Games 44-47 Black tries 5...♘bd7. The key feature of games in this chapter is that Black will meet a capture on f6 by recapturing with a piece (usually the bishop). The more dynamic, but also more risky, plan of ...g7xf6 is considered in the next chapter.

> ### Game 38
> ### Tebb-M.Gurevich
> ### *4NCL 1998*

1 e4 e6 2 d4 d5 3 ♘c3 ♘f6 4 ♗g5 dxe4 5 ♘xe4 ♗e7 6 ♗xf6 ♗xf6

The more dynamic recapture 6... gxf6 is the subject of Chapter 6.

7 ♘f3

For the alternative 7 c3 see Game 43.

7...0-0 8 ♕d2

This queen move is popular here. Other tries can be found in Games 41 and 42.

8...♘d7

The immediate fianchetto with 8...b6 is seen in Game 40.

9 0-0-0 b6 10 ♗d3

White points the bishop directly at the kingside. For 10 ♗c4 see Game 39.

10...♗b7 11 h4

This is certainly White's most direct try in what is a major parting of the ways. More subtle approaches are as follows:

a) 11 ♕e3 (both this and 11 ♕e2 inhibit Black's ...c7-c5 by unveiling the rook on d1) 11...♕e7 12 ♔b1 ♖fd8 13 ♘fg5 c5 14 dxc5 ♗xe4 15 ♘xe4 ♘xc5 16 ♘xc5 bxc5 was fine for Black in Kavalek-Fichtl, Kosice 1961.

b) 11 ♕e2 ♗e7 (11...♕e7 is interesting, as in the previous example) 12 h4 ♘f6 13 ♘eg5 ♗xf3 14 ♘xf3 ♕d6 15 ♘e5 c5 16 dxc5 ♕xc5 17 ♔b1 ♖ad8 18 ♗c4 ♘d5 19 ♗xd5 exd5 20 ♘d3 with a slight edge for White in Sakaev-Kacheishvili, Ubeda 2001.

c) 11 c3 ♗e7 12 h4 c5! (In Topalov-Dreev, Linares 1995, White developed a strong attacking position after 12...♘f6 13 ♘eg5 ♗xf3 14 gxf3 ♔h8 15 ♔b1 ♕d6 16 ♖dg1 h6 17 ♘e4 ♘xe4 18 fxe4 e5 19 f4. The text is far more incisive, offering a pawn sacrifice to accelerate the queenside counterplay.) 13 dxc5 ♕c7 14 ♘eg5 (14 ♕c2 h6 15 cxb6 axb6 16 ♔b1 ♖a5 17 ♘ed2 ♖fa8 gave Black excellent counterplay in Solozhenkin-Dizdar, Paris 1996) 14...♘f6 15 ♕c2 h6 16 ♖de1 ♗xf3 17 ♘xf3 ♗xc5 with equality in Topalov-Dreev, Moscow 1996.

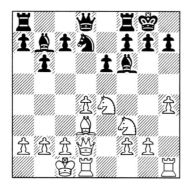

11...♗e7 12 ♕f4

Other possibilities are:

a) 12 ♔b1 ♘f6 13 ♘xf6+ ♗xf6 14 ♘g5 h6 15 ♘h7 ♖e8 16 ♘xf6+ ♕xf6 was already uncomfortable for White in Harris-Dokhoian, Philadelphia 1990.

b) 12 ♘fg5 h6 13 ♖h3 has been tried by some wild Englishmen, but Black's position proves to be very durable after 13...♖c8! (13...♘f6 14 ♘xf6+ ♗xf6 15 ♘h7 ♖e8 16 ♘xf6+ ♕xf6 17 g4 e5 18 ♗b5! gave White the initiative in another Hebden game against Machulsky) 14 ♔b1 c5 15 dxc5 bxc5 16 ♕e2 (Hebden-Kaidanov, Hastings Challengers 1990) and now 16...♕b6 would certainly not be worse for Black.

c) 12 ♖h3 (Chandler-Dolmatov, Hastings 1990) should probably be met by 12...♖c8 as in the Hebden-Kaidanov game above.

12...♘f6 13 ♘xf6+

In the game Fressinet-Tukmakov, Salona 2000, Black answered 13 c4 with 13...c5!? 14 dxc5 ♕b8!? The continuation showed that the pressure Black obtains with this thematic pawn sacrifice can even continue into the endgame: 15 ♘xf6+ ♗xf6 16 ♕xb8 ♖fxb8 17 cxb6 axb6 18 ♔b1 ♗xf3 19 gxf3 h5 with the better chances for Black despite his pawn minus. Positions with opposite-coloured bishops tend to favour the side with the initiative.

Alternatively 13 ♘eg5 ♗xf3 14 ♘xf3 ♕d6 15 ♘e5 c5 16 dxc5 ♕xc5 left Black fully equal in Nunn-M.Gurevich, Belgrade 1991.

13...♗xf6 14 ♘g5 h6

This looks more incisive than 14...g6, though that too looks eminently playable. Hector-Liiva, Stockholm 1993, continued 15 ♗e4 ♗d5 16 ♔b1 ♗g7 17 ♘f3 ♕f6 18 ♕e3 ♗xe4 19 ♕xe4 c5 with quite a good position for Black.

15 ♗h7+

White can simplify the position with 15 ♘h7 ♖e8 16 ♘xf6+ ♕xf6 17 ♕xf6 gxf6, but the resulting position is by no means easy. After 18 f3 f5 one plan for Black is to bring his king to f6 and put a rook on the g-file.

15...♔h8 16 ♗e4 ♗xe4 17 ♘xe4 ♗e7 18 c4 ♕d7 19 ♔b1 ♖ad8 20 ♖d3?!

Far too ambitious. White should just centralise his other rook with 20 ♖he1.

20...♕c6 21 ♖c1 f5 22 ♘d2 e5!

It was also possible to capture on g2 but Gurevich's move is far more convincing. Black liquidates his weakness on e6 and clears the e-file for major piece action.

23 ♕xe5 ♗xh4 24 d5 ♕c5 25 ♖h1 ♕xf2

Very cold-blooded. White gets nothing.

26 ♖dh3 ♖de8 27 ♕c3 ♗f6 28 ♖xh6+?

Sheer desperation, but the position is hopeless in any case.

28...gxh6 29 ♖xh6+ ♔g7 30 ♕h3 ♕xd2 31 ♖h7+ ♔g8 0-1

White has run out of attacking pieces. This is an instructive example of how to win with Black in this opening.

Game 39
Van den Doel-M.Gurevich
Wijk aan Zee 1999

1 e4 e6 2 d4 d5 3 ♘c3 ♘f6 4 ♗g5 dxe4 5 ♘xe4 ♗e7 6 ♗xf6 ♗xf6 7 ♘f3 0-0 8 ♕d2 ♘d7 9 0-0-0 b6 10 ♗c4

For 10 ♗d3 see the previous main game.

10...♗b7

Gurevich is about to demonstrate that

Black need not worry about the possibility of his opponent playing d4-d5 – which means that Black can do without the passive 10...c6 after which 11 ♕e3 (11 g4!? ♗e7 12 g5 ♗b7 13 ♕f4 ♕b8 14 ♕h4 was also very dangerous for Black in Velimirovic-Cosma, Niksic 1994) 11...♕c7 12 ♘xf6+ ♘xf6 13 ♘e5 a5 14 c3 a4 15 a3 ♖a5 16 ♗a2 c5 17 ♖he1 left White with a strong and well-centralised position in Kindermann-Dreev, Nussloch 1996.

11 d5!?

White can also just protect the knight on e4 with either rook or queen, but Black does not experience great difficulties in either case:

a) 11 ♖he1 ♗d5 12 ♗d3 (12 ♗xd5 exd5 13 ♘xf6+ ♘xf6 was just equal and drawish in Finkel-M.Gurevich, European Club Cup, Belgrade 1999, whereas 12 ♕d3 c6 13 ♗b3 b5 14 ♗xd5 cxd5 15 ♘xf6+ ♘xf6 16 ♕xb5 gave Black a tremendous attack down the b- and c- files in Wedberg-Nielsen, Reykjavik Zonal 2000) 12...c5 13 c4 ♗b7 14 dxc5 (14 d5!? exd5 15 cxd5 c4 16 ♗c2 b5 17 ♔b1 ♕b6 18 ♕f4 ♖ad8 led to a complex struggle in Reinderman-M.Gurevich, Andorra Zonal 1998) 14...♕e7! (a thematic pawn sacrifice which opens lines against White's king – 14...bxc5 15 ♘xf6+ ♕xf6 16 ♕c2 g6 17 ♗e4 was slightly better for White in Hübner-Short, Novi Sad Olympiad 1990) 15 ♘xf6+ ♘xf6 16 cxb6 axb6 17 ♔b1 ♖a5 and Black had a strong initiative for the sacrificed pawn in David-M.Gurevich, Amsterdam 2000.

b) 11 ♕f4 ♗d5 (11...♗xe4 12 ♕xe4 ♗e7 13 ♘e5 ♘f6 14 ♕f3 ♘d5 15 ♔b1 ♕d6 16 ♖he1 a6 17 ♗d3 b5 was also very reasonable for Black in Kindermann-Chernin, Dortmund 1990, but 11...♗e7 is dangerous for Black because of 12 d5) 12 ♗d3 (12 ♗xd5 exd5 is fine for Black) 12...♗e7 13 c4 ♗b7 14 g4!? (attempting to improve on Hübner-M.Gurevich, Germany 1992, which went 14 h4 ♘f6 15 ♘e5 a6 16 ♘xf6+ ♗xf6 17 ♗e4 ♗xe4 18 ♕xe4 ♗xe5 19 dxe5 ♕e7 with an equal position) 14...♘f6 15 ♘xf6+ ♗xf6 16 ♗e4 ♗xe4 17 ♕xe4 ♕e7! 18 h4 ♕b4! and Black had excellent counterplay in the game Bologan-M.Gurevich, Belfort 1998.

11...b5!? 12 ♗b3

The only decent move for White. After 12 ♗xb5 exd5 13 ♘xf6+ ♘xf6 14 ♖he1 c5 Black is doing very nicely and 12 dxe6? bxc4 wins a piece because the knight on e4 is hanging.

12...c5 13 ♘d6

Once again 13 dxe6? loses a piece – this time because of 13...♗xe4 14 exf7+ ♔h8 15 ♕xd7 ♕xd7 16 ♖xd7 ♗xf3 17 gxf3 c4 trapping the bishop.

13...♗xd5 14 ♗xd5 exd5 15 ♕xd5 ♘b6

15...♖b8!? was also worth considering.

16 ♕e4!

16 ♕xc5? ♘a4 is immediately disastrous and 16 ♕c6 is also bad because of 16...♗xb2+ 17 ♔xb2 ♕f6+ 18 ♔c1 ♘c4 19 ♕xb5 ♘xd6. The only other move worth considering for White was 16 ♕b3, but then 16...♕c7 17 ♘xb5 ♕c6 leaves Black with very dangerous attacking chances due to the open b-file and powerful bishop on f6.

16...♘a4

Gurevich also suggested 16...♕d7!? in his notes.

17 ♘e5 ♕b6 18 ♕d5

18 ♘dxf7? loses to 18...♕e6 19 ♔b1 ♖ae8 20 f4 ♖xf7.

18...♖ad8 19 f4

This time around 19 ♘exf7? is bad because of 19...♗xb2+ 20 ♔d2 ♕a5+ 21 c3 (21 ♔e3 ♗d4+ will leave White's king without a good square) 21...♕xc3+ 22 ♔e2 ♕c4+ 23 ♘xc4 ♖xd5 24 ♖xd5 ♘c3+ etc.

19...c4 20 ♔b1 ♕c7 21 ♖he1

Once again, snatching the b5-pawn gives Black very strong play on the b-file: 21 ♘xb5 ♖xd5 22 ♘xc7 ♖xd1+ 23 ♖xd1 ♖b8 is very strong despite the absence of queens.

21...a6 22 g4 ♗xe5 23 fxe5

White could also consider 23 ♕xe5. Now Black's knight heads for e6 from where it nicely blockades White's e-pawn.

23...♘c5 24 ♖f1 ♘e6 25 ♖f3 ♕c5 26 ♕xc5 ♘xc5 27 b4?!

27 b3 was better.

27...♘d7 28 ♖e3 ♘b6 29 g5 ♖d7 30 ♖a3?!

And here White should simplify with 30 e6. As the game goes Black is slightly better. **30...♘a4 31 ♖f3 ♖e8 32 ♖df1 ♖xe5 33 ♘xf7 ♖e8! 34 ♔c1 c3 35 ♘e5 ♖de7 36 ♘d3 ♘b6 37 ♘f2 ♘d5 38 ♘d1 ♘xb4**

In time trouble Black snatches a pawn and lets his opponent off the hook. He should have played 38...♖e1 39 ♖xe1 ♖xe1 40 a3 ♖g1 41 h4 ♖h1 when White is in deep trouble.

39 ♘xc3 ♖c7 40 ♔b2 ♖d7 41 ♖f4 ♘c6 42 a4 bxa4 43 ♘xa4 ♖d6 44 ♘c5 h6

45 gxh6 ☖xh6 46 ⓩxa6 ☖xh2 47 ☖1f2 ½-½

Game 40
Kindermann-Bareev
Pardubice 1994

---

1 e4 e6 2 d4 d5 3 ⓩc3 ⓩf6 4 &g5 dxe4 5 ⓩxe4 &e7 6 &xf6 &xf6 7 ⓩf3 0-0 8 ∰d2 b6

The idea behind this order of moves is to avoid the line in which White's bishop comes to c4 after 8...ⓩd7 9 0-0-0 b6 10 &c4, though it is arguable whether this is so fearsome for Black. The negative side of 8...b6 is demonstrated in the current game. Black has also played 8...&e7 in this position which avoids the exchange of the dark-squared bishop but loses valuable time. For example:

a) 9 &d3 b6 10 ⓩeg5!? was an interesting plan that was used in Gelfand-Bareev, Linares 1992, the game continuing 10...h6 11 &h7+ ⓓh8 12 &e4 &xg5! 13 ⓩxg5 c6 14 ⓩf3 &b7 15 ⓩe5 ∰c7 16 ∰f4 ⓓg8 17 ∰g3 and now 17...☖c8 intending ...ⓩd7 would have steered the game to safe waters for Black (rather than 17...ⓩd7?! 18 ⓩxc6 ∰xg3 19 hxg3 ⓓh8 20 0-0-0 as played in the game).

b) An interesting recent example of this line was seen in Ehlvest-Khalifman, Bali 2000, which went 9 0-0-0 ∰d5!? (Khalifman was on the other side of this position in Khalifman-Bareev, Belgrade 1993, that game continuing 9...ⓩd7 10 &c4 a6!? 11 &b3 c6 12 ∰f4 b5 13 h4 ☖a7 14 ⓩeg5 ⓩf6 15 c3 ∰c7 16 ⓩe5 c5 17 &c2 cxd4 and now 18 ∰xd4! would have been White's best) 10 ⓩc3 ∰a5 11 ⓩe5 &b4 12 ⓩc4 &xc3 13 ⓩxa5 &xd2+ 14 ☖xd2 b6 15 ⓩc4 &b7 16 ⓩe3 ⓩd7 17 &b5 ⓩf6 18 f3 ☖fd8 19 ☖hd1 ⓓf8 ½-½.

9 ⓩxf6+!

First played by Chandler, this virtually forces Black into making a dubious

exchange sacrifice.

9...∰xf6 10 &d3 &b7

After 10...h6 11 &e4 White has an unpleasant bind on the position.

11 ⓩg5 h6

11...g6?! weakens Black's kingside and gives White a strong attack after 12 0-0-0 ⓩc6 (and not 12...∰xd4? 13 ⓩxh7) 13 h4 ⓩxd4 14 h5, as in Sax-M.Gurevich, Manila Interzonal 1990.

12 ⓩh7 ∰xd4 13 ⓩxf8 ⓓxf8

Psakhis later suggested the line 13...∰xb2!? 14 &h7+ ⓓh8 15 0-0 ⓩa6 16 ⓩxe6 ⓓxh7 which he felt gave Black enough for a draw. This idea has either been ignored or gone unnoticed as nobody seems to have tried it in practice.

14 c3 ∰h4

14...∰e5+ 15 &e2 ⓩc6 16 0-0 ☖d8 17 ∰e1 left Black with very little compensation in Almasi-Dreev, Tilburg 1994.

15 g3!

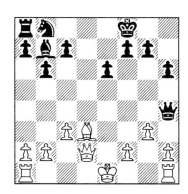

This makes it difficult for Black to obtain compensation. After the older 15 0-0-0 &xg2 16 ☖hg1 &c6 Black has two pawns for the exchange and a solid position.

15...∰f6 16 ☖f1 ⓩd7 17 f4 ⓩc5 18 0-0-0 &d5

Black now faces a grim defensive struggle to save half a point. His last move deviates from the stem game in this line, Chandler-D.Prasad, Novi Sad Olympiad 1990. That encounter continued 18...a5 19 &c2 &c6 20

♕e3 a4 21 ♖d4 ♕e7 22 f5 and now 22...♕f6 intending 23 ...e5 would have kept White at bay.

19 c4 ♘xd3+ 20 ♕xd3 ♗c6 21 ♕d4?!

White should want to keep the queens on so 21 g4 was better. Black in turn should take the opportunity to exchange.

21...♔e7?! 22 ♕e3 ♕f5 23 g4!

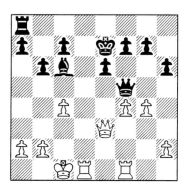

Starting the process of softening up Black's king.

23...♕xg4 24 ♕e5 ♖c8 25 ♖g1 ♕h4 26 ♖xg7 ♕xh2 27 ♖e1! ♗d7 28 c5! ♕f2 29 c6 ♗e8 30 ♕xe6+ ♔f8 31 ♕e5

The spectacular 31 ♖xf7+ ♗xf7 32 ♕xc8+ ♔g7 33 ♕g4+ ♗g6 34 ♕d7+ ♗f7 35 ♕d2 would have been stronger, but White is winning in any case.

31...♖d8

Sacrificing the queen for two rooks with 31...♕xe1+ 32 ♖xe1 ♔xg7 would also be quite hopeless for Black after 33 ♕e5+.

32 ♖gg1 ♕c5+ 33 ♖xc5+ bxc5 34 ♖e5 ♖d4 35 ♖xc5 ♖xf4 36 ♖g3 ♖f1+ 37 ♔c2 ♖f2+ 38 ♔b3 f5 39 ♖e3 f4 40 ♖e1 h5 41 ♖f5+ ♗f7+ 42 ♔c3 h4 43 ♖h1 ♖f3+ 44 ♔d4 h3 45 ♔e4 ♖f2 46 ♖xh3 ♔g7 47 ♖xf4 ♖xb2 48 ♖a3

48 ♖g3+ would have been more accurate.

48...♖c2

Black could hold out a bit longer with 48...♖b4+ 49 ♔e3 ♖b6.

49 ♖g3+ ♗g6+ 50 ♔d5 ♖xa2 51 ♔e6 1-0

Game 41
Leko-Khalifman
Budapest 2000

1 e4 e6 2 d4 d5 3 ♘c3 ♘f6 4 ♗g5 dxe4 5 ♘xe4 ♗e7 6 ♗xf6 ♗xf6 7 ♘f3 0-0 8 ♗c4

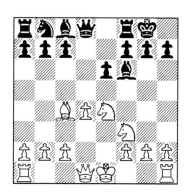

A natural developing move which envisions putting the queen on e2 in some lines. 8 ♕d3 is seen in Game 42.

8...♘c6!?

Attempting to reveal the dark side of White's plan by playing for an early ...e6-e5. The traditional mode of development is to play 8...♘d7 though this is quite dangerous for Black after 9 ♕e2 ♗e7 10 0-0-0!? (10 0-0 c5 11 d5 exd5 12 ♗xd5 ♘b6 13 ♗b3 ♕c7 was fine for Black in Smirin-Lputian, Wijk aan Zee 1993) with the game Topalov-Kramnik, Monaco 1997, proceeding 10...c6 11 h4 b5 12 ♗d3 ♕c7 13 ♔b1 ♘f6 (13...c5!? 14 dxc5 ♘xc5 looks interesting, offering a pawn to open lines against White's king) 14 ♘xf6+ ♗xf6 15 ♕e4 g6 16 h5 ♗b7 17 hxg6 hxg6 18 ♘e5 ♖fd8 19 ♕g4 (the immediate 19 ♘xg6 is met by 19...♖xd4, but now this is a threat) 19...♗xe5 20 dxe5 ♕xe5 21 ♗xg6! with a very dangerous attack.

9 c3

9 ♘xf6+ led to a quick draw after 9...♕xf6 10 0-0 e5 11 ♘xe5 ♘xe5 12 dxe5

♕xe5 13 c3 in Balashov-Dreev, Elista 1995. In the game J.Polgar-Shirov, Prague match 1995, White attempted to inhibit Black's intended ...e6-e5 by playing 9 ♗b5 but this has the drawback that it loses valuable time. Shirov in fact found a nice tactic with 9...♗d7 10 ♕d2 (10 ♘c5 ♗e8! 11 ♘xb7? ♕b8 is not to be recommended for White) 10...♗e7 11 0-0 ♘e5! and after 12 ♘xe5 ♗xb5 13 c4 ♗a6 was already slightly better on account of his bishop pair.

9...e5 10 d5

10 dxe5 ♘xe5 11 ♘xf6+ ♕xf6 12 ♘xe5 ♕xe5+ was probably an attempt to achieve a quick handshake in the game Spassky-Shirov, Paris/Internet 2000, but after 13 ♕e2 ♖e8! 14 ♕xe5 ♖xe5+ 15 ♔d2 ♗e6! 16 ♗xe6 ♖d8+ 17 ♔c2 ♖e2+ 18 ♔b3 fxe6 Black was already much better. Pushing on to d5 is the only serious option for White.

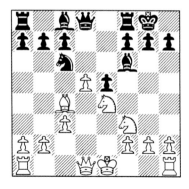

10...♘b8

This has been the most popular choice, but Black's position is certainly not easy in either the game continuation or Short-Gurevich in the note to White's 12th move. He might therefore have to consider the two other knight moves in this position:

a) 10...♘e7 11 ♘xf6+ gxf6 and now:

a1) Short-M.Gurevich, 4NCL 2000, went 12 ♘h4 ♘g6 13 ♕h5 ♕d7 14 h3 and now Gurevich annotated his 14...♘xh4 as being a dubious move but without suggesting an improvement; I suspect that he wants to

play 14...b5 against his next unsuspecting opponent with the idea that 15 ♗d3 is answered by 15...e4! 16 ♗xe4? ♖e8 winning a piece.

a2) 12 ♕d2 ♔h8 13 0-0-0 ♗g4 14 ♗e2 ♕d6 15 ♘h4 ♖g8 16 g3 ♖ad8 when Black stood well in the game Anand-Shirov, Sydney (Olympic Exhibition) 2000.

b) 10...♘a5!? might appeal to those with a more exotic taste in chess moves but it could be quite playable. Baklan-Goloshchapov, Ordzhonikidze Zonal 2000, continued 11 ♗d3 b6 12 h4!? and now 12...♗b7! was the correct move (rather than 12...g6 13 h5 ♗g4 14 ♕d2 ♗g7 15 hxg6 hxg6 16 ♘fg5 as played in the game).

11 ♕e2

Aiming to castle long is the only way that White can really trouble his opponent. Instead 11 0-0 ♗g4 12 h3 ♗xf3 13 ♕xf3 ♗e7 14 ♗b5 a6 15 ♗a4 ♘d7 16 ♖ad1 ♗d6 17 b4 ♘f6 18 ♘xf6+ ♕xf6 19 ♕xf6 gxf6 20 ♗c2 a5 produced a drawish-looking endgame in Ivanchuk-Ehlvest, Reggio Emilia 1990.

11...♗f5 12 0-0-0

This is certainly not the only move, since White has tried no less than three alternatives of which Short's play in 'c' looks like the most dangerous for Black:

a) After 12 0-0 Black can equalise with 12...♗xe4 (12...♘d7 13 ♖ad1 ♗xe4 14 ♕xe4 ♘c5 also looked fine for Black in Hernandez-Shirov, Merida 2000) 13 ♕xe4 ♕d6 14 ♖ad1 ♘d7 15 ♗b5 ♘b6!? (15...♘c5 is also possible) 16 ♖fe1 a6 17 ♗d3 g6, as in Sutovsky-Psakhis, Pula Zonal 2000.

b) 12 ♘g3 ♗g4 13 h3 ♗xf3 14 ♕xf3 ♘d7 15 ♘e4 ♗e7 16 0-0-0 ♗d6 17 g4 ♖b8 18 g5 b5 produced a double-edged struggle which Black eventually won in Leko-Shirov, Frankfurt 2000.

c) White obtained a much improved version of this in Short-M.Gurevich, Shenyang 2000, after 12 ♗d3 ♗xe4 13

♗xe4 ♘d7 14 0-0-0 ♗e7 15 g4 ♗d6 16 ♔b1 ♖b8 17 h4 with the makings of a very strong attack on the kingside.

12...♘d7 13 ♘g3 ♗g6 14 ♗d3!

A considerable improvement on Bologan-M.Gurevich, Belfort 1999, in which Black obtained excellent play after 14 h4 e4! 15 ♘xe4 ♖e8 16 ♘xf6+ ♕xf6 17 ♕d2 ♘b6 and after the further 18 ♗b3 ♕f5 19 ♗c2 ♕xc2+ 20 ♕xc2 ♗xc2 21 ♔xc2 ♖ad8 won back his pawn. By preventing the freeing 14...e4, Leko keeps Black bottled up.

14...♗xd3 15 ♕xd3 ♘c5 16 ♕e3 b6 17 h4!?

17 ♘e4 was also better for White but the text is much sharper.

17...♖e8

17...e4!? 18 ♘xe4 ♖e8 would have given Black some compensation for his pawn and certainly a lot more freedom. Now it gets a bit grim.

18 ♘e4 ♘xe4 19 ♕xe4 g6 20 g4 ♗g7 21 h5

Black's problems stem from the fact that his bishop has been made 'bad' by the inhibiting effect of the e4-pawn. Both 21 g5 and 21 ♘d2 were quite good too.

21...♕f6

Activating the 'bad bishop' with 21...♗h6+ 22 ♔b1 ♗f4 runs into 23 hxg6 hxg6 24 ♘d4! threatening to hop into c6 or even e6.

22 hxg6 hxg6 23 ♘d2! c6

Capturing the pawn on f2 would see a dramatic increase in the pressure after 23...♕xf2 24 ♖df1 ♕c5 25 ♕f3 ♕e7 26 ♘e4 ♖ad8 27 g5. In fact Black would be utterly helpless in this line.

24 dxc6 ♖ac8 25 f3 ♖xc6

Black should certainly take the opportunity to exchange queens given the vulnerability of his king and the strength of the queen and knight team. In any case White would have a clear advantage after 25...♕xc6 26 ♕xc6 ♖xc6 27 ♘e4 as the

attempt by Black to free his position with 27...f5? is met by 28 gxf5 gxf5 29 ♘d6 ♖f8 30 ♖h5, forcing strategic capitulation with 30...f4.

26 ♕e2 ♕e6 27 ♔b1

27...e4?

Black forcibly unleashes the bishop on g7 but gains little compensation for his pawn. In retrospect it would have been better to try and do this with 27...f5!? 28 gxf5 gxf5, leaving Black's king a bit open but keeping material parity. White would continue with 29 ♖dg1 (or maybe 29 ♘f1!? to come to e3 or g3).

28 ♕xe4 ♕c8 29 ♕d3 ♖d8 30 ♕e2 ♖e6

30...♖xc3? 31 bxc3 ♕xc3 32 ♘b3 defends everything.

31 ♘e4 ♖xd1+

Or 31...f5 32 ♖xd8+ ♕xd8 33 gxf5 gxf5 34 ♕c4 ♔f7 35 f4!

32 ♕xd1 ♕c6 33 ♕d3 a5 34 ♖d1 ♗e5 35 ♕e3 ♕c7?!

Allowing the rook to come into d5 makes it easier for White.

36 ♖d5 ♗g7 37 ♕d3 ♖e8 38 ♖d7 ♕e5 39 a4 ♖f8 40 ♕d5 ♕f4 41 ♘d6 ♗e5 42 ♘c4 ♗c7 43 ♕c6 ♗d8 44 ♖b7 ♔g7 45 ♘xb6

The harvest of pawns commences. Black's case is hopeless.

45...♗xb6 46 ♖xb6 ♖d8 47 ♖a6 ♕d2 48 ♕e4 ♖d5 49 ♖a7 g5 50 ♔a2 ♖c5 51 ♕d4+ ♕xd4 52 cxd4 ♖d5 53 ♔b3 1-0

Game 42
Milos-Shirov
Las Vegas 1999

1 e4 e6 2 d4 d5 3 ♘c3 ♘f6 4 ♗g5
dxe4 5 ♘xe4 ♗e7 6 ♗xf6 ♗xf6 7 ♘f3
0-0 8 ♕d3

An interesting alternative to the usual 8 ♕d2, though it does have a slightly artificial feel. For 8 ♗c4 see the next game.
8...♘d7
The natural move and probably the best. 8...♘c6?! is an attempt to take advantage of the awkward position of White's queen (with a subsequent lunge to b4) though it has the drawback of blocking Black's c-pawn. Speelman-Nogueiras, Lucerne 1989, continued 9 0-0-0 ♗e7 10 a3! ♕d5 11 ♘c3 ♕a5 12 ♕e3 ♖d8 13 ♗d3 g6 14 ♗e4 ♗d7 15 h4 h5 16 ♘d2 (16 d5!?) 16...♕b6 17 ♘b3 ♘a5 18 ♘xa5 ♕xa5 and now 19 g4! would have launched a very dangerous attack.
9 0-0-0 ♗e7
Freeing the f6-square for the knight but losing time. More usual is 9...b6 and after 10 h4 ♗b7:
a) 11 ♘eg5 can be answered by the energetic 11...g6 12 ♕e3 c5!? (12...h6 13 ♘e4 ♗g7 was also okay for Black in J.Polgar-Bareev, Madrid 1994, but Gurevich's pawn offer is altogether more

challenging) 13 dxc5 (13 ♗b5 a6 14 ♗xd7 ♕xd7 15 dxc5 ♕a4! gives Black excellent compensation for his pawn) 13...♕e7 14 h5 ♗xf3 15 ♘xf3 ♖fc8 with excellent play.
b) In a subsequent game from the same match, Shirov chose 11 ♘fg5 and play saw 11...♗xe4 (11...♗xg5+ was Black's earlier choice after which Milos probably intended 12 hxg5 ♗xe4 13 ♕xe4 ♕xg5+ 14 ♔b1 anyway) 12 ♕xe4 ♗xg5+ 13 hxg5 ♕xg5+ 14 ♔b1 ♘f6 15 ♕c6 and White had barely adequate compensation for his pawn.
10 h4! ♘f6 11 ♘fg5 ♘xe4 12 ♕xe4 g6
12...♗xg5+ 13 hxg5 ♕xg5+ 14 f4 ♕g6 15 ♕f3 gives White a strong initiative for the pawn, but this might have been preferable to the game continuation, after which White soon develops a very strong attack.
13 ♗c4 ♖b8 14 ♕e3 ♗f6 15 f4 b5 16 ♗b3 a5 17 h5 ♗xg5 18 hxg6?!

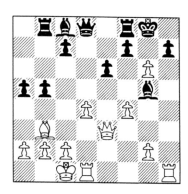

This is certainly a spectacular move, but after Black's simple reply White must have regretted giving his opponent the f-file. The immediate 18 fxg5 was better.
18...fxg6
18...a4 was suggested by Milos in his notes, but it seems to be bad because of 19 fxg5 axb3 20 ♖xh7 fxg6 21 ♖dh1 bxa2 (both 21...♕d5 22 ♖h8+ ♔f7 23 ♕f4+ ♕f5 24 ♕xc7+ ♔e8 25 ♖xf8+ ♕xf8 26 ♕xb8 and 21...♖f1+ 22 ♖xf1 ♔xh7 23 ♕e5 look winning for White) 22 ♖h8+ ♔f7 23 ♖1h7+ ♔e8 24 ♖xf8+ ♔xf8 25 ♕f4+ followed by

mate. Note that 18...♗f6 loses to 19 ♕h3.

19 fxg5 ♕e7 20 ♖df1

20 ♖he1 looks more natural.

20...♗d7 21 a3 a4?

After this the endgames are much more dangerous for Black because of the danger of White's king coming in via b4. It would have been better to simplify with 21...♖xf1+ 22 ♖xf1 ♖f8.

22 ♗a2 ♖xf1+ 23 ♖xf1 ♖f8 24 ♖xf8+ ♔xf8 25 ♕f4+ ♔e8

25...♕f7 26 ♕xf7+ ♔xf7 27 ♔d2 ♔e7 28 ♔c3 ♔d6 29 ♔b4 clearly illustrates the problem with Black's 21st.

26 ♔d2 b4

A desperate lunge before White's king comes to c3.

27 ♕e5 ♔d8 28 ♕h8+ ♗e8 29 ♕f6 bxa3 30 bxa3 ♕xf6

After 30...♔d7 White should play 31 ♕xe7+ ♔xe7 32 c4! e5 33 c5! exd4 34 ♔d3 when Black's bishop is bad and his pawns (especially a4) are weak. Note that 34 ♔d3 ♗f7 35 ♗xf7 ♔xf7 36 ♔xd4 ♔e6 37 ♔e4 wins for White because he takes the opposition.

31 gxf6 ♔d7?

Losing on the spot. Black's last chance to stay on the board was with either 31...♗d7 or 31...♗f7.

32 d5! 1-0

32 d5 e5 33 d6 cxd6 34 f7 wins Black's bishop.

Game 43
Topalov-Bareev
Linares 1994

---

1 e4 e6 2 d4 d5 3 ♘c3 ♘f6 4 ♗g5 dxe4 5 ♘xe4 ♗e7 6 ♗xf6 ♗xf6 7 c3

This apparently innocent-looking move conceals megalomaniac intent. By delaying the development of his knight to f3, White hopes to establish a better grip on e5 by advancing his f-pawn to f4. The drawback of this is that it uses a lot of time and

creates potential weaknesses should Black break out.

Occasionally White has played 7 ♘xf6+ ♕xf6 8 ♘f3 which immediately gets back the bishop pair and hopes to keep a small space advantage. But the problem with this plan is that Black finds it all too easy to free his game with ...c7-c5 and/or ...e6-e5. An example of Black equalising and then going on to outplay his opponent was Prokes-Tartakower, Budapest 1929, which is worth giving in full because of the instructive way Black sets about making something out of nothing: 8...0-0 9 ♗d3 ♘d7 10 0-0 c5 11 c3 cxd4 12 cxd4 e5! (Black frees his game completely; 12...b6 is dubious because of 13 ♕c2 h6 14 ♗e4 ♗a6 15 ♗xa8 ♗xf1 16 ♔xf1 ♖xa8 17 ♕c6 with strong pressure) 13 dxe5 ♘xe5 14 ♘xe5 ♕xe5 15 ♕c2 g6 16 ♖fe1 ♕f6 17 ♗e4 ♗e6! (rather more than freeing Black's game – White has to be careful that he doesn't slip into an inferior position) 18 ♗xb7 ♖ab8 19 ♕c7 ♕xb2 20 ♗e4 ♖b4 21 ♕c2 ♖c8 22 ♕xb2 ♖xb2 23 a4 a5 (Black is now clearly better – White's a-pawn is fixed on a light square and Black's rooks are much more active) 24 h3 ♔g7 25 ♗d3 ♖c3 26 ♖e2 ♖xe2 27 ♗xe2 ♔f6 28 ♗b5 ♔e7 29 ♖d1 ♖b3 30 ♖d4 ♖b4 31 ♖d1 ♗b3 32 ♖a1

32...♔d6 33 ♔f1 ♔c5 34 ♔e1 ♔d4 35 ♔d2 ♗d5 (enabling Black's rook to come to the seventh rank) 36 g3 ♖b2+ 37 ♔e1

♗b3 38 h4 f6 39 ♗a6 ♔c3 40 ♗b5 ♔b4 41
♗d7 ♖a2 42 ♖b1 ♔c3 43 ♖c1+ ♖c2 44 ♖b1
♖b2 45 ♖c1+ ♗c2 46 h5 ♖b7 47 ♗c6 ♖e7+
48 ♔f1 ♔b2 49 ♖xc2+ (forced because of
49 ♖e1 ♗d3+) 49...♔xc2 50 hxg6 hxg6 51
f3 ♔b3 52 g4 ♖c7 53 ♗e8 g5 54 ♔f2 ♔c3
55 ♗b5 ♔d4 56 ♔g3 ♔e3 57 ♗e8 ♖c1 58
♗b5 ♖g1+ 59 ♔h2 ♔f2 60 ♗c6 ♖c1 61
♗d5 ♖c7 62 ♗e4 ♖g7 0-1. A very finely
played endgame by Black.

7...♘d7 8 ♕c2

A new move at the time of the game, but
not particularly effective. 8 f4 0-0 9 ♘f3 b6
10 ♗d3 ♗b7 11 0-0 c5 12 dxc5 ♘xc5 13
♘xc5 bxc5 14 ♕c2 g6 left Black rather
more than equal in Boll-Dreev, Tilburg
1993. 8 ♘f3 is probably White's best,
though this defeats the object of playing 7
c3.

8...e5! 9 dxe5?!

White should try 9 0-0-0!?

**9...♘xe5 10 f4 ♘g6 11 g3 0-0 12 ♗d3
♕d5! 13 a3??**

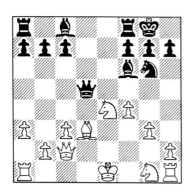

Overlooking a brilliant combination. 13
♘xf6+? is also bad because of 13...gxf6 14
0-0-0 ♕xh1 15 ♗e4 ♗f5!; but 13 ♘e2
avoids the immediate danger.

13...♘xf4 14 ♘xf6+

The point of Bareev's combination is
that 14 gxf4 is answered by 14...♗h4+ 15
♔f1 (or 15 ♔e2 f5 16 b3 ♔h8) 15...f5,
Black emerging the exchange up after 16
♘d2 ♕xh1 17 ♘df3 ♗e7 etc.

14...gxf6 15 ♗xh7+ ♔g7! 16 ♕e4 ♖e8!

Fantastic chess! Both 16...♕xe4+ 17
♗xe4 ♖e8 and 16...♘d3+ would be better
for Black, but he has bigger fish to fry.

17 ♕xe8 ♗f5 18 ♕xa8

It's too late to turn back – 18 ♕e7 ♘d3+
19 ♔f1 ♗xh7 wins the rook on h1 and 18
♕a4 ♘d3+ 19 ♔f1 ♗xh7 20 ♕d1 ♖e8!
leaves White without a decent move.

18...♕e4+ 19 ♔f2

Through lack of a good alternative
White's king decides to head for the hills.
Both 19 ♔f1 ♕g2+ 20 ♔e1 ♘d3+ 21 ♔d1
♗g4+ and 19 ♔d1 ♕c2+ 20 ♔e1 ♘d3+ lead
to mate.

**19...♕g2+ 20 ♔e3 ♘d5+ 21 ♔d4 ♕d2+
22 ♔c5 ♕e3+! 23 ♔c4**

Instant death follows 23 ♔xd5 ♗e6 mate
and 23 ♔b5 ♕b6+ 24 ♔c4 ♘e3 mate.

23...♘b6+ 0-1

Now 24 ♔b3 ♕e6+ also leads to mate.

Game 44
J.Polgar-Bareev
Hastings 1993

**1 e4 e6 2 d4 d5 3 ♘c3 ♘f6 4 ♗g5
dxe4 5 ♘xe4 ♘bd7**

This line is less popular than 5...♗e7 but
is nevertheless quite playable

6 ♘f3

In this game we see a slightly unusual
move order. The position after Black's
seventh move is more commonly reached
via 6 ♘xf6+ ♘xf6 7 ♘f3 h6.

6...h6 7 ♘xf6+ ♘xf6 8 ♗e3

The plan of maintaining the pin with 8
♗h4 is seen in Game 45.

8...♗d6

A natural and perfectly playable move ...
if Black follows up correctly. There is an
interesting alternative in 8...a6 with which
Black prepares to fianchetto his queen's
bishop without having to worry about
checks on b5. He also avoids committing
his king, keeping the option of castling

queenside. Zhang-M.Gurevich, Cap d'Agde 2000, continued 9 ♘e5 b6 10 c3 ♗b7 11 ♕a4+ ♘d7 (and not 11...b5 12 ♗xb5+) 12 c4 ♗d6 13 0-0-0 ♕e7 14 f4 ♗xe5 15 dxe5 0-0-0 16 ♗e2 g5 with excellent counterplay.

9 ♕d3

A rather exotic-looking move with violent intent. In subsequent games in this line White tended to prefer the natural 9 ♗d3 but without setting the world on fire. The game Almasi-Hübner, Baden 1999, continued 9...♕e7 (Hübner was on the opposite side of this position in the game Hübner-Nogueiras, Elista Olympiad 1998, and evidently prefers to keep the option of a queenside fianchetto rather than bringing his queen's bishop to c6 via d7. That game went 9...♗d7 10 ♕e2 ♕e7 11 0-0 0-0 12 c4 c5 13 ♖ad1 ♖fd8 14 ♔b1 ♗a4 15 b3 ♗c6 16 ♘e5 ♗e4 17 ♗xe4 ♘xe4 18 ♖d3 with a very slight edge for White.) 10 0-0 0-0 11 ♖e1 b6 12 c4 ♗b7 13 d5 ♖ae8 14 h3 ½-½.

9...b6 10 ♘e5 ♗b7

White's reply severely interferes with White's development. Black should get his king out of the way with 10...0-0 and only after 11 0-0-0 complete the fianchetto of his bishop (11...♗b7).

11 ♕b5+ ♘d7 12 0-0-0 a6 13 ♕b3?!

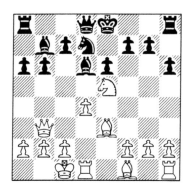

Polgar later felt that 13 ♕e2! 0-0 14 f4, intending ♖g1 and g2-g4, would have been even stronger. Over the next few moves Black manages to exploit the poor position

of White's queen and develops excellent counterplay.

13...b5! 14 c4

Polgar tries to prevent Black's bishop from becoming entrenched in the centre. 14 f4 ♗d5 15 ♕d3 0-0 is very comfortable for Black.

14...0-0 15 f4

Naturally White refuses the pawn offer as 15 cxb5 ♗d5 16 ♗c4 ♘b6 17 ♗xd5 ♘xd5 would see lines opening up in front of her king.

15...♗e4 16 c5 ♗e7 17 ♗d3 ♗xg2!

A cold-blooded and correct decision. Opening lines in front of the king may seem very risky but then risk is inevitable in such a sharp position. After 17...♗xd3 18 ♕xd3 ♘f6 19 g4 ♕d5 20 g5 hxg5 21 fxg5 ♘e4 22 ♖hg1 White's attack is very dangerous in any case.

18 ♖hg1 ♗d5 19 ♕c2 f5 20 ♘g6 ♖e8

In her notes to the game Polgar suggested 20...♖f7 21 c6 ♘f6 22 ♘e5 ♖b8 (counterattack rather than passive defence) 23 ♖g6 ♖b6 24 ♖dg1 ♘g4, though this is far from clear after 25 ♖6xg4 (or 25 ♖1xg4 fxg4 26 f5).

20...♖f6!? was another interesting line, intending simply to eliminate the dangerous knight (White's key attacking piece) with an exchange sacrifice.

21 c6

The weakness of the c6-pawn gives Black more chances for counterplay. White should prefer the immediate 21 ♕e2.

21...♘f8 22 ♘e5 ♗h4?

Black in turn goes astray. He should have played 22...♗f6 23 ♕e2 ♖e7, meeting 24 ♕h5 with 24...♕e8 25 ♕xh6 ♗xe5 26 fxe5 ♕xc6+.

23 ♕e2!

23 ♖xg7+ doesn't quite work after 23...♔xg7 24 ♖g1+ ♔h7 25 ♗xf5+ exf5 26 ♕xf5+ ♔h8 27 ♘f7+ ♗xf7 28 ♕xf7 ♗g5.

23...♕f6 24 ♕h5 ♖ed8

With 24...♖e7 Black could hope for 25

♘g6? (White should prepare this with 25 ♖df1) 25...♘xg6 26 ♖xg6 ♗f3! Now White comes crashing through.

25 ♖xg7+! ♔xg7

Or 25...♕xg7 26 ♖g1.

26 ♖g1+ ♔h8

26...♔h7 27 ♘g4 ♕g6 28 ♕xh4 is equally deadly.

27 ♘f7+ ♔h7 28 ♘xh6 1-0

Black is mated after 28 ♘xh6 ♕xh6 29 ♕f7+ ♔h8 30 ♕g8.

> ## Game 45
> ### Rozentalis-Vaganian
> *Budapest 1996*

1 e4 e6 2 d4 d5 3 ♘d2 dxe4 4 ♘xe4 ♘d7 5 ♘f3 ♘gf6 6 ♘xf6+ ♘xf6 7 ♗g5 h6

Here we arrive at the same position as in the previous game, but via a Rubinstein move order. For the immediate 7...c5 see Game 47.

8 ♗h4 c5 9 ♗e2 ♗d7

One of the main ideas behind placing the bishop on e2 is that after 9...cxd4 10 ♕xd4 ♕xd4 11 ♘xd4 White brings the bishop to f3 and obtains quite serious pressure against Black's queenside.

10 0-0 ♕b6?

This over-ambitious move could have had unexpectedly serious consequences. Black should play either 10...♗e7 or 10...cxd4 11 ♕xd4 ♗c6.

11 ♘e5! cxd4 12 ♗xf6

White is tempted by the possibility of making Black's king wander and thereby misses a golden opportunity. In fact he could have won on the spot with 12 ♗h5! ♘xh5 13 ♕xh5 g6 14 ♘xg6! etc.

12...gxf6 13 ♘xd7 ♔xd7 14 c3 ♖d8 15 ♕a4+ ♔c7 16 cxd4 ♔b8!

Finally reaching sanctuary on the queenside. Black is now okay.

17 ♖fd1 ♕b4 18 ♕c2 ♖xd4

The start of a cold-blooded sequence of moves with which Vaganian contests the initiative. He invites a white rook to come to d7, correctly envisioning that it can be repulsed.

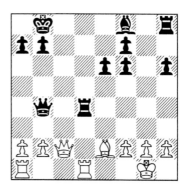

19 ♖xd4 ♕xd4 20 ♖d1 ♕b6 21 ♖d7 ♗c5 22 ♗f3 ♖c8! 23 g3

When he played his 18th move, Vaganian must have seen that 23 ♖xb7+ is met by 23...♕xb7 24 ♗xb7 ♗xf2+ 25 ♕xf2 ♖c1+ 26 ♕f1 ♖xf1+ 27 ♔xf1 ♔xb7 when Black emerges with a winning king and pawn endgame.

23...♖c7 24 ♖d8+ ♖c8 25 ♖d3

Exchanging rooks with 25 ♖xc8+ would have made it easier to draw. Now White must suffer.

25...♕c7 26 ♗c3 ♕d6 27 ♔g2

And not 27 b4 ♗xf2+! 28 ♔xf2 ♕d4+ etc.

27...♖c7 28 ♕h7 ♕f8 29 ♕e4 f5 30 ♕e5 ♗d6 31 ♕b5 a6 32 ♕b3 ♗c5

32...♕c8 was probably better. Now White's pieces become active and any winning chances fade away.

33 ♕d1 ♕h8 34 a4 ♕e5 35 ♕d2 ♕f6 36 ♖c4 e5 37 ♕d5 ♕e7 38 ♗h5 ♗d4 39 ♖xc7 ♕xc7 40 b3 ♔a7 41 ♗xf7 ♕b6 42 f3 ♕c7 43 ♕c4

The exchange of queens leads to a draw, and White should certainly be satisfied with that result. Trying to improve the king with 43 ♔h3? runs into the highly unpleasant 43...♕c2.

43...♛xc4 44 ♗xc4 ♚b8 45 ♗d3 ♚c7
46 ♗xf5 a5 47 ♚f1 ♚d6 48 ♚e2 ♚e7
49 ♚d3 ♚f6 50 ♗c8 b6 51 ♚c4 ♗g1
52 ♚b5 ♗f2 53 ♚c6 ♗g1 ½-½

Game 46
Kasparov-Shirov
Frankfurt 2000

---

1 e4 e6 2 d4 d5 3 ♘c3 ♘f6 4 ♗g5
dxe4 5 ♘xe4 ♘bd7 6 ♘f3 ♗e7 7 ♘xf6+
♗xf6 8 h4

8...0-0

Black can also try delaying castling:

a) 8...a6!? 9 ♕d2 b5 10 0-0-0 ♗b7 11
♖h3 ♗e7 12 ♗d3 f6 13 ♗f4 ♗d5 14 ♕e2
c6 15 ♗e4 ♚f7 16 ♘d2 ♘f8 was an
interesting plan of blockade that Black tried
in the game De Firmian-Seirawan, USA
Championship, Salt Lake City 1999. Black
plays ...a7-a6 because the immediate 8...b6?
is answered by 9 ♗b5 ♗b7 10 ♘e5.

b) 8...h6 9 ♗xf6 leaves Black with two
ways of playing the position:

b1) 9...♘xf6 10 ♕d2 b6 (Black should
probably castle at this point and only play
...b7-b6 on his next move) 11 0-0-0 (or 11
♗b5+ ♗d7 12 ♗d3) 11...♗b7 12 ♘e5 0-0
13 ♗d3 c5! 14 dxc5 ♕c7 15 ♖he1 (15 cxb6
♕xb6 would give Black excellent play on
the c- and b-files) 15...♗xg2?? (Korchnoi is
famous for his cold-blooded defence, but
on this occasion opening the g-file proves

suicidal; 15...bxc5 was correct, with a
double-edged fight in prospect) 16 ♖e2
♚h8 17 ♖g1 ♗d5 18 ♕f4 ♕xc5 19 ♖e3 1-0
Anand-Korchnoi, Wijk aan Zee 2000. Black
is defenceless, e.g. 19...♖ac8 20 ♖eg3 ♘h5
21 ♕xh6+!! gxh6 22 ♖g8+ ♖xg8 23 ♘xf7
mate.

b2) 9...♕xf6 (Black aims to free his game
with ...e6-e5, a plan which tends to lead to
drawish positions in which he is slightly
worse) 10 ♕d2 0-0 11 0-0-0 e5 12 ♖e1 (12
dxe5 ♘xe5 13 ♘xe5 ♕xe5 14 ♗c4 ♗e6 15
♖de1 ♕c5 16 ♗xe6 fxe6 gave Black a
slightly inferior but tenable rook endgame
in Degraeve-Speelman, Istanbul Olympiad
2000) 12...exd4 13 ♕xd4 ♕xd4 14 ♘xd4
♘b6 15 ♘b5 c6 16 ♘d6 ♖d8 17 ♗d3 ♚f8
18 ♘xc8 ♖axc8 19 ♗f5 ♖b8 20 g3 gave
White the slightly better endgame in Leko-
Korchnoi, Tilburg 1998.

c) 8...c5 9 ♕d2 (9 dxc5 ♕a5+ 10 c3 ♕xc5
11 ♗e3 ♕c7 12 ♘g5 b6 13 ♗b5 a6 14 ♗e2
♗b7 15 ♕c2 ♘c5 16 ♗xc5 ♕xc5 17 ♘e4
♕e5 18 ♘xf6+ gxf6 19 0-0-0 ♗xg2 was
much better for Black in Sax-Korchnoi,
Lucerne 1989, though he later managed to
lose) 9...cxd4 10 0-0-0 e5?! (10...0-0 is safer)
11 ♖e1 0-0 12 ♘xe5 ♖e8? (Black should
play simply 12...♘xe5 13 ♖xe5 ♗e6 with
only slightly the worse game) 13 ♘xf7!
♖xe1+ (13...♚xf7 14 ♗c4+ ♚f8 15 ♖xe8+
♕xe8 16 ♖e1 gives White a winning attack)
14 ♕xe1 ♚xf7 15 ♗c4+ ♚f8 16 ♕e6
♗xg5+ 17 hxg5 ♕xg5+ 18 ♚b1 ♘e5 19
♕g8+ ♚e7 20 ♖e1 ♗d7 21 ♕xa8 ♕d2 22
♖xe5+ ♚f6 23 a3 ♚xe5 24 ♕b8+ ♚f5 25
♕f8+ 1-0 Timman-Korchnoi, Tilburg 1991.

9 ♗d3

9 ♕d2 e5 (this equalises, though Black
could also play for a more complex game
with 9...b6!?) 10 ♗xf6 ♕xf6 11 0-0-0 exd4
12 ♕xd4 ♕xd4 13 ♘xd4 ♘f6 14 ♘b5 ♗f5
15 ♗d3 (and not 15 ♘xc7 ♖ac8) 15...♗xd3
16 ♖xd3 ♖fc8 17 ♖hd1 ♚f8 18 ♖c3 c6 19
♘d6 ♖c7 with an equal position in Lutz-
Korchnoi, Zurich 1999.

9...c5 10 ♕e2 cxd4 11 ♕e4 g6 12 0-0-0 ♕a5?

A new but dubious idea. Black should play 12...e5 after which 13 ♗xf6 ♕xf6 14 ♗b5 ♖d8 (14...♕e6!? is a suggestion of Kostakiev) 15 ♖he1 gives White adequate compensation for his pawn, but no more than that. Another rapidplay game, Kasparov-Anand, Kopavogur 2000, continued 15...♕b6 (Black can also play 15...a6!? when Balashov-Kruppa, Elishta 2000, continued 16 ♗xd7 ♗xd7 17 ♕xe5 ♕xe5 18 ♖xe5 ♗c6 ½-½) 16 ♗c4 ♘c5 17 ♕xe5 ♗e6 18 ♗xe6 ♘xe6 19 h5 d3 20 hxg6 hxg6 21 ♖h1 ♘g7 22 cxd3 ♕xf2 23 ♖d2 ♖ac8+ 24 ♔b1 ♕c5 (the position is equal) 25 ♕f4 ♘h5 26 ♕h6 ♕f8 27 ♕g5 ♕c5 28 ♕h6 ½-½.

13 ♗xf6 ♘xf6 14 ♕xd4 ♘h5

An interesting move which certainly makes a fight of it. 14...♔g7 15 h5 would win immediately.

15 a3 ♖d8

The endgame arising after 15...♕b6 16 ♕xb6 axb6 17 ♖he1 would be much better for White due to his vastly superior development and the weakness of Black's b-pawns.

16 ♕e3 ♗d7 17 g4 ♘f6 18 ♕f4

According to Shirov, 18 h5! would have been even stronger. He offers the following variations as proof: 18...♘xg4 19 ♕f4 e5 (19...♘xf2 20 hxg6 fxg6 21 ♕h6 wins) 20 ♕g5 h6 (20...f6 21 ♕h4 g5 22 ♘xg5 is devastating) 21 ♕e7 ♕d5 22 hxg6 ♕xf3 23 ♗e4 ♕f4+ 24 ♔b1 fxg6 (24...♖f8 25 ♗xb7 ♗e6 26 ♗xa8 ♖xa8 27 f3! ♕xf3 28 ♖hf1 winning) 25 ♗xg6 ♕f6 26 ♖xd7 with a huge advantage in the coming endgame.

18...♘d5 19 ♕h6 ♘f6 20 ♘g5?!

This seems very strong but it lets Black off the hook. White could still transpose into the variation given above with 20 h5! ♘xg4 21 ♕f4.

20...♗c6 21 ♗xg6 hxg6?

Black should play 21...fxg6 after which

22 ♘xe6 ♖xd1+ 23 ♖xd1 ♔f7 leaves White with nothing better than a draw by repetition with 24 ♘g5+ ♔g8 25 ♘e6 ♔f7 etc.

22 ♘xe6 fxe6 23 ♕xg6+ ♔h8 24 ♕xf6+ ♔h7 25 ♖he1

25 g5 looks very strong but Shirov pointed out an amazing defence in 25...♗xh1 26 g6+ ♔h6 27 g7+ ♔h5! (and not 27...♔h7? 28 g8♕+ ♖xg8 29 ♖d7+).

25...♖xd1+ 26 ♖xd1 ♕c5! 27 g5 ♖f8 28 ♕h6+ ♔g8 29 ♕xe6+ ♔g7??

The proverbial final error. 29...♔h8 leaves White with nothing clear.

30 ♕h6+??

Kasparov in turn misses his chance, at least this time around. 30 ♖d6 would win.

30...♔g8 31 ♕g6+ ♔h8 32 ♕h6+ ♔g8 33 ♕e6+ ♔g7??

Once again missing 33...♔h8. This time Kasparov gets it right.

34 ♖d6 ♗e8 35 ♕e7+ 1-0

Game 47
Leko-Korchnoi
Wijk aan Zee 2000

---

1 e4 e6 2 d4 d5 3 ♘c3 ♘f6 4 ♗g5 dxe4 5 ♘xe4 ♘bd7 6 ♘xf6+

A much quieter treatment than 6 ♘f3.

6...♘xf6 7 ♘f3 c5

The choice between playing this immediately and preceding it with 7...h6 seems largely a question of taste. The main argument against 7...h6 is 8 ♗e3 (see J.Polgar-Bareev), though this is far from convincing.

8 ♗b5+

Certainly White's most forceful move but if White's initiative is neutralised he will have further freed Black's game with exchanges. 8 ♗c4 has been the most popular alternative, e.g. 8...♕a5+ 9 c3 ♗e7 10 0-0 0-0 11 ♖e1 ♖d8 12 ♖e5 ♕b6 13 ♕e2 h6 (An argument against interpolating ...h6 on move seven? 13...cxd4 14 ♘xd4 h6 15 ♗h4 ♘d5 16 ♗xe7 ♘xe7 17 ♖e1 left Black under some pressure in Shirov-Topalov, Monaco 1997) 14 ♗xf6 gxf6 15 ♖h5 ♗f8 16 dxc5 ♕c7 17 ♖e1 ♗g7 18 h3 b6 19 ♘h2 ♗b7 20 ♘g4 and was agreed drawn in Morozevich-Korchnoi, Wijk aan Zee 2000. The final position is very sharp indeed and it is surprising that neither of these two great fighters wished to continue.

8 ♗e2 leads to similar play to the next game.

8...♗d7 9 ♗xd7+ ♕xd7 10 ♕e2 ♗e7?!

Black seems to obtain a very reasonable position in this game, but this is not the only move. 10...cxd4 11 0-0-0 ♗c5 is another good line, the game Almasi-Ehlvest, Biel 1996 continuing 12 ♕e5 ♖c8 13 ♘xd4 ♕c7 14 ♕xc7 (14 ♗xf6 gxf6 15 ♕xf6 loses after 15...♗xd4 with mate on c2) 14...♖xc7 with equality.

11 dxc5

In an earlier game against Korchnoi, Leko played 11 0-0-0 but after 11...0-0 12 dxc5 ♕a4 13 ♔b1 ♗xc5 14 ♗xf6 gxf6 15 ♘e1 ♖fd8 16 ♘d3 ♗f8 Black had no problems (Leko-Korchnoi, Vienna 1996).

11...0-0

After 11...♗xc5 12 ♘e5 ♕a4 13 0-0 0-0 14 ♗xf6 gxf6 15 ♕f3 Black found himself in big trouble in the game Hracek-

Slobodjan, Koszalin 1999. In fact he lasted just another four moves: 15...f5 (15...fxe5 16 ♕g3+ ♔h8 17 ♕xe5+ ♔g8 18 ♕xc5 wins a pawn) 16 ♖ad1 ♗e7 17 ♕xb7 ♖fe8 18 ♖d3 f4 19 ♖d7 ♗f6 and 1-0.

12 ♘e5 ♕d5 13 0-0 ♗xc5 14 ♖fe1 ♘d7 15 ♘f3 f6??

A quite uncharacteristic blunder from Korchnoi who loses a pawn for zero compensation. Both 15...♖fc8 16 ♖ad1 ♕c6 and 15...♕c6 look rather equal.

16 ♖ad1 ♕c6 17 ♕xe6+ ♕xe6 18 ♖xe6 fxg5 19 ♖xd7 g4 20 ♖e5!

A simple refutation.

20...♖ad8

Korchnoi might have missed the fact that 20...♖ac8 is answered by 21 ♖g5, winning the g4-pawn, as 21...gxf3 is met by 22 ♖gxg7+ ♔h8 23 ♖xh7+ ♔g8 24 ♖dg7 mate.

21 ♖xd8 ♖xd8 22 ♘e1 ♗d4 23 ♖b5 ♗b6 24 c4 ♖d1 25 ♔f1 ♖c1 26 b3 ♔f8 27 a4 ♗d4 28 ♔e2 b6 29 ♖d5 ♗f6 30 ♘d3 ♖c3 31 ♖b5 h5 32 ♔d2 h4 33 ♘f4 h3 34 g3

Korchnoi's attempts to complicate have come to nought.

34...♔g8 35 ♘d5 ♖f3 36 ♔e2 ♗d4 37 ♘e3 ♗c5 38 b4 ♗f8 39 a5 bxa5 40 bxa5 a6 41 ♖b8 ♔f7 42 ♘xg4 ♖f5 43 f4 1-0

Summary

5...♘bd7 is currently less popular than 5...♗e7 and tends to be a bit more passive. But Black's position is ultra-solid and it seems that he can more or less neutralise 6 ♘xf6+ and he gets to trade punches after the sharp 6 ♘f3 ♗e7 7 ♘xf6+ ♗xf6 8 h4.

If Black opts for 5...♗e7 then he must certainly know what he's doing, yet countless attempts by the world's most dangerous attacking players have failed to make a lasting impression on Black's fortress-like position. In the main line White seems to be hitting his head against a brick wall, especially when Black is Mikhail Gurevich.

The current fashion is to try and eke out an edge with 8 ♗c4, hoping for 8...♘d7 9 ♕e2. But this doesn't look like the end of the world for Black and he can avoid the perils of Leko-Khalifman (Game 41) with 10...♘e7. Upcoming battles in the Burn variation may well centre on this very line.

1 e4 e6 2 d4 d5 3 ♘c3 ♘f6 4 ♗g5 dxe4 5 ♘xe4

5...♗e7

    5...♘bd7

        6 ♘f3

            6...h6 7 ♘xf6+ ♘xf6 *(D)*

                8 ♗h4 – *Game 44*; 8 ♗e3 – *Game 45*

            6...♗e7 – *Game 46*

        6 ♘xf6+ ♘xf6 7 ♘f3 *(D)*

            7...h6 – *Games 44 and 45 (by transposition)*; 7...c5 – *Game 47*

6 ♗xf6 ♗xf6

    6... gxf6 – *Chapter 6*

7 ♘f3

    7 c3 – *Game 43*

7...0-0 *(D)* 8 ♕d2

    8 ♗c4 – *Game 41*; 8 ♕d3 – *Game 42*

8...♘d7

    8...b6 – *Game 40*

9 0-0-0 b6 10 ♗d3

    10 ♗c4 – *Game 39*

10...♗b7 – *Game 38*

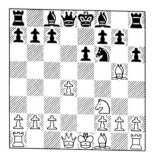
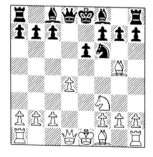
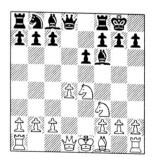

     7...♘xf6   *7 ♘f3*   *7...0-0*

CHAPTER SIX

The Burn Variation: 4 ♗g5 dxe4 5 ♘xe4 ♗e7 6 ♗xf6 gxf6

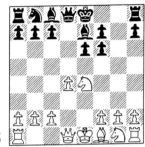

1 e4 e6 2 d4 d5 3 ♘c3 ♘f6 4 ♗g5 dxe4 5 ♘xe4 ♗e7 6 ♗xf6 gxf6

Recapturing with the pawn on f6 leads to an altogether more dynamic and double-edged game then the solid 6...♗xf6 (see Chapter 5, Games 38-43). Black covers the e5- square and obtains an open g-file. On the other hand Black's king will only be able to reside on the kingside under exceptional circumstances (generally speaking Black tries to castle long) and his pawn structure might get shredded should White manage to play a later d4-d5.

Many Black players opt to include both 6...♗xf6 and 6...gxf6 in their repertoire, the choice of line depending on the occasion, and also who their opponent is.

White usually plays 7 ♘f3 and then Games 48-50 see various White tries after the popular move 7...a6, while Games 51-53 witness attempts by Black to get by, for the moment at least, without ...a7-a6.

Game 48
Sutovsky-Morozevich
Pamplona 1998

1 e4 e6 2 d4 d5 3 ♘c3 ♘f6 4 ♗g5 dxe4 5 ♘xe4 ♗e7 6 ♗xf6 gxf6 7 ♘f3

This is far and away the most popular move, but White has tried numerous alternatives:

a) 7 g4?! attempts to combine a kingside fianchetto with the restraint of Black's ...f6-f5 idea, but it is far to extravagant to be good. Black can simply play 7...♗d7 8 ♗g2 ♗c6 threatening ...f6-f5.

b) 7 c3 f5 8 ♘g3 c5 9 ♗b5+ ♗d7 10 ♗xd7+ ♕xd7 11 ♘f3 ♘c6 12 dxc5 ♕xd1+ 13 ♖xd1 ♗xc5 brought about an endgame in which White had to play carefully to hold the balance in Ljubojevic-Lautier, Manila 1990.

c) 7 ♕d2 prepares queenside castling and in some cases intends to come to h6 with the queen. Black should meet this plan with 7...b6 8 ♗b5+ (giving Black a useful tempo for ...c7-c6, but 8 ♗c4 ♗b7 is embarrassing) 8...c6 9 ♗c4 ♗b7 10 0-0-0 b5!? 11 ♗e2 ♘d7 12 ♘f3 ♕c7 13 ♖he1 0-0-0 (preparing ...a7-a6 followed by ...c6-c5 – which White now tries to prevent) 14 ♕h6 ♖dg8 15 g3 f5! 16 ♘ed2 ♗f8 when Black had more space and the bishop pair in Renet-Andersson, Cannes 1989.

d) 7 g3 (Fischer's favourite line which Black should meet energetically) 7...f5! 8 ♘c3 ♗f6 9 ♘ge2?! (9 ♘f3 is probably better, but then 9...c5 10 dxc5 ♕a5 11 ♕d2 ♗d7 12 ♘d4 ♕xc5 13 0-0-0 ♗xd4 14

♕xd4 ♕xd4 15 ♖xd4 was fine for Black in Psakhis-King, Dortmund 1989) 9...♘c6 10 d5 exd5 11 ♘xd5 (after 11 ♕xd5 Black's most promising line is probably 11...♗e6!? 12 ♕b5 0-0 13 ♕xb7 ♘a5, an interesting pawn sacrifice recommended by Soltis) 11...♗xb2 12 ♗g2 (offering an exchange sacrifice that it would be unwise to accept) 12...0-0 13 0-0 ♗e5 (13...♗h8?! 14 ♘ef4 ♘e5 15 ♕h5 gave White compensation for the pawn in Fischer-Petrosian, Candidates match 1971) 14 ♖b1 ♘a5 15 ♕e1 c6 16 ♖d1 ♖e8 17 ♘df4 ♕c7 18 ♘h5 ♘c4 and White was struggling to find decent compensation in Bellon-Marovic, Medina del Campo 1990.

e) 7 ♗c4 is an interesting move after which 7...a6 (7...f5?! is risky because of 8 ♘g3 ♗f6 9 c3, when White prevents the ...c7-c5 break and may play his knight or queen to h5 next move; while 7...b6 8 ♘f3 transposes into the next game, Almasi-Andersson) 8 a4 (8 ♘f3 b5 transposes into Bakre-D.Prasad, given as a note within Sutovsky-Morozevich) 8...♘d7 9 ♘f3 c5 10 0-0 was the game Leko-Bunzmann, Hamburg 1999, and now 10...cxd4 11 ♘xd4 ♘b6 would have led to a complex struggle with chances for both sides.

f) 7 ♘e2 aims to bring the knight to f4, but it loses time and this is far from being a secure post. Here 7...b6 8 ♘f4 f5 9 ♘g3 ♕d6 10 ♕f3 ♘c6 11 0-0-0 ♗b7 gave Black a very active position in Zagoryansky-Ufimtsev, Moscow 1949.

7...a6

This ubiquitous little move has been very fashionable recently. Black stops anything landing on the b5-square, prepares a pawn storm should White castle queenside and in many cases will play ...b7-b5, stopping White from establishing a pawn on c4 and thus keep control of d5. This plan of c2-c4 and d4-d5 is White's main plan against 6...gxf6. Against Sutovsky 7...a6 is an especially good idea as the young Israeli

grandmaster has been scoring heavily against 7...b6 with 8 ♗c4 ♗b7 9 ♕e2 followed by castling short, e.g. 9...c6 10 0-0 ♕c7 (the position is extremely dangerous for Black – 10...♘d7 looks bad because of 11 ♘h4! 0-0 12 ♘g3 f5 13 ♘hxf5 exf5 14 ♘xf5 ♗f6 15 ♕h5 ♗g7 16 ♕g4 ♕f6 17 ♘xg7 ♕xg7 18 ♕xd7 winning in Sutovsky-Hoffman, Villa Martelli 1997) 11 ♘g3 ♘d7 (11...b5!? 12 ♗b3 ♘d7 might be an improvement, intending to meet 13 ♘f5 exf5 14 ♖fe1 with 14...♘b6) 12 ♘f5!? exf5 13 ♖fe1 ♘f8 14 ♘h4 ♘g6 15 ♘xf5 h5 16 ♕f3 ♔f8 17 ♘xe7 ♘xe7 18 ♕xf6 ♘g6 19 ♖e5 and White's attack just kept on coming in Sutovsky-Volkov, Isle of Man 2000.

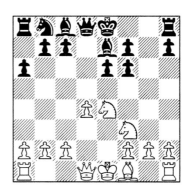

8 ♕d2

8 ♗c4 can now by met by 8...b5 9 ♗b3 ♗b7 10 ♕e2 ♗d5 with Bakre-D.Prasad, Calcutta 2000, continuing 11 ♗xd5 ♕xd5 12 0-0 0-0 13 a4 ♘c6 with a very solid position for Black. 8 g3 is seen in Game 49 and 8 c4 in Game 50.

8...b5

Alternatively there is 8...f5 9 ♘g3 (or 9 ♘c3 b5 ½-½ W.Watson-Anand, Palma de Mallorca 1989) 9...♘d7 10 ♘h5 h6 11 0-0-0 ♘f6 12 ♘xf6+ ♗xf6 13 ♔b1 b5 14 g3 ♗b7 15 ♗g2 ♕d6 16 ♖he1 0-0-0 with equality in Perunovic-Antic, Yugoslav Championship, Subotica 2000.

9 ♕h6

The game Klovans-P.Nielsen, Istanbul

Olympiad 2000, was also interesting: 9 0-0-0 &b7 10 &d3 ②d7 (10...&d5 11 &b1 ②c6 also looks reasonable) 11 &b1 &d5 12 ₩h6 c6 13 ₩g7 ᙏf8 14 ₩xh7 f5 15 ②c3 ②f6 16 ₩h3 ②g4 when Black's active pieces gave him compensation for the pawn.

9...&b7 10 &d3

10 ₩g7 ᙏf8 11 ₩xh7 f5 offers Black excellent compensation for his pawn.

10...②d7

As usual Black must be wary of letting his opponent's pieces in with a premature 10...f5?! Nurkic-Muratovic, Bihac 1999, was good for White after 11 ②eg5 &xf3 12 ②xf3 &f8 13 ₩e3 ₩d5 14 0-0 ②d7 15 a4.

11 ②g3

11 0-0-0 f5 12 ②eg5 &xg5+ 13 ②xg5 ₩f6 14 ₩h5 ₩g6 15 ₩h4 0-0-0 gave Black a good game in Wedberg-P.Nielsen, New York Open 2000.

11...f5 12 ②h5 &f8 13 ₩e3?

Presumably Sutovsky thought that this prevented Black's next move. He is certainly in for a big surprise. 13 ₩f4 ᙏg8 is also uncomfortable for White so he should head for equality with 13 ②g7+ &xg7 14 ₩xg7 ₩f6 15 ₩xf6 ②xf6 16 &e2.

13...②f6! 14 ₩e5?

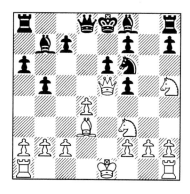

Heading straight for Black's ambush. White should bail out with 14 ②xf6+ ₩xf6 15 &e2, though Black is already better because of the two bishops

14...②xh5!!

Morozevich must have prepared this well in advance. 14...&e7 is bad because of 15 &xf5.

15 ₩xh8 &xf3 16 gxf3 ②f6

Imprisoning White's queen and threatening ideas such as ...₩d5, ...0-0-0 (or ...&e7) followed by ...&h6. The queen can be saved, but at a very heavy cost.

17 ᙏg1

This loses, but what can White do? Morozevich gave the lines 17 0-0-0 &e7 18 &b1 ₩d5; 17 d5 &e7 18 &f1 0-0-0; and 17 c3 &e7 18 ᙏg1 ₩d5 19 ᙏg8 (otherwise ...&h6 as usual) 19...₩xf3 winning.

17...₩xd4 18 ᙏg8 &e7 19 &f1 &g7! 20 ₩xg7

Giving up the queen with 20 ᙏxa8 &xh8 21 ᙏxh8 ②g4! 22 fxg4 ₩xh8 is also hopeless for White.

20...ᙏxg8 21 ₩h6 ₩xb2 22 ᙏe1 ₩c3 23 ₩h4 c5 24 ᙏd1 c4 25 &xf5 ₩xf3!

25...exf5 26 ₩f4 would keep White in the game.

26 ₩d4 ②d5 0-1

After 27 ₩c5+ (27 &e4 ②e3+) 27...&f6 28 ₩d4+ &xf5 White runs out of checks.

Game 49
Kasparov-M.Gurevich
Sarajevo 2000

1 e4 e6 2 d4 d5 3 ②c3 ②f6 4 &g5 dxe4 5 ②xe4 &e7 6 &xf6 gxf6 7 ②f3 a6 8 g3

Adopting a formation which challenges one of the main points of the 7...a6 and 8 ...b5 plan. White fianchettoes his king's bishop and gradually prepares for c2-c4.

8...b5

Morozevich himself switched to 8...②c6!? in his game against Milos at the Istanbul Olympiad, 2000. That game went 9 &g2 e5 10 d5 ②b4 11 ②c3 c6 12 dxc6 ₩xd1+ 13 ᙏxd1 bxc6 14 a3 ②d5 15 ②xd5 cxd5 16 ᙏxd5 0-0 17 0-0 &e6 18 ᙏd2 ᙏab8 19 b4 a5 when Black's pressure on the queenside was compensation for the pawn.

Nigel Short has played 8...f5 9 ♘c3 ♗f6 (he also tried the immediate 9...c5 against Glek in an Internet blitz game, 2000: 10 d5 ♕b6 11 ♖b1 ♗f6 12 ♗g2 0-0 13 0-0 ♖d8 14 ♖e1 ♘c6 with complex play) 10 ♕d2 (10 ♗g2 c5 11 dxc5 ♕a5 12 0-0 ♕xc5 was fine for Black in Madl-Maric, Halle 2000) 10...c5 11 d5 0-0 12 0-0-0 b5 13 dxe6 ♕xd2+ 14 ♘xd2 fxe6 15 ♗g2 ♖a7 with approximate equality in De la Villa-Short, Pamplona 2000.

9 ♗g2 ♗b7 10 ♕e2 ♘d7

Black has an alternative in 10...♗d5, but Morozevich had an unpleasant experience in this line after 11 ♘c3 (11 ♘ed2 ♘d7 12 0-0 0-0 13 ♖fd1 ♘b6 14 c3 ♘a4 15 ♘f1 c6 16 ♘e3 intending ♕c2, b2-b3 and c2-c4 was another promising plan that was used in Glek-Volkov, Korinthos Open 2000) 11...c6 12 0-0-0 ♘d7 13 ♔b1 ♘b6 14 ♖he1 ♕c7 15 ♘h4 h5 16 f4 f5 17 ♘f3 0-0-0 18 ♘e5 (Leko-Morozevich, Frankfurt 1999).

11 0-0 0-0 12 ♖fd1

Improving on the game J.Polgar-Morozevich, Wijk aan Zee 2000, in which Black had good play after 12 ♖ad1 ♗d5 13 ♖fe1 ♔h8 14 ♘fd2 c6 15 c4 bxc4 16 ♘xc4 a5. Kasparov had no doubt done his homework on this line and frees the f1-square for his knight.

12...♗d5 13 c3 f5 14 ♘ed2 c5 15 dxc5 ♘xc5 16 ♘f1!

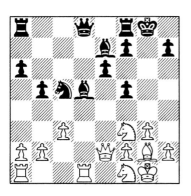

Preparing a dangerous exchange sacrifice.

16...♕c7 17 ♖xd5! exd5 18 ♘e3 ♗f6!

18...♖fe8 19 ♘d4 gives White superb compensation. Gurevich knows he must eliminate one of White's knights.

19 ♘d4 ♗xd4! 20 cxd4 ♘e4 21 ♘xd5

Surprisingly this is not White's best. After the game Kasparov felt that 21 ♗h3 would have been better – Black's weaknesses are not going to run away.

21...♕d6 22 ♘e3 ♕f6 23 ♕h5 ♖ad8 24 ♘xf5 ♘d6 25 ♘e3?

Before playing this, White should protect his d-pawn with 25 ♕g4+. Now Black is better.

25...♕xd4! 26 ♖d1 ♕g7?

Missing a golden opportunity with 26...♕xb2! 27 ♕g5+ ♕g7! 28 ♕xg7+ ♔xg7 29 ♖xd6 ♖xd6 30 ♘f5+ ♔f6 31 ♘xd6 ♔e5, when Black's active king is a menace. After the text, all hell breaks loose.

27 ♖d5 ♔h8 28 ♕d1 ♘b7 29 b4 ♖xd5 30 ♕xd5 ♘d8 31 ♕d6 ♘e6 32 ♕xa6 ♘d4 33 h4 f5 34 ♘d5 ♘e2+ 35 ♔f1 f4! 36 ♔xe2 fxg3 37 ♕d6 ♕b2+?

In time trouble Black slips up. 37...♖xf2+ 38 ♔e3 ♖xg2 39 ♕b8+ ♕g8 40 ♕e5+ is a draw by perpetual check.

38 ♔d3 ♖xf2 39 ♕b8+ ♔g7 40 ♕xg3+ ♔h8 41 ♕b8+ ♔g7 42 ♕c7+ ♔f8

Black's king is unable to escape – 42...♔h6 loses to 43 ♕d6+ ♔h5 (43...♔g7 44 ♕e7+ ♔h8 45 ♕d8+ ♔g7 46 ♕g5+

transposes into the game) 44 ♘f4+ ♖xf4 45 ♕xf4 ♕xg2 46 ♕g5+! ♕xg5 47 hxg5 ♚xg5 48 a4 winning.

43 ♕e7+ ♚g8 44 ♕g5+ ♚h8 45 ♗e4!

A deadly quiet move. White has calculated that his king can escape the checks.

45...♕c2+ 46 ♚d4 ♕d2+

Or 46...♕c4+ 47 ♚e5 etc.

47 ♚c5 ♕xg5 48 hxg5 ♖xa2 49 ♚xb5 ♖e2 50 ♘c3 ♖e3 51 ♚c4 ♖g3 52 b5 ♖xg5 53 b6 1-0

Game 50
Shirov-Topalov
Sarajevo 2000

---

1 e4 e6 2 d4 d5 3 ♘c3 ♘f6 4 ♗g5 dxe4 5 ♘xe4 ♗e7 6 ♗xf6 gxf6 7 ♘f3 a6 8 c4

This direct and natural way move is an attempt to exploit the time lost by 7 ...a6. White is playing for d4-d5.

8...f5 9 ♘c3 ♗f6!

In Wang Zili-Dreev, Shenyang 1999, Black played 9...c5 10 d5 ♗f6, but then 11 ♕c2 was quite good for White. With Topalov's move order the queen must go to the inferior d2-square.

10 ♕d2

After 10 ♕c2 Black can play 10...♗xd4 11 0-0-0 c5.

10...c5

Shirov suggested that 10...0-0 would be better, and he probably intended to meet this with 11 g4!? fxg4 12 ♖g1.

11 d5

The thematic move, obtaining a passed pawn and driving a wedge through Black's position. 11 dxc5 ♕a5 12 ♗e2 ♕xc5 was fine for Black in Kovalevskaya-Maric, Women's World Cup, Shenyang 2000.

11...0-0 12 0-0-0 e5

12...♗g7!? is an interesting alternative, not blocking the bishop's diagonal.

13 h4 b5 14 d6 ♘c6?!

Allowing the d-pawn to advance turns out to be mistaken. Black later improved on this with 14...♗e6!? in the game Belotti-Radjabov, St Vincent 2001, and obtained a strong attacking position after 15 ♘d5 (Shirov suggested 15 g4!? fxg4 16 ♗d3 ♗g7 17 ♘g5 as being slightly better for White) 15...♗xd5 16 ♕xd5 ♘d7 17 ♘d2 ♗g7 18 ♖h3 ♕f6.

15 d7 ♗b7 16 ♕d6!

Topalov must have underestimated this idea. White puts his biggest piece right in Black's guts.

16...e4 17 ♘d5 ♗g7 18 ♘g5 ♘d4

18...h6 is met by 19 cxb5 axb5 20 ♗xb5 when the black position is falling apart at the seams.

19 ♘e7+ ♚h8 20 ♖h3?!

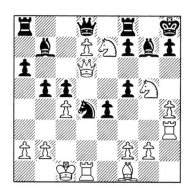

An inaccurate order of moves according to Shirov, who later discovered an interesting defensive try for Black. White should play 20 ♚b1! first, after which 20...b4 (20...f4 21 ♖h3 transposes back into the game) 21 ♗e2 is winning for White because 21...♘xe2 is answered by 22 ♕xc5 threatening ♕xf5.

20...f4?!

20...b4! would have set White a very difficult problem (Black wants to defend by playing ...a6-a5 and ...♖a6) but White can still develop a winning attack with 21 ♖g3! a5 22 ♖xd4! cxd4 23 ♕f4 (threatening ♕xf5) 23...♕xd7 24 ♘xf5 etc.

21 ♔b1 b4 22 ♗e2 f3

After 22...♘xe2 Shirov gave 23 ♕xc5 ♘d4 (23...f5 24 ♘e6) 24 ♖xd4 ♗xd4 25 ♕f5! ♔g7 26 ♘g8! By interposing 22 ...f3 Black hopes to get his knight back to defend. Unfortunately for him, one knight is not enough to stem the flow of White's pieces.

23 gxf3 ♘xe2 24 ♕xc5 ♘f4 25 ♕f5 ♘g6 26 h5 ♕xe7 27 hxg6 1-0

Game 51
Kaplan-Bronstein
Hastings 1975

1 e4 e6 2 d4 d5 3 ♘c3 ♘f6 4 ♗g5 dxe4 5 ♘xe4 ♗e7 6 ♗xf6 gxf6 7 ♘f3

7...♘d7

An interesting and flexible move which develops a piece and maintains options of ...c7-c5, ...f6-f5 or a queenside fianchetto with ...b7-b6. An old favourite of Bronstein, Nigel Short has recently been using it. The moves 7...b6, 7...f5 and 7...a6!? will be covered in later games.

8 ♕d2

In Short's games White has tried several other moves:

a) 8 ♗c4 c5 9 0-0 (9 d5 ♘b6 10 ♗b5+ ♗d7 11 ♕e2 ♗xb5 12 ♕xb5+ ♕d7 13 ♕xd7+ ♔xd7 14 dxe6+ fxe6 was very comfortable for Black in Tseshkovsky-Bronstein, USSR Championship, Moscow

1981) 9...0-0 10 ♖e1!? (10 c3 cxd4 11 cxd4 ♘b6 12 ♗b3 ♗d7 followed by bringing the bishop to c6 is just equal) 10...♘b6 11 ♗f1 cxd4 12 ♘xd4 ♔h8 13 c3 e5?! (had Short seen the reply he would probably have played 13...f5) 14 ♕h5! (Shirov-Short, Las Vegas 1999) and now 14...exd4? loses on the spot to 15 ♘xf6! ♗xf6 16 ♗d3.

b) 8 ♗d3 c5 9 0-0 0-0 10 ♕d2 f5 11 ♘xc5 ♘xc5 12 dxc5 ♗f6 (12...♗xc5 13 ♕h6 ♗e7 14 ♖ad1 is very dangerous for Black) 13 c3 ♗d7 and Black had good compensation for the pawn in Rogers-Short, Novi Sad Olympiad 1990.

c) 8 g3 c5 9 ♗g2 ♕b6 10 0-0 cxd4 11 ♘xd4 0-0 12 ♘c3 ♘e5 13 ♘b3 ♗d7 gave Black a solid game in Sutovsky-Short, Bugojno 1999.

8...c5!?

Certainly the sharpest move, though Bronstein avoided the chance to repeat this in a later game. He was probably well aware of the possible danger. In Van den Abbeele-Bronstein, Brussels 1995, he adopted the solid plan of 8...c6 9 ♗d3 b6 10 0-0-0 ♗b7 11 ♖he1 ♕c7 12 ♕h6 0-0-0. Another intriguing plan of development was tried in Benjamin-Seirawan, Los Angeles 1991: 8...♘f8 9 0-0-0 c6 10 ♗c4 h5 11 h4 ♕c7 12 ♖he1 ♗d7. This super-solid approach seems to have gone unnoticed by theory.

9 d5

The critical move, which coupled with the improvement on White's next spells danger for Black. 9 0-0-0 cxd4 10 ♕xd4 ♕b6 was fine for Black in J.Polgar-Short, Pamplona 1999.

9...f5 10 dxe6?!

In B.Ivanovic-Zviaginsev, Yugoslavia 2000, White improved on this with 10 ♘c3 ♗f6 (10...e5!?) 11 0-0-0 0-0 12 g4! and obtained a very dangerous attack.

10...fxe4 11 exd7+ ♕xd7 12 ♕c3?

Far too optimistic. White should play for equality with 12 ♕xd7+ ♗xd7 13 ♘e5.

12...0-0 13 ♘d2 ♕f5 14 0-0-0 ♕xf2

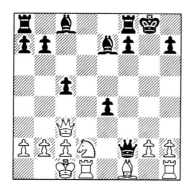

White probably overestimated his chances in this position. The lack of pawn cover in front of Black's king is far less important than the mighty bishop pair.

15 ♘xe4 ♕f4+ 16 ♘d2 ♗g4 17 ♖e1 ♗g5

A vicious pin, which prevents White from properly mobilising his forces.

18 ♗d3 ♖ae8 19 ♖ef1 ♕e3 20 h3 ♗e2!
21 ♖f5 ♗h6 22 ♗xe2 ♕xc3! 23 bxc3
♖xe2 24 ♖d5 ♖xd2!

Initiating a really elegant combination that forces zugzwang.

25 ♖xd2 ♖d8 26 ♖hd1 c4 0-1

White will eventually run out of pawn moves after which he will be forced to leave the rook on d2 undefended.

Game 52
Almasi-Andersson
Ubeda 1997

---

1 e4 e6 2 d4 d5 3 ♘c3 ♘f6 4 ♗g5
dxe4 5 ♘xe4 ♗e7 6 ♗xf6 gxf6 7 ♘f3

7 ♗c4 b6 8 ♘f3 ♗b7 would transpose back into the game.

7...b6

The solid line which aims first of all to tuck Black's king away on the queenside.

8 ♗c4

8 ♗b5+?! c6 9 ♗c4 is a surprisingly common inaccuracy which gives Black the useful ...c7-c6 move on a plate.

8...♗b7 9 ♕e2 c6 10 0-0-0 ♕c7 11
♖he1 ♘d7 12 ♔b1 0-0-0

Castling immediately is not mandatory. Black can also keep his options open with 12...h5 13 ♘c3 ♘f8, as in Goloshchapov-Volkov, Novgorod 1999.

13 ♗a6

13...♗xa6

Black has tinkered with a number of different moves in this position but the respective strategies are basically the same. White exchanges light-squared bishops and then tries to engineer a central breakthrough with c2-c4 and d4-d5. Black, on the other hand, will try to restrain d4-d5 and perhaps even attack the d4-pawn with a subsequent ...f6-f5 and ...♗f6.

Another plan for Black is to try and generate play on the half-open g-file. One thing he should be quite wary of, however, is playing ...f6-f5 prematurely. This weakens his central control and invites a White knight to step in to e5. Here are some of the alternatives:

a) 13...♖he8 14 ♗xb7+ ♔xb7 15 c4 (the passive 15 c3 has also been played but should hardly trouble Black after 15...♘f8 followed by ...♘g6.) 15...♘f8 16 ♕c2 f5! 17 ♘c3 ♗f6 18 ♖e3 ♗e7 19 ♖ed3 ♘g6 20 d5 ♖ed7 21 ♕a4 ♘e7 22 dxc6+ ♘xc6 23 ♘b5 ♖xd3 24 ♖xd3 ♕b8 25 ♕d1 ½-½ Korchnoi-Andersson, Reykjavik 1988.

b) 13...♖hg8!? 14 ♘g3 (14 g3 f5 15 ♘ed2

h5 gave Black good play on the kingside in Lanka-Budnikov, St Petersburg 1993) 14...♗b4!? 15 c3 ♗f8 16 ♗xb7+ ♔xb7 17 c4 ♔b8 produced a delicately balanced game in Van der Wiel-M.Gurevich, Wijk aan Zee 1990.

c) 13...♘f8!? 14 ♗xb7+ ♔xb7 15 g3 ♘g6 16 c4 f5! 17 ♘c3 ♗f6 started to give White problems with his d-pawn in Janovsky-Savchenko, Moscow 1991.

d) 13...f5? is bad because of 14 ♗xb7+ ♔xb7 15 ♘eg5 ♖df8 16 d5! when White had achieved his breakthrough very easily in Timman-Andersson, Yerevan Olympiad 1996.

e) Last but not least Black played 13...b5!? in Neelakantan-Speelman, Calcutta 1998. Black's idea is that White will not be able to achieve his thematic c2-c4 and d4-d5 breakthrough. The game continued 14 ♗xb7+ ♔xb7 15 c4 bxc4 16 ♕xc4 ♘b6 17 ♕b3 ♔a8 18 ♖c1 ♖b8 19 ♕c2 ♖hc8 with approximate equality.

14 ♕xa6+ ♔b8

After the king move White's best is to retreat the queen anyway. This is probably slightly stronger than 14...♕b7 which forces White's queen back to its best square after 15 ♕e2.

15 g3

The queen is optically impressive on a6 but nothing more. 15 ♕e2 is probably White's best after which 15...♖he8 (Black tried 15...♖hg8!? in Christiansen-Andersson, FIDE World Championship, Groningen 1997, and 15...♘f8!? is also possible) 16 c3 (16 a3 ♗f8 17 c4 h6 18 ♘c3 f5 19 d5 ♗g7 was tried in Hellers-Andersson, Eksjo 1993) 16...♘f8 17 g3 f5 18 ♘ed2 ♘g6 19 ♘c4 was marginally more comfortable for White in Leko-Andersson, Ubeda 1997.

15...f5 16 ♘ed2 h5!

The thematic means of gaining counterplay after White's g2-g3. 16...♗f6 17 ♕e2 was slightly better for White in Sokolov-Andersson, Bar 1997, when

White's knights honed in on e5.

17 ♕e2 h4 18 ♘c4 hxg3 19 hxg3 ♗f6 20 ♖d3 b5?!

Although this is often a good idea, in this case White builds quick pressure against c6. Black should settle for the solid 20...♖he8.

21 ♘cd2 ♘b6 22 ♖c1 ♖d5 23 c4 bxc4 24 ♘xc4 ♔a8

A further mistake. Black should exchange White's knight before it comes to e5 as he does not get adequate compensation for his pawn.

25 ♘ce5 ♕b7 26 ♘xc6 ♖c8 27 ♖dc3 ♘a4 28 ♖c4 ♘b6 29 ♖4c2 ♖d7 30 ♘a5 ♖xc2 31 ♖xc2 ♕e4 32 ♘b3 ♕xe2 33 ♖xe2 ♖d8 34 ♖c2 ♘d5 35 ♘a5 ♖h8 36 a3 a6 37 ♔a2 ♔a7 38 ♘c4 ♖h7 39 ♖c1 f4 40 gxf4 ♘xf4 41 ♘d6 ♘d3?!

41...♘d5 was better when Black should still be able to hold the draw.

42 ♖c7+ ♔b6 43 ♘e8 ♖h8 44 ♖xf7 ♗xd4 45 ♘xd4 ♖xe8 46 ♖f6 ♘c5 47 f4 ♔b7 48 b4 ♖d8 49 ♘xe6 ♖d2+ 50 ♔b1 ♘e4 51 ♖h6 ♖f2 52 ♔c1 ♔a7 53 ♖h3 ♔b6 54 ♔d1 a5 55 bxa5+ ♔xa5 56 ♔e1 ♖a2 57 ♖e3 ♘f6 58 ♘d4! ♔g4 59 ♖g3 ♘f2 60 f5 ♘e4 61 ♖e3 ♘g5 62 f6 ♔b6 63 ♖c3 ♖g2 64 ♖c6+ ♔b7 65 ♖c5 ♘f7 66 ♘e6 ♔b6 67 a4 ♖g4 68 a5+ ♔a6 69 ♘c7+ ♔a7 70 ♘d5 ♔a6 71 ♔d2 ♖a4 72 ♘c7+ ♔b7 73 ♔e3 ♔a7 74 ♘e6 ♘h6 75 ♔d3 ♔a6 76 ♖h5 ♖a3+ 77 ♔c4 ♘f7 78 ♘c7+ ♔b7 79 ♖h7 ♘e5+ 80 ♔b5 ♖b3+ 81 ♔c5 ♖d3 82 ♘d5+ 1-0

Game 53
Pavlovic-Sakaev
Vrnjacka Banja 1998

1 e4 e6 2 d4 d5 3 ♘c3 ♘f6 4 ♗g5 dxe4 5 ♘xe4 ♗e7 6 ♗xf6 gxf6 7 ♘f3 f5!?

Black's most energetic and direct treatment which leads to ultra-sharp positions. As discussed in the notes to

Kaplan-Bronstein, White can avoid this possibility if he plays 7 ♗c4 provided he is happy about having his bishop on c4 in the 7 ♘f3 a6 and 7 ♘f3 b6 lines.

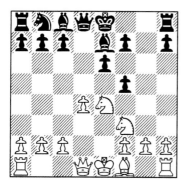

8 ♘c3

White wants to meet Black's intended ...c7-c5 with d4-d5, but retreating the knight to g3 is also interesting and requires great care on Black's part: 8 ♘g3 c5 (in Zhu-Bareev, Rome 1990, Black played 8...♘d7!? and after 9 ♗c4 c5 10 ♕e2?! ♘b6 11 ♗b5+ ♔f8!? 12 dxc5 ♘d5 had very strong play) 9 ♗b5+ (9 ♕d2 cxd4 10 0-0-0 h5 11 h4 ♘c6 12 ♗b5 ♗d7 13 ♘xd4 ♗f6 left Black with a good game in Hoi-Sax, Lugano 1989; while 9 ♗c4 cxd4 10 ♘xd4 ♘c6 11 ♘xc6 ♕xd1+ 12 ♖xd1 bxc6 was also very comfortable for Black in Short-Dizdar, Bundesliga 1990/91) 9...♗d7 10 ♗xd7+ ♕xd7 11 d5 exd5 12 ♕d3 ♘c6 13 0-0-0 f4! 14 ♘h5 0-0-0! (an important improvement over the 14...♕g4 15 ♕xd5 ♖d8 16 ♕f5 of Shabalov-Savchenko, USSR Championship, Tbilisi 1989).

8...♗f6 9 ♕d2

9 ♗c4 is questionable because of 9...♘c6 10 d5 (10 ♘e2 ♘a5 11 ♗d3 c5 was fine for Black in Kovalev-Luther, Hamburg 1993, as was 10 ♗b5 ♕d6 11 ♕d2 ♗d7 12 ♕h6 ♕e7 13 0-0-0 0-0-0 in Rohde-Speelman, London 1984) 10...♘a5.

9...c5

This time 9...♘c6 10 ♗b5 would be

good for White, but 9...0-0!? is an interesting alternative. Gipslis-Chernin, St John 1988, continued 10 g4 fxg4 11 ♖g1 e5! 12 ♗d3 ♗g7 13 dxe5 ♔h8 14 0-0-0 f5! with complex play.

10 d5

The only move to really trouble Black. The alternatives are dealt with as follows:

a) 10 0-0-0 cxd4 11 ♘xd4 ♘c6 12 ♗b5 ♗d7 13 ♘xf5!? exf5 14 ♕d6 ♗e5! (14...♗e7 15 ♖he1 makes it difficult for Black to unravel) 15 ♖he1 ♕g5+! 16 ♔b1 0-0-0 17 ♖xe5! ♗e6! (17...♘xe5 18 ♘d5) 18 ♕c5 ♖xd1+ 19 ♘xd1 ♖d8 20 ♘c3 ♕xg2 with equality in Liberzon-Botvinnik, Moscow Team Championship 1966.

b) 10 dxc5 ♘d7 11 ♗b5 0-0! 12 c6 bxc6 13 ♗xc6 ♖b8 gives Black good compensation for his pawn according to Suetin.

c) 10 ♗b5+ ♗d7 11 dxc5 (11 ♗xd7+ ♘xd7 12 0-0-0 ♕a5 13 ♔b1 0-0-0 was already getting difficult for White in Sax-Andersson, Reggio Emilia 1988/89) 11...a6 12 ♗xd7+ ♘xd7 13 ♘a4 (13 0-0-0 ♕c7 14 ♕d6 ♖c8 recovered the pawn in A.Sokolov-Andersson, Brussels 1988) 13...♕c7 14 0-0-0 ♘xc5! 15 ♘xc5 ♕xc5 16 ♕d7+ ♔f8 17 ♕d6+ ♕xd6 18 ♖xd6 ♖g8 19 g3 ♔e7! was fine for Black in Wedberg-Andersson, Haninge 1988.

10...0-0

After 10...exd5 simply 11 ♕e3+ wins back the pawn with advantage.

11 0-0-0 e5 12 h4

Preparing to put the knight on g5. In Saulin-Kiriakov, Moscow 1999, 12 ♔b1 also led to a razor-sharp struggle after 12...♘d7 13 g4!? e4 14 ♘g1 fxg4 15 ♘xe4 ♗g7 16 h3 ♕b6 17 c3 ♘e5 18 hxg4 ♗xg4 19 ♖e1 ♖fe8.

12...♘d7

Black has also played 12...♗g7, but after 13 d6 (White can also play a waiting move with 13 ♔b1, after which he met 13...a6 with 14 d6 in Timoshenko-Navrotescu,

Caciulata 1992) 13...♗e6 14 ♘g5 ♘c6, the position of the knight on c6 did not prove that helpful in Klovans-Dizdar, Groningen 1991. That game continued 15 g4 ♘d4 16 gxf5 ♗xf5 17 ♗d3 ♕d7 18 ♗xf5 ♕xf5 19 ♘d5 ♔h8 20 c3 ♘c6 21 ♘e3 ♕d7 22 ♕d5 when White was taking control. 12...a6?! has also been seen, but in such a sharp position such a relaxed build-up looks rather slow.

13 ♖g1

White has also played 13 d6 ♘b6 14 ♕e3 (14 ♘g5 h6 15 ♘h3 ♗g7 16 ♕e3 ♕xh4 was good for Black in Kuzutovic-Dizdar, Croatian Championship, Makarska 1994, while 14 ♘b5 ♗d7 15 ♘c7 ♖c8 16 ♕e3 ♖xc7! 17 dxc7 ♕xc7 gives Black good compensation for the exchange, according to Sakaev) 14...e4 15 ♘g5 ♗d7 16 g4! ♗d4 17 ♖xd4 cxd4 18 ♕xd4 f6 was very messy in Lau-Sakaev, Dortmund 1991.

13...e4 14 ♘g5 ♘e5 15 ♗e2

Sakaev gave 15 f3 h6 16 ♘h3 ♗g7 17 fxe4 ♕xh4 as an alternative – which is also very complicated.

15...h6 16 ♘h3 ♗g7 17 ♘f4 b5!?

Certainly consistent but possibly not the best. Black can also play 17...♕xh4 after which the attempt to smash through the kingside with 18 g4 does not really work after 18...fxg4 19 ♘xe4 ♗f5 20 ♖h1 ♕d8

21 ♘g3 ♗g6 (Sakaev).

18 g4

18 ♘xb5 ♕b6 obviously gives Black compensation (and not 18...♖b8 because of 19 ♘h5 ♗h8 20 ♕xh6).

18...b4 19 ♘a4 fxg4 20 ♘h5

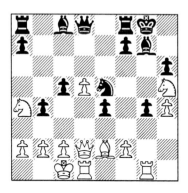

20...♕a5?

This apparently natural move is a mistake according to Sakaev. Black should keep his pieces centralised with 20...♕d6 21 ♕f4 f5 22 ♘xc5 a5 when Black can give his king additional protection with ...♖a7 (and not 22...♗h8? 23 ♘e6! ♗xe6 24 ♕xh6!).

21 ♘xg7 ♔xg7 22 b3 f5 23 ♕e3 ♗d7 24 f4! ♘g6 25 ♘xc5 ♖ad8 ½-½

White is clearly better now and should keep playing.

Summary

6...gxf6 has been all the rage of late, with attention being centred on Morozevich's 7...a6. Whether or not this is a passing phase remains to be seen. The plan of 8 g3 from Kasparov-Gurevich (Game 49) seems to have a certain amount of venom and we may see some developments in 8...♘c6!? as opposed to the 'natural' 8...b5.

Black's position still looks quite playable in the older 7...b6 lines, as Ulf Andersson and Mikhail Gurevich have repeatedly shown. It may be a bit easier to play White, but this can't really be called an advantage. I quite like the idea of repositioning Black's knight with 12 or 13...♘f8!? and these middlegames should be studied quite carefully if Black wants to play this line. The other plan which needs to be handled carefully is Sutovsky's idea of castling kingside and trying to sac one of his knights!

Black has also been doing well with 7 ♘f3 f5!?, with ultra-sharp opposite-side castling positions arising after 8 ♘g3. White can try to side-step this with 7 ♗c4, though this cuts out the Kasparov-Gurevich plan should Black adopt the Morozevich idea of 7...a6.

1 e4 e6 2 d4 d5 3 ♘c3 ♘f6 4 ♗g5 dxe4 5 ♘xe4 ♗e7 6 ♗xf6 gxf6 *(D)*

7 ♘f3 *(D)* **a6**
      7...♘d7 – *Game 51*; 7...b6 – *Game 52*; 7...f5 – *Game 53*
8 ♕d2 *(D)*
      8 g3 – *Game 49*; 8 c4 – *Game 50*
8...b5 – *Game 48*

6...gxf6

7 ♘f3

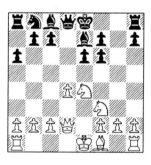

8 ♕d2

CHAPTER SEVEN

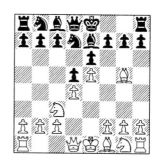

Main Line with 4 ♗g5 ♗e7 5 e5 ♘fd7

1 e4 e6 2 d4 d5 3 ♘c3 ♘f6 4 ♗g5 ♗e7 5 e5 ♘fd7

With 4...♗e7 Black responds to the threat of 5 e5 in the most obvious way – by unpinning the knight. In turn, White now has to answer the renewed threat to the e4-pawn, and the natural continuation 5 e5 ♘fd7 is the subject of this chapter. Deviations from this sequence are included in the 'odds and ends' of Chapter 9.

Following 4...♗e7 5 e5 ♘fd7 the traditional battleground has been 6 ♗xe7 ♕xe7 7 f4 (Games 54-59). As opposed to the immediate 4 e5 ♘fd7 both sides have profited from the exchange on e7. White has traded off the 'bad' bishop that might be hampered by the pawn chain on the dark squares. For Black the removal of a piece relieves the cramp somewhat.

After the obligatory ...c7-c5, Black has two main strategies: (1) to attack on the queenside with combinations of ...c5-c4, ...♕b6-4, ...♘d7-b6-a4, ...♘c6-a5-c4; and (2) to assault the centre with ...f7-f6, a move which is often compulsory as a defensive measure in any case. White also has two ways to play: (1) to attack on the kingside, using the bishop sacrifice on h7 or a pawn advance such as f4-f5-f6; or (2) to play for central control, bringing the rooks to the

central files and putting a knight on d4 or e5 (after ...f7-f6, e5xf6) or both, aiming for an advantageous endgame with the superior minor piece, knight vs. light-squared bishop.

The second half of this chapter (Games 60-63) sees a different approach for White (and hence also for Black). Instead of capturing on e7 White supports the ♗g5 with the h-pawn by 6 h4!?, when a subsequent exchange of bishops on g5 will give White a half-open h-file. Black can win a pawn by taking twice on g5, but in that case White will gain time to build up an initiative by attacking the black queen, and in the short term Black's counterplay will be severely reduced.

Game 54
Glek-Morozevich
Russian Championship 1998

---

1 e4 e6 2 d4 d5 3 ♘c3 ♘f6 4 ♗g5 ♗e7 5 e5 ♘fd7 6 ♗xe7 ♕xe7 7 f4

This is the normal continuation. White protects the e5-pawn in advance of Black's undermining thrust ...c7-c5. Also, in the event of ...f7-f6 (or ...f7-f5) White can play e5xf6, when the f-pawn controls the e5-square, supporting a possible outpost and helping to fix the black e6-pawn as backward. Other seventh moves are considered in the notes to Game 59.

7...0-0

7...a6 and other moves are also seen in Game 59.

8 ♘f3 c5

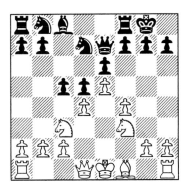

Transpositions are rife in these variations. This game features 9 ♕d2 ♘c6 10 dxc5 with 10...♕xc5 11 0-0-0. The next game sees 10...♘xc5 11 0-0-0, which may move on to Game 56 (10...f6) should Black follow with 11...f6. Game 57 has the alternative main line 9 dxc5 ♘c6 with 10 ♗d3, instead 10 ♕d2 would return to 9 ♕d2. Similarly, an early ♗d3 by White in Game 54 or 55 may transpose to Game 57, though the move order is perhaps inaccurate. 9 ♗d3 cxd4 leads to unique positions in Game 58, but other black ninth moves allow White to return to Game 57 with d4xc5. Finally, 7...a6 (Game 59) can also enter the loop, should Black subsequently castle short.

9 ♕d2 ♘c6

Since White has held back d4xc5 Black can pre-empt the exchange by capturing on d4. This is usually dealt with via 9...♘c6 10 0-0-0 cxd4, but as 10 dxc5 is more usual, it makes more sense, if Black wants to play this way, to capture on d4 immediately, i.e. 9...cxd4 10 ♘xd4 ♘c6 11 0-0-0 ♘b6 and then 12 ♕e3 is standard; the queen overprotects e5 in case of ...f7-f6 and allows

the bishop come to d3. It is a mistake for Black to try to exchange queens as White's central dark-square control guarantees a good endgame, e.g. 12...♗d7 13 ♔b1 ♕c5 14 h4 ♖ac8 15 ♖h3 ♘a5 16 ♘b3! ♕xe3 17 ♖xe3 ♖ac4 18 ♖f3 f6 19 exf6 ♖xf6 20 ♘d4 ♖cf8 21 ♗xc4 ♘xc4 22 b3 ♘d6 23 ♖e3 b5 (23...♖xf4 24 ♘xe6 leaves Black with an isolated queen's pawn) 24 a3 a5 25 g3 with total control in Larsen-Bareev, Hastings 1990/91.

However, 12...♘xd4 13 ♕xd4 ♗d7 followed by ...♖fc8 and ...♘c4 gives Black a reasonable game, e.g. 14 ♗d3 ♖fc8 15 ♘e2 ♘c4 16 ♗xc4 ♖xc4 17 ♕d2 ♖ac8 18 ♘d4 ♖xc2+! 19 ♘xc2 ♗a4 20 b3 ♗xb3 21 axb3 ♕a3+ with perpetual check in Nemet-Züger, Suhr 1991. For this reason White might consider avoiding exchanges and retreating with 12 ♘f3, intending ♗d3.

10 dxc5

White scuttles the centre and rules out the aggressive ...c5-c4, maintaining his knight on f3 for the time being to control d4 and e5.

In the old main line White castled long immediately, 10 0-0-0, waiting to see what Black intended before deciding whether to capture on c5. 10...a6 is reasonable, passing the ball back, when the usual 11 dxc5 ♘xc5 transposes to 10 dxc5 ♘xc5 11 0-0-0 a6 in the next game. However, Black can change the nature of the game by 10...c4!, and although White's attack appears to be further along, Black has an important resource ...f7-f6! in answer to f4-f5, gaining time for counterplay. Nor need Black fear the knight sortie ♘c3-b5-d6, as shown by the following variations:

a) 11 ♘b5 ♘b6 12 h4 ♗d7 13 ♘d6 ♖ab8 14 f5 f6 15 ♕f4 exf5 16 g3 ♘c8 17 ♘b5 ♘b6 18 ♘d6 ♘c8 19 ♘b5 ♘b6 20 ♘c3?! ♖be8 21 ♖e1 ½-½ Bologan-Gleizerov, Calcutta 1999.

b) 11 f5!? f6! 12 fxe6 ♘b6 (not 12...♕xe6 13 ♘b5! and 14 ♘c7) or 11...♖b8!? 12 ♕f4 f6 13 fxe6 ♘b6 (not 13...♕xe6 14 ♗xc4 bxc4 15 d5).

c) 11 g4 ♖b8 12 ♘b5 ♘b6 13 ♘d6 ♗d7 14 c3 (or 14 f5 f6! 15 ♕f4 ♘c8) 14...♘c8 15 ♘xc8 ♖fxc8 16 ♕c2 f6 17 h4 b5 18 ♔b1 b4 19 cxb4 (Gallagher-Crouch, Krumbach 1991) and in *Informator* 52 Crouch gave 19...♘xb4 20 ♕c3 ♘xa2! 21 ♔xa2 ♖b3 22 ♕e1 ♖xf3 as the simplest win.

d) 11 h4 ♖b8 12 ♘b5 ♘b6 13 g4 ♗d7 14 ♘d6 ♘c8 15 f5 ♘xd6 (or 15...f6!?) 16 f6 gxf6 17 exd5 ♕xd6 18 ♕f4 (if 18 ♕h6 ♖fe8!? 19 ♕xf6 ♕e7 20 ♕f4 e5 or 20 ♕h6 ♕f8) 18...♕e7 19 ♕f4 fxg5 20 hxg5 f6 with an unclear position in Viaud-Carleton, correspondence 1992-94.

10...♕xc5

This is the most aggressive recapture. Black prevents his opponent from castling short and intends a queenside assault when the white king goes long. 10...♘xc5 is seen in the next game and 10...f6 in Game 56.

11 0-0-0

White does not achieve anything by delaying castling:

a) 11 ♗d3 f6 12 exf6 ♘xf6 (or 12...♖xf6!? intending ...♘f8) 13 0-0-0 ♖b8 (or 13...♗d7 14 ♖he1 ♖ac8) 14 ♔b1 b5 15 ♘e2 ♔h8 16 ♕e1 (16 ♕c3) 16...b4 17 ♕h4 ♔g8 18 ♖he1 ♖b6 19 ♘c1 g6 20 ♘b3 ♕d6 21 ♘bd4 ♘xd4 22 ♘xd4 ♕c5 23 ♘b3 ♕c7 24 g3 ♖d6 25 ♕g5 ♗a6 ½-½ Klovans-Nikolenko, Pardubice 1995.

b) 11 a3!? (intending 11...♘b6?! 12 b4 ♕e7 13 ♗d3 and 0-0 with advantage) can be met by 11...a6 12 ♗d3 f6! (12...b5!?) 13 exf6 ♘xf6 14 0-0-0 b5 16 ♘e2 ♔h8 (Peptan-Matveeva, Yugoslavia 1997) and the inclusion of a2-a3 ...a7-a6 is clearly in Black's favour.

11...♘b6

Here 11...a6 12 ♘e2 b5 would transpose to 7...a6 (Game 59) but White can play more strongly with 12 ♗d3! and if 12...b5? the sacrifice is very strong: 13 ♗xh7+! ♔xh7 14 ♘g5+ ♔g8 15 ♕d3 ♖e8 (or 15...♖d8 16

♕h7+ ♔f8 17 ♕h8+! ♔e7 18 ♕xg7 ♖f8 19 ♘xe6! ♔xe6 20 ♖xd5 and wins) 16 ♕h7+ ♔f8 17 ♕h5! ♘d8 18 ♘h7+ ♔g8 19 ♖d3 ♕e7 (19...♕c4 20 ♘e2!) 20 ♖h3 f6 21 ♘xf6+! ♖xf6 22 exf6 1-0 Chandler-Agnos, London Lloyds Bank 1989.

White is also in control after 12...f6 13 exf6 ♘xf6 14 ♖he1, and this applies equally to 11...f6 12 exf6 ♘xf6 when White gains the advantage after 13 ♘d4!? ♕xd4 (Stetsko gives 13...♖b8 14 g3 b5 15 ♘xc6 ♕xc6 16 ♗g2 b4 17 ♘e2) 14 ♕xd4 ♘xd4 15 ♖xd4 a6 16 g3 ♗d7 17 ♗g2 b5 18 ♖e1 ♖ae8 19 a3 g6 20 ♖d2 ♖c8 21 ♘e2 ♘h5 22 ♘d4 as in Sutterer-Mayer, World Senior Championship 1993.

12 ♔b1

After 12 ♗d3 Black should probably opt for 12...♘c4!, since after 12...♗d7, apart from 13 ♔b1 transposing, White can sacrifice with 13 ♗xh7+! ♔xh7 14 ♘g5+ ♔g8 15 ♕d3 ♖fe8 16 ♕h7+ ♔f8 17 ♖he1! and then if 17...♕b4 18 ♕h8+ ♔e7 19 ♕h4 ♔d8 20 ♘xe6+ ♔c8 21 a3 ♕e7 22 ♘g5 f6 (Van der Wiel-Korchnoi, Amsterdam 1991) White can gain the advantage with 23 exf6 ♕xf6 24 ♖xe8+ ♗xe8 25 ♘xd5 ♘xd5 26 ♖xd5 (Korchnoi). In Nielsen-Ulibin, Mamaia 1991, Black tried 17...♘c4!? 18 ♕h8+ ♔e7 19 ♕h4 ♖h8 20 ♘h7+ f6 21 exf6+ ♔d8 22 fxg7+ ♔c7 23 gxh8♕ and here the players prematurely agreed a draw.

White's other option is to advance the h-pawn to weaken the enemy kingside by 12 h4 ♗d7 13 h5 ♖ac8 (or 13...♖fc8) 14 h6 g6. The slowness of this plan enables Black to generate sufficient counterplay on the queenside. For example, 15 ♘h2 ♘b4 16 a3 ♕a5! 17 axb4 ♕a1+ 18 ♘b1 ♗a4 19 ♗d3 ♗b3 20 ♕f2 ♘a4 21 ♔d2 ½-½ Jakobetz-Frilli, correspondence 1995.

12...♗d7 13 ♗d3

It is still a little early yet for 13 ♘b5 as after 13...♘a4 14 ♘d6?! f6! the knight is insecure on d6. Hjartarson-Brynell, Stockholm 1996, continued 15 ♗e2 fxe5 16 fxe5 ♘xe5 17 ♘xe5 ♕xd6 18 ♘xd7 ♕xd7 and Black had an extra pawn. White does better to play 14 ♘bd4 ♕b6 15 ♘b3 and then 15...a5! (threatens ...♘xb2!) 16 c3 f6 17 exf6 ♖xf6 18 ♗d3 ♖af8 19 g3 e5 20 ♘g5 (or 20 ♘xe5 ♘xe5 21 fxe5 ♖f2 22 ♗e2 ♗g4 with counterplay – Ulibin) 20...g6! 21 ♗c2 (if 21 ♗xg6 hxg6 22 ♕xd5+ ♖6f7 23 ♘xf7 ♖xf7 24 ♕c4 ♕f2! intending 25 ♕xa4 ♘d4! 26 ♕xa5 ♗f5+ with a draw) 21...d4 22 ♘e4 ♖6f7 23 fxe5 dxc3 24 ♘xc3 ♘xe5 was unclear in Borik-Blauert, German Bundesliga 1997.

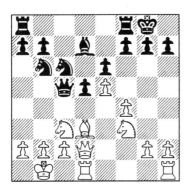

13...♘a5?!

Black prevents the ♘c3-b5 manoeuvre and prepares to attack with ...♘ac4. However, this is perhaps the worst of Black's tries at this point and he does better to play:

a) 13...♘b4 prevents both 14 ♘b5 and

14 ♗xh7+ (by keeping the white queen from d3). However, after 14 a3 a5 15 ♖hf1! ♖fc8 16 ♕f2 ♘xd3 17 cxd3 White achieved a good endgame following both 17...♕xf2 18 ♖xf2 ♘a4 19 ♖c2 ♘xc3+ 20 ♖xc3 ♖xc3 21 bxc3 ♖c8 22 ♔b2 f6 23 ♖e1 ♔f7 24 ♔c2 ♔e7 25 ♔d2 fxe5 26 ♖xe5 (Campora-Züger, Bern 1992) and 17...♘a4 18 ♘xa4 ♗xa4 19 ♕xc5 ♖xc5 20 ♖c1 b6 21 ♘d4 ♖ac8 22 b3 ♗d7 23 ♔b2 (Almasi-Züger, Horgen 1995).

b) 13...♖ac8 negates the sacrifice more subtly: if 14 ♗xh7+ ♔xh7 15 ♘g5+ ♔g8 16 ♕d3 ♖fe8 17 ♕h7+ ♔f8 the king is able to thread his way through to the queenside ...♔e7-d8-c7-b8. Sax-Timman, Rotterdam 1989, concluded 18 ♕h5 ♔e7 19 ♘xf7 ♘a5! 20 ♘d6 ½-½. However, putting a rook on c8 encourages ♘c3-b5 as ♘d6 comes with tempo: 14 ♘b5! f6 15 exf6 ♖xf6 16 ♘bd4! ♘xd4 17 ♘xd4 ♘a4 18 ♘b3 ♕c7 (18...♕b6 19 ♖he1) 19 g3 e5 20 fxe5 ♕xe5 21 ♕c1 ♖f2 22 ♖de1 ♕f6 23 ♖hf1 and Black's initiative was not enough to outweigh his inferior structure in Naiditsch-Blauert, Budapest 1998.

c) 13...♖fc8 also prevents the ♗xh7+ sacrifice because the black king already has room to run, but after 14 ♘b5! and 15 ♘d6 the rook is missing from the f-file to support the ...f7-f6 break.

14 ♗xh7+!

The quieter 14 b3 is also reasonable. After 14...♖fc8 15 ♘e2 ♘ac4 16 ♕c3! ♘e3 17 ♕xc5 ♖xc5 18 ♖dg1 ♘g4 19 ♖c1! a5 20 h3 ♘f2 21 ♖hf1 ♘xd3 22 cxd3 ♖ac8 23 ♖xc5 ♖xc5 24 ♖c1 ♖xc1+ 25 ♔xc1 White was on top in Madl-Hagarova, Ostrava 1999.

14...♔xh7 15 ♘g5+ ♔g8 16 ♕d3

White has played the sacrifice in three games so far, the first of which was Tong Yuanming-Ulibin, Beijing 1996, which went 16...♖fc8 17 ♕h7+ ♔f8 18 ♕h8+ ♔e7 19 ♕xg7 ♖d8 20 ♘xf7+ ♔c7 21 ♘d6 ♘ac4 22 ♘xc4 ♖g8 23 ♕h7 ♘xc4 24 ♘xd5+ exd5

25 e6 ♖ad8 26 g3 ♕b6 27 b3 ♘e3 28 exd7 ♘xd1 and Black won.

However, in this line White can play more strongly with 18 f5! (Glek) 18...exf5 19 ♕h8+ ♔e7 20 ♕xg7 ♗e6 21 ♘xe6 ♔xe6 22 ♕f6+ ♔d7 and now rather than 23 ♕xf7+ ♔c6 24 ♘xd5 when 24...♘ac4! continues Black's attack (25 ♘e7+ ♔b5 26 ♘xc8+ ♖xc8), White should play 23 ♘xd5! ♕xc2+ (not 23...♘xd5? 24 ♕xf7+ ♔c6 25 ♕e6+) 24 ♔a1 ♘xd5 25 ♕xf7+ ♔c6 26 ♖c1 when the queen and pawns are better than the rook and knights in the endgame. Black cannot deviate from this line: if 20...♔d8? 21 ♘xf7+ ♔c7 22 e6! ♗xe6 23 ♘g5+, or 20...♘ac4 21 ♘xf7 ♔e8 22 ♘d6+ ♘xd6 23 ♖xd5! wins.

16...♖fe8 17 ♕h7+ ♔f8

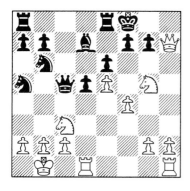

With the rook on e8 the 18 f5 variation does not work: Black could simply capture 24 ♘xd5? ♘xd5! as White does not have 25 ♕e6+.

This apart, the rook is worse placed on e8, as it might later be taken with check and Black is without latent threats against c2. Thus the straightforward 18 ♕h8+ ♔e7 is good for White. Glek later suggested 19 ♕h4!? ♖h8! 20 ♘h7+ ♔e8 21 ♘f6+ gxf6 22 ♕xh8+ ♕f8 23 ♕xf6 ♘ac4 24 ♖d3 ♕b4 25 b3 or 25 ♘d1 as slightly better for White. This was tested in Grabics-Matveeva, Istanbul 2000, and White could find nothing better than perpetual check: 25 b3 ♘a3+ 26 ♔b2 ♗b5 27 ♖g3 ♘d7 28 ♖g8+

♘f8 29 ♖g7 ♖c8 30 ♕xf7+ ♔d8 31 ♕f6+ ♔e8 32 ♕f7+ etc. However, *Fritz* comes up with 29 ♘xd5! exd5 30 e6 and after 30...♘c4+ 31 ♔a1 ♕e7 32 ♖xf8+! ♕xf8 33 bxc4 ♗xc4 34 exf7+ ♔d7 35 ♖e1 the advancing the g-pawn will win the game.

White can also play 19 ♕xg7! ♔d8 20 ♘xf7+ ♔c7 21 ♘d6 ♘ac4 22 ♘cb5+! ♔b8 23 ♘xc4 ♕xc4 24 ♘d6 ♕xf4 25 ♖hf1 with a 'significant advantage' according to Finkel, who also notes 21...♖ed8 22 ♕e7! ♔c6 23 ♘e2 ♖e8 24 ♘d4+ ♕xd4 25 ♘xe8 ♕c5 26 ♕xc5+ ♔xc5 27 ♘f6 and 19...♖f8? 20 ♘ce4! dxe4 21 ♘xe4 ♕b4 22 ♕f6+ ♔e8 23 ♘d6+ ♕xd6 24 exd6 ♘c6 25 h4 as winning for White.

Instead White decides to force a draw:
18 ♘ce4?! dxe4 19 ♘xe4 ♕c6 20 ♖d6 ♕b5 21 ♕h8+ ♔e7 22 ♕h4+ ♔f8

If Black really wanted to win he could try 22...f6!? 23 exf6 ♔d8 24 f7+ ♔c7 25 fxe8♕ ♖xe8 26 b3 ♘ac4 27 ♖d4 (Glek) and then 27...e5!? (Finkel) with complications. But White could have his draw anyway with 23 ♘xf6 ♘ac4 24 ♘xd7+ ♔f7 25 ♕h5+ etc.

23 ♕h8+ ♔e7 24 ♕h4+ ♔f8 ½-½

Game 55
Labutin-Ulibin
Kstovo 1997

1 d4 e6 2 e4 d5 3 ♘c3 ♘f6 4 ♗g5 ♗e7 5 e5 ♘fd7 6 ♗xe7 ♕xe7 7 f4 0-0 8 ♘f3 c5 9 ♕d2 ♘c6 10 dxc5 ♘xc5

By recapturing on c5 with the knight, Black keeps options open regarding where to play on the board. In this game he goes for the queenside with ...a7-a6 and ...b7-b5, whereas in Game 56 Black opts to challenge the white centre with ...f7-f6.

This flexibility also serves Black well should his opponent now attempt a 9 dxc5 main line with 11 ♗d3. Then 11...f6! 12 exf6 ♕xf6 13 g3 shows White's move order to be inaccurate, on account of Alekhine's suggestion 13...♘xd3+! intending 14 cxd3 e5! (for which see the note to 13 0-0 in Game 57).

11 0-0-0 a6

With ...a7-a6 Black prevents the sortie ♘b5 and prepares a queenside pawn advance. The position after 11...a6 might also arise via 7...a6 8 ♘f3 c5 9 ♕d2 ♘c6 10 dxc5 ♘xc5 11 0-0-0 b5 12 ♕e3 and then 12...0-0. Starting with 7...a6 is more flexible as Black can hold back ...0-0 until the most suitable moment. But White does have other options against 7...a6, such as 8 ♕g4 or 8 ♕h5, which Black might not want to bother with and which 7...0-0 renders ineffectual. The ramifications of 7...a6 are covered in Game 59.

Returning to the current game: here 11...f6 12 exf6 ♕xf6 13 g3 is another route to 10...f6 positions in Game 56. 11...♗d7!? is a waiting move; Black may yet play either ...f7-f6 or ...a7-a6. The easiest reply for White is 12 ♕e3! so that if ...f7-f6 Black is unable, after e5xf6, to recapture with the queen since the knight hangs; while if Black chooses 12...a6 he is committed to an early ...♗d7 when he might prefer to play ...b7-b5.

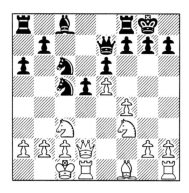

12 ♕e3

This useful move has several points. White can follow with ♗f1-d3 threatening ♗xh7+ etc., and if ...♘xd3 c2xd3 White will aim for an advantageous endgame, playing ♔b1, ♘e2 and ♖c1. The queen is well placed on e3, overprotecting e5 in preparation for Black's ...f7-f6 or White's own advance f4-f5. Finally, there is a positional threat of 13 ♖xd5!? exd5 14 ♘xd5, as in Aseev-Hölzlein, Würzburg 1990, after 12...f5? 13 ♖xd5! b6 (if 13...exd5 14 ♘xd5 ♕d8 15 ♕xc5 ♗e6 16 ♗c4 ♔h8 17 ♘g5 with a huge advantage) 14 ♖d6 ♗b7 15 ♗e2 ♕c7 16 ♖hd1 ♘d8 17 g4! with a won position for White.

White can also play 12 ♔b1, preparing for the opening of the c-file after an exchange on d3. However, Black may not oblige, preferring the advance 12...b5 13 ♗d3 b4 14 ♘e2 a5 intending ...♗a6. In Klovans-Kviriashvili, Pardubice 1996, this plan was extremely effective after 15 h4 ♗a6 16 h5? b3! 17 ♘c1 ♗xd3 18 ♘xd3 ♘b4 19 ♘xb4 axb4 20 ♘d4 ♕a7 21 a3 bxc2+ 22 ♕xc2 bxa3 23 b4 ♘e4 24 ♖h3 ♖fc8 0-1. The alternative, 13 ♕e3, is considered via 12 ♕e3 b5 13 ♔b1 below.

More often White plays 12 ♗d3 immediately and then if 12...f6 (or 12...f5) 13 exf6 ♕xf6 14 g3 Black has wasted a move on ...a7-a6 in a 10...f6 line, c.f. 14 ♗d3 in the notes to 14 ♘d4 in Game 56. However, Black can improve by delaying ...f7-f6. After 12...♗d7 13 ♕e3 f6! White is unable to play as desired with 14 exf6 ♘xd3+ 15 cxd3?! ♕xf6 16 g3? because of 16...d4, while after 15 ♖xd3 or 15 ♕xd3 ♕xf6 16 g3 Black gains time with ...♗e8-g6. Instead 13 ♘e2 ♖ac8 14 ♔b1 ♘xd3 15 cxd3 f6! 16 ♘ed4 (or 16 exf6 ♕xf6 17 ♕e3 ♗e8) 16...♘xd4 17 ♘xd4 fxe5 18 fxe5 ♕h4 was fine for Black in Dolmatov-Bareev, Sochi 1988. The same applies to 12...b5 13 ♕e3 f6 (see below), but here White has 13 ♘e2, intending to establish a knight on d4. *ECO* quotes Gligoric-Stahlberg, match 1949, which continued 13...♗b7 14 ♘fd4 ♘xd4 15 ♘xd4 when White's central control gives him the edge.

12...b5!

This obvious advance has a hidden

subtlety which White fails to notice: it clears the second rank for the queen. For instance, White can no longer consider 13 ♖xd5? exd5 14 ♘xd5 since 14...♕a7! keeps hold of the ♘c5. Aseev-Bareev, Lvov 1990, saw instead 12...♖d8!? 13 ♘e2 ♗d7 14 ♘ed4 ♖ac8 15 ♔b1 ♘a5 16 ♗d3 ♘c4 17 ♗xc4 dxc4 18 g4 ♘a4 19 c3 b5 with mutual chances.

13 f5?!

This logical move, threatening f5-f6, was one of the above-mentioned purposes of 12 ♕e3. Unfortunately it is incorrect at this juncture due to Black's unexpected reply.

Instead 13 ♗d3 gives Black a choice. 13...f6 is okay since, as noted above, 14 exf6 ♘xd3+ 15 cxd3?! ♕xf6 16 g3? fails to 16...d4, while after 14 ♘e2 b4 15 ♔b1 a5 16 exf6 ♖xf6 17 ♖de1 ♕d6 18 ♘e5 ♗a6 Black began to take over the initiative in Khalifman-Stojanovic, Ubeda 1997. Black has also fared well with 13...♘xd3+ 14 cxd3 ♗b7!? intending ...♖fd8, ...d4, or if 15 ♘e2 d4!? with good compensation for the pawn. Lindgren-Trapl, correspondence 1992, saw 15 ♖d2 ♖fd8 16 d4 ♖ac8 17 ♔b1 ♘a5 18 ♕d3 ♗c6 19 ♘g5 f5 20 g4 ♖f8 21 ♖g2 ♗e8 22 h4 b4 23 gxf5 ♖xf5 and Black was better.

13 ♔b1 also lacks punch. As noted before, the point of ♔b1 is to anticipate ...♘xd3, which cannot occur unless the bishop goes to d3. Furthermore, 13 ♔b1 allows Black to establish his knight on e4 by 13...b4 14 ♘e2 ♘e4, and this lead to easy equality in Short-Korchnoi, Thessaloniki Olympiad 1988, after 15 ♘g3 ♕c5! 16 ♕xc5 ♘xc5 17 ♗d3 a5 18 ♖he1 ♗a6 19 ♗xa6 ♖xa6, though a subsequent accident cost Black the game. Finkel suggests 15 g4 as a possible improvement, but this has not yet been tried.

13...♕a7!

An unusual and strong resource – Black removes the queen from e7 with tempo by threatening ...♘b3+.

14 ♘d4

With this move White gives up his kingside ambitions as the queen can hardly do anything on her own, but there doesn't seem to be anything better. Black is for preference after 14 ♕g5 f6 15 exf6 ♖xf6 16 dxe6 ♗xe6, while if 14 ♕f4!? exf5 15 ♘xd5 ♘e4 16 ♖g1 ♗e6 17 ♘e3 (Finkel) then 17...♖fd8 is strong, e.g. 18 ♗d3 ♘f2 or 18 g4 ♘b4! 19 a3? ♕xe3+! 20 ♕xe3 ♘a2+ and mates, or if 18 ♖xd8+ ♖xd8 19 ♗d3 g5! 20 ♘xg5 ♖xd3! 21 cxd3 ♘xe5! with decisive threats of ...♘xd3, ...♘g6 and ...♕xe3.

14...♘xd4 15 ♕xd4

Finkel suggests 15 ♖xd4!? exf5 16 ♘xd5 ♗e6 17 ♗e2 ♘e4 18 ♘f4 ♗xa2 19 g4 with counterplay. This is certainly more adventurous than taking with the queen. If 19...♘c5 20 gxf5 ♖ad8 21 ♖hd1 (not 21 ♖xd8? ♘b3+) 21...♕c7 (threat: ...♘b3+) 22 ♖b4 and White hangs on.

15...exf5 16 ♘xd5 ♗e6 17 ♗e2 ♗xd5 18 ♕xd5 ♘e4 19 ♖he1 ♕e7!

Simple chess – Black intends to drive the white queen away and win the e5-pawn.

20 ♗f3 ♖ad8 21 ♕c6 ♖c8?!

21...♕xe5 wins a safe pawn, whereas the text allows White to maintain material equality.

22 ♕b6?!

White should therefore take the a-pawn and may still survive after 22 ♕xa6 and either 22...♕xe5 23 ♗xe4 fxe4 24 ♕d6;

22...♕c5 23 ♗xe4 fxe4 24 ♖d2; or 22...♖a8 23 ♕xb5 ♖xa2 (or 23...♖fb8 24 ♗xe4!? ♖xb5 25 ♗xa8) 24 c3.

22...♕xe5 23 g3 ♖c4

The rook switches to frontal attack by 24...♖b4 or if 24 ♕xa6 ♖a4. Exchanging rooks does not help White: 24 ♖d8 g6 25 ♖xf8+ ♔xf8 and the a-pawn still cannot be taken due to 26 ♕xa6? ♖a4 27 ♕c8+ ♔g7 and Black wins after either 28 a3 ♖xa3!; 28 c3 ♖c4 and ...♖xc3+; 28 ♗xe4 ♖xa2! 29 ♔d2 fxe4; or 28 ♕c3!? ♕xc3 29 bxc3 ♖xa2.

24 ♖e2?

White prepares to defend b2 by c2-c3. However...

24...♖b4 25 c3 ♖xb2!

...Black takes it anyway.

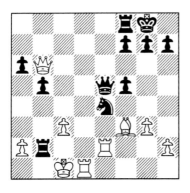

26 ♖xb2 ♕xc3+ 27 ♔b1 ♕xf3 28 ♕d4?

The only defence was 28 ♖c1 intending 28...♘c3+ 29 ♔a1 ♘a4 30 ♕f2!, though Black is clearly better with three pawns for the exchange. After 28 ♕d4 Black simply has three pawns for nothing.

28...♘c3+ 29 ♔c1 ♘xd1 30 ♕xd1 ♖c8+ 0-1

Game 56
Mrdja-Gleizerov
Turin 2000

---

1 e4 e6 2 d4 d5 3 ♘c3 ♘f6 4 ♗g5 ♗e7 5 e5 ♘fd7 6 ♗xe7 ♕xe7 7 f4 0-0 8 ♘f3 c5 9 ♕d2 ♘c6 10 dxc5 f6 11 exf6 **♕xf6 12 g3 ♘xc5 13 0-0-0**

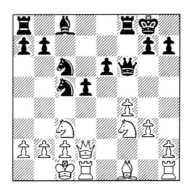

This line has recently seen a revival. The diagram position can arise by a variety of routes. Gleizerov has favoured the direct 10...f6 as in this game, but 10...♘xc5 11 0-0-0 f6 12 exf6 ♕xf6 13 g3 is also often seen, as is 9 dxc5 f6 10 exf6 ♕xf6 11 g3 ♘c6 12 ♕d2 ♘xc5 13 0-0-0.

The pawn structure defines White's strategy: to control the central dark-squares and thus the black d- and e-pawns. The backward e6-pawn is an obvious target, either for direct attack or for the thrust f4-f5 to undermine the d5-pawn. As the e6-pawn can only be advanced if White goes wrong, losing his grip on the position, Black will work around the centre, re-routing the bishop to a more active post on the kingside via d7 and e8. The black rooks will typically be posted on the c- and d-files.

Instead of 13 0-0-0 in the game, 13 ♗d3 is also possible transposing to 9 dxc5, but White's move order is inaccurate – as is explained in the notes to Game 57.

13...♖d8

A necessary preliminary. If immediately 13...♘d7?! 14 ♘xd5! exd5 15 ♕xd5+ ♘e6 16 ♕xd7 (not 16 ♘g5 ♖ad8 17 ♗h3 ♖fe8 18 ♖he1 ♘cd4 19 ♕e4 ♕f7 20 f5 ♗c6 21 fxe6 ♕g6 22 ♕c4 b5 with an unclear position) 16...♖fd8 17 ♕xb7 ♖ab8 18 ♖xd8+ ♘exd8 19 ♕d7 ♖xb2+ 20 ♔d2 and Black has insufficient compensation.

By ...♖d8 Black prepares development with ...♗d7-e8, prevents ♕e3 due to ...d5-d4, and supposedly threatens 14...♘e4 since 15 ♘xe4? dxe4 wins material.

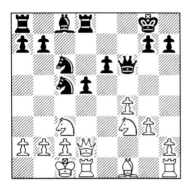

14 ♘d4

ECO's recommendation, intending 14...♘e4 15 ♕e3 with a slight advantage (Keres, Euwe).

a) 14 ♗d3 is preferred in *NCO*, though White has not shown much against Black's standard plan of 14...♗d7 15 ♖he1 ♖ac8 16 ♔b1 ♗e8 17 ♘e5 ♘xe5 18 ♖xe5 ♘d7 19 ♖ee1 and White had nothing in Mukhaev-Gleizerov, Tomsk 1998; Black in fact played for the win after 19...♗h5 (19...♗f7) 20 ♗e2 ♗g6!? (20...♗xe2) 21 ♗g4 ♖c6 22 ♕d4 ♕xd4 23 ♖xd4 ♔f7 24 f5?! exf5 25 ♗f3 ♘f6 26 ♘xd5 f4! 27 ♖e2 fxg3 28 hxg3 ♖cd6. Instead 17 ♕f2 ♘xd3 18 ♖xd3 ♗g6 lead to a quick draw in Gallagher-Weinzettl, Pula 2000, following 19 ♖d2 ♘a5!? (19...b6) 20 ♕d4 ♘c4 21 ♖de2 ♕f8 22 ♘e5 ♕b4 23 ♘xc4 ♖xc4 24 ♕e5 ♖c6 25 a3 ♕c4 26 ♖d2 ♖dc8 ½-½.

White has several other options:

b) 14 ♕f2 used to be thought good, since if 14...♘e4?! 15 ♘xe4 dxe4 16 ♘d2 White gains the advantage, or if 14...b6 White has gained a tempo on 14 ♕e1 ♗d7 15 ♗g2 ♗e8 16 ♕f2. However, the absence of a major piece on the e-file, plus the latent pin on the f-file gives Black the chance to break with 14...d4! 15 ♘b5 e5 which scored two

crushing wins for the Czech correspondence IM, Milan Mraz: 16 ♗c4+ ♗e6 17 ♕f1 d3! 18 ♗xe6+ ♕xe6 19 ♘c7? ♕xa2 20 ♘xa8 ♘e4 0-1 (Khoklov-Mraz, correspondence 1992) and 16 ♘c7 ♕f7! 17 ♘xa8 ♕xa2 18 ♕g2 e4! 19 ♘d2 ♕a1+ 20 ♘b1 d3 21 ♗xd3 exd3 0-1 (Kunz-Mraz, correspondence 1994). Best play appears to be 16 ♘g5! ♔h8 (not 16...♗f5? 17 ♗c4+ ♔f8 18 g4 ♗g6 19 ♘c7 winning material in Sadvakasov-R.Bagirov, Istanbul Olympiad 2000) 17 h4 (or 17 ♗c4 ♖f8) 17...♖f8 18 ♕f3 exf4 19 ♘xh7!? ♔xh7 20 ♕h5+ ♕h6 21 ♕xc5 fxg3+ 22 ♔b1 ♗g4 with an unclear position.

c) 14 ♕e1 keeps control of e5 and the knight out of e4. Gleizerov again outplayed two opponents following 15 ♗b5 ♖ac8 16 ♗xc6 ♗xc6 17 ♘d4 ♗e8 18 ♕e5 ♕xe5! 19 fxe5 ♔f7 and then 20 h4 ♔e7 21 h5 ♘e4! 22 ♘xe4 dxe4 23 h6! gxh6 24 ♘e2?! (24 ♖xh6) 24...♖xd1+ 25 ♔xd1 h5! (Sochko-Gleizerov, Stockholm 2000); the front h-pawn blocks White's play down the file and grants an endgame advantage to Black, who ground out a win in 86 moves. Black was also better after 20 ♘db5 ♗xb5 21 ♘xb5 ♘e4 22 ♖he1 ♔e7 23 ♘xa7?! ♖c5 in Grabarska-Gleizerov, Koszalin 1999, and won after 24 a4 ♖a8 25 ♘b5 ♖xa4 26 ♘a3 b5 27 ♘b1 b4 28 ♖e3 ♖a8 29 ♘d2 ♖a1+ 30 ♘b1 ♖a8 31 ♘d2 ♖a1+ 32 ♘b1 ♖c4 33 ♖f1? ♖xb1+ 0-1.

Gleizerov notes 15 ♗g2 as an improvement. In fact, this worked out well for White in Machulsky-Stetsko, Moscow 1981, after 15...♗e8 16 ♕f2 b6 17 ♘d4 ♘xd4 18 ♕xd4 ♖ac8 19 ♖he1 ♗g6 20 ♗h3 ♖c6? 21 ♕xf6 gxf6 22 f5! For Black either 19...♗f7 or 20...♗f7 was necessary.

d) 14 ♗g2! is also possible immediately, since there is no need to prevent ...♘e4. In fact 14...♘e4 is probably a mistake. After 15 ♕e3! ♘xc3 16 ♕xc3 ♕xc3 17 bxc3 ♗d7 18 ♖he1 Black has great difficulties defending the centre and both the white f-pawn and front c-pawn are useful levers. Voitsekhovsky-Volkov, Smolensk 1997, continued 18...h6 19 ♘e5 ♘xe5 20 ♖xe5 ♔f7 21 c4 ♗c6 22 ♗h3 dxc4 23 ♗xe6+ ♔f6 24 ♗xc4 and White had won a pawn. Otherwise after 14...♗d7 15 ♖he1 has saved time on 14 ♕e1.

14...♗d7

Keres and Euwe's assessment of 14...♘e4 15 ♕e3 was confirmed in J.Berry-V.Hybl, correspondence 1976, which continued 15...♘xc3 16 ♕xc3 ♗d7 17 ♗g2 ♖ac8 18 ♖he1 b6 19 ♘xe6 ♗xe6 20 ♕xf6 gxf6 21 ♖xe6 and White had won a pawn.

15 ♕e3

Again 15 ♗g2 seems better. Soentges-Hampel, correspondence 1992-97, continued 15...♗e8 16 ♕e3 ♘xd4 17 ♕xd4 ♖ac8 18 ♕xf6 gxf6 when White advanced thematically 19 f5! d4 20 ♘e4 ♘xe4 (if 20...♗c6 21 ♘xc5 ♗xg2 22 ♘xe6) 21 ♗xe4 e5 22 ♗xb7 with an extra pawn. If instead 16...♖ac8 17 ♘xc6 ♖xc6 18 ♘xd5! exd5 19 ♗xd5+ ♔h8? (or 19...♘e6 20 ♖he1) 20 ♗xc6 ♖xd1+ 21 ♖xd1 ♕xc6 22 ♕e7 wins for White.

15...♖ac8 16 ♗e2?!

After this less than incisive move Black is able to reinforce his central defences. 16 ♗g2 still looks better.

16...♗e8 17 ♗g4 ♗f7 18 ♖he1 ♘xd4 19 ♕xd4 ♖c6

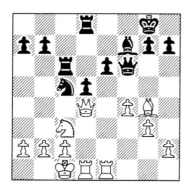

Black's policy of over-protection leaves

White rather at a loss. If here 20 ♕xf6 gxf6 21 f5 Black can simply play 21...e5 since d5 is well defended. White proceeds to do nothing much for the next few moves while Black continues to reorganise his forces.

20 ♔b1 a6 21 a3 h6 22 ♖e5 ♖dd6 23 h4 ♘d7 24 ♖e3 ♗g6 25 ♗h3

25 ♕xf6 ♘xf6 26 ♗f3 and White still has a hold over the central dark squares. Black cannot play 25...gxf6?! due to 26 f5! exf5 27 ♗f3 and d5 drops off.

25...♕f7 26 ♗f1

White might at least have attempted to do something on the kingside, e.g. 26 g4 b5 27 f5 to undermine the d5-pawn.

26...♘c5 27 ♖ee1 ♘b3!?

27...b5 was also worthwhile, but Black wants to keep the b-file open for his rook. Plus, ...♘b3 shows nice psychology: White will be aware that he has not done much constructive, and Black teases him by exploiting White's nondescript a2-a3 and ♔b1.

28 ♕f2

It was preferable to play 28 ♕e5 intending g2-g4, f4-f5. Black cannot then play 28...♘a5 29 g4 ♘c4? 30 ♗xc4 since the ♖d6 hangs, while if 28...♗f5 29 ♗d3 ♗xd3 30 ♖xd3 White still has a grip on e5.

28...♘a5 29 ♗d3 ♘c4 30 ♕d4?!

Better was 30 ♗xc4 ♖xc4 31 ♖d4.

30...♗h5 31 ♘e2 ♕c7 32 ♔a2 ♖d8 33 ♖c1 e5!

When Black can achieve this advance with impunity then White has clearly gone wrong.

34 fxe5 ♘xe5 35 ♖f1 ♘xd3 36 ♕xd3 d4!?

An odd decision. Black is okay after this move, but 36...♗g6 was simpler, with an extra pawn after 37 ♕d2 ♖xc2 38 ♖xc2 ♕xc2 39 ♕xc2 ♗xc2 40 ♘d4 ♗e4.

37 ♘f4?

Probably short of time, White sees ghosts. It was essential to capture 37 ♘xd4, when if 37...♖c4 then not 38 c3 ♖dxd4!, but

38 ♖f4 as 38...g5 fails to 39 hxg5 hxg5 40 ♕f5 gxf4 41 ♕g5+. Black would have to try 37...♖cd6 38 c3 (if 38 ♖f4 g5! now works since Black has ...♗g6 after ♕g5+) 38...♗f7+ 39 b3 a5 40 a4 b5! 41 ♕xb5 ♖b8 42 ♖xf7 (if 42 ♕f5 ♗xb3+ 43 ♘xb3 ♕c4) 42...♔xf7 43 ♖f1+ ♔g8 44 ♕c4+ ♕xc4 45 bxc4 and White has better chances to hold the game.

37...♗f7+ 38 ♔b1?!

38 b3 ♖c3 is not much of an improvement.

38...♗c4 39 ♕f3 ♗xf1

The exchange up Black won easily.

40 ♕xf1 d3 41 ♘xd3 ♕xg3 42 h5 ♖f6 43 ♕h1 ♕f3 44 ♕h4 ♖d5 45 ♕c4 ♔h7 46 ♖g1 ♖xh5 47 ♕c7 ♖f7 0-1

Game 57
Ulibin-R.Bagirov
Dubai 2000

---

1 e4 e6 2 d4 d5 3 ♘c3 ♘f6 4 ♗g5 ♗e7 5 e5 ♘fd7 6 ♗xe7 ♕xe7 7 f4 0-0 8 ♘f3 c5 9 dxc5

By capturing early on c5 White is able to follow with ♗d3 and castle short. The immediate 9 ♗d3 can transpose to the current game after, for example, 9...♘c6!? 10 dxc5 or 9...f6 10 exf6 ♕xf6 11 g3 ♘c6 12 dxc5 ♘xc5. But it allows Black to change the play with 9...cxd4!? leading to different positions in Game 58.

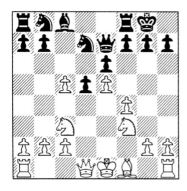

9...♘c6

Once again there are many transpositional possibilities. After 9...♘c6 10 ♕d2 would return to 9 ♕d2 in Games 54-56. If 9...♘xc5 10 ♗d3 f5 11 exf6 ♕xf6 12 g3 ♘c6 is another route to move 12 below, while 10 ♕d2 ♘c6 is again Game 55. Similarly 9...f6 (or 9...f5) 10 exf6 ♕xf6 11 g3 ♘c6 12 ♗d3 ♘xc5 was the actual move order in Ulibin-Bagirov, while 12 ♕d2 ♘xc5 is Game 56.

Finally, 9...♕xc5!? attempts to avoid the current game in favour of a return to Game 54 after 10 ♕d2 ♘c6 or 10...♘b6 11 0-0-0 ♘c6. White can refuse the transposition with 10 ♗d3!? and in Rodriguez-Comas Fabrego, Linares 1997, he held a slight plus after 10...♕e3+ 11 ♘e2 ♘c6 12 ♕d2 ♕xd2+ 13 ♔xd2 ♘c5 14 ♖he1 ♗d7 15 ♘ed4. The alternative 10 ♕d4 is less testing following 10...♘b6 11 ♗b5 (or 11 ♕xc5 bxc5 12 ♘b5 ♘c6) 11...a6 12 ♗xd7 ♗xd7 13 0-0-0 ♖a7 14 ♔b1 ♘c6 15 ♕d2 and White had merely lost time in Zhelnin-Gleizerov, Russian Team Championship 1997, which continued 15...♖a5!? 16 b3 ♖c8 17 ♘e2 ♘c6 18 ♘ed4 a5 19 ♘xc6 ♗xc6 20 ♘d4 ♕e7 21 ♖he1 ♗d7 22 ♖e3 a4 23 b4 a3 with an unclear position.

10 ♗d3

As noted above, 10 ♕d2 returns to 9 ♕d2 ♘c6 10 dxc5 lines in Games 54-56.

10...f6

There is little point in 10...f5!? which gives White a choice between 11 exf6 transposing, and 11 0-0!? as seen in Plachetka-Bareev, Trnava 1989. The game continued 11...♘xc5 12 ♘e2 ♗d7 13 ♘ed4 ♗e8 14 ♕d2 ♘e4 15 ♕e3 ♗h5 16 a3 ♗xf3 17 ♘xf3 a5 18 c4! with pressure against the centre, and after 18...♕c5 19 ♕xc5 ♘xc5 20 cxd5 ♘xd3 21 dxc6 bxc6 22 ♘d4 ♖fe8 23 ♖f3 ♘xb2 now 24 ♘xc6! ♖a6 25 ♖c1 would have been clearly better for White according to Plachetka.

11 exf6 ♕xf6

The best move, prompting the

weakening of White's kingside light squares. Instead 11...♘xf6 12 ♕d2 ♕xc5 would reach the note to move 11 in Game 54, although this move order gives White more options, either for 12 0-0 ♕xc5+ 13 ♔h1, or 12 ♕e2 and 13 0-0-0.

Capturing with the rook is also inferior as White does not have to make any concessions. Thus 11...♖xf6 12 ♕d2 ♘xc5 13 0-0 is clearly worse than after 11...♕xf6, an assessment which has not changed since Bronstein-Yanofsky, Saltsjöbaden Interzonal 1948. Alternatively, 12...♕xc5 would prevent White from castling short, but in ...♕xc5 positions (see Game 54) Black does not play ...f7-f6 so soon, if at all.

12 g3 ♘xc5 13 0-0

The most accurate move. 13 ♕d2 allows Black to break immediately with 13...♘xd3+ intending 14 cxd3 e5! (Alekhine), e.g. 15 0-0 (if 15 ♘xd5 ♕d6 and ...exf4) 15...♗h3 16 ♖fe1 ♖ae8 17 ♘xd5 ♕d6 18 ♘c3 exf4 19 ♖xe8 ♖xe8 20 ♕xf4 ♕xd3 21 ♖d1, as in Virovlansky-Driamin, St Petersburg 1998. Or if 14 ♕xd3 ♗d7 (intending ...♗e8-g6) 15 ♘g5 ♕f5 is okay.

13...♗d7 14 ♕d2

White prepares to grip the e5-square by ♖ae1. If instead 14 ♕e2!? Black can initiate favourable exchanges by 14...♘d4 15 ♘xd4 ♕xd4 16 ♕f2 ♕b4 17 a3 ♕b6 and after 18 b4 ♘xd3 19 cxd3 d4! 20 ♘e4 e5 Black had freed both his position and his bishop in Simagin-Ljublinsky, Sochi 1952.

White has also tried 14 ♗b5!?, intending to remove the knight from c6 so that the white queen can take up residence on d4. However, Black can thwart the plan by 14...d4! and if 15 ♗xc6 (15 ♘e2 ♖ad8) 15...dxc3 16 ♗xd7 cxb2 17 ♖b1 ♖ad8 18 ♕d6 (or 18 ♘e5 ♘xd7 19 ♘xd7 ♕e7) 18...♘xd7 19 ♕b4 b6 20 ♕xb2 ♕e7 21 ♖be1 ♘c5 and Black drew without difficulty in Jenni-R.Bagirov, Biel 2000.

14...♘xd3

Black intends to break with ...e6-e5 while

it is still possible. It is necessary to take the bishop first since if 14...e5? loses a pawn to 15 ♘xd5 ♕d6 16 ♗c4. Anything else and White will play 15 ♖ae1 with a positional advantage, e.g. 14...♗e8 15 ♖ae1 ♗g6 16 ♗xg6 ♕xg6 17 ♘e5 or 15...♖ad8 16 ♘e5 ♘xe5 17 ♖xe5 ♗f7 18 ♘d1 ♘d7 19 ♖ee1 d4+ 20 ♕e3 ♕xe3+ 21 ♖xe3 (Keres-Lilienthal, USSR Championship 1949).

15 cxd3

15 ♕xd3 is inferior due to 15...♗e8 and the bishop arrives at g6 with tempo, enhancing Black's counterplay. With 15 cxd3, if 15...♗e8 16 ♖ae1 grips e5 again. Hence Black plays:

15...e5! 16 ♖ae1

The immediate 16 ♘xd5 is no good since after 16...♕d6 the knight must retreat when 17...exf4 regains the pawn. 16 ♘xe5 ♘xe5 17 fxe5 ♕xe5 18 d4 ♕h5 also gives White nothing. By 16 ♖ae1 White adds pressure to e5, while if 16...exf4 17 ♘xd5 ♕d6 the knight is now able combine retreat and recapture with 18 ♘xf4.

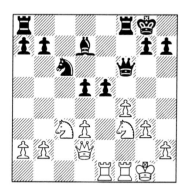

16...exf4!?

Of his own accord Black falls in with his opponent's scheme, sacrificing a pawn for active piece play.

The alternative, 16...♗h3 17 ♖f2 d4 18 ♘e4 ♕f5, leads to great complications. For a start, White can win the black queen by 19 ♘xe5 ♘xe5 20 fxe5 ♕xe5!, but after 21 ♘f6+ ♕xf6 22 ♖xf6 ♖xf6 and 23...♖af8 the white pieces are impotent, tied to defence of f1. De Firmian-Chernin, New York Open 1988, saw instead 21 ♖xf8+ ♖xf8 22 ♘f2 ♕h5 23 ♕b4 ♗g2! 24 ♕xd4 ♗c6 and again the threats on the light squares were enough to draw the game.

In A.Rodriguez-Stojanovic, Linares 1997, White tried 19 ♘fg5!? ♗g4! (not 19...exf4? 20 ♕c1!) 20 h3 ♗xh3 21 ♖h2 exf4 22 ♖xh3 h6 23 gxf4 hxg5 24 ♕h2 ♕g4+ 25 ♔h1 ♕xf4 26 ♖h8+ ♔f7 27 ♘d6+ and obtained a winning position after 27...♕xd6? 28 ♕xd6 ♖xh8+ 29 ♔g2 ♖h6 30 ♕d5+ ♔f8 31 ♖f1+ ♖f6 32 ♕d6+ ♔e8 33 ♖xf6 gxf6 34 ♕e6+ ♘e7 35 ♕xf6. However, after 27...♔f6! White has no more than a draw by 28 ♖h6+ g6 29 ♘e4+ ♔g7 30 ♖h7+ ♔g8 (Fröberg-A.Gaujens, correspondence 1997-98), while if 27 ♕h5+ it is not clear how White continues after 27...♔e6 28 ♘xg5+ ♔d6!

Fritz improves on this for White with the subtle 19 ♕c1!?, and if 19...exf4 20 ♘fg5! when the prospect of ♖xf4 and ♕c4+ creates serious problems for Black, or if 19...♗g4 20 ♘xe5! since the bishop no longer controls f1. A.Bartsch-Scruton, email 1997, saw 19...♕d7 20 ♕c4+ ♔h8 21 ♘c5 ♕c7 22 ♘g5 (threatening ♘xh3 and ♘e6) 22...b5 (or 22...♗f5 23 ♘ce6 ♕a5 24 ♖fe2) 23 ♕xb5 ♕b6 24 ♕c4 ♘a5 25 ♘f7+ and Black resigned.

17 ♘xd5 ♕d6

17...♕f7?! 18 ♘xf4 ♕xa2 is inconsistent. Black gets the pawn back but cedes all counterplay; after 19 d4 ♕a5 20 ♕xa5 ♘xa5 21 ♖e7 White was in control in A.Rodriguez-Chernin, Subotica Interzonal 1987.

18 ♘xf4 ♗g4 19 ♕e3

19 ♕c3!? is another possibility, aiming to combine ♘g5 and ♕c4+ with new threats, for instance, 19...♖ad8 20 ♕c4+ ♔h8 21 ♘g5 is strong. G.Coleman-O'Neale, correspondence 1997-98, saw 19...♗xf3 20 ♖xf3 ♘d4 21 ♖f2 ♖ac8 (if now 21...♖ad8 22 ♕c4+ ♔h8 23 ♖e4 threatens 24 ♖xd4!

♕xd4 25 ♕xd4 ♖xd4 26 ♘g6+) 22 ♕a5 ♖f5 23 ♕a4 g5 24 ♖e4! ♘b5 25 ♕b3+ ♔h8 26 ♕e6 ♖cf8 27 ♘h3 and White consolidated.

19...♖ad8

19...♗xf3 allows White more activity after 20 ♕xf3! ♕d4+ 21 ♔f2 ♖ad8 22 ♖e4, as in Brunner-Züger, Prague 1989.

20 ♘g5

Better than 20 ♖f2 h6 21 h4 ♖f7 22 ♘d2 ♕b4 23 ♘e4 ♘d4 with a dynamic position for Black in Arnason-Bareev, Sochi 1988.

20...h6 21 ♘e4 ♕b4

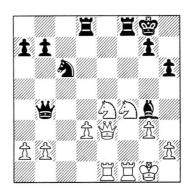

The black player reached this same position again later in the year. Kadhi-R.Bagirov, Abu Dhabi 2000, saw 22 ♘g6?! ♖xf1+ 23 ♖xf1 ♕xb2 24 ♕f4, when after 24...♗e6 25 ♘f8 ♘d4! 26 ♔h1 ♗f5 27 g4 ♖xf8 28 gxf5 ♘xf5 Black still had his all his counterplay and was now a pawn up as well.

22 h3

This was first seen in Kovalevskaya-Ulibin, St Petersburg 1995, continuing 22...♗c8 23 ♖f2 ♘d4 24 ♖ef1 ♗f5 25 g4 ♗xe4 26 ♕xe4 ♖fe8 27 ♕g6 ♕d6 28 ♕xd6 ½-½. Presumably Ulibin had some White improvement in mind, or else thought the final position was worth playing on. Whatever, Black wisely makes a different response.

22...♗f5 23 ♖f2 ♘e5!?

Rather than adopt a blockading strategy with ...♘d4 Black resorts to a tactical defence, threatening 24...♞xd3 25 ♞xd3 ♜xd3 when White cannot recapture as the ♜e1 hangs.

24 a3 ♛a5 25 ♞c5

Having driven the queen back 25 d4 was now possible, since if 25...♜xd4 26 b4 ♛d8 27 ♞c5 ♜e8 28 ♜fe2 threatens 29 ♛b3+ and 29 ♞fe6 maybe with g3-g4 thrown in, e.g. 29...♚h7 30 g4 ♝c8 31 ♞fe6 ♝xe6 32 ♛xe5. However, 25...♞c4! 26 ♛c3 ♞xc3 27 ♞xc3 g5! 28 ♞fd5 ♝xh3 improves for Black; if 29 ♞f6+ ♚g7 30 ♜e7+ ♚g6 31 ♞cd5 ♞b6 defends.

25...♜de8 26 ♞ce6?!

White sees that after 26 ♞fe6 ♝xe6 27 ♜xf8+ ♜xf8 28 ♞xe5 ♝xh3 is drawish, and 27 ♛xe5? ♝f7 even wins for Black since the ♜e1 hangs again. By using the c5-knight White keeps h3 defended, while after 26...♝xe6 27 ♛xe5 opposes queens. Unfortunately, Black does not have to capture on e6.

26...♞xd3! 27 ♞xd3 ♜xe6 28 ♞e5 ♜ef6

Black is content to have regained his pawn and rejects complications following 28...♝xh3 29 ♜xf8+ ♚xf8 30 ♛e4 h5! Now the game proceeds to a draw.

29 b4 ♛a6 30 h4 ♝e6 31 ♜xf6 ♜xf6 32 ♜d1 ♚h7 33 g4 ♚g8 34 ♚g2 ♜f8 35 ♚g3 ♛b5 ½-½

Game 58
Szilagyi-Harding
correspondence 1987

---

1 e4 e6 2 d4 d5 3 ♞c3 ♞f6 4 ♝g5 ♝e7 5 e5 ♞fd7 6 ♝xe7 ♛xe7 7 f4 0-0 8 ♞f3

8 ♝d3 c5 9 ♞f3 is the same thing as current game. Instead 8 ♛d2 c5 9 ♞f3 or 9 dxc5 ♞c6 10 ♞f3 reaches ♛d2 lines in Games 54-56.

8 ♛h5 is artificial, since after 8...c5 9 ♞f3 cxd4 10 ♞xd4 ♞c6 11 ♝d3 g6 12 ♞xc6 bxc6 13 ♛h6 f6 14 exf6 ♛xf6 15 0-0 ♜b8 Black was better in Okolotowicz-Friedman, Toronto 1998.

8...c5 9 ♝d3

An unpretentious move, setting up to sacrifice immediately on h7. Unfortunately for White, even if Black does not prevent it, the sacrifice does not seem all that strong.

The sortie with 9 ♞b5 is now ineffective as 9...a6! creates a home for the rook, i.e. 10 ♞c7? ♜a7 and the knight is trapped. J.Olivier-Gleizerov, Metz 1999, saw 10 ♞d6 cxd4! 11 ♝d3 f6 12 ♞xc8 ♜xc8 13 exf6 ♛xf6 and White had used several moves in order to capture Black's problem bishop on its home square. Nevertheless, this was better than 12 0-0 ♞c6 13 ♛e2 ♞c5 14 ♜ae1 ♝d7 15 a3 ♝e8 16 g4 fxe5 17 ♞xe8? e4 18 b4 ♞xd3 19 cxd3 exf3 0-1 D.Walker-R.Shaw, British Championship 1999.

9...cxd4!?

Showing no fear, Black not only ignores the bishop sacrifice but even encourages it.

9...♞c6!? is also okay as the sacrifice 10 ♝xh7+ is only good enough for a draw: 10...♚xh7 11 ♞g5+ ♚g6! 12 ♛g4 (if 12 ♛d3+ f5 13 ♛h3 ♞f6! 14 exf6 gxf6 and the black queen defends laterally) 12...f5 (not 12...♞dxe5? 13 dxe5 ♞xe5 14 ♛g3 f5 15 ♞f3+ winning in Finnie-Simmons, correspondence 1995-96, nor 12...f6? 13 ♞xd5! exd5 14 f5+) 13 ♛g3 (if 13 ♛h4 ♞f6 14 g4 fxg4 15 exf6 gxf6 16 ♞ge4 f5) 13...cxd4 14 ♞xe6+ (if 14 ♞e2 ♜h8) 14...♚h6 15 ♞xf8 ♝xf8 16 ♞xd5 ♛c5 and Black survives. White should probably return to the main lines of Game 57 by 10 dxc5!

9...f6 (or 9...f5) also allows White to play normal lines following 10 exf6 ♕xf6 (10...♖xf6!? 11 ♕d2 cxd4 12 ♘xd4 ♘c6 13 ♘f3 ♕b4! might be worth trying) 11 g3! when 11...♘c6 12 dxc5 ♘xc5 13 0-0 or 11...cxd4 12 ♘xd4 ♘c6 13 ♘f3 ♘c5 14 0-0 transposes again to Game 57 (9 dxc5). Bronstein's imaginative 11 ♘g5!? has proved to be unsound after 11...♕xf4! 12 ♗xh7+ ♔h8 13 ♕h5 ♘f6! 14 ♘f7+ ♖xf7 15 ♕xf7 ♔xh7 and White has insufficient compensation. If 16 ♖f1 (as suggested in *Informator* 45) then 16...♕h4+ 17 g3 (or 17 ♖f2 cxd4 18 ♘e2 ♘c6) 17...♕xd4 18 ♘e2 (or 18 ♖f4 ♕g1+ 19 ♔d2 ♕xh2+) 18...♕xb2 19 ♖d1 ♘g4! 20 ♕h5+ ♘h6 stopping all threats (G.Berry-Megier, correspondence 1992-94). Or if 13 ♕d2!? ♕xd2+ 14 ♔xd2 ♖f2+ 15 ♘e2 (or 15 ♔e1 ♖xg2 16 h4 ♘c6!) 15...♘f8! 16 ♗d3 c4 17 ♖af1 ♖xf1 18 ♖xf1 (Kostakiev-Strelkov, correspondence 1988) then 18...♔g8! preventing ♖f7 and Black is clearly better.

10 ♗xh7+

10 ♘xd4!? is possible when 10...♘c6 11 ♘f3! can again return to normal lines by 11...♘c5 or 11...f6 12 exf6 ♕xf6 13 g3. Martinez Penalver-Deak, San Agustin 1997, saw instead 11...♕b4!? 12 ♗xh7+ ♔xh7 13 ♘g5+ ♔g6 14 ♕d3+ f5 when 15 ♘xe6! d4 (or 15...♖e8 16 ♕g3+ ♔f7 17 ♕xg7+ with perpetual) 16 a3 ♕xb2 17 ♘d5! ♘dxe5! 18 ♕g3+ ♘g4 19 ♘xf8+ ♔f7 20 0-0 ♔xf8 21 ♕d3 would have been unclear.

10...♔xh7 11 ♘g5+ ♕xg5?!

11...♔g6! again seems sufficient after 12 ♕d3+ (not 12 ♕g4? f5 13 exf6 ♘xf6) 12...f5 13 exf6+ (if 13 ♕h3 ♘f6! 14 exf6 gxf6 defends laterally again) 13...♖xf6 14 ♘h7+ ♔f7 15 ♘g5+ ♔f6 etc (not 15...♔d8? 16 ♕g6+). White can play on with 14 ♕xd4+ ♔g6 15 ♕d3+ ♔f6 16 ♘h7+ ♔f7 17 ♘xf8 but has no actual advantage (17...♕xf8 intending ...♔g8).

12 fxg5 dxc3

Black has three pieces for the queen and after 13 ♕d3+ ♔g8 14 ♕xc3 would have good play with 14...♘c6 and ...♘dxe5.

13 ♕h5+!

White intends to lift his queen's rook to the h-file and attack before Black has time to develop his queenside.

13...♔g8 14 0-0 ♘xe5

Not 14...g6? 15 ♕h6 followed by ♖f4 and ♖h4; while if 14...cxb2 15 ♖ae1 ♘c6 (or 15...b1♕ 16 ♖xb1 ♘xe5 17 ♖b3) 16 ♖e3 b1♕ 17 ♖h3! ♕xf1+ 18 ♔xf1 f6 19 g6 fxe5+ 20 ♔g1 ♖f1+ 21 ♔xf1 ♔f8 22 ♕h8+ ♔e7 23 ♕xg7+ wins.

15 ♖ae1 ♘g6?!

Black has better chances to defend after 15...♘bc6 16 ♖e3 g6 17 ♕h4 ♖d8 18 ♖h3 ♔f8.

16 ♖e3 e5 17 g4

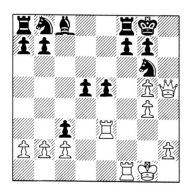

17...♖d8?!

No better is 17...♖e8 18 ♖h3 ♖e6 19 ♕h7+ ♔f8 20 ♖h6 ♘e7 (or 20...♘f4 21 ♕h8+ ♔e7 22 ♕xc8 gxh6 23 ♕xb7+) 21 g6! f6 22 ♕h8+ ♘g8 23 ♖h7 ♖e7 24 ♖xg7! 1-0 Teichmeister-Krecmer, correspondence 1988-89, since 24...♖xg7 25 ♖xf6+ ♔e8 26 ♕xg7 wins.

The only way Black can prolong the game is to return a piece by 17...♗xg4 18 ♕xg4 cxb2 though White is clearly for preference.

18 ♖h3 ♖d6 19 ♕h7+ ♔f8 20 ♖h6! ♖f6

Hoping for 21 gxf6?? gxh6. Instead Bernard-Dermann, Dortmund 1989, concluded 20...♚e8 21 ♕xg7 ♗e6 22 ♖xg6 1-0, while in Tait-Crouch, Nottingham 1990, after an hour's thought Black decided simply to resign.

21 ♖xf6! 1-0

Game 59
King-Short
Birmingham 4NCL 2001

---

1 e4 e6 2 d4 d5 3 ♘c3 ♘f6 4 ♗g5 ♗e7 5 e5 ♘fd7 6 ♗xe7 ♕xe7 7 f4

Although 7 f4 has been the featured move in all the main games, it is not White's only possibility. Several other moves are worth noting.

a) Firstly, 7 ♘b5, to which Black should answer 7...♘b6! and then:

a1) 8 c3 a6 9 ♘a3 was popular in the early years of the 20th century. Black has a solid reply in 9...c5 10 ♘c2 (or 10 f4 ♘c6) 10...♘c6 11 f4 ♘a4 12 ♖b1 b5, or a more dynamic one in 9...f6!? with a few lines:

a11) 10 exf6 gxf6 11 ♕h5+ ♕f7 12 ♕h4 e5.

a12) 10 ♕h5+ g6 11 ♕h4 (11 exf6? ♕xa3) 11...fxe5.

a13) 10 ♗d3 fxe5 11 ♕h5+ (11 dxe5 c5) 11...♚d8 12 dxe5 ♘a4.

a14) 10 f4 fxe5 11 dxe5 (11 fxe5 ♕h4+) 11...0-0.

a15) 10 ♘f3 ♘8d7 11 exf6 ♕xf6 12 ♗d3 e5!

a2) 8 a4!? is sharper: 8...a6 9 a5 axb5 10 axb6 ♖xa1 11 ♕xa1 and now 11...0-0 (or 11...♘c6 12 c3 0-0) 12 bxc7 ♕xc7 13 ♗d3 ♘c6 14 c3 b4 was equal from Spielmann-Maroczy, Vienna 1908, to Borgo-Gleizerov, Bolzano 1999. Black also has an interesting piece sacrifice in 11...c6! (intending to win the b6-pawn by a future ...♘d7) 12 ♕a8 ♕b4+ 13 c3 (if 13 ♚e2 ♕a4 14 ♕xb8 ♕xc2+ with a draw, not 13 ♚d1? ♕xd4+ and 14...♕xe5) 13...♕xb2!? (13...♕a4 14 ♕xb8 ♕a1+ is also good for a draw) 14 ♘e2 b4 15 ♕xb8 0-0 16 cxb4 ♕xb4+ 17 ♚d1 c5! 18 ♕c7 ♕a4+ 19 ♚d2 ♗d7 20 ♚e3 ♖c8 21 ♕xb7 cxd4+ 22 ♘xd4 ♖c3+ 23 ♗d3 g5!? (23...♖xd3+ is another draw) 24 ♕b8+ ♚g7 25 ♕d8 and Black finally decided to force a draw: 25...♖xd3+ 26 ♚xd3 ♕c4+ 27 ♚e3 ♕c3+ 28 ♚e2 ♕b2+ 29 ♚d3 ♗b5+ 30 ♘xb5 ♕xb5+ 31 ♚d2 ½-½ Ljubojevic-Korchnoi, Belgrade 1987.

b) If White wants to play ♕d2 main lines (Games 54-56) then 7 ♕d2 is an interesting move order, holding back f2-f4 for a while. As usual 7...c5 is a mistake due to 8 ♘b5, while if 7...a6 White can try 8 ♘d1!? c5 9 c3 ♘c6 10 f4 when ...a7-a6 is just a wasted move. This 19th century idea was seen again recently in Sakaev-Volkov, New Delhi 2000, which continued 10...cxd4 11 cxd4 g5!? 12 fxg5 h6 13 ♘f3 hxg5 14 ♘f2! ♖g8 15 h3 f6 16 exf6 ♘xf6 17 0-0-0 ♘e4 18 ♘xe4 dxe4 19 ♘e5 ♘xe5 20 dxe5 ♗d7 21 ♚b1 0-0-0 22 ♕e3 ♗c6 23 ♖c1 ♕c7 24 ♕a7 with the big threat of 25 ♗xa6! bxa6 26 ♖xc6 ♕xc6 27 ♖c1, and White won.

After 7...0-0 the plan with 8 ♘d1 is now ineffective – after 8...c5 9 c3 ♘c6 10 f4 cxd4 11 cxd4 f6! 12 ♘f3 fxe5 13 fxe5 ♖xf3! 14 gxf3 ♕h4+ 15 ♕f2 ♘xd4, with the f- and e-pawns dropping off Black will get three pawns for the exchange (Harmonist-Tarrasch, Frankfurt 1887). 8 ♘ce2 is a safer version since after 8...c5 9 c3 ♘c6 10 f4 cxd4 11 cxd4 f6 12 ♘f3 fxe5 13 fxe5 then 13...♖xf3? fails to 14 gxf3 ♕h4+ 15 ♔d1, but Black has nothing to fear after 13...♘b6 14 ♘g3 ♗d7 (Keres, Euwe). White cannot improve on 8 f4 c5 9 ♘f3 transposing into normal lines with ♕d2. Instead, as after 7 f4 0-0 8 ♘f3 c5, 9 ♘b5 is poor due to 9...a6 when 10 ♘c7? loses the knight after 10...♖a7, and otherwise ...f7-f6 demolishes White's centre.

Finally, in Shirov-M.Gurevich, New Delhi 2000, Black tried 7...♘c6!? 8 f4 ♘b6 9 ♘f3 ♗d7 10 ♗d3 a6 11 0-0 f6 12 exf6 ♕xf6 13 ♕e3 0-0-0 14 a4 ♗e8 15 a5 ♘d7 16 f5?! exf5 17 ♘xd5 ♕d6 18 c4 ♗g6 19 ♘h4 f4! 20 ♖xf4 and now 20...♗xd3 21 ♕xd3 ♘f4! would have won material after 22 ♘xb4 ♕xf4, 22 ♘f5 ♕xf4 or 22 ♕d2 ♘xd5 23 cxd5 g5.

c) The direct 7 ♕g4 can be met simply by 7...0-0! 8 ♘f3 c5 9 ♗d3 cxd4 (9...f5?! 10 ♕g5! showed up weaknesses at c7, d6 and e6 in Senff-Mork, Budapest 1998) 10 ♗xh7+ (if 10 h4 f5!) 10...♔xh7 11 ♘g5+ ♕xg5 (or 11...♔g8 12 ♕h5 ♕xg5) 12 ♕xg5 dxc3 13 bxc3 ♘c6 14 f4 ♖h8 15 0-0 ♘c5 16 ♖f3 ♔g8 17 ♖d1 ♘e4 18 ♕g4 b5 with an unclear position in Michel-Rellstab, Bad Elster 1937.

7...a6

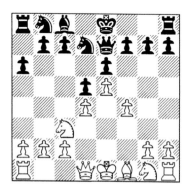

The first point of 7...a6 is to prevent the incursion at b5 and thus enable ...c7-c5. Black also prepares the later advance ...b7-b5 and refuses to commit the king for the time being. The king may go short if and when Black deems it appropriate, or he may go long.

The immediate 7...c5? 8 ♘b5 is clearly bad, though Black keeps falling for this – perhaps because ♘b5 is an unexpected move in the opening. If Black covers c7 then the king will have to move following ♘d6. The exchange sacrifice is insufficient: 8...0-0 9 ♘c7 cxd4 (or 9...f6 10 ♘f3 ♘xe5 11 ♘xa8 ♘xf3+ 12 ♕xf3 cxd4 13 0-0-0 Keres) 10 ♘xa8 f6 11 ♘f3 fxe5 12 fxe5 ♘c6 13 ♗d3 ♘dxe5 14 0-0 ♘g4 15.♘d2 with a clear advantage in Levenfish-Fahrni, Carlsbad 1911.

8 ♘f3

Alternatively:

a) White sometimes develops the queen first. 8 ♕d2 c5 9 dxc5 ♘c6 10 0-0-0 ♕xc5 11 ♘f3 b5 transposes below.

b) If 8 ♕g4 0-0 9 ♗d3 (if 9 f5 f6!) 9...c5 10 f5! cxd4 11 f6 ♘xf6 12 ♕h4 h6 13 exf6 ♕xf6 14 ♕xf6 gxf6 15 ♘a4 ♘d7 16 b3 b5 17 ♘b2 e5 18 ♘e2! ♘c5 (if 18...e4 19 ♘xd4 cxd3 20 ♘xd3 ♖e8+ 21 ♔d2 ♘e5 22 ♖hf1 ♘xd3 23 cxd3 the white knight dominates) 19 0-0 ♘xd3 20 ♘xd3 and the piece was better than the pawns in Hjartarson-Bricard, Iceland-France 1993. Black can improve by playing ...f7-f5 himself. Hjartarson suggests 9...f5 10 exf6 ♕xf6 12 ♘f3 c5 13 ♘g5 as unclear. Simpler still is 8...f5 9 exf6 ♘xf6 10 ♕g5 ♘c6!? 11.0-0-0 ♗d7 12 ♘f3 0-0-0 13 ♘e5 ♖hg8 14 ♗e2 h6 15 ♘xc6 ♗xc6 16 ♕e5 ♘d7 and White was unable to utilise the e5-weakness in Krantz-Carleton, correspondence 1987. Black subsequently broke with first ...g7-g5 and later ...e6-e5.

c) 8 ♕h5!? c5 9 ♘f3 cxd4 10 ♘xd4 ♘c6 11 0-0-0 led to White's advantage in Van der Wiel-Moskalenko, Belgrade 1988, after 11...♘xd4 12 ♖xd4 ♘b6 (if 12...b5 13 f5!) 13 ♗d3 ♕c5 14 ♘e2 ♗d7 15 ♕g5 g6 16 ♕f6 ♖g8 and now 17 g4! (Moskalenko). It is better to delay the exchange on d4 and play first 11...♞b6. For example, 12 ♚b1 ♝d7 13 h4 and now 13...♞xd4 14 ♖xd4 ♛c5 15 ♛d1 ♝b5 16 ♝e2 0-0 was fine for Black in Van Mil-Kuijf, Dutch Championship 1992.

8...c5

8...b5 is best followed by 9 ♝d3 c5 10 dxc5 ♛xc5 11 ♛d2 ♞c6 reaching 11 ♝d3 in the notes to the game. If instead 10...♞xc5 11 0-0 or 9...♞b6 10 0-0 c5 11 dxc5 Black has merely shown his hand at an early stage. The continued queenside advance ...b5-b4 allows White to consolidate the centre and attack with f4-f5, as in Schuh-Schmittdiel, Vienna 1991: 9 ♝d3 b4 10 ♞e2 a5 11 0-0 c5 12 c3 (12 c4!? is also worth considering) 12...♝a6 13 f5 bxc3 14 bxc3 ♞c6 15 ♝xa6 ♖xa6 16 ♛d2 cxd4 17 cxd4 0-0 18 ♖ac1 exf5 19 ♞f4 ♞db8 20 ♞xd5 with a clear advantage to White.

9 dxc5

9 ♝d3 is dubious due to 9...cxd4 10 ♞xd4 (10 ♞e2 ♛b4+ is similar) 10...♛b4! 11 ♞de2 ♛xb2 12 0-0 ♛b6+ 13 ♚h1 ♞c6 with an extra pawn in Lasker-Levenfish, Moscow 1925.

King in fact inverted his 9th and 10th moves, playing 9 ♛d2 ♞c6 10 dxc5. Throwing in 10 0-0-0 also makes little difference after 10...b5 11 dxc5 ♞c6, unless Black opts to close the queenside with 10...c4!? This is supposed to be bad as it allows White to attack the centre immediately with 11 f5! However, in Shirov-Morozevich, Frankfurt 2000, Black quickly evacuated to the queenside by 11...♞b6! 12 fxe6 fxe6 13 h4 ♝d7 14 h5 0-0-0. After the further 15 h6 gxh6 16 ♖xh6 ♖dg8 17 ♛f4 ♝e8 18 ♛f6 ♝g6 19 g4?! ♛e8 20 ♝g2 ♖f8 21 ♛h4, having negated the kingside threats Black took over the initiative on the queenside: 21...♞b4 22 ♖d2 ♞a4 23 a3 ♞xc3 24 bxc3 ♛a4! 25 cxb4 ♛xa3+ 26 ♚d1 ♖xf3! 27 ♛e7? (though if 27 ♝xf3 ♛xf3+ 28 ♚c1 ♛a3+ 29 ♚d1 ♖f8 or 28 ♖e2 ♝xc2+) 27...♖e3 and Black won.

9...♞c6

9...♞xc5 10 ♛d2 ♞c6 and 9...♛xc5 10 ♛d2 ♞c6 again transpose below. Against the latter theory recommends 10 ♛d4 following the famous game Konstantinopolsky-Lilienthal, Moscow 1936: 10...♞c6 11 ♛xc5 ♞xc5 12 ♝d3 ♚e7 13 ♚d2 h6 14 ♞e2 ♝d7 15 ♞ed4 ♖ac8 16 ♖ae1 ♖c7 17 g4 ♞b4 18 a3 ♞bxd3 19 cxd3 ♖hc8 20 ♖c1 ♚d8 21 h4 ♞a4 22 ♖xc7 ♖xc7 23 b3 ♞b6 24 h5 and White invaded on the kingside. However, 10...b6 seems okay for Black, as after 7...0-0 in Game 57.

10 ♛d2

If 10 ♝d3 then 10...♛xc5! prevents kingside castling and then 11 ♛d2 yet again transposes below. 10...♞xc5 is slightly inferior as it allows White more flexibility in development. Olivier-Soln, Mitropa Cup 1999, saw 11 0-0 ♞xd3 12 cxd3 0-0 13 ♛d2 f5 14 exf6 ♛xf6 15 g3 ♝d7 16 ♖ae1 and White was better; while in El Taher-Sorial, Cairo Zonal 2000, Black fell for 11...0-0? 12 ♝xh7+! ♚xh7 13 ♞g5+ ♚g6 14 ♛g4 ♞xe5 15 ♛h4 f5 16 ♖ae1 ♞e4 17 ♛h7+ ♚f6 18 ♞cxe4+ dxe4 19 ♞xe4+ ♚f7 20 fxe5 and White won.

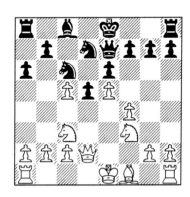

10...♛xc5

The alternative recapture, 10...♞xc5, is very similar to two variations examined previously: 7...0-0 8 ♞f3 c5 9 ♛d2 ♞c6 10 dxc5 ♞xc5 11 0-0-0 a6 (Game 55) and 4 e5

♘fd7 5 f4 c5 6 ♘f3 ♘c6 7 ♗e3 a6 8 ♕d2 b5 9 dxc5 ♗xc5 10 ♗xc5 ♘xc5 (Games 24-26).

Then 11 0-0-0 0-0 transposes directly in to Game 55. However, Black can delay castling in favour of 11...b5 12 ♗d3 b4 13 ♘e2 a5 14 ♘ed4 ♘xd4 15 ♘xd4 when Miljanic has shown the attributes of Black's position: 15...0-0 16 ♔b1 ♗b7 17 ♖he1 ♘e4 18 ♕e3 a4 19 ♗xe4 dxe4 20 ♘e2 ♗d5 21 ♖d4 ♖fc8 22 ♖c1 ♕a7 23 c4? ♗xc4 24 ♖xe4 ♗xe2 25 ♕xe2 ♖xc1+ 26 ♔xc1 ♕g1+ winning (Brajovic-Miljanic, Cetinje 1996) and (by transposition) 15...♗d7!? 16 ♔b1 a4 17 ♕e3 0-0 18 ♖he1 ♖fb8 19 g4? (better 19 f5 ♘xd3 20 cxd3 exf5 with equality) 19...b3! 20 cxb3 axb3 21 a3? ♘a4 22 ♕d2 ♘xb2! 23 ♕xb2 ♖xa3 24 ♘e2 ♖a2 25 ♕c3 ♕a3 26 ♘c1 ♖c8 27 ♕d4 ♖cc2 0-1 Vujosevic-Miljanic, Tivat 1997.

Castling short seems preferable for White against ...♘xc5. Compared with the 4 e5 line mentioned above, Black has swapped ...♕d8 and ...b7-b5 for just ...♕e7 and should stand comparatively worse. Indeed, after 11 ♗d3 and 12 0-0, Black has struggled to challenge White's dominance in the centre. For example, 11...0-0 12 0-0 f5 13 exf6 ♕xf6 14 g3 ♗d7 15 ♖ae1 ♗e8 16 ♘e5 ♖c8 17 ♖f2 ♘xe5 18 ♖xe5 ♖c6 19 ♗f1 ♘d7 20 ♖e1 (Stefansson-Hjartarson, Icelandic Championship 1995) or 11...b5 12 0-0 b4 13 ♘e2 0-0 14 ♘ed4 ♘xd4 15 ♘xd4 ♘e4 16 ♕e3 ♗b7 17 a3 a5 18 axb4 axb4 19 ♘b3 f6 20 ♕b6! (Kovacevic-Antic, Yugoslav Team Championship 2001) with advantage to White in both cases.

11 0-0-0

With this move White plans to attack in the middlegame, centralising a knight in support of f4-f5.

11 ♗d3 is also important, especially as the bishop may already have been deployed to b3; i.e. 10...♕xc5 11 ♕d2. After the usual 11...b5 then 12 0-0-0 again returns to 11 0-0-0 (see the note to 12 ♘e2 below).

White has another option in 12 a3!? preparing ♕f2 to take control of d4 (12 ♕f2 would be answered by 12...♕b4!). However, Black can achieve adequate counterplay with a timely ...f7-f6 and/or ...b7-b5-b4. For example, Piuva-Carleton, correspondence 1992-94, went 13...0-0 14 ♕xc5 ♘xc5 15 ♔d2 b4 16 axb4 ♘xb4 17 ♘d4 f6 18 exf6 ♖xf6 19 g3 g5 20 ♘ce2 with an unclear position. Bologan-Short, Buenos Aires 2000, saw 13...h6 14 h4 0-0 15 ♕xc5 ♘xc5 16 b4 ♘d7 17 ♔d2 ♘b6 18 ♘e2 ♘c4+ 19 ♗xc4 dxc4 20 ♘fd4 ♖ad8 21 ♔e3 ♘e7 22 ♔f2 ♘d5 23 ♖hd1 ♖de8 24 g3 and now at last 25...f6! 25 ♘f3 g5 26 hxg5 hxg5 27 exf6 gxf4 28 gxf4 ♖xf6 and the game was soon drawn.

If Black tries 11...♘b6, White can again play either 12 0-0-0 (see the next note), or 12 a3 and if 12...♘c4 13 ♗xc4 ♕xc4 14 b3 ♕c5 15 ♘a4 ♕e7 16 c4 dxc4 17 ♘b6 ♖b8 18 ♘xc4 0-0 with advantage to White in Morovic Fernandez-Alvarado, Las Palmas 1995, which concluded 20 0-0 ♗b7 21 ♖ac1 ♘a7 22 f5 exf5? 23 ♘xf5 ♕e6 24 ♕g5 g6 25 ♘3d4 ♕b6 26 ♕h6 1-0.

Sometimes White opts immediately for 11 a3 b5 12 ♕f2, but this has little independent significance as White generally plays ♗d3 fairly soon in any case, e.g. 12...♗b7 13 ♗d3 or 13 ♕xc5 ♘xc5 14 0-0-0 0-0 15 ♗d3.

11...b5

Not wanting to be predictable, Short has also played 7...0-0, and here 11...♘b6!? which theory frowns on due to Kindermann-Franke, German Bundesliga 1989: 12 ♗d3 ♗d7 13 ♔b1 ♘a5 14 b3 ♖c8 15 ♘e2 ♘c6 16 c3 halting Black's counterplay, after which White attacked on the kingside with g2-g4. Possibly Short would instead have castled long, as he was encouraged to do in Hernandez-Short, Merida 2001, after 12 h4 ♗d7 13 ♖h3 h6 14 ♖g3 ♖g8 15 h5 0-0-0 16 ♔b1 f6 17 exf6 gxf6 18 ♖xg8 ♖xg8 19 f5 e5 20 ♘xd5 (if 20

Wxh6 ♗xf5 21 Wf6 ♖f8 and 22...d4)
20...♘xd5 21 Wxd5 Wxd5 22 ♖xd5 ♗xf5
23 ♖d6 ♖d8 24 ♖xd8+ ♔xd8 with a
favourable endgame for Black.

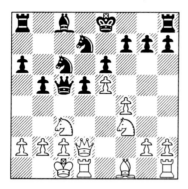

12 ♘e2

The generally recommended move for
White. Since the knight will have to move
anyway after ...b5-b4 White moves it in
advance and prepares to establish a knight
on d4.

12 ♗d3 is also important. With ...0-0
instead of ...b7-b5 then 12 ♗d3 is very
strong, threatening ♗xh7+ (see 11...a6 in
Game 54). Here, however, Black is not so
obliging with the king and continues either
12...b4, followed by ...a6-a5 and ...♗a6, or
else 12...♘b6 with ideas of ...♘b4, ...♗d7
and ...0-0-0, ...♖b8 and ...♘c4, or ...b5-b4
and ...♘a4. For example, 12...b4 13 ♘e2 a5
14 ♔b1 ♗a6 as in 15 h4 a4 16 ♗xa6 ♖xa6
17 Wd3 ♖b6 18 ♖h3 Wa5 19 ♘fd4 ♘xd4
20 ♘xd4 ♘c5 21 Wg3 0-0 22 f5 ♘e4 23
We1 exf5 24 ♘xf5 (Gunnarsson-
Thorhallsson, Icelandic Championship
2000) when Black should have played
24...♗e6!; or 12...♘b6 13 h4 b4 14 ♘e2
♗d7 15 ♔b1 h6 16 ♘g3 ♘a4 17 ♔a1 ♘c3
18 ♖de1 (not 18 bxc3 bxc3 19 Wc1 ♖b8
etc.) 18...Wa5 19 a3 ♖b8 20 f5 ♘b5 21
♗xb5 ♖xb5 22 fxe6 fxe6 23 ♘h5 bxa3 24
b3 Wxd2 25 ♘xd2 0-0 with a winning
endgame in Savanovic-Raicevic, Niksic
1996.

12...0-0

Mostly Black plays both ...b5-b4 and
...0-0 at some point. Short starts with ...0-0,
whereas other players have mostly played
...b5-b4 first, but it makes little difference.
In either case White will play 13 ♘ed4 and
throw in ♔b1 and h2-h4 at some point.
ECO gives 12...b4 13 ♘ed4 ♘xd4 14 ♘xd4
0-0 15 ♔b1 a5 16 h4 with a slight advantage
to White in A.Rodriguez-Moskalenko,
Holguin 1989. The game continued
16...Wb6 17 ♗d3 ♗a6 18 We3 ♗xd3 19
cxd3 b3 20 a3 ♖fc8 21 ♖he1 ♘c5 22 f5
♘a4 23 ♖d2 ♖ab8 24 f6 Wd8 25 Wf4 ♘c5
26 ♖e3 ♘d7 27 ♖g3 g6 28 ♖d1 ♔h8 29 h5
Wc7 30 Wh6 and White won. Kindermann-
Mueller, German Championship 1996,
deviated with 15 h4 a5 16 h5 a4 17 ♔b1
Wb6 18 g4 ♘c5 19 ♗g2 ♗a6 20 ♖h3 b3 21
cxb3 axb3 22 a3 ♗c4 23 f5 and after 23...f6?
24 ♘xe6 ♘xe6 25 fxe6 Wxe6 26 ♗xd5
♗xd5 27 Wxd5 Wxd5 28 ♖xd5 fxe5 29
♖xb3 White won the endgame.

12...♘b6, and ...♘b6 in general, no
longer achieves anything for Black.
Following 13 ♘ed4 ♘xd4 13 ♘xd4 or
13...♗d7 14 ♘xc6 ♗xc6 White will be
happy to answer ...♘c4 with ♗xc4, keeping
the favourable minor piece for the
endgame.

13 ♘ed4 ♗b7!?

A slightly unusual development in these
positions. On the long diagonal the bishop
supports the possible manoeuvre ...♘d7-c5-
e4. Meanwhile Black clears the back rank in
preparation for his 16th move.

14 h4 ♘xd4 15 ♘xd4 b4 16 ♖h3

One of the points of h2-h4, though not
always appropriate. Better was 16 h5 and if
16...♖ae8 17 g4 f6?! 18 f5! or 17...Wb6 18
♗g2.

16...♖ae8!

Rather than wait while White prepares
f4-f5, Black plans to take the fight to his
opponent in the same sector with the move
...f7-f6.

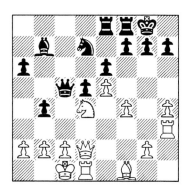

17 ♖e3 ♕b6 18 ♔b1 f6 19 ♘f3 a5 20 ♕d4?!

Trading queens is a routine plan when White controls the centre, but here it is inappropriate as White cannot maintain his control. With hindsight it looks better to support the f-pawn by 20 g3.

20...fxe5 21 ♘xe5

21 ♕xb6 ♘xb6 22 fxe5 ♘c4 is also fine for Black.

21...♕xd4 22 ♖xd4 ♘xe5 23 ♖xe5 ♖f5!

This is the point: White cannot maintain his grip on e5, for if 24 ♖ee1? ♖ef8 25 g3 Black has 25...e5! since the bishop on f1 is undefended.

24 a3?!

Voluntarily wrecking his own pawn structure. Better was 24 ♖xf5 exf5 25 ♔c1 and if 25...♖e4 26 c3 when the game should be drawn.

24...♖xe5 25 fxe5 bxa3 26 bxa3

Black has the initiative in the endgame since the white pawns are more scattered and vulnerable.

26...♗c6 27 g3 ♔f7 28 ♗d3 g6 29 ♔c1 ♔e7 30 ♔d2 ♖b8 31 ♖f4 ♗b5 32 ♗xb5 ♖xb5 33 h5?!

Seeking to create some weaknesses to attack but, more significantly, opening up a route for the black king to infiltrate. It was better to wait with 33 ♖a4 or 33 ♔d3.

33...gxh5 34 ♖h4 ♔f7 35 ♖xh5 ♔g6 36 ♖h4 ♖b7 37 ♖f4 ♖f7 38 ♖xf7?

Suicidal – White had to keep rooks on. It was preferable to sit tight with 38 ♖g4+ ♔h5 39 ♖a4 and if 39...♔g5 40 ♖xa5 ♔f5 41 ♖a4 ♔xe5 42 ♔e3.

38...♔xf7 39 ♔e3

White is a tempo short after 39 c4 dxc4 40 ♔c3 ♔g6 41 ♔xc4 ♔f5 42 a4 ♔xe5 43 ♔b5 ♔d5 44 ♔xa5 ♔c5! and the e-pawn quickly queens.

39...♔g6 40 ♔f4

Again if 40 ♔d4 ♔f5 41 a4 h5 42 ♔c5 (or 42 c3 ♔g4) 42...♔xe5 43 ♔b5 ♔d4 44 ♔xa5 ♔c5! and wins.

40...h5 41 a4 ♔h6 0-1

And White resigned since his king must give way after 42 c3 ♔g6 or 42 g4 h4 43 c3 ♔g6 44 g5 h3.

Game 60
Khalifman-Gulko
Reykjavik World Cup 1991

---

1 e4 e6 2 d4 d5 3 ♘c3 ♘f6 4 ♗g5 ♗e7 5 e5 ♘fd7 6 h4!?

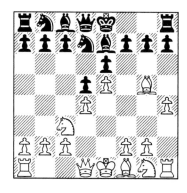

White offers a pawn in order to reduce Black's counterplay to a minimum. Albin, Alekhine and Chatard have all had their names attached to this move, although of the older players Bogolyubov and Euwe were more frequent adherents.

6...♗xg5

Acceptance is usually the critical test of a gambit, if not obligatory. The numerous declinations are seen in Games 61-63.

7 hxg5 ♕xg5 8 ♘h3

This is the usual move. White has tried others, e.g.

a) 8 ♕h5 ♕e7 9 ♕g4 f5 10 ♕h3 ♘f8 11 0-0-0 ♗d7 12 g4 fxg4 13 ♕xg4 ♘c6 14 ♖g5 ♖g8 15 ♘ge2 0-0-0 with no problems for Black in Velimirovic-Kovacevic, Yugoslavia 1989.

b) 8 ♘b5 ♕d8 9 ♕g4 g6 10 0-0-0 a6 11 ♘c3 c5 12 f4 ♘c6 13 dxc5 ♘xc5 14 ♘f3 ♗d7 15 ♖h6 ♕e7 16 ♗d3 0-0-0 17 ♕g5 ♕f8 18 ♕h4 ♔b8 19 ♔b1 ♖c8 20 ♖xh7 ♖xh7 21 ♕xh7 regaining the pawn, but Black had organised good queenside counterplay: 21...♘b4 22 ♕h1 ♘a4 23 ♘xa4 ♗xa4 24 b3? ♕c5 25 ♖c1? ♕a5 26 a3 ♗xb3 27 ♔b2 ♘xc2 0-1 Velimirovic-Antic, Yugoslav Team Championship 1999.

c) The most significant alternative is 8 ♕d3!?, an idea of GM Hector's which does not appear in any theoretical tome to date.

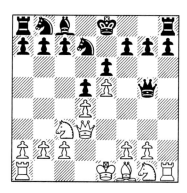

By hitting the h7-pawn White seeks to prompt ...g7-g6 and bind the kingside with ♖h6 before Black has time for ...h7-h5 (c.f. the note to 10...♘xd4 in the game). 8 ♕d3 is clearly set for a higher profile after its recent use (albeit in a rapidplay game) by the 13th World Champion. Three replies have been seen:

c1) 8...♘c6? 9 ♘f3 ♕g6 10 ♕xg6 fxg6 11 ♘b5 ♔e7 12 ♘xc7 ♖b8 13 ♘b5 ♘b6 14 c3 ♗d7 15 ♗d3 ♘a5 16 b3 ♗xb5 17 ♗xb5

h6 18 ♘h4 ♖hc8 19 ♖h3 g5 20 ♘g6+ ♔f7? (20...♔d8) 21 ♖f3+! ♔xg6 22 ♗d3+ (forcing mate) 22...♔h5 23 ♖h3+ ♔g4 24 f3+ ♔f4 25 ♔f2 g4 26 g3+ 1-0 Kasparov-Korchnoi, Zurich rapidplay 2001 (26...♔g5 27 f4 mate).

c2) 8...h5 9 ♘f3 ♕e7 10 g4 g6 11 gxh5 gxh5 12 ♕e3 ♘b6 13 0-0-0 ♗d7 14 ♗e2 ♘c6 15 ♕f4 0-0-0 16 ♖dg1 and White had full compensation for the pawn in Hector-Brynell, Gothenburg 1999.

c3) 8...g6 9 ♘f3 ♕e7 10 ♕e3 and then 10...♘c6 11 0-0-0 ♘b6 12 ♖h6 ♗d7 13 ♕g5 ♕xg5+ 14 ♘xg5 ♔e7 15 ♘xh7 ♖ac8 16 f4 ♘b8 17 ♗d3 ♘a4 18 ♘xa4 ♗xa4 19 ♖dh1 c5 20 dxc5 ♖xc5 21 ♘g5 ♖xh6 22 ♖xh6 ♗e8 (Hector-Brynell, Malmo 1993) when 23 ♗xg6! fxg6? 24 ♖h7+ ♔f8 25 ♖xb7 is strong. Black may do better with a standard plan: 10...a6! 11 0-0-0 c5 12 dxc5 (12 ♘e2!?) 12...♕xc5 13 ♘d4 ♘c6 14 f4 ♘xd4 15 ♖xd4 b5 16 ♕d2 ♗b7 17 ♖h3 ♘b6 18 ♘d1 ♖c8 19 ♘e3 ♘d7 20 ♗e2 ♕e7 21 ♗d3 ♕c5 22 ♗e2 with a draw in Nataf-Thorhallsson, Bermuda 1999.

8...♕e7

8...♕h6 is less reliable as after 9 g3 White can build a strong initiative by advancing the kingside pawns. This was shown in Riumin-Makogonov, USSR Championship 1934, following 9...c6 10 ♗d3 g6 11 f4 b6 12 ♕e2 a5 13 0-0-0 ♕g7 14 g4 ♗a6 15 f5 ♗xd3 16 ♕xd3 g5 17 ♕e3 h6 18 ♖h2 ♘f8 19 ♖dh1 ♖h7 20 ♘a4 ♘bd7 21 ♕c3 ♖c8 22 f6 ♕g6 23 ♘xb6 ♘xb6 24 ♕c5 ♖c7 25 ♕xb6 and White won. And again in Khalifman-Heyken, Germany 1993, 9...a6 10 f4 g6 11 ♕f3 ♕f8 12 0-0-0 ♘c6 13 f5!? ♘b6 (13...gxf5) 14 ♘g5 ♕g7 15 fxg6 ♕xg6 16 ♕f4 h6 17 ♗e2 ♘b4 18 ♖d2 ♔e7 19 ♘f3 ♗d7 20 ♕h4+ f6 21 a3 ♘c6 22 ♗d3 ♕g7 23 ♘e2 ♗e8 24 ♘f4 ♗f7 25 ♖e2 ♖af8 26 ♖he1 ♘d8 27 ♗f5 and White won quickly.

9 ♘f4

From f4 the knight may later sacrifice

itself on d5 or probe the kingside from h5. Black already needs to be careful. For instance, 9...f5? and 9...f6? are immediately refuted by 10 ♘g6, while the seemingly solid 9...♘f8?! was demolished in the famous game Alekhine-Fahrni, Mannheim 1914: 10 ♕xg4 (threatening ♕xg7 or ♘xd5) 10...f5 11 exf6 gxf6 12 0-0-0 c6 13 ♖e1 ♔d8 14 ♖h6 e5 15 ♕h4 ♘bd7 16 ♗d3 (16 ♘xd5 is also strong) 16...e4 17 ♕g3 ♕f7 18 ♗xe4 dxe4 19 ♘xe4 ♖g8 20 ♕a3 ♕g7 21 ♘d6 ♘b6 22 ♘e8 ♕f7 23 ♕d6+ 1-0.

Ever since Alekhine's game 9 ♘f4 has been considered the main line. However, Black has sorted out some good defences, so more attention has recently been given to other ideas for White, such as 8 ♕d3 above; or here 9 ♕g4!?, preparing quick castling, and then:

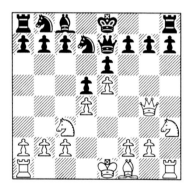

a) 9...f5 (not 9...f6? 10 ♘f4 ♘f8 11 ♘cxd5!) with a pleasant choice for White between 10 exf6!? ♘xf6 11 ♕g3 (Short) 11...♘c6 12 0-0-0 a6 13 ♘g5 ♕d6 14 f4 ♗d7 15 ♗d3 ♖g8 16 ♗xh7 ♘xh7 17 ♖xh7 ♕f8 18 ♕g4 ♕f6 19 f5 exf5 20 ♕h5+ g6 21 ♘xd5! and wins (Asanov-Hernando Rodrigo, Santa Clara 1999); 10 ♕g3 ♘c6 11 0-0-0 ♘f8 12 ♘f4 ♕f7 (12...♗d7 13 ♘fxd5!) 13 ♗e2 ♗d7 14 ♗h5! g6 15 ♗xg6 ♘xg6 16 ♕xg6 hxg6 17 ♖xh8+ ♔e7 18 ♖xa8 with an advantage (A.Ivanov-Crouch, Netherlands 1992); and 10 ♕h5+ g6 11 ♕h6 ♘f8 12 ♘f4 c6 13 0-0-0 b6 with a solid but passive position. In the latter variation Black is also worse after 10...♕f7 11 ♕xf7+ ♔xf7 12 ♘b5 ♘a6 13 ♘g5+ ♔e7 14 ♖xh7 ♖xh7 15 ♘xh7 ♘b6 16 ♘a3 ♗d7 17 ♗xa6 bxa6, as in Klip-Korchnoi, Dutch League 1992.

b) 9...g6! is more solid, offering a return to main lines after 10 ♘f4. However, White can deviate by 10 ♘g5!?, attacking h7 and leaving f4 free for the queen or f-pawn. 10...♘f8? loses to 11 ♘xd5, while after 10...h5 11 ♕f4 White can attack the h-pawn with g2-g4, as for example, in Bezgodov-Hmadi, Tunis 1997, which continued 11...♘c6 12 0-0-0 ♘b6 13 g4 ♗d7 14 gxh5 gxh5 15 ♗e2 0-0-0 16 ♖xh5 ♖xh5 17 ♗xh5 ♘c4 18 a3 (not 18 ♗xf7? ♕b4) 18...♖g8 (or 18...♖h8 19 ♗e2) 19 ♘h7 (not 19 ♘xf7? ♗e8) 19...♘6a5 20 ♗e2 f5 21 ♘f6 ♖g7 22 b4 c6 23 ♘b1! ♘xa3 24 ♘xa3 ♕xb4 25 ♘b1 and White won. No better is 11...c5? 12 ♘b5 or 11...a6 12 g4! c5 13 gxh5 cxd4 14 hxg6! ♖xh1 15 g7 wins.

In P.Adams-Tait, correspondence 2000-01, Black prepared ...c7-c5 by 11...♘f8!? (the idea is 12 g4 f6!) 12 0-0-0 a6 13 ♗d3 c5 14 dxc5 ♘c6, but White exploited the time-consuming nature of this plan by sacrificing for an impressive win: 15 ♖he1 ♕xc5 16 ♘xf7! ♘dxe5 17 ♖xe5 ♘xe5 18 ♕xe5 ♔xf7 19 ♘e4! ♕e7 20 ♘d6+ ♔g8 21 ♗xg6 ♕g7 22 ♕xh5 ♖xf2 23 ♘e8! ♕h8 24 ♕g5 ♗d7 25 ♘c7 ♖c8 26 ♘xd5! exd5 27 ♕xd5+ ♔g7 28 ♕xd7+ ♔xg6 29 ♕g4+! ♔f7 30 ♖d7+ ♔f8 31 ♕b4+ ♔g8 32 ♕b3+ ♔f8 33 ♕a3+ 1-0 as Black finally saw that mate follows 33...♔g8 34 ♕g3+ ♔f8 35 ♕xf2+ etc.

Another try is 10...h6!? 11 ♗d3 ♘c6 (still not 11...♘f8? 12 ♘xd5) 12 0-0-0 ♘f8 13 ♘f3 (instead 13 ♖h4 ♘xd4!? 14 ♘xf7 ♔xf7 15 ♕xd4 ♕g5+ is unclear) 13...♗d7 14 ♖h2 0-0-0 15 ♖dh1 h5 16 ♕f4 with a kingside bind in Bartel-Ulibin, Bydgoszcz 2001, although White let it slip following 16...♖g8 17 ♘g5?! ♗e8 18 ♗b5?! ♘xd4 19 ♕xd4

♕xg5+ 20 f4 ♕h6 21 ♗xe8 ♖xe8 22 g4
♘d7 23 gxh5?! g5! 24 ♖xa7 gxf4 25 ♘a4
f3+ 26 ♔b1 b6 27 ♕a8+ ♘b8 28 c4? ♕e3
0-1.

White can also consider 12 ♘xf7!? ♔xf7
13 ♗xg6 ♔g7 (if 13...♔g8 14 ♗h5+ ♔f8 15
♕f4+ or 13...♔f8 14 0-0-0) 14 ♖h5! with
good compensation for the piece. Play
might continue 14...♘d8 15 0-0-0 ♘f7 16 f4
♔f8 17 f5, or 14...♘f8 15 ♗e8+! ♔h7 16
0-0-0 (threatening ♖xh6+) 16...♕g7 17 ♕h3,
or 14...♔g8 15 0-0-0 ♘f8 16 ♗e8+ ♕g7 17
♕h3 ♗d7 18 ♗xd7 ♕xd7 19 ♖d3.

9...♘c6!

This move has caused White the most
problems. Although the knight blocks the c-
pawn, the pawn break is not ruled out
altogether – Black hopes to consolidate by
...♘b6, ...♗d7 and ...0-0-0, after which the
c6-knight can move and ...c7-c5 advanced.

Furthermore, Black has trouble with an
early ...c7-c5, firstly because of the familiar
knight sally to b5, but also because of
potential white sacrifices on d5.

For example, if 9...a6 10 ♕g4 g6 11 0-0-0
c5? 12 ♕g3! (not yet 12 ♘cxd5? exd5 13
♘xd5 ♘b6!) 12...cxd4 13 ♘cxd5! exd5 14
♘xd5 ♕c5 15 c4! (threatening 16 e6 or 16
b4) with a very dangerous attack, or
12...♘b6 13 dxc5 ♕xc5 14 ♗d3
(threatening ♗xg6) 14...♕f8 15 ♗e4!
(threatening ♗xd5) 15...dxe4 16 ♘xe4
♘8d7 (Bogolyubov-Spielmann, Stockholm

1919) when 17 ♘d6+! ♔d8 (or 17...♔e7 18
♕h4+) 18 ♘h3! intending ♘g5 is strong.
White also gained a clear advantage after
11...♘b6 12 ♗d3 ♘8d7 13 ♖h6 ♘f8 14
♔b1! ♗d7 15 ♘h5! 0-0-0 16 ♘f6 in
Müllner-Iqbal Ahmed, correspondence
1989. 15...f5 16 exf6 gxh5 17 ♕g7 was no
better, while if 15...gxh5 16 ♕g7 ♘g6 17
♗xg6 because if ♔b1 Black does not have
the resource 17...♕g5+.

Sometimes Black plays first 9...g6 to
prevent ♘h5 and in advance of ♕g4.
However, White can exploit this move
order by 10 ♗d3! threatening 11 ♗xg6, as
for example in Goldberg-Bohn, German
Bundesliga 1994: 10...♘b6 11 ♗xg6! ♘c6
(or 11...♕g5 12 ♖h5! ♕xf4 13 g3) 12 ♗xh7
♕g5 13 g3 ♗d7 (or 13...♕f5 14 ♕h5) and
now 14 ♕d3! 0-0-0 (if 14...♕g7 15 ♘h5! or
14...♘b4 15 ♕e2 ♕f5 16 ♖h5) 15 0-0-0
♕g7 16 ♘ce2 intending c2-c3, ♕c2
consolidates. Or 10...♕g5 11 ♕d2 a6 12
♗xg6! ♘xe5 (12...fxg6 13 ♘xe6) 13 ♖h5
♘c4 (if 13...♘f3+ 14 gxf3! ♕g1+ 15 ♔e2
♕xa1 16 ♗xf7+! ♔xf7 17 ♘fxd5! wins –
Baburin) 14 ♖xg5 ♘xd2 15 ♗d3 ♘c4 16
♘cxd5! exd5 17 ♘xd5 ♘b6 18 ♘xc7+ ♔f8
19 ♘xa8 ♘xa8 20 ♔d2 and White won in
the game Velimirovic-Stojanovic, Yugoslav
Championship 1996. Even worse is
10...♘f8? due to the familiar 11 ♘cxd5!
exd5 12 ♘xd5 ♕d8 13 ♘f6+ ♔e7 14 ♕f3
c6 15 0-0-0 ♗e6 16 d5! and wins (Banas-
Kafka, Czechoslovakia 1975).

10 ♕g4

This involves sacrificing the d-pawn. If
White does not want to do that then 10
♕d3 should be chosen, when 10...g6 11
0-0-0 ♘b6 12 ♕g3 h5! transposes to 10
♕g4 g6 11 0-0-0 h5 12 ♕g3 ♘b6 in the
next note.

Other moves are easier on Black. After
10 ♗b5 ♕b4! 11 ♘fe2 (if 11 ♗xc6 bxc6 12
a3 ♕c4 or 12 ♖h3 ♖b8 intending ...c7-c5)
11...♕xb2 12 a3 ♘xd4 13 ♖a2 ♘xc2+ 14
♔f1 ♕b3 15 ♖xc2 a6 16 ♘d4 ♕xa3 17

♖h3 ♕b4 and Black was clearly better in Hellsten-Brynell, Malmo 1995. Or if 10 ♕d2 Black need not weaken the kingside but can play 10...b6 (or 10...♘f8!? intending ...♗d7) 11 ♘b5 (if 11 ♘h5 ♖g8 12 ♗d3 ♘f8) 11...♘f8 12 ♘h5 ♖g8 13 0-0-0 a6 14 ♘c3 ♗b7 15 f4 0-0-0 16 g4 f6 17 g5 f5 and Black slowly consolidated in R.Watson-Giulian, correspondence 1984-85.

10...♘xd4!

Black can avoid complications by playing 10...g6. Following 11 0-0-0 White intends to blockade the h-pawn by ♖h6 and build up on the kingside. This plan, if allowed, gives White more than enough for the pawn, for instance 11...♘b6 (not 11...b6? 12 ♘cxd5! exd5 13 ♘xd5 ♕d8 14 e6 or 11...♘f8 12 ♕g3 ♕b4 13 ♗b5 ♗d7? 14 ♘xd5! and wins) 12 ♖h6 ♗d7 13 ♗b5 and then if 13...0-0-0 14 ♗xc6 ♗xc6 15 ♖dh1 and White regains the pawn with advantage; similarly 13...♘a5 14 ♖dh1, or if 13...♘b4 14 ♗xd7+ ♘xd7 15 ♖dh1 ♘f8 16 a3 ♘a6 17 ♘b5! ♕d7 18 a4 ♘b4 19 ♘h5! gxh5 20 ♕g7 with a clear advantage to White in Loskutov-Iljushin, St Petersburg 2000.

So Black should play 11...h5! to block the h-file. This advance is often risky because it loosens the kingside pawn structure, setting Black up for sacrifices either on g6 or for the sequence ♘fxd5 e6xd5, ♘xd5 ♕d8, e5-e6! But here the sacrifices don't work: after 12 ♕g3 ♘b6 13 ♗d3 ♗d7 then if 14 ♗xg6? ♖g8 or 14 ♘xg6? fxg6 15 ♗xg6+ ♔d8 16 ♖xh5 ♖xh5 17 ♗xh5 ♔c8 intending ...♔b8, ...a7-a6, ...♔a7 and Black keeps the extra piece. White probably has to be content with 12 ♕f3 ♘b6 13 g4 h4 14 ♘h3 ♗d7 15 g5 0-0-0 16 ♕f4 intending ♘g1-f3 (Sax) with a level game.

11 0-0-0

If 11 ♕xg7?! ♕f8 and White remains a pawn down, e.g. 12 ♕xf8+ ♔xf8 13 0-0-0 c5 14 ♖h5 ♘c6 15 ♖e1 a6 16 ♘h3 b5 17 f4 h6 18 g4 f6 19 exf6 ♘xf6 20 ♖h4 (Beake-Tait, Notts League 1998) and now 20...♘e7!

intending ...♘g6 with a clear advantage.

11...♘f5

Black has another option in 11...c5!?, when the sacrifice is unsound: 12 ♘fxd5? exd5 13 ♘xd5 ♕xe5! and if 14 ♗b5 ♔f8! 15 ♗xd7 f5 or 14 ♖h5 f5! wins. White does have some unexpected tricks after 14 ♗c4!?, e.g. 14...0-0? 15 ♖xh7! and wins or 14...♘b6 15 ♕h4 ♘xc4 16 ♖he1 0-0 (if 16...♘e2+ 17 ♖xe2 ♕xe2 18 ♘c7+) 17 ♖xe5 ♘xe5 18 ♘e7+ ♔h8 19 ♕xh7+! mating, but in the latter line 15...♕d6! is strong, or even 14...♔f8!?

Black also has the advantage after 12 ♖e1 ♕f8, or 12 ♗b5 ♘xb5 13 ♘xb5 ♔f8, or 12 ♖xd4 cxd4 13 ♘b5 ♔f8. So White must play 12 ♕xg7 ♕f8 13 ♕g5! with some compensation.

12 ♘fxd5!

White has to sacrifice further to justify his play. Not, however, 12 ♘cxd5? due to 12...♘xe5!

12...exd5

Black must accept as 12...♘xe5? 13 ♕a4+ ♗d7 14 ♘xe7 ♗xa4 15 ♘xf5 or 12...♕c5? 13 b4 ♕xf2 14 ♘e4 ♕e3 15 ♘xc7+! ♔f8 16 ♘xf2 wins for White, while if 12...♕d8 13 ♘e3! ♘xe3 (13...g6 14 ♘xf5 exf5 15 ♕d4) 14 ♕xg7 (14 fxe3!?) 14...♘xd1 15 ♕xh8+ ♔e7 16 ♕xd8+ ♔xd8 17 ♔xd1 ♘xe5 18 ♖xh7 with advantage.

13 ♘xd5

Not 13 ♕xf5? ♘b6.

13...♕xe5!

Very few players have had the nerve to play this move, but it is certainly best. Not 13...♕c5? 14 ♕xf5 ♘b6 15 e6 ♗xe6 16 ♘f6+ wins, while if 13...♘xe5 White has a choice of promising lines:

a) 14 ♕e4 ♕d6 (14...♘d6 15 ♕e3) 15 f4 c6 (15...♗e6 16 fxe5 ♗xd5 17 ♖xd5 ♕e6 18 ♖d3) 16 ♘b6! ♕b8 (16...♘g3 17 ♕e3) 17 ♘xc8 ♖xc8 18 ♗d3.

b) 14 ♕a4+ ♗d7 15 ♗b5 ♕d6 (15...♗xb5 16 ♕xb5+ c6 17 ♘xe7 cxb5 18 ♘xf4) 16 ♗xd7+ ♘xd7 17 ♘b6 ♕xb6 18 ♕xd7+ ♔f8 19 ♕xf5 with the advantage, e.g. 19...♕e6 20 ♕xe6 fxe6 21 ♖d7 ♖e8 22 ♖hd1 ♖e7 23 ♖d8+ ♖e8 24 ♖1d7.

c) 14 ♕e2 ♕d6 15 f4 ♘g3 (not 15...f6? 16 fxe5 fxe5 17 ♕h5+) 16 ♕e3 ♘xh1 (16...♘xf1!? 17 ♖hxf1 ♗e6) 17 fxe5 ♕d8 (17...♕h6!?) 18 ♘f6+ gxf6 19 ♖xd8+ ♔xd8 20 ♕d4+ ♔e8 21 ♗b5+ c6 22 exf6 ♗d7 (not 22...♘g3 23 ♕d6 ♘f5 24 ♗xc6+) 23 ♗d3 (Timmerman-Carleton, correspondence 1992-93) when Black had to try 23...♘g3 24 ♕d6 (or 24 ♕e5+) 24...♔d8 25 ♕xg3 (Cimmino) with two rooks for the queen, e.g. 25...♗e6 26 ♕d6+ ♔c8 27 ♗xh7 ♖d8 28 ♕a3 ♔c7.

14 ♗b5!

The only move. 14 ♘xc7+? ♕xc7 15 ♕xf5 ♘f6, 14 ♗c4? ♘f6 and 14 ♗d3? ♘f6 are winning for Black, while if 14 f4 ♘f6 15 fxe5 (not 15 ♗b5+? c6 16 ♕f3 ♕b8!) 15...♘xg4 16 ♘xc7+ ♔e7 17 ♘xa8 ♘f2 regains the rook with advantage.

14...0-0 15 ♗xd7

Black is also okay after 15 f4 ♕e6 16 ♕xf5 ♕xf5 17 ♘e7+ ♔h8 18 ♘xf5 ♘f6 or 15 ♖he1 ♘f6 16 ♕c4 ♕xd5! 17 ♖xd5 ♘xd5 18 ♕xd5 c6 with rook, bishop and knight for the queen.

15...♘h6?!

Black could have played for a win with 15...♗xd7 16 ♕h5 f6! (Gulko) since if 17 ♕xh7+? ♔f7 18 ♕h5+ g6 19 ♕h7+ ♘g7 he keeps the piece, i.e. 20 ♘b6 (20 ♖he1 ♖h8,

20 f4 ♕f5) 20...♗g4 21 ♘xa8 ♗xd1 22 ♖xd1 ♕f5 23 ♕h2 ♖xa8 24 ♕xc7+ ♔g8. Or if 17 ♖he1 ♘g3! 18 ♕xe5 (18 ♖xe5? ♘xh5 19 ♖xh5 ♗g4) 18...fxe5 19 ♘e7+ (19 fxg3 ♗g4) 19...♔f7 20 ♖xd7 ♔e6 21 ♖d5 ♖xf2 22 ♖dxe5 ♔f7 still with the extra pawn.

16 ♕g3

White can win the queen after 16 ♕h4 ♗xd7 17 ♖he1 ♘f5 18 ♕h5 ♕d6 19 ♘e7+ ♘xe7 20 ♖xd6 cxd6 21 ♖xe7 ♗c6 though is unlikely to make any progress against the rook and bishop. With 16 ♕g3 White gives up his attack to regain the pawn and there is nothing left to play for.

16...♕xg3 17 ♘e7+ ♔h8 18 fxg3 ♗xd7 19 ♖xd7 ♘g4 20 ♖xc7 b5 21 ♖h4 ♘f6 22 ♘f5 a6 23 a4 ½-½

Game 61
Nataf-Ulibin
Stockholm Rilton Cup 1999

---

1 e4 e6 2 d4 d5 3 ♘c3 ♘f6 4 ♗g5 ♗e7 5 e5 ♘fd7 6 h4 c5

This is the critical declination. Black ignores the bishop on g5 and plays to undermine the enemy centre straightaway. The one drawback is that ...c7-c5 weakens the queenside dark squares which White can probe with ♘b5.

7 ♗xe7!

This is a useful preliminary to the knight

sally. White intends to follow up with ♘b5 only after the natural recapture 7...♕xe7.

The immediate 7 ♘b5? allows Black to attack the centre by 7...f6! If 8 exf6 ♘xf6 White has lost the d6-outpost, while 9 ♗f4 0-0 10 ♘c7 fails to 10...♘d8. Black is also for preference after 9 dxc5 ♗xc5 10 ♗d3 0-0 or 9 ♘f3 ♘c6 and 10...a6.

For this reason White has attempted to justify the line by sacrificial means: 8 ♗d3 intending 8...fxg5 9 ♕h5+ ♔f8 10 hxg5 ♗xg5? 11 ♘d6. However, Black can refute this by 8...a6 9 ♕h5+ ♔f8 and then if 10 ♖h3 axb5 11 ♗h6 ♘xe5! (making room for the king; 11... ♕c7 is also good) 12 dxe5 (if 12 ♗xg7+ ♔xg7 13 ♖g3+ ♔f8) 12...gxh6 13 ♖f3 c4 14 ♕xh6+ (or 14 exf6 cxd3 15 fxe7+ ♔xe7 16 ♖f7+ ♔d6 17 ♘f3 ♘c6) 14...♗e8 15 ♕g7 ♖f8 16 ♗xh7 ♕c7 17 exf6 ♕e5+ and Black wins (Zlotnik). No better is 10 ♘d6 ♗xd6 11 exd6 cxd4 12 ♗xh7 ♘e5 13 ♗f4 ♕xd6 14 ♘e2 ♘bc6 15 0-0-0 ♗d7 16 ♗xe5 ♘xe5 17 f4 ♗e8 18 fxe5 ♗xh5 19 exd6 ♖xh7 20 ♖d2 ♗xe2 21 ♖xe2 ♔f7 and Black won in Murey-Bricard, Paris 1994.

Nor is 7 ♕g4 effective, due to 7...♔f8! 8 ♘f3 (or 8 ♗xe7 ♕xe7 9 ♘b5 cxd4 10 ♘c7? ♘xe5) 8...♘c6 9 ♕f4 (or 9 ♘b5 cxd4) 9...cxd4 10 ♘b5 after either 10...♕a5!? 11 ♔d1 h6 12 ♗xe7+ ♔xe7 (Zlotnik) or 10...f6! 11 exf6 ♘xf6 12 ♘bxd4 ♗d6 (Stetsko).

7...♔xe7!

After 7...♕xe7?! White proceeds with 8 ♘b5! aiming at c7 and d6. Black can prevent ♘c7 by ...♔d8 or ...♕d8, but both 8...♔d8 9 f4 and 8...♕d8 9 ♘d6+ ♔e7 are just inferior versions of 7...♔xe7. So Black has tried to justify the variation by sacrificing the exchange at a8. The direct 8...cxd4 9 ♘c7+ ♔d8 10 ♘xa8 ♘c6 (if 10...♕b4+ 11 ♕d2) 11 ♘f3 ♕b4+ 12 ♕d2 ♕xd2+ (or 12...♕xb2 13 ♖d1) 13 ♔xd2 ♘xe5 14 ♘xe5 ♘xe5 (Kraatz-Stader, correspondence 1983) and now 15 ♖h3 (Nogueiras and Sieiro) intending ♖a3 wins for White. So Black has concentrated upon

8...0-0 9 ♘c7 cxd4 10 ♘xa8. Unfortunately no continuation seems satisfactory for Black:

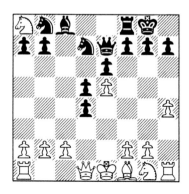

a) 10...♕b4+ 11 ♕d2 ♕xb2 12 ♖d1 ♘c6 13 ♘f3 ♗c5 14 ♗d3 ♗d7 15 ♘c7 ♖c8 16 ♘xd5! exd5 17 0-0 ♗g4 (17...♖xa2 18 ♕f4) 18 ♕f4 ♗xf3 19 ♕xf3 ♘xd3 20 cxd3 ♕xa2 21 ♖a1 ♕d2 22 ♕xd5 (Keller-Heidenfeld, Enschede 1961) and if 22...♕xd3 23 e6!

b) 10...♘c6 11 ♘f3 f6 12 ♘xd4 ♘dxe5 (if 12...fxe5 13 ♘xe6! ♕xe6 14 ♘c7 and 15 ♕xd5) 13 ♗e2 ♘xd4 14 ♕xd4 ♘c6 15 ♕d2 ♕d6 16 0-0 ♗d7 17 c4 d4 18 b4 ♖xa8 19 c5 ♕d5 20 ♗f3 ♕c4 21 ♖fc1 ♕xb4 22 ♕xb4 ♘xb4 23 ♗xb7 (Zezulkin-Malorov, Krasnodar 1998).

c) 10...f6 11 ♕xd4 ♘c6 (11...fxe5 12 ♕d2) 12 ♕d2 fxe5 13 0-0-0 ♘f6 14 f3 ♕d6 15 ♘h3 (or 15 ♘e2 ♗d7 16 ♘c3 ♖xa8 17 ♘e4) 15...♗d7 16 ♗b5 ♖xa8 17 ♖he1 and White is better; i.e. 17...♘d4 18 ♗xd7 ♘xd7 19 f4 ♘c6 20 ♔b1 ♕e7 21 f5 d4 22 fxe6 ♕xe6 23 ♘g5 ♕d5 24 c3 ♘f6 25 cxd4 ♘xd4? (25...exd4) 26 ♘f3 ♘xf3 27 ♕xd5+ ♘xd5 28 gxf3 ♖d8 29 ♔a1 1-0 Vitolins-Koopmann, Porz 1991.

d) 10...♘xe5 11 ♕xd4 ♘bc6 (11...♘ec6 12 ♕d2 e5 13 0-0-0 ♗e6 14 f4) 12 ♕d2 ♕d6 (12...b6 13 ♗e2 ♗b7 14 ♘xb6 axb6 15 ♘f3) 13 ♗e2 ♗d7 14 h5 f6 15 0-0-0 ♘f7 16 f4 ♖xa8 17 ♘f3 (Khalifman-Levin, Riga 1988).

8 f4

This has always been the standard plan for White, hoping to show that the awkwardness of Black's ...♔e7 outweighs the now wasted move 6 h4 in 6 ♗xe7 ♕xe7 7 f4 type positions. However, White has not managed to prove an advantage with this plan. It may be because other players foresaw Ulibin's novelty on move 10 that White has tried doing without f2-f4. This leaves the e5-pawn vulnerable but, if captured, White obtains open lines and attacking chances against the black king. To this end four moves have been ventured:

a) 8 ♘f3 cxd4 9 ♕xd4 ♘c6 and after 10 ♕f4 ♕c7 11 0-0-0 ♘dxe5 (threatening ...♘d3+) 12 ♕g3 (or 12 ♔b1 ♕b8) 12...♔f8 13 ♘b5 ♕b8 14 ♘xe5 ♕xe5 15 f4 ♕f6 Black was better in Chigvintsev-Ulibin, Tomsk 1997. White has also tried 10 ♕d2 ♘dxe5 11 ♘xe5 ♘xe5 12 0-0-0 f6 13 g4 ♗d7 14 f4 ♘c6 15 ♘xd5+!? exd5 16 ♕xd5 ♕c7 17 ♗c4 ♖ae8 18 ♕f7+ ♔d8 19 ♖xd7+ ♕xd7 20 ♖d1 ♘d4 21 ♕xd7+ ♔xd7 22 ♗b5+ ♔c7 23 ♗xe8 ♘e2+ 24 ♔d2 ♘xf4 with a level endgame in Manca-Gleizerov, Montecatini Terme 1997.

b) 8 ♕g4 ♔f8 9 ♘f3! cxd4 (or 9...♘c6 10 ♕f4) and then 10 ♘b5 ♘c6 11 ♕f4 ♕a5+ (if 11...f6 12 exf6 ♘xf6 13 ♘c7! ♕xf4 14 ♘xe6+ regains the pawn with advantage) 12 ♔d1 ♕b6 13 g4! (preparing 14 ♘d6 f6 15 exf6 ♘xf6 16 g5) 13...h6 14 ♖g1 g5 15 hxg5 hxg5 16 ♕xg5 a6 17 ♘d6 gave White a very

strong attack in Loskutov-Chuprikov, Smolensk 2000. The game ended abruptly 17...♘cxe5? 18 ♘xe5 ♕xd6 19 ♕d8+ ♔g7 20 ♕xh8+! 1-0. No better is 13...♔g8 14 ♘d6 f6 15 exf6 ♘xf6 16 g5 ♕xb2 17 ♖c1 e5 (the only move) 18 ♘xe5 ♘xe5 19 ♕xe5 ♗g4+ 20 f3! ♗xf3 21 ♗e2 ♗xe2 22 ♕xe2 ♘e4 23 ♘xe4 dxe4 24 ♕c4+ and wins.

White can also try 10 ♕xd4 ♕b6 11 ♕f4!? (if 11 ♕xb6 axb6! 12 0-0-0 ♘c6 13 ♖e1 d4 14 ♘b5 ♖xa2) 11...♕xb2 12 ♔d2! ♕xa1?! (12...♘c6 13 ♖b1 ♕a3 is safer) 13 ♘g5! when Black's defence consists of a string of only moves: 13...♘xe5 14 ♕xe5 ♘c6 15 ♕d6+ ♔g8 16 ♕c7 ♗d7 17 ♕xd7 ♘e5 18 ♕c7 b5! 19 ♕xe5 b4 (or 19 a3 a5). So perhaps 8...♘c6 is better, when 9 dxc5 ♔f8 10 f4 ♕a5 (intending ...d5-d4), 9 ♕xg7 ♘xd4, or 9 ♕g5+ ♔f8 10 ♕xd7+ ♘xd8 11 f4 b6! (Situru-Hübner, Yerevan Olympiad 1996) don't offer White anything. Instead 9 ♘f3! cxd4 10 ♘b5 ♔f8 11 ♕f4 or 10...♕a5+ 11 ♔d1 ♔f8 12 ♕f4 returns to 8...♔f8 above, but Black might try 10...♕f8!? 11 ♕f4 ♔d8 12 0-0-0 f6.

c) 8 ♕h5!? ♘c6 9 dxc5 and now rather than 9...♘dxe5 10 0-0-0 g6?! 11 ♕h6 f6 12 ♕g7+ ♘f7 13 ♘e4 f5 14 ♘g5 ♕f8 15 ♕c3 with a clear advantage to White in Frolov-Gleizerov, St Petersburg 1995, Black should prefer 9...♕a5 10 0-0-0 (if 10 ♕g5+ ♔f8 or 10 ♗b5 ♘dxe5 11 0-0-0 d4) 10...d4 11 ♘b5 (11 ♘b1 ♕xa2) 11...♕xa2 12 ♕g5+ ♔f8 13 ♘xd4 h6! 14 ♕f4 ♘dxe5 with an unclear position.

d) 8 dxc5!? ♘xe5 9 ♕e2 was Sakaev-Ulibin, Dubai 2000, which continued 9...♘bc6 10 0-0-0 ♔f8 11 f4 ♘d7 12 ♘f3 ♘xc5 13 ♔b1 (13 f5!?) 13...b5 14 ♕e3 ♕b6 15 ♖xd5 exd5 16 ♘xd5 ♕d8 17 ♕xc5+ ♘e7 18 ♘c3 a6 19 ♗e2 ♗e6?! 20 ♖d1 ♕c8 21 ♕b4 h5 22 ♘d4 ♖h6 23 ♗f3 ♖a7 24 f5 ♗c4 25 ♘c6 ♖xc6 26 ♗xc6 ♔g8 27 ♗e4 ♘xf5 28 ♕a5 ♖d7 29 ♖xd7 ♕xd7 30 b3 ♗f1 31 ♕xa6 and White won; but 19...♗b7 20 ♖d1 ♕c8 would have held for Black.

Gormally-Summerscale, York Vikings 2000, saw instead 12...♕e7!? 13 g4 (13 f5!?) 13...h5 14 g5 g6 15 ♘e5 ♘dxe5 16 fxe5 ♕xc5 17 ♗g2 ♘d4 18 ♕d3 ♘f3 and Black consolidated his defences.

Black can also decline the pawn by 8...♘c6, when 9 f4, 9 ♕g4 and 9 ♕h5 transpose to 8 f4 ♘c6, 8 ♕g4 ♘c6 and 8 ♕h5 ♘c6 respectively, while 9 ♕e2 ♕a5! or 9 ♘f3 ♘dxe5 10 ♘xe5 ♘xe5 11 ♕e2 ♘c6 12 0-0-0 ♔f8 are unclear.

8...♕b6

Black has two other reliable moves:

a) 8...♘c6 9 dxc5 (if 9 ♘f3 a6 10 ♕d2 b5 prepares a queenside initiative) 9...♕a5! (better than 9...♗xc5 10 ♕g4! ♔f8 11 0-0-0 with advantage) 10 ♕d2 (or 10 ♘f3 ♗xc5 11 ♕d2) 10...♗xc5 11 ♘f3 ♖d8 12 ♘d4 ♔f8 13 0-0-0 ♕b6! 14 h5 ♘e4 15 ♕e3 ♘xd4 16 ♘xd4 ♘xc3 (not 16...♘g3? 17 ♘a4! ♕d4 18 ♕d4 ♘h1 19 f5) 17 ♕xc3 ♔g8 and Black was okay in Tait-Micklethwaite, correspondence 2000-01.

b) 8...cxd4 9 ♕xd4 ♕b6 (if 9...♘c6 10 ♕d2 Black is merely behind on 8...♘c6 9 dxc5 with ♕d2) 10 ♕xb6 (if 10 ♕d2!? ♕xb2! 11 ♖b1 ♕a3 12 ♖b3 ♕a5 13 ♖b5 ♕d8 14 f5 ♘c6 is safe enough) 10...♘xb6 White has a nominal advantage though all the games have been drawn, e.g. 11 h5 h6 12 ♘b5 ♘c6 13 ♘f3 ♗d7 14 b3 a6 15 ♘bd4 ♘xd4 16 ♘xd4 ♘c8 17 ♔d2 ♘a7 18 c3 ½-½ Nunn-Seirawan, Cannes rapidplay 1992.

9 ♘a4

Again White has alternatives:

a) 9 ♘f3 allows Black to force a draw by 9...♕xb2! 10 ♘b5 a6 11 ♖b1 (11 ♘c7? ♕c3+ 12 ♔f2 ♖a7) 11...♕xa2 12 ♖a1 ♕b2 13 ♖b1 etc. as in Maksimovic-Ulibin, Chelyabinsk 1990. Instead 10...♕b4+ 11 ♔f2 a6 12 ♘c7 ♖a7 13 c4 ♔d8! leads to very interesting play, e.g. 14 cxd5 ♔xc7 15 a3 ♕a5 16 d6+!? ♔d8 17 d5 intending ♘g5 (Nogueiras and Sieiro), or 14 ♘xd5 exd5 15 cxd5 cxd4 16 ♖c1!? (Minev) 16...b6 17 ♖c4

♕a3 18 ♕c2 ♕e3+ 19 ♔g3 ♘c5 20 ♖xd4 ♖c7 21 ♗c4 ♗b7 22 ♖e1 ♕a3 23 ♕f5 b5 24 d6 bxc4? 25 dxc7+ ♔xc7 26 ♕xf7+ ♔b6 27 ♖xc4 ♘bd7 28 ♖b1+ 1-0 Wibe-J.Szalai, correspondence 1994.

b) 9 ♖h3!? defends the ♘c3, rendering 9...♕xb2? suicidal because of 10 ♖b1 ♕a3 11 ♘xd5+ and wins. But other moves are more than okay for Black: e.g. 9...cxd4 10 ♘b5 d3 11 ♕xd3 ♕xg1 12 ♕g3 ♘c6 13 ♕xg7 ♖f8 14 ♕xh7 ♘c5 15 0-0-0 ♘e4; or 9...♘c6 10 dxc5 ♘xc5 11 ♘ge2 ♖d8! 12 ♘d4 ♕b4! 13 ♘xc6 bxc6 14 ♕d2 ♕b8 15 b3 d4 and Black stood better in Tait-P.Adams, correspondence 2000-01.

9...♕a5+

9...♕c6 10 ♘xc5 ♘xc5 11 dxc5 ♕xc5 12 ♕d2 ♘c6 13 ♘f3 ♗d7 14 h5 h6 15 0-0-0 ♖ac8 16 ♔b1 ♕a5 17 ♕xa5 ♘xa5 is not so bad for Black either. It was not because of the opening that White won in Velimirovic-Miljanic, Yugoslav Team Championship 1992.

10 c3

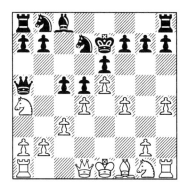

10...b6!

Black prepares the exchange of light-squared bishops by ...♗a6. This is a typical device in the French, so it is perhaps surprising that 10...b6 was actually a novelty here.

10...♘c6 was Black's choice previously, when Keres proposed the following pawn sacrifice: 11 ♘f3 cxd4 (not 11...b5? 12

♘xc5 ♘xc5 13 dxc5 b4 14 ♘d4!) 12 b4!
♘xb4 (declining the pawn by 12...♕c7 13
♘xd4 a6 14 ♖h3 gives Black a very passive
position) 13 cxb4 ♕xb4+ 14 ♔f2 b5 15
♗xb5 ♕xb5 16 ♘xd4 ♕a6?! 17 ♕b3 with a
strong attack for White. R.Hall-Valerio,
correspondence 1993-95, quickly concluded
17...♗b7 (if 17...f6 18 ♖hc1 fxe5 19 ♖c6) 18
♕b4+ ♔d8 19 ♖hc1 ♖c8 20 ♖xc8+ ♔xc8 21
♖c1+ 1-0, since after 21...♔d8 (21...♔b8 22
♖xc6) 22 ♘xc5 ♘xc5 23 ♖xc5 and 24 ♖a5
♕c4 25 ♕d6 ♔e8 26 ♘e2 wins.

Black can improve with 16...♕c4!?
(preventing ♕b3) and then if 17 ♖h3!
(intending ♖c3) 17...♘b6! 18 ♘b2 ♕c5 19
♖c1 ♘c4, but it is easier not to enter this
line at all.

11 ♔f2

White can prevent ....♗a6 by playing
either 11 a3 or 11 ♖b1, since if 11...♗a6??
12 b4 wins the queen. However, after
11...c4! the threat of ...b6-b5 forces White to
re-open the queenside by 12 b4 and Black is
fine after the *en passant* capture, e.g. 11 a3 c4
12 b4 cxb3 13 ♕xb3 ♗a6 14 ♗xa6 ♘xa6
15 ♘e2 ♖hc8 16 0-0 g6 17 ♘b2 b5 18 ♘d3
♕a4! 19 ♕b1 ♘b6 20 ♕e1 ♘c4 with
advantage to Black in A.Hunt-Sarkar, Witley
1999.

**11...♗a6 12 ♘f3 ♗xf1 13 ♖xf1 ♘c6 14
♔g1 g6**

Black emphasises the solidity of his
position, ruling out any f4-f5 breaks.

15 b3

Preparing a2-a3. If immediately 15 a3
then Black plays 15...c4 again.

15...♖ac8 16 a3 cxd4 17 cxd4

Not 17 ♘xd4? b5.

17...b5 18 ♘c5 ♘xc5 19 b4

After 19 dxc5 ♕c3! 20 b4 a5 attacks the
pawn chain. 21 ♕e1 ♕xe1 22 ♖fxe1 axb4
23 axb4 ♖a8 does not ease the pressure,
while if 21 ♕e2 axb4 22 ♖fc1, intending
22...♕b3 23 a4!? bxa4 24 ♖ab1 with
perpetual against the queen, Black has the
resource 22...♘d4! keeping the advantage.

19...♕a4!

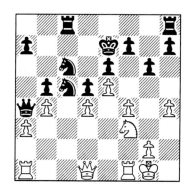

Black gains the initiative on the
queenside after the queen exchange.

20 bxc5

Or 20 dxc5 ♕xd1 21 ♖fxd1 ♖c7 22 ♘d4
♘xd4 23 ♖xd4 a5 intending ...♖a8 and
...♖ca7 when Black will invade down the a-
file.

**20...♕xd1 21 ♖fxd1 ♖b8 22 ♖db1 ♖b7
23 ♔f2 ♖hb8 24 ♖a2**

White can do little but wait for Black to
prepare his breakthrough.

**24...a5 25 ♔e3 b4 26 ♖ab2 a4 27 axb4
a3 28 ♖b3 ♖xb4 29 ♖xb4 ♖xb4 30 ♖a1
♖b3+ 31 ♔d2 ♘b4 32 ♘e1 a2 33 ♘c2?**

Losing immediately, though Black is still
better after 33 ♔c1 ♖c3+ 34 ♔b2 ♖e3
(threatening ...♖xe1) and then 35 ♘c2 ♖e2
36 ♔c3 ♖xc2+ 37 ♔xb4 ♖xg2, when 38
♔b3 ♖d2 39 ♖xa2 ♖xd4 40 ♖a7+ ♔f8 and
...♖c4, or 35 ♘f3 ♖e2+ 36 ♔b3 ♘d3 or 36
♔c3 ♘c6 37 ♘e1 ♖e3+ 38 ♔d2 ♖e4 are in
Black's favour.

**33...♖b1 34 ♔c3 h5! 35 g3 ♔d8! 36
♔d2 ♔c7 37 ♔c3 ♔b8 38 ♔d2 ♘xc2
39 ♖xa2 ♘xd4 0-1**

Game 62
Degraeve-M.Gurevich
Belfort 1997

**1 e4 e6 2 d4 d5 3 ♘c3 ♘f6 4 ♗g5 ♗e7
5 e5 ♘fd7 6 h4 a6**

Black prevents the knight sortie to b5 and intends to assault the centre with ...c7-c5 at the earliest opportunity. Therefore White must proceed on the kingside with all haste.

7 ♕g4

Defending the bishop and threatening ♗xe7 and ♕xg7.

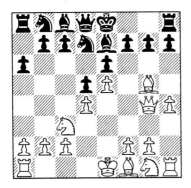

7...♗xg5!?

The most combative move, if extremely risky as White gains the h-file and a forward infantryman with which to prod the kingside. Nevertheless, while the statistics are with White, who scores 67% from 112 games in my database, the theoretical status is less clear.

Other moves give Black a passive position or worse. 7...c5? misses the threat of 8 ♗xe7 and 9 ♕xg7, while both 7...g6 8 ♗xe7 ♕xe7 9 h5 and 7...f6 8 ♗f4 merely weaken Black's kingside.

The same applies to 7...f5?! 8 ♕h5+ g6 (or 8...♔f8 9 ♘h3 and ♘f4) 9 ♕h6 ♗xg5 (not 9...♔f7? 10 h5! ♗xg5 11 hxg6+ ♔g8 12 gxh7+ ♔f7 13 ♕h5+ ♔g7 14 ♘f3 ♗e7 15 ♘xd5! exd5 16 ♕h6+ ♔f7 17 e6+ mates, or otherwise ♘xe7 and ♘g5 wins) 10 hxg5 and now 10...♔f7, intending ...♘f8, ...♖g8-g7, is supposedly the most solid formation, although this looks atrocious and White has a simple plan of attack in ♘ge2-f4 and g2-g4. For example, 11 ♘ge2 ♘f8 12 ♘f4 ♖g8 13 0-0-0 ♖g7 14 g4 fxg4 15 f3 gxf3 16 ♖d3

♔g8 17 ♖xf3 c5 18 ♗d3 ♕e8 19 ♗xg6 ♘xg6 20 ♘h5 ♕e7 21 ♘f6+ ♔h8 22 ♖fh3 ♘f8 23 ♘e2 ♗d7 (or 23...b6 24 ♘f4 ♖a7 25 ♘xh7!) 24 ♘f4 ♗e8 25 ♘xe6 1-0 Zanlungo-Salas Romo, correspondence 1963; while if 14...c6 15 ♗g2 ♔g8 (Hacker-Faisst, correspondence 1991) it is hard to see how Black can survive after 16 gxf5 exf5 17 ♗xd5+! cxd5 18 ♘cxd5.

7...♔f8 is also passive. The straightforward 8 ♗xe7+ ♕xe7 9 f4 c5 10 dxc5 ♘c6 11 0-0-0 ♘xc5 12 ♘f3 is clearly a good (for White) version of a 6 ♗xe7 main line. Or White can take a more aggressive approach, as in Hector-Wikstrom, Norrköping 1996, which saw: 8 ♘f3 c5 9 dxc5 ♘c6 10 ♘a4!? (better than 10 ♕f4 ♕c7! 11 ♗xe7+ ♔xe7 12 0-0-0 ♘dxe5 with an unclear position) 10...♘dxe5 11 ♘xe5 ♘xe5 12 ♗xe7+ ♕xe7 13 ♕g3 f6 14 f4 ♘c6 15 0-0-0 ♗d7 16 ♗e2 ♔f7 17 ♖he1 ♘b4 18 ♕b3 a5? (better is 18...♗xa4 19 ♕xb4 ♗c6) 19 ♘b6 ♖ad8 20 f5 g6 21 ♘xd7 ♕xd7 22 a3 ♘c6 23 fxe6+ ♕xe6 24 ♗f3 1-0.

Black has also tried 7...h5!? intending 8 ♗xe7?! hxg4 9 ♗xd8 ♔xd8, or otherwise to block the kingside after 8 ♕g3 ♗xg5 9 hxg5 g6. Nevertheless, White can break in with a timely g2-g4, as for example after 10 0-0-0 b5 11 ♕e3 ♖g8 12 f4 ♘b6 13 ♘f3 ♕e7 14 ♘h2 ♘8d7 15 g4 hxg4 16 ♘xg4 ♗b7 (Rytshagov-Bykhovsky, Cappelle la Grande 1993) when 17 ♘f6+ ♘xf6 18 exf6 is clearly better for White. No better is 8...g6 9 0-0-0 c5 10 dxc5 ♘c6 11 ♘f3 ♘xc5 12 ♕f4 ♗xg5 13 ♘xg5 ♕e7 14 ♖h3 ♘d7, when Bauer-Ruf, Metz 1998, concluded 15 ♖xd5! 0-0 (if 15...exd5 16 ♘xd5 ♕f8 17 ♖e3! and 18 e6) 16 ♖xd7 ♗xd7 17 ♘ge4 ♔g7 18 ♘f6 ♖h8 19 ♖d3 ♖ad8 20 ♘ce4 ♗c8 21 ♖d6 ♕c7 22 ♘g5 ♖df8 23 c3 1-0.

8 hxg5 c5

The only consistent follow-up, as anything else would leave Black with a passive position. For example, 8...g6 9 ♗d3

♕e7 10 ♘f3 c5 11 dxc5 ♘c6 12 0-0-0 ♘xc5 (if 12...♘dxe5 13 ♘xe5 ♘xe5 14 ♕d4) 13 ♕f4 ♗d7 14 ♖h6 with a clear advantage in Bogolyubov-Maroczy, San Remo 1930.

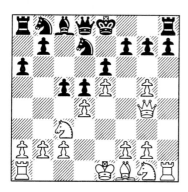

9 ♘f3

The direct attack 9 g6!? f5 (not 9...fxg6 10 ♖xh7!) has not proved conclusive. After 10 ♕g3 h6 11 ♘f3 Black is able to escape the worst with 11...0-0! 12 0-0-0 ♘c6 13 ♘e2 cxd4 14 ♘exd4 f4! 15 ♘xc6 bxc6 16 ♕h4 ♕xh4 17 ♖xh4 c5, as in Khalifman-M.Gurevich, Moscow TV 1987. Instead 10 ♕f4 is critical, supporting the d4-pawn and a possible rook sacrifice on h6 should Black castle short. The position White is aiming at follows 10...h6 11 dxc5 0-0?! 12 0-0-0 ♘c6 (if 12...♘xc5 13 ♗c4! ♕e8 14 ♖xd5! exd5 15 ♖xh6!) 13 ♘f3 ♘xc5 (if 13...♕e8 14 ♘xd5! exd5 15 ♖xd5) 14 ♗c4! with sacrifices pending at d5 and h6. Black has to play 14...♕e8 15 ♖xd5 ♘e4 (not 15...exd5? 16 ♖xh6!) 16 ♘d4 when wild tactics arise.

For example, 16...b5? 17 ♘xc6 ♕xc6 18 ♘xe4 exd5 19 ♘f6+! ♖xf6 20 exf6 dxc4 21 f7+ ♔f8 22 ♖xh6 wins (I.George), or 16...♕xg6 17 ♘xc6 bxc6 18 ♖dd1 ♘xc3 19 bxc3 ♕xg2? 20 ♖dg1 ♕e4 21 ♗xe6+! ♗xe6 22 ♖xg7+! wins, or 16...♘e7? 17 ♖d8! ♖xd8 18 ♘xe6 ♕d2+ 19 ♕xd2 ♘xd2 20 ♔xd2 ♗xe6 21 ♗xe6+ ♔h8 22 ♗f7 with a clear advantage (I.George-Corfield, correspondence 1988-89). Black does better with

either 16...♘xd4 17 ♖xd4 ♘xc3 18 bxc3 ♕xg6 19 ♖d3 ♕xg2 20 ♖xh6 gxh6 21 ♖g3+ ♕xg3 22 ♕xg3+ ♔h7 or 16...♘xc3 17 ♖xh6! ♘e2+! 18 ♘xe2 gxh6 19 ♕xh6 ♕e7 20 ♘f4 ♕g7 21 ♕h5 ♖e8! 22 ♖d6 ♘xe5 23 ♘xe6 ♗xe6 24 ♗xe6+ ♖xe6 (24...♔f8 25 f4 ♔e7 26 ♖b6) 25 ♖xe6 when White has adequate compensation (I.George), but maybe no more than that after 25...♘c4 26 c3 ♕d7.

Furthermore, Black can avoid this line, if desired, by 11 dxc5 ♘c6 12 ♘f3 ♘xc5 13 0-0-0 ♕c7! when Bos Swiecik-Lissowska, Polish Women's Championship 1991, continued 14 ♔b1 (14 g4!?) 14...♖f8 15 ♘d4? ♕xe5 16 ♕xe5 ♘xe5 17 ♖e1 ♘e4 18 f3 ♘xc3+ 19 bxc3 ♘xg6 20 ♘xe6 ♗xe6 21 ♖xe6+ ♔f7 and Black was better. Other move orders can also be circumvented: 11 ♘f3 ♘c6 12 0-0-0 cxd4 or 11 0-0-0 ♘c6 12 dxc5 ♘xc5 13 ♘f4 ♘e4!

With 9 ♘f3 White keeps options open, holding back g5-g6 until it might more inconvenience Black.

Another possibility is 9 dxc5!? and after 9...♘xe5 (or 9...♘c6 10 0-0-0! ♘dxe5 11 ♕g3) 10 ♕g3 ♘bc6 11 0-0-0 White has good compensation for the pawn, e.g. 11...♕e7 12 f4 ♘d7? 13 ♘xd5! exd5 14 ♖e1 with a clear advantage in Pliester-Giulian, Edinburgh 1988, or 11...♕a5 12 f4 ♘g6 13 f5 (13 ♗d3!?) 13...♘ge5 14 g6 (if 14 f6 ♖g8! 15 ♕h4 gxf6 16 gxf6 ♗d7 and ...0-0-0) 14...fxg6 15 fxg6 h6 16 ♖h5 (T.Thiel-J.Jenssen, Balatonbereny 1994) when 16...♘d7 intending ...0-0 or ...♘f6 was essential.

9...♘c6

Black has another possibility in 9...cxd4!? 10 ♕xd4 ♘c6 11 ♕f4 ♕c7 12 0-0-0 ♘dxe5 (threatening ...♘d3+) and if 13 ♘xe5 ♕xe5 14 ♕xe5 ♘xe5 15 ♖e1 (Arencibia-Hernandez Castillo, Santiago 1993) then 15...d4! equalises after 16 ♘d5 exd5 17 ♖xe5 ♗e6 or 16 ♘e2 ♘c6 17 ♖h4 ♗d7 18 ♘xd4 ♘xd4 19 ♖xd4 ♗c6. White might prefer to keep the tension by 13 ✜b1!? planning ♖e1. Black has also tried 11...♕b6!? 12 0-0-0 ♕xf2 13 ♖d2 ♕c5 14 g6 fxg6 15 ♗d3 ♖f8? (15...♔d8 offers more resistance) 16 ♕g3 ♕e3 17 ♖xh7 ♘dxe5 18 ♗xg6+ ♔d8 19 ♗e4! intending ♗xd5 with a huge attack in Mirumian-Supatashvili, Ankara 1995.

10 dxc5

10 g6 is again possible when, after 10...f5 11 ♕g3! h6, the fact that Black has not yet castled allows White to play 12 ♘g5! attacking and then:

a) 12...♗e7 13 ♘f7 ♖f8 (not 13...0-0? 14 ♘xh6+) 14 ♘e2 cxd4 15 0-0-0 ♘c5 16 ♘xd4 with a clear advantage to White. Landa-Gleizerov, Bled 1990, continued 16...♘e4 17 ♕e3 f4 18 ♕e1 ♕c5 19 c3 ♘e7 20 ♗d3 ♘xg6 21 ♘d6+ ♗xd6 22 ♗xg6+ ♘f7 23 ♘f5 exf5 24 e6 ♔e7 25 ♗xf7 ♕d6 26 ♖d2 f3 27 gxf3 ♗d7 and now 28 ♖g1! g5 29 ♖h1 ♖h8 30 exd7+ ♔xf7 31 ♕d1 would have won (Landa).

b) 12...♘xd4 13 ♘f7! ♕a5 14 0-0-0 ♖g8 (again not 14...0-0? 15 ♘xh6+) 15 ✜b1 b5 (perhaps 15...♘b5!?) 16 ♕h4 b4 17 ♖xd4!? cxd4 18 ♘xd5! exd5 19 ♘d6+ ♔f8 20 ♘xf5 ♘f6 21 exf6 ♗xf5 22 ♕f4 with compensation in Passos-Dutra Neto, correspondence 1993.

10...♘dxe5 11 ♘xe5 ♘xe5 12 ♕g3

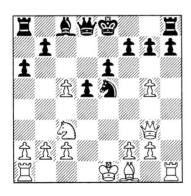

12...♘g6?!

The knight blockades the g5-pawn but is itself a target on g6. 12...♘d7 was stronger when 13 g6 h6 14 gxf7+ ♔xf7 doesn't achieve much for White, nor does 13 ♕e3 ♕e7, while in B.Ivanovic-Shaboian, Pula 1990, Black defended after 13 0-0-0 ♘xc5 14 g6 fxg6 15 ♖xh7 ♖xh7 16 ♕xg6+ ♔f8 17 ♕xh7 ♕g5+ 18 ♖d2 ♕h6 and eventually won as his higher-rated opponent overpressed.

13 0-0-0 ♗d7

13...♕e7 allows Black to defend against 14 ♗d3 by 14...♕xc5 15 ♗xg6 fxg6 16 ♕e5 0-0! (Finkel) since if 17 ♕h2 ♖xf2 18 ♕xh7+ ♔f8 or 17 ♖d2 ♖f5! 18 ♕h2 h5 19 gxh6 ♖h5. Instead 14 ♕e3! increases the pressure, and if 14...♗d7 15 ♗xg6 fxg6 16 ♖he1 wins the d5-pawn, or 14...0-0?! 15 f4 and Black is in trouble down the h-file.

14 ♗d3 ♕b8 15 ♕e3 ♘e7

Black cannot play 15...♕e5? because of 16 ♘xd5! exd5 (or 16...♕xd5 17 ♗xg6 ♕xa2 18 ♗xf7+!) 17 ♕xe5+ ♘xe5 18 ♖de1 f6 19 gxf6 gxf6 20 f4 and White won in Hector-J.Hansen, Gausdal 1987.

16 ♗xh7 g6 17 ♗xg6!

Clearly Black cannot capture with the f-pawn so he is forced to give up his defences on the e-file.

17...♖xh1 18 ♖xh1 ♘xg6 19 ♘xd5 ♗c6 20 ♘b6 ♗xg2?

20...♖a7 was obligatory when there is no immediate win for White.

21 ♖h6!

Threatening the decisive 22 ♖xg6 fxg6 23 ♕xe6+ etc.

21...♔e7 22 ♕d4

Black has no defence to ♕f6+. If 22...e5 the queen comes round via 23 ♕g4 ♗c6 24 ♕f5.

22...♕d8 23 ♕f6+ ♔e8 24 ♘xa8 ♕a5 25 ♕c3 ♕xa2 26 b3 ♗e4 27 f3 ♗xc2 28 ♕xc2 ♕a1+ 29 ♔d2 ♕d4+ 30 ♕d3 ♕f2+ 31 ♔d1 ♕g1+ 32 ♔c2 ♕xc5+ 33 ♕c3 ♕xg5 34 ♖h2 ♔f8 35 ♘b6 ♕b5 36 ♘c4 ♔e7 37 ♔b2 ♘f4 38 ♖d2 ♘d5 39 ♕e5 ♕c5 40 ♕d4 ♕c7 41 ♘e3 1-0

Game 63
Zezulkin-Lempert
Czestochowa 1991

1 e4 e6 2 d4 d5 3 ♘c3 ♘f6 4 ♗g5 ♗e7 5 e5 ♘fd7 6 h4 0-0

A disdainful move – Black continues as if 6 h4 did nothing at all. There are another two more moves that need to be examined:

a) The first, 6...f6!?, is probably too sharp. White has a strong response in 7 ♕h5+!, the point being that 7...g6 8 exf6! gxh5 9 fxe7 or 8...♘xf6 9 ♕e2 leaves Black very weak on the dark squares. The alternative, 7...♔f8, has obvious drawbacks – after 8 exf6 ♘xf6 (if 8...♗xf6 9 ♘h3! ♕e8 10 ♕g4 – Suetin) 9 ♕e2 (aiming at the weak e5-square) 9...c5 (if 9...♗b4 10 ♖h3!) 10 dxc5 and Black has struggled after 10...♘a6 (10...b6!?) 11 ♘f3 ♘xc5 12 0-0-0 b5 13 ♕e3 b4 14 ♘b5! ♗d7 15 ♘e5 ♗e8 16 ♘d4 ♕b6 17 ♗d3 ♖c8 18 ♖he1 a5 19 ♘g4 h5 (if 19...♘xg4 20 ♗xe7+ ♔xe7 21 ♕g5+) 20 ♗f5! ♘xg4 (if 20...hxg4 21 ♘xe6+ wins) 21 ♘xe6+ ♕xe6 22 ♗xe7+ ♔xe7 23 ♕g5+ ♘f6 24 ♗xe6 ♘xe6 25 ♖xd5 ♗f7 26 ♖xe6+ 1-0 Vitomskis-Carleton, correspondence 1996-97.

b) The second, 6...h6

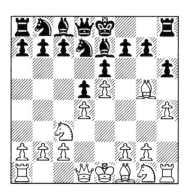

offers a normal position (following 7 ♗xe7 ♕xe7) with the two h-pawn moves thrown in. Opinion is divided as to whom this inclusion favours more. For White, h2-h4 is often useful, allowing a rook lift via h3. On the downside the white kingside is somewhat weakened, which Black might later try to exploit by ...f7-f6 e5xf6 ♘xf6! Also ...h7-h6 rules out the sacrifice on h7 and any knight sally to g5.

After 7 ♗xe7 ♕xe7 Stetsko offers 8 f4 0-0 9 ♘f3 c5 10 ♕d2 ♘c6 11 0-0-0 f6! 12 exf6 ♘xf6 intending ...♘h5, even 13 ♖e1 ♘h5!? since 14 ♘xd5 gains a pawn only temporarily. Or if 8 ♕g4 0-0 he proposes ...f7-f5 and ...c7-c5, for example 9 ♘f3 (or 9 0-0-0 c5 10 f4 ♘c6 11 ♘f3 f5) 9...f5 10 ♕f4 c5 11 0-0-0 (Trajkovic-Malesevic, Novi Sad 1988) and then 11...♘c6! 12 ♘b5 a6 13 ♘d6 cxd4. *ECO* prefers 8 f4 0-0 9 ♘f3 c5 10 dxc5 'with a slight advantage'. None of these variations have received serious testing.

White can decline the discussion in two ways:

b1) 7 ♕h5!? and then *ECO* gives 7...a6 8 0-0-0 c5 9 dxc5 ♘xc5 10 ♘f3 as slightly better for White, or if 7...g6 8 ♗xe7 ♕xe7 9 ♕g4 with a clear advantage. In the latter line, though, *Fritz* finds a trick in 9...♕b4!? intending 10 0-0-0 ♘xe5. White has sufficient compensation but no more than that after 11 ♕g3 ♘c4 12 ♗xc4 ♕xc4. White should prefer 9 ♕e2 and f2-f4, 0-0-0, ♘f3, etc.

b2) 7 ♗e3 c5 8 ♕g4 when Hellers-Bareev, Gausdal 1986, saw 8...g6 9 ♘f3 ♘c6 (9...cxd4!?) 10 dxc5 ♘xc5 (if 10...♘dxe5 11 ♘xe5 ♘xe5 12 ♕g3 with compensation) 11 0-0-0 a6 12 ♗xc5 ♗xc5 13 ♘e4 ♗e7 14 ♕f4 b5 15 ♘d6+! ♗xd6 16 exd6 ♖a7? (15...f6 16 ♕g3) 17 ♘d4! ♔d7 (17...♘xd4 18 ♕xd4 forks the rooks) 18 ♗xb5 axb5 19 ♕xf7+ 1-0. 8...♔f8 is more solid. *ECO* also gives 9 ♘f3 ♘c6 10 0-0-0 cxd4 11 ♗xd4 as clearly better for White, but Black might try either 10...f5!? (Sokolsky) along the lines of (line 'b1', or 10...cxd4 11 ♗xd4 ♘xd4 12 ♖xd4 b5!?

(Stetsko) with queenside counterplay after 13 ♘xb5 ♕b6 or 13 ♗xb5 ♖b8 and ...♕b6.

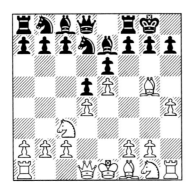

7 ♗d3

This is the most direct attempt at refutation, planning 8 ♘h3 and ♗xh7+ etc. White has a quieter alternative in 7 ♕g4 f5 (not 7...c5?! 8 ♗h6 g6 9 h5 with a strong attack) 8 ♗xe7 ♕xe7 9 ♕g5! with a slight plus after 9...♕xg5 10 hxg5 c5 11 ♘b5 ♘c6 12 0-0-0, or 9...♕b4 10 0-0-0 c5 11 ♕e7 ♕b6 12 ♘a4 ♕c6 13 ♘xc5 ♘xc5 14 ♕xc5 ♕xc5 15 dxc5 ♘d7 16 ♘f3 ♘xc5 (Hebden-Gurevich, 4NCL 1998).

7...f5?!

Black blocks the b1-h7 diagonal in advance of ♗f1-d3, but it seems a little inconsistent now to be worrying about the opponent's moves. Better to continue as planned with 7...c5! and then:

a) 8 ♕h5 g6 9 ♕h6 and either 9...cxd4 10 ♘f3 ♘xe5! 11 ♘xe5 dxc3 12 ♘xg6 with a draw, or 9...♘c6! (Euwe) when 10 ♗xe7 ♕xe7 11 h5 cxd4 12 hxg6 fxg6 13 ♗xg6 hxg6 14 ♕h8+ ♔f7 15 ♖h7+ ♔e8 16 ♖xe7+ ♘xe7 is good for Black, while 10 f4 ♘xd4 11 h5 ♘f5! 12 ♗xf5 gxf5 is unclear.

b) 8 ♘h3 and now the threat of 9 ♗xe7 ♕xe7 10 ♗xh7+ must be answered. Not 8...h6? 9 ♗xh6! gxh6 10 ♕g4+ ♔h8 11 ♘g5 (or 11 ♕h5 ♔g7 12 ♘f4 and 13 ♖h3) 11...♕b6 12 ♕h5 ♔g7 13 ♖h3 wins; but 8...g6! seems okay. Relange-M.Gurevich, Belfort 1997, continued 9 f4 cxd4 10 ♘e2

♕a5+! 11 ♕d2 (if 11 ♔f1 f6) 11...♕xd2+ 12 ♔xd2 ♗b4+ 13 ♔d1 f6 14 ♗h6 when 14...♖f7!? 15 h5 (or 15 exf6 ♘xf6 16 ♘xd4 ♘g4) 15...fxe5 16 hxg6 hxg6 17 ♘g5 e4 would have been good for Black according to Gurevich.

8 ♘h3

8 g4!? c5 9 gxf5 cxd4 10 f6 is perhaps over-sharp: the compulsory sacrifice 10...♗xf6! (not 10...gxf6? 11 ♗xh7+ etc.) 11 exf6 ♘xf6 gives Black strong play for the piece with an advancing centre and greater co-ordination, e.g. 12 ♘ce2 e5 13 f3 ♕b6 14 c3 ♕xb2 15 cxd4 ♘c6 16 ♕b1? (better 16 ♗xf6 ♖xf6 17 ♕b1 or 16 dxe5) 16...♘b4 17 ♘c1? ♘xd3 18 ♘xd3 ♕g2 19 dxe5 ♕xh1 and Black won in Shabalov-Supatashvili, USSR 1985.

After this debacle White switched to 8 exf6 ♘xf6 9 ♘f3 c5 10 dxc5 ♘c6 11 ♕e2 ♗xc5 12 0-0-0 and White has good chances here too. Shabalov-Budnikov, Leningrad 1989, continued 12...♗d7 13 ♔b1 a6 14 h5 ♕e7 15 ♘h4 ♕f7 16 ♗g6!? ♕e7? (the only defence was 16...hxg6 17 hxg6 ♕e8 18 ♗xf6 ♖xf6 19 ♕h5 ♘e7) 17 h6 gxh6 18 ♗xh6 hxg6 19 ♘xg6 ♕f7 20 ♘h8 ♕e7 21 ♖d3 ♗d6 22 f4 ♘h7 23 ♘g6 ♕f6 24 ♖g3 ♔f7 25 ♕h5 ♖g8 26 ♘f8+ ♔e7 27 ♖xg8 ♖xf8 28 ♖xf8 1-0.

8...♘c6

It is too late now for 8...c5? 9 ♘f4 ♘b6 10 dxc5. Khalifman-Ulibin, Sochi 1989, saw instead 8...♘a6 9 ♗xa6 bxa6 10 ♘a4 with a slight advantage. White can aim for more with 9 g4! (Nesis) 9...♘b4 10 gxf5 exf5 (not 10...♘xd3+? 11 ♕xd3 ♗e7 12 ♕xe7 ♖xf5 13 ♘xd5) 11 ♘f4 or even 11 ♗f1!? and White is clearly better.

9 ♘e2

Not now 9 g4? ♘xd4.

9...♘b4

More active than 9...♘b6 when Vigfusson-Carleton, correspondence 1995-97, saw 10 c3 h6 11 ♗xe7 ♘xe7 12 ♘hf4 ♕e8 13 ♖g1 ♘c4 14 ♕c2 c5 15 g4 cxd4 16 cxd4 ♗d7 17 g5 hxg5 18 ♖xg5 ♖c8 19 ♗xc4 ♖xc4 20 ♕b3 and White was better.

10 ♘ef4 ♘xd3+ 11 ♕xd3 ♘b6 12 0-0-0

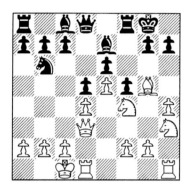

12...♗d7?!

Naïve development does not fit the bill since White is about to launch a huge attack by ♖g1 and g2-g4. Black needed to generate some quick counterplay. For example, 12...♘c4 13 ♖hg1 c5 14 g4 ♕a5 15 ♔b1 ♕b4 and 12...c5 13 dxc5 ♘c4 14 ♖he1 ♕a5 or 14 ♔b1 b6!? are quite messy. Nevertheless White can hope for some advantage after either 12...♘c4 13 ♕g3!? intending to attack with 14 ♘h5 or 14 h5, 15 ♘g6; or if 12...c5 13 ♕a3!? ♖e8 (or 13...♘c4 14 ♗xe7 ♕xe7 15 ♕xc5 ♕xc5 16 dxc5 ♘xe5 17 ♖he1) 14 dxc5 ♘c4 15 ♕c3, e.g. 15...♕c7 16 ♗xe7 ♖xe7 17 ♖xd5! or 15...b6 16 b3 ♘a5 (or 16...♘a3 17 ♔b2 ♘b5 18 ♕g3) 17 ♖hg1 intending g2-g4.

13 ♖hg1 ♘c4 14 g4 c5 15 dxc5?

This slip gives Black time to create counterplay. White's other idea was much stronger: 15 ♗h6! gxh6 (not 15...♕a5? 16 gxf5 ♕xa2 17 ♖xg7+ ♔h8 18 ♖xh7+! ♔xh7 19 f6+ mates) 16 gxh5+ ♔h8 17 fxe6 ♗xe6 (or 17...♕b6 18 b3 ♗xe6 19 ♘g6+ hxg6 20 ♕xg6 ♖f7 21 ♘f4) 18 ♘g6+! hxg6 19 ♕xg6 (Zezulkin) when 19...♖f7 20 ♘f4 ♕f8 21 ♘xe6 ♕g8 22 ♕h5! ♕h7 23 ♖g6 wins.

15...♕a5! 16 ♔b1 ♕xc5?

A serious mistake which returns the tempo to his opponent. Black had to play

16...♗xg5! (Zezulkin) 17 hxg5 (not 17 ♘xg5? ♘xb2! 18 ♔xb2 ♕b4+) 17...fxg4 and then if 18 ♘xd5 ♕b5 19 ♘e7+ ♔f7 20 b3 ♘a3+ and ...♕xd3, or 18 g6 h6 19 ♘xd5 ♕b5 (not 19...♕xc5? 20 ♘f6+!, though 19...♗b5!? is possible) 20 ♘e7+ ♔h8 21 b3 ♘a3+ 22 ♔b2 gxh3! 23 ♕xd7 ♘c4+ 24 ♔c1 ♕xc5 when 25 bxc4 ♕a3+ 26 ♔b1 ♕b4+ is perpetual check.

17 gxf5 ♖xf5 18 ♗f6!

Not wasting any more time.

18...♗f8

White is also better after:

a) 18...g6? 19 ♘xg6 ♗xf6 (not 19...hxg6? 20 ♖xg6 ♔f7 21 ♖g7+) 20 ♘e7+ ♔h8 21 ♘xf5 ♘xe5 22 ♘h6! since if 22...♘xd3? 23 ♘f7 mate.

b) 18...♗xf6 19 exf6 g6 (not 19...♖xf6? 20 ♘h5 ♖f7 21 ♘g5) 20 h5 (not now 20 ♘xg6? hxg6 21 ♖xg6+ ♔f7!) 20...♕b4 (or 20...♘e5 21 ♕e2 ♕c4 22 ♕e3) 21 b3 ♘a3+ 22 ♔b2 ♘c4+ 23 ♔a1 ♘e5 24 ♕g3.

c) 18...♖xf6 19 exf6 ♗xf6 20 ♘h5 (if 20 ♘g5 ♗xg5 21 ♖xg5 ♕b4 22 ♕d4 ♘a3+! 23 ♔c1 ♕xd4 24 ♖xd4 ♘b5 and Black has chances to defend after ...♖f8 and ...♘e4) 20...♖f8 21 ♘g5 ♗xg5 22 ♖xg5 ♖f7 23 ♘xg7 ♔f8 (23...♖xg7? 24 ♖dg1) 24 ♕c3.

19 ♕g3 ♖xf6

19...♕b6 leads to an unexpected draw after 20 ♘d3? g6 21 h5 ♖xh5 22 ♘hf4 ♗h6! 23 ♘xh5 ♘a3+, but simply 20 b3 leaves White on top, e.g. 20...♘d6 (or 20...♘a3+ 21 ♔b2) 21 ♗xg7 ♘e4 22 ♕g4 ♔f7 23 ♖d3.

20 exf6 ♖c8 21 f7+!

White takes the simplest route to victory. If 21...♔h8 22 ♘g6+ hxg6 23 ♕xg6.

21...♔xf7 22 ♘g5+ ♔e8

If 22...♔g8 23 ♕d3 or 22...♔e7 23 ♘xd5+! wins.

23 ♘gxe6 ♕b4 24 ♕c3

And Black is lost after 24...♕xc3 25 bxc3 ♗a3 26 ♘xg7+ ♔f7 27 ♖xd5. Instead he hastens the end by blundering.

24...♘a3+? 25 ♕xa3 1-0

Summary

In the 6 ♗xe7 ♕xe7 main lines 9 dxc5 ♘c6 10 ♗d3 seems to create most problems for Black. With 9 ♕d2 ♘c6 10 dxc5 the flexible line 10...♘xc5 11 0-0-0 a6 may be Black's best. Against 10...♕xc5 or the currently popular 10...f6, White can again hope for some advantage. Whereas with 9 ♗d3 White has nothing better than a return to 9 dxc5 lines, and Black can avoid the transposition if desired. 7...a6 is not played quite so often, but can be recommended for Black due to its flexibility, particularly as regards king deployment. For White, if ♕d2 main lines are intended after 7...0-0, then 7 ♕d2 is worth considering, when 7...a6 can be met by 8 ♘d1!? c5 9 c3.

The Chatard Attack, 6 h4, remains sound as White gets sufficient compensation if the proffered pawn is accepted. Black is okay as well after 6...♗xg5 7 hxg5 ♕xg5, but this position requires patient handling in defence. For more immediate counterplay Black should decline the pawn, to which end the pseudo-classical 6...c5 7 ♗xe7 ♔xe7! is the safest choice. Other moves, such as 6...a6 or 6...0-0, up the stakes so that any inaccuracy in the defence can lead to Black being demolished.

1 e4 e6 2 d4 d5 3 ♘c3 ♘f6 4 ♗g5 ♗e7 *(D)* **5 e5 ♘fd7**

6 ♗xe7
> 6 h4 *(D)*
>> 6...♗xg5 7 hxg5 ♕xg5 – *Game 60*
>> 6...c5 – *Game 61*; 6...a6 – *Game 62*; 6... 0-0 – *Game 63*

6...♕xe7 7 f4 0-0
> 7...a6 – *Game 59*

8 ♘f3 c5 *(D)* **9 ♕d2**
> 9 dxc5 – *Game 57*; 9 ♗d3 – *Game 58*

9...♘c6 10 dxc5 ♕xc5
> 10...♘xc5 – *Game 55*; 10...f6 – *Game 56*

11 0-0-0 – *Game 54*

4...♗e7

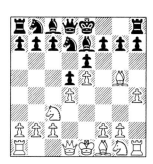

6 h4

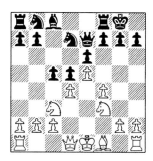

8...c5

CHAPTER EIGHT

The McCutcheon Variation
4 ♗g5 ♗b4

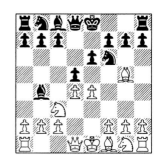

1 e4 e6 2 d4 d5 3 ♘c3 ♘f6 4 ♗g5 ♗b4

Whereas in the Burn variation (4...dxe4) and Classical proper (4...♗e7) White can count on at least a positional plus due to greater space or some strategic control, that is not the case in the McCutcheon where the assessments are generally 'equal' or 'unclear'. So it is surprising that 4...♗b4 has not, hitherto, been seen more frequently on the tournament stage. Partly this was due to the popularity of the Winawer (3...♗b4), of which the McCutcheon has been regarded as an ugly sibling – as someone once said of the variation: 'both players stand worse'. When 3...♘f6 again came to be played more often in the 1980s, White's overwhelming preference was for 4 e5; while if 4 ♗g5 was ventured then Black opted in the main for 4...dxe4.

At the turn of the millennium, however, the McCutcheon is having a second youth. In the early 20th century, Alekhine and Marshall were fond of 4...♗b4, and now it appears regularly in games by such uncompromising players as Morozevich, Korchnoi, Vaisser and Mikhail Gurevich. The most persistent practitioner is GM Igor Glek who has defended the McCutcheon for many years.

The main line occurs after 5 e5 h6 6 ♗d2

♗xc3 7 bxc3 ♘e4 8 ♕g4 as seen in Games 64-66. Since White has not proved any advantage here, deviations are common. The remaining games in this chapter see: 7 ♗xc3 (Game 67), 6 ♗e3!? (Game 68), 6 exf6 (Game 69), 5 exd5 (Game 70) and 5 ♘e2 (Game 71).

Game 64
B.Svensson-Brynell
Swedish Championship 1990

---

1 e4 e6 2 d4 d5 3 ♘c3 ♘f6 4 ♗g5 ♗b4 5 e5 h6 6 ♗d2 ♗xc3

Virtually forced, so that the attacked knight can come to e4. 6...♘fd7?! 7 ♕g4 ♔f8 and 7...♔f8 are both very passive, while if 7...g6 Black has weakened the kingside dark squares without getting anything from White in return.

7 bxc3

White views this recapture not so much as weakening the queenside as reinforcing the centre; a white rook may later utilise the half-open b-file. Black of course begs to differ.

7...♘e4 8 ♕g4!

Hitting g7 and exploiting the absence of Black's dark-squared bishop. Since 8...0-0? is not possible due to 9 ♗h6, Black is forced to make a concession: either to weaken the dark squares by advancing the g-pawn or to misplace the king with ...♔f8. 8 ♕g4 is the starting position for the main line of the McCutcheon. Earlier deviations are covered in Games 67-71, as noted in the introductory remarks to this chapter.

White does not have to play 8 ♕g4 but nothing else creates any problems for Black. In the Winawer (3...♗b4) White has positional continuations (e.g. a2-a4, ♘f3) based on dark-square control, but these are ineffective in the McCutcheon as White's own dark-squared bishop is about to be removed, e.g. 8 ♗d3 ♘xd2 9 ♕xd2 c5 10 f4 (if 10 ♘f3 c4 or 10 dxc5 ♕c7) 10...♘c6 11 ♘f3 ♕a5 12 h4 h5 13 ♖b1 c4 14 ♗e2 ♕xa2 15 ♔f2 ♕a3 16 ♖bg1 ♗d7 17 g4 hxg4 18 ♖xg4 ♕f8 19 ♖hg1 g6 20 ♖h1 0-0-0 and White had nebulous compensation for the pawn, though he managed to draw in Degraeve-Radziewicz, Cappelle la Grande 1998.

White sometimes retreats 8 ♗c1, but after 8...♘xc3 or 8...c5 9 ♗d3 ♘xc3 then ♕d1-g4 is necessary after all in order to justify the sacrifice.

8...g6

The alternative, 8...♔f8, is seen in Game 66.

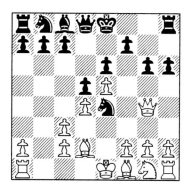

9 ♗d3

The first major point of departure. Sometimes White plays first 9 h4 or 9 ♘f3,

but these soon return to main lines after 9...c5 10 ♗d3 ♘xd2 11 ♔xd2.

The only significant alternative is 9 ♗c1, by which White keeps the dark-squared bishop at the cost of a pawn. After 9...c5 10 ♗d3 it is risky to play 10...cxd4 11 ♘e2 dxc3 12 ♗xe4 dxe4 13 ♘xc3. De Vreugt-Glek, Wijk aan Zee 1999, continued 13...♕d4!? 14 ♗b2 ♗d7 15 ♖b1 ♗c6 16 0-0 ♕c4 17 ♕g3 ♘d7 18 ♗a3 ♘c5 19 ♘d1 ♘a4 20 ♕f4 0-0-0 21 ♘e3 ♕a6 22 ♕xf7 ♖he8 23 ♗d6 ♗d7 24 ♖b4 and White won.

It is safer for Black to play 10...♘xc3 11 dxc5 ♕a5 12 ♗d2 ♕a4! and if 13 ♕f3 ♘e4! 14 ♗xe4 ♕xe4+ (or 14...dxe4 15 ♕c3 ♗d7) 15 ♕xe4 dxe4 16 ♘e2 ♗d7 and ...♗c6, or 13 h3 ♘e4 (13...h5!? – Keres) 13 h3 ♘e4 14 ♘e2 ♘xc5 15 ♕f3 ♕d7 16 0-0 b6 17 a4 ♗a6 18 a5 ♗xd3 19 cxd3 ♘b3 with mutual chances in Arbakov-D.Gurevich, USSR 1978.

If immediately 9...♘xc3 then 10 ♗d3 c5 transposes, but White can also try 10 ♕h3!? ♘a4 11 ♕b3 ♘b6 12 ♘f3 ♘c6 13 h4 ♗d7 14 ♕c3 with dark-square control as compensation in Chandler-Glek, German Bundesliga 1995.

9...♘xd2 10 ♔xd2 c5 11 ♘f3

White has two major alternatives:

a) 11 ♕f4, eyeing the kingside dark-square weaknesses. Black can play according to taste either 11...♘c6 (transposing below after 12 ♘f3) or 11...♗d7 (for which see Game 65). Instead 11...cxd4 12 cxd4 ♕a5+ 13 c3 seems premature while White can still support the centre with ♘e2. Nevertheless, Kindermann-Piskov, German Bundesliga 1996, ended in a draw after 13...b6 14 h4 ♗a6 15 ♗xa6 ♕xa6 16 ♘e2 ♘d7 17 ♖hb1 ♖c8 18 ♖b4 ♖c4 19 ♖xc4 ♕xc4 20 ♕e3 ♔e7 21 ♕d3 ♖c8 22 ♕xc4 ♖xc4 ½-½.

b) 11 h4 with possibilities of h4-h5 to attack the kingside at some point. 11...♗d7 is again in Game 65, while 11...♘c6 12 ♘f3 transposes below, though White has other options:

b1) 12 ♕f4 cxd4 13 cxd4 ♕a5+ 14 c3 and again the plan with ...b7-b6 and ...♗a6 lacks force while White can still has ♘e2, so Sutovsky-Glek, Essen 2000, saw 14...b5! 15 ♕f6 ♖f8 16 ♘e2 b4 17 ♖hc1 ♗a6 18 ♗xa6 ♕xa6 19 cxb4 ♘xb4 20 ♕f3 ♘c6 21 ♖c5 ♘a5 22 ♖ac1 ♖b8 23 ♔e1 ♘c4 24 ♘f4 ♕a4 with an unclear position. The game ended entertainingly with 25 ♘d3 g5 26 ♕f6 ♕xa2 27 ♔f1 ♘d2+ 28 ♔g1 ♘e4 29 ♖c7 ♘xf6 30 exf6 ♕d2 31 ♖e7+ ♔d8 32 ♖cc7 ♕xd3 ½-½.

b2) 12 h5 g5 13 f4 is the most direct but Black seems okay, e.g. 13...♕a5 14 fxg5 cxd4 15 ♔e2 ♕xc3 16 ♘f3 ♗d7 17 ♕f4 (17 g6 0-0-0 is unclear) 17...0-0-0 18 g4 hxg5 19 ♘xg5 f6 20 ♕xf6 ♖hf8 21 ♘f7 ♖xf7 22 ♕xf7 ♘xe5 23 ♕f4 ♘c4 24 ♗xc4 e5 25 ♕f3 ♕xc2+ 26 ♔e1 dxc4 and Black's pawns were much faster in Wedberg-Brynell, Stockholm 1990.

11...♘c6

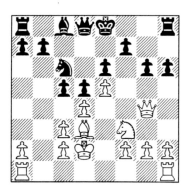

The traditional and natural method for Black, further attacking the centre. The modern development with 11...♗d7 is seen in Game 65. 11...♕c7 has a trick defence in mind: 12 h4 cxd4 13 cxd4 ♘c6 14 ♕f4 and now 14...f5! exploiting the pin on the e5-pawn. After 15 ♕g3 ♘e7 16 ♖hc1 ♗d7 17 ♔e2 ♗c6 18 ♘g1 0-0-0 19 ♘h3 ♕d7 20 a4 ♔b8 21 a5 ♗b5 22 ♘f4 ♖c8 23 ♖ab1 ♘c6!? 24 ♔e3? ♗xd3 25 cxd3 ♖hg8 Black assumed the initiative with ...g6-g5 in

Aseev-Dolmatov, USSR Championship 1989.

12 ♕f4

In this game Black plays 12...cxd4 13 cxd4 ♕a5+! This plan is also viable against other moves. For example:

a) 12 h4 cxd4 13 cxd4 ♕a5+ 14 ♔e3 b6 15 ♕f4 ♗a6 16 a3 ♖c8 17 ♖hc1 ♘e7 18 g4 ♖c3 19 ♘d2 g5 20 ♕f6 ♘g6 21 h5? (21 ♘b1 was necessary) 21...♕b5! 22 hxg6? ♖xd3+ 23 ♔e2 ♖e3+ 24 ♔xe3 ♕e2 0-1 Balcerak-Glek, Senden 1998.

b) 12 ♖ab1 cxd4 13 cxd4 ♕a5+ 14 ♔e2 (if 14 ♔e3 b6 15 ♕f4 ♗a6 16 ♖hc1 ♕a3!) 14...b6 15 ♖hc1 (15 ♕f4 ♗a6 16 h4 returns to the main game) 15...♗a6 16 a3? ♕xa3 17 ♖a1 ♗xd3+ 18 cxd3 ♕b2+ 19 ♔e3 ♘e7 20 ♖cb1 ♕c2 21 ♘e1 ♕c3 22 ♔e2 ♘f5 23 ♖a4 0-0 and having failed to win or draw against the queen White was just a pawn down in Kayumov-Glek, Dubai 2001.

Against 12 ♖hb1, however, 12...cxd4 13 cxd4 ♕a5+ 14 c3 b6 is less good as White can play 15 a4! ♗a6 16 ♗b5. Gallagher-Schwartzman, Bern 1990, continued 16...♖c8 17 ♕f4 ♔f8 18 ♕e3 ♔g7 19 ♘g1 ♖c7 20 ♘e2 ♖hc8 21 g4 ♘e7 22 h4 ♗b7 23 h5 g5 24 ♖a3 a6 25 ♗d3 b5 26 f4! gxf4 27 ♕xf4 with a big advantage.

Instead Black can consider 12...c4!? 13 ♗e2 b6 14 h4 ♗d7 15 ♘h2 ♕e7 16 h5 0-0-0 17 hxg6 f6 18 ♘f3 fxe5 19 ♘xe5 ♘xe5 20 dxe5 h5 21 ♕d4 ♖dg8 22 a4 ♗c6 23 a5 b5 with a sound position in Sutovsky-Daly, Isle of Man 1999.

12...cxd4

This is the most direct and safest choice. Other moves give White a better chance for advantage.

a) 12...♕c7 13 h4?! f5! equalising in Fischer-Rossolimo, US Championship 1965, but 13 ♕f6 ♖g8 14 h4 is good for White.

b) 12...c4!? 13 ♗e2 ♗d7 is a bit stodgy, though it led to an unusual game in Busemann-I.Carlsson, correspondence

1994: 14 h4 ♕e7 15 ♘h2 0-0-0 16 ♘g4 h5 17 ♘f6 ♕a3 18 f3 ♘a5 19 ♖hb1 ♗a4 20 ♕g5 b5 21 g4 ♘c6 22 gxh5 gxh5 23 ♕e3 ♘e7 24 f4 ♘f5 25 ♕g1 a5 26 ♕c1 ♕f8 27 ♕e1 ♕a3 28 ♕c1 ♕f8 29 ♕e1 ♖h6 30 a3 ♖xf6 31 exf6 e5 32 ♗f1 exd4 33 ♗h3 dxc3+ 34 ♔xc3 d4+ 35 ♔b2 c3+ 36 ♔a2 ♖e8 37 ♗xf5+ ♔c7 38 ♕h1 ♕c5 39 ♗d3 b4 and remarkably Black found sufficient play to draw a rook down.

c) 12...♕a5 13 h4 may arise via different move orders (i.e. h2-h4, ♘f3 and ♕f4 might be played in any order). Here 13...cxd4 14 ♘xd4 ♘xd4 15 ♕xd4 is passive (c.f. 12...cxd4 13 ♘xd4 below) as White can build up an initiative on the queenside, e.g. 15...♗d7 16 ♖hb1 ♗c6 17 ♖b4 0-0-0 18 ♖ab1 ♖d7 19 a4 as in Hebden-Vaisser, Bern 1992.

If instead 13...b6 White can play on either side of the board: 14 h5 gxh5 15 ♖xh5 ♗a6 16 ♗xa6 ♕xa6 and now 17 ♖xh6 ♖xh6 18 ♕xh6 0-0-0, though Black drew in Kovalev-Glek, German Bundesliga 1994. Or 14 ♖hb1 ♗a6 15 a4 ♗xd3 16 cxd3 a6 17 dxc5 ♕xc5 18 d4 ♕c4?! (though 18...♕a5 19 ♔d3 ♖c8 20 ♕c1 g5 21 ♕b2 gxh4 22 ♕xb6 was still good for White in Aseev-Piskov, Berlin 1991) 19 ♕f6 ♖h7 20 ♖xb6 ♔f8 21 ♖ab1 ♖c8 22 ♕e1!? ♔g8 (if 22...♕xc3+ 23 ♔f1 ♘xd4 24 ♘xd4 ♕xd4 25 ♔g1 intending ♖b8 or ♖xe6) 23 ♖1b3 ♘a5 24 ♘d2 ♕c7 25 ♖b1 ♘c4 26 ♖b7 ♕c6 27 ♖b8 ♖g7? 28 ♕d8+ 1-0 Chandler-Fernandes, Santo Antonio 2001.

13 cxd4

Supposedly White is slightly better here, but in truth Black has very few worries – and after 13...♕a5+! in the database Black scores 82% with no losses at all.

Instead 13 ♘xd4!? was tried in Przewoznik-Cichocki, Polish Championship 1990, and after 13...♗d7 14 ♘b5 ♔f8 15 h4 ♔g7 16 ♘d6 f5 17 exf6+ ♕xf6 18 ♕xf6+ ♔xf6 19 ♘xb7 e5 20 ♘c5 White had the advantage. But Black is okay with 13...♘xd4

14 cxd4 ♕a5+ and 15...b6 etc., or if 14 ♕xd4 ♕g5+!? or 14...♗d7.

13...♕a5+!

The results make this almost compulsory, and whatever White's response Black will follow with 14...b6 planning to exchange light-squared bishops with ...♗a6. Without this White can hope for an advantage. For example, 13...♕c7 14 ♕f6! ♖g8 15 ♖ab1 ♗d7 16 h4 ♖c8 17 ♔e2 ♘e7 18 ♕f4 ♗a4 19 ♖hc1 ♖h8 20 ♕f6 ♖g8 21 h5 (Kindermann-Knaak, Dortmund, 1991; or 13...♗d7 14 h4 (14 ♕f6!?) 14...♖c8 15 h5 gxh5 16 ♖xh5 ♕a5+ 17 ♔e2 ♘b4 and rather than 18 ♔f1 ♗b5 19 ♗xb5+ ♕xb5+ 20 ♔g1 with an unclear position (Bryson-C.Williams, correspondence 1984-85), instead 18 ♘g5 looks good for White.

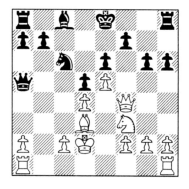

14 ♔e2

In Lanc-Vavrak, Austrian Team Championship 1999, White tried to attack the kingside but Black's play on the other side was much swifter: 14 ♔e3 b6 15 h4 ♗a6 16 ♕f6 ♖g8 17 ♖ab1 ♖c8 18 h5 gxh5 19 ♖xh5 ♗xd3 20 cxd3 ♕xa2 21 ♖c1 ♕b2 22 ♖g1 ♘b4 23 ♖xh6 ♕c2 24 ♖e1 ♕xd3+ 25 ♔f4 ♖c4 26 ♖h8 ♖xd4+ (mate in six) 27 ♘xd4 ♕xd4+ 28 ♔f3 ♕g4+ 29 ♔e3 ♕e4+ 30 ♔d2 ♕d3+ 0-1.

White does better to contest matters on the queenside by 14 c3 b6 15 a4 ♗a6 16 ♗b5 ♗xb5 17 axb5 ♕xb5 18 ♖hb1 ♕c4 19 ♖xb6, so in N.Johnson-D.Phillips, correspondence 2000, Black chose to force a draw with 19...0-0! 20 ♕xh6 (or 20 ♖b7 ♖ab8) 20...♘xd4! 21 ♘xd4 axb6 ½-½. After 22 ♘xe6! perpetual follows either 22...fxe6 23 ♕xg6+ or 22...♖a2+ 23 ♖xa2 ♕xa2+ 24 ♔c1.

14...b6 15 ♖hd1

A sensible precaution. The attacking gesture 15 ♕f6 ♖g8 16 h4 again led to disaster in Wahlbom-Brynell, Swedish Championship 1998: 16...♗a6 17 ♕f4 ♖c8 18 ♖hc1 ♘b4 19 ♕d2 ♖xc2! 20 ♖xc2 ♗xd3+ 21 ♕xd3 ♘xd3 22 ♖c8+ ♔d7 23 ♖xg8 ♕a6 24 ♔e3 ♕a3 25 ♖f1 ♘c1+ 0-1.

15...♗a6 16 ♔f1 ♖c8 17 ♔g1 ♗xd3 18 cxd3 ♕a3 19 h4

Having removed his king to safety White now starts something on the kingside. Unfortunately the h-pawn thrust lacks potency without the rook behind it on h1.

19...♕e7 20 ♖ac1 ♔d7!

Black seeks the endgame so that he can safely advance his a- and b-pawn duo.

21 ♖c3 ♘b4 22 ♖xc8 ♔xc8 23 a3 ♘c6 24 ♖c1 ♔b7 25 ♖c3 ♖c8 26 ♕c1

Not 26 ♕xh6? ♘xe5! 27 ♖xc8 ♘xf3+ 28 gxf3 ♔xc8 and White's pawn structure is the worst imaginable.

26...♕f8 27 g3 ♘e7 28 ♖xc8 ♘xc8 29 ♔g2 ♘e7 30 ♕f4 ♘c6 31 ♕f6 b5

With the rooks gone Black starts his pawns going.

32 g4 a5 33 ♕f4 a4

34 ♘d2?

Better was 34 ♕c1 since it is suicide to let the a-pawn go. 34...♕xa3 35 ♕f7+ ♔e7 36 ♕xg6 a3 37 ♘b3 a2 intending ...♕a3 again is already good. Black throws in a *zwischenzug* to strengthen his hand even more.

34...g5! 35 hxg5 hxg5 36 ♕xg5 ♕xa3 37 ♕g8 ♔e7! 0-1

38...a3 39 ♘b3 a2 will follow and White cannot cover all of ...♕a3, ...♕b4 and ...♘xd4.

Game 65
Sutovsky-Zifroni
Israel 2000

---

1 e4 e6 2 d4 d5 3 ♘c3 ♘f6 4 ♗g5 ♗b4 5 e5 h6 6 ♗d2 ♗xc3 7 bxc3 ♘e4 8 ♕g4 g6 9 ♗d3 ♘xd2 10 ♔xd2 c5 11 ♘f3 ♗d7!?

This is the currently popular method of development. Black intends to follow with ...♗c6, ...♘d7, ...♕e7 covering his weaknesses at b7, f6 and f7, and then castle long. This scheme is quite new – too recent to make it into Harding's 1991 book – and appears to stem from a brief note by Fischer in his *My 60 Memorable Games*: '11...B-Q2 12 PxP deserves testing', though the plan is not explicitly defined.

11...♗d7 can also be played against other 11th moves. 11 ♕f4 ♗d7 12 ♘f3 ♗c6 13 h4 ♘d7 is another route to the game. Similarly 11 h4 ♗d7 12 ♘f3, while 12 h5!? g5 13 f4 ♘c6 14 fxg5 ♕xg5+ 15 ♕xg5 hxg5 16 ♔e3 g4! and Black defended in Leko-Short, Batumi 1999: 17 ♖f1 ♔e7 18 ♖h4 ♖ag8 19 ♖b1 b6 20 ♗e2 cxd4+ 21 cxd4 f5 22 exf6+ ♔xf6 23 ♖f1+ ♔e7 24 ♖xg4 ♖xg4 25 ♗xg4 ♘xd4 26 ♔xd4 ½-½, since Black regains the material after 26...e5+ and 27...♗xg4.

One drawback of playing ...♗d7-c6 immediately is that it weakens e6, which White can try to exploit by sacrificing

♗d3xg6. While the sacrifice is not decisive it does allow White either to force a draw or try for more with three pawns for the piece. It was presumably in order to avoid this that Zifroni played 11...♛e7, reaching the game after the further 12 h4 ♝d7 13 ♛f4 ♝c6 14 ♘h2 ♘d7, but would have had to do something else against 12 ♖ab1 or 12 ♖hb1. Black can also insert ...c5-c4 before ...♝c6, but this is obviously committal.

Again Black should be aware that 11 ♖b1 prevents Black's plan of development with ...♝d7. Instead 11...♘c6 12 ♘f3 cxd4 13 cxd4 ♛a5+ reaches positions in the previous game.

12 h4

White has tried other moves:

a) 12 ♛f4 ♝c6 13 h4 ♘d7 is the current game.

b) 12 dxc5!? ♛e7 13 ♖ab1 ♝c6 14 h4 ♘d7 15 ♖he1 ♘xc5 16 ♘d4 ♖c8 17 ♘xc6 bxc6 18 ♖b4 a5 19 ♖bb1 0-0 20 h5 ♛g5+ 21 ♛xg5 hxg5 and Black was okay in Spassky-Relange, French Team Championship 1991.

c) 12 ♖ab1 ♝c6 and then Klovans-Glek, German Bundesliga 1998, saw 13 ♖he1 ♛e7 14 h4 ♘d7 15 dxc5 ♘xc5 16 ♘d4 0-0-0 17 ♖b4 ♛c7 18 ♛f4 f5 19 ♛e3 a5 20 ♖b2 ♘e4+ 21 ♔c1 ♝d7 22 ♝xe4 dxe4 23 f4 ♔b8 24 ♖d1 ♖c8 25 ♘e2 ♝c6 26 ♖d6 ♝d5 27 ♘d4 ♛xc3 28 ♛xc3 ♖xc3 29 ♘xe6 ♝xe6 30 ♖xe6 g5 with an unusual endgame.

Here, though, White gets the chance for 13 ♝xg6!? fxg6 14 ♛xe6+ ♛e7 15 ♛xg6+ (15 ♛c8+ ♔d8 ½-½ Stefanova-Hamdouchi, Pulvermuele 2000) 15...♔d8 16 e6! intending ♖he1, ♘e5 (Gara-Goczo, Hungarian Women's Championship 1999). Black may be able to defend but has little chance to win.

12...♝c6 13 ♛f4

13 ♝xg6!? is again possible. If Black wants to avoid this then 12...♛e7 should be preferred, especially as ...♝d7-c6 can no longer be prevented.

13...♘d7

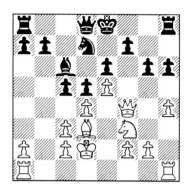

14 ♘h2

Intending ♘h2-g4 to attack the weak dark squares f6 and h6. Previously White had floundered for a plan in the face of Black's flexible, prophylactic development. For example:

a) 14 ♖h3 ♛e7 15 dxc5 0-0-0 16 ♘d4 ♘xc5! 17 ♖b1 (if 17 ♘xc6 bxc6 18 ♖b1 ♖d7! intending ♖b7) 17...♛c7 18 ♛f6 ♖hf8 19 f4 ♘e4+! 20 ♝xe4 dxe4 21 ♖b4 ♖d7! 22 ♔c1 ♖fd8 23 a3 a5!? (23...♛a5! 24 ♔b2 ♛c5 25 ♘xc6 bxc6! 26 ♖xe4?! a5! with an attack on the b-file having prevented the rook returning to b4) 24 ♖c4 ♛b6 25 ♖e3 ♔b8 26 ♖e1? (In time trouble White capitulates; the only defence was 26 ♘xc6+ bxc6 27 ♖d4) 26...♝d5 27 ♖a4 ♖c8 (27...♝a2 is also very strong) 28 ♔d2 ♛b2 29 ♖e3 ♝b3! (exploiting multiple pins) 30 ♖xa5 ♖xd4+! 0-1 Spraggett-Glek, Cappelle la Grande 1998.

b) 14 ♖he1 ♛e7 15 a4?! c4! 16 ♝e2 a5 (fixing the a-pawn as a target for attack, threatening ...♘b6) 17 ♖a2 0-0-0 18 ♘h2 g5 19 hxg5 ♛xg5 20 ♛xg5 hxg5 21 ♘g4 ♖h7 22 g3 ♔c7 23 ♝f3 ♖f8 24 ♔e3 f5 25 exf6 ♘xf6 26 ♘e5 ♘d7 27 ♝g4 ♔d6 28 ♘xd7 ♝xd7 29 ♖aa1 ♖h2 30 ♖e2 ♝c6 and White was reduced to passive defence (Degraeve-M.Gurevich, Belfort 1998).

c) 14 dxc5 ♛e7 15 ♘d4 ♘xc5 16 f3 ♝d7 17 a4 a6 18 a5 ♖c8 19 g4 ♖c7 20 g5 h5 21

♕f6 ♖g8 22 ♖hb1 ♗c8 23 ♕xe7+ ♔xe7 24 ♖b4 ♖d8 and a draw by shuffling was soon agreed in Olivier-Sharif, Lyon 1995.

14...♕e7!

After 14...♕a5 15 ♘g4 cxd4 16 ♕xd4 0-0-0 17 ♖he1 ♘c5 18 ♕b4! ♕b6 19 ♕xb6 axb6 20 ♖eb1 d4 21 f3 White was always slightly better in Madl-Feigin, Recklinghausen 1999, though the game was drawn.

15 ♘g4 0-0-0!

Rather than try and defend the h-pawn Black sacrifices it for the initiative. Werner-Bohnenblust, Bern 1999, had seen 15...♕f8 16 ♘f6+ ♘xf6 17 ♕xf6 ♖g8 18 h5 and White was better. 15...h5? is worse because of 16 ♘f6+! ♘xf6 17 ♕xf6 ♕xf6 18 exf6 and the white king will march forward strongly on the dark squares.

16 ♘xh6

If 16 ♘f6 Sutovsky gives 16...cxd4 17 cxd4 ♘b6 or 16...g5!? 17 hxg5 hxg5 18 ♕xg5 ♖hg8 as unclear. Wynn Zaw Htun-Hoang Thanh Trang, Vietnam 2000, saw instead 16...cxd4 17 cxd4 ♕b4+ 18 ♔e3 ♘b6 19 ♖ab1 ♕a4 20 ♘g4 ♘c4+ 21 ♔e2 ♘a3 22 ♖b3 g5 23 ♖xa3!? (if 23 ♕xf7 ♕xd4) 23...gxf4 24 ♖xa4 ♗xa4 25 ♔f3 with good compensation since the knight is a strong piece.

16...f5!

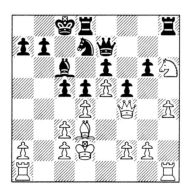

This is the novelty, probably prepared at home. Black attempts to corral the knight,

while if White captures the pawn the black knight rushes to f6 and e4 creating strong counterplay.

17 exf6

If 17 g4 Sutovsky's notes include an entertaining draw: 17...cxd4! 18 cxd4 fxg4 19 ♘f7 ♖df8 20 ♗xg6 ♖hg8 21 h5 ♖g7 22 h6! ♖xg6 23 h7 ♖xf7 24 h8♕+ ♖f8 25 ♕hxf8+ ♘xf8 26 ♖h8 ♕b4+ 27 ♔d1 ♔c7 28 ♖xf8 ♖h6! 29 ♖f7+ ♔b6 30 ♕xh6 ♕xd4+ 31 ♕d2 ♕xa1+ 32 ♕c1 ♕xe5 33 ♕e3+ ♕xe3 34 fxe3.

17...♘xf6 18 ♘g4

18 f3!? does not prevent the black knight coming forward. Black can play anyway 18...cxd4 19 cxd4 ♘e4+! since 20 fxe4 dxe4 21 ♗xe4? loses to 21...♖xd4+. Or if 20 ♔e2 ♕b4 with threats on the dark squares.

18...♘e4+ 19 ♗xe4 dxe4

With the white king to be opened up by ...c5xd4 Black has full compensation for the pawn. In fact White must play carefully to keep the game level.

20 ♘e5! cxd4 21 ♘xc6 bxc6 22 ♖ab1

Aiming for counterplay against the black king. It was also possible to capture 22 ♕xe4 and if 22...dxc3+ 23 ♔e1 (not 23 ♔xc3? ♕a3+ 24 ♔c4 ♕a4+ winning the queen) 23...♕d6 24 ♖h3 defends, e.g. 24...♖h5 25 ♔f1 or 24...♕d5 25 ♕xd5 exd5 26 ♔e2 intending ♔d3.

22...dxc3+ 23 ♔e1

Exposing the king to attack 23 ♔xc3!? would be risky, e.g. after 23...♕g7+ 24 ♔b3 ♖h5 (intending ...♖b5) 25 a4 ♖c5 with a heavy piece pincer movement.

23...♕d6! 24 ♕xd6

Forced. Not now 24 ♕xe4? since Black has gained a tempo (on 22 ♕xe4) so that 24...♖h5 25 ♔f1 ♖e5 or 25 f4 ♖f5 26 g3 e5 is very strong.

24...♖xd6 25 ♖h3!

Again the only move, since otherwise Black infiltrates on the d-file by 25 ♖b3 ♖hd8 or 25 ♖d1 ♖xd1+ 26 ♔xd1 ♖d8+.

25...e3!?

A last attempt to win by 26 fxe3? ♖d2.

26 ♖xe3! ♖xh4 27 ♖b3 ♖h1+ ½-½

After 28 ♔e2 ♖d2+ 29 ♔f3 ♖xc2 30 ♖bxc3 ♖xc3 31 ♖xc3 Black will not keep the extra pawn for long as he his own are too weak.

Game 66
Anand-Korchnoi
Dos Hermanas 1999

---

1 e4 e6 2 d4 d5 3 ♘c3 ♘f6 4 ♗g5 ♗b4 5 e5 h6 6 ♗d2 ♗xc3 7 bxc3 ♘e4 8 ♕g4 ♔f8!?

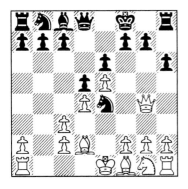

Long thought to be inferior, 8...♔f8 has recently been revived by Korchnoi. Black refuses to weaken the dark squares by 8...g6, hopes to defend the king with moves such as ...♖g8, ...♗d7-e8, meanwhile creating counterplay on the queenside with ...c5-c4, ...a7-a5 and ...b7-b5-b4.

9 ♗d3

9 h4 c5 10 ♗d3 ♘xd2 11 ♔xd2 is another route to move 11 in the game, but then Black has an alternative in 9...f5!? 10 exf6 ♕xf6. The game move 9 ♗d3 avoids this by hitting the knight straightaway, but gives Black another possibility in 9...♘xd2 10 ♔xd2 ♕g5+!? Similarly, if White wants to play 11 ♘f3, then 9 ♘f3 c5 10 ♗d3 ♘xd2 11 ♔xd2 is the simplest route as Black will not deviate – although White might: Zsu.Polgar-Korchnoi, Munich Schuhplattler

2000, saw instead 10 ♕f4 c4!? 11 ♗e2 ♘c6 12 0-0 ♘xd2 13 ♕xd2 ♔e8!? 14 g3 ♔d7 15 ♘h4 ♔c7 16 f4 g6 17 ♘g2 h5 18 ♘h4 ♕e7 19 ♘f3 ♕a3 20 ♘g5 ♘d8 21 h3 and at last came 21...b5 22 ♖ab1 ♖b8 23 ♔g2 ♗d7 24 g4 hxg4 25 hxg4 a5 with the initiative on the queenside.

The pawn sacrifice 9 ♗c1, hoping to cause problems with a later ♗a3, is not dangerous after 9...c5 10 ♗d3 ♘xc3 11 dxc5 ♕a5 12 ♗d2 ♕a4! (c.f. 8...g6 9 ♗c1).

9...♘xd2 10 ♔xd2 c5

Presumably Anand did not fear 10...♕g5+!?, as he gives the note 11 ♕xg5 hxg5 12 ♖f1 without assessment. The g5-pawn is an obvious target for f2-f4 or h2-h4 or ♘h3, and certainly the statistics favour White who scores a healthy 71% after 10...♕g5+.

11 h4

11 ♘f3 often arises via 9 ♘f3 c5 10 ♗d3 ♘xd2 11 ♔xd2, when 11...c4 12 ♗e2 ♘c6 is thematic.

The position after 13 h4 b5 14 a3 ♗d7 arose in two more of Korchnoi's games. J.Polgar-Korchnoi, Wijk aan Zee 2000, saw 15 ♕f4 ♔e7! 16 h5 ♗e8 17 ♘h4 a5 18 ♕g3 ♖g8 19 ♕e3 ♗d7 20 f4 b4 21 ♖hb1 bxc3+ 22 ♕xc3 ♕c7 23 g4 ♖gb8 24 f5 ♕a7 25 f6+ gxf6 26 exf6+ ♔xf6 27 ♖f1+ ♔e7 28 ♖f4 a4 29 ♗xc4!? dxc4 30 d5, when *Fritz* suggests 30...e5!? but it is very complicated to risk over-the-board. For instance, after 31 dxc6 exf4 32 ♖e1+ ♔e6 33 ♘f5+ ♔d8 34 ♕f6+ ♔c7 35 ♕e7+ ♔b6 36 ♕b4+ Black would have to foresee the subtlety 36...♔a6! so that after 37 ♕xa4+ ♔b6 38 ♕b4+ ♔xc6 39 ♕d6+ ♔b5 40 ♖e5+ does not win because the king can now go to a4. Understandably Korchnoi took the safer path 30...♕a5 31 dxc6 ♗xc6 32 ♕xa5 ♖xa5 and the game was drawn. Three months later, Christiansen-Korchnoi, Reykjavik 2000, saw instead 15 h5 a5 16 ♖hb1 ♖b8 17 ♕f4 ♔e7 18 g4 ♕f8 19 ♕e3 ♔d8!? 20 ♘e1 ♔c7 and only then did Black initiate queenside play with

...b5-b4.

White can also play 13 a4. Short-Morozevich, German Bundesliga 1998, continued 13...♗d7 14 h4 a6 15 ♕f4 b5 16 g4 b4 17 cxb4 ♘xb4 18 c3 ♘c6 19 ♖hb1 ♖b8 20 ♗d1 ♘a5 21 ♔e1 ♘b3 22 ♗xb3 cxb3 23 ♕c1! intending ♕a3 and White gained the upper hand. However, Khalifman-Short (!), Merida 2001, saw instead 13...a6 14 ♖hb1 ♖b8 15 h4 b5 16 axb5 axb5 17 ♕f4 ♕e7 18 ♕e3 ♔e8 19 h5 ♔d8 20 ♘g1 b4 21 f4 ♗d7 22 cxb4 ♖xb4 23 ♖xb4 ♕xb4+ 24 ♕c3 ♕xc3+ 25 ♔xc3 ♔c7 and the game was soon drawn.

If Black delays ...c5-c4 White may decide to prevent it by taking on c5. For example, 11...♘c6 12 dxc5! ♕a5 13 ♕f4 ♕xc5 14 ♘d4 ♗d7 15 ♖hb1 when White takes the initiative on the queenside, as in Leko-Hübner, Dortmund 2000, following 15...b6 16 a4 ♘a5 17 ♗a6 ♗c8 18 ♗b5 ♕e7 19 ♘c6 ♘xc6 20 ♗xc6 ♖b8 21 a5 with a clear advantage; or 15...♘d8! 16 a4 ♖c8 17 ♖b3 a6 18 h4 ♖c7 19 g4 ♘c6 20 ♘xc6 ♗xc6 and now Morozevich-Vallejo Pons, Pamplona 1999, continued 21 ♕b4 ♕xb4 22 cxb4 ♗d7 23 ♖c3 ♖xc3 24 ♔xc3 ♔e7 25 ♔d4 h5! with counterplay for Black. Hence Morozevich later preferred 21 h5 keeping control of the position, though Black is not easy to break down.

But note that 11 dxc5?! would have been too soon as Black has 11...♘d7!, e.g. 12 ♘f3 ♘xc5 13 ♕d4 b6 14 h4 ♗a6 15 ♕b4 ♔g8 16 a4 ♖c8 and Black was already better in Medvegy-Salmensuu, Stockholm 2001.

11...c4

Declaring his intentions forthwith. In a later game Korchnoi played first 11...♘c6 12 ♘f3 then 12...c4 13 ♗e2 as in the previous note. However, 12 ♖h3 c4 13 ♗e2 would transpose back to the game and Black has had no success with anything else.

12 ♗e2 ♘c6 13 ♖h3 ♖g8

A small novelty, the point of which is seen in the next note. Previously Black had

played immediately 13...b5 and if 14 ♖g3 ♖g8, 14 ♖f3 a5 or 14 ♕f4 ♗d7 15 ♗h5 ♗e8.

14 ♕f4

Against 14 ♖f3 Korchnoi made use of ...♖g8 to play 14...♔e7!? Jenni-Korchnoi, Zurich rapidplay 2001, continued 15 ♘h3 ♕a5 16 ♕f4 ♖f8 17 ♖g3 ♖g8 18 ♗h5 ♘d8 19 ♖e1 b5 20 a3 ♕xa3 21 ♖xg7 ♖xg7 22 ♕f6+ ♔d7 23 ♕xg7 b4 24 ♖e3 b3 25 ♖e1 ♖b8 26 ♘f4 ♕a2 27 ♗xf7 ♕xc2+ 28 ♔e3 ♕e4+ 0-1.

14...♗d7 15 ♗h5 ♗e8

First defending f7, and allowing Black to play 16...f5 due to the opposition of bishops.

16 ♘e2 f5 17 g4?!

Anand later recommended 17 ♗xe8! ♔xe8 18 g4 ♘e7 19 ♖g1! with the initiative.

17...♘e7 18 ♖g1 ♗xh5

Black could of course have played this a move sooner.

19 gxh5 ♕e8

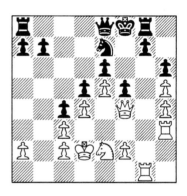

To judge from Anand's notes this whole game is a series of inaccuracies. Here he thinks Black should have played first 19...♖c8! to answer 20 ♕f3 with 20...♔f7; similarly in the game, after 19...♕e8 20 ♕f3 ♖c8 21 ♘f4 he prefers 21...♔f7! 22 ♖hg3 ♖c6. The black queen can just as easily defend g7 from f8, and on the back rank can more easily switch to defend the queenside if necessary.

However, Black's position is very solid in any case. White certainly has no way in on the kingside as Anand discovers as he aimlessly triples on the g-file.

22 ♖hg3 ♖a6 23 ♕g2 ♕f7 24 ♕f1

White's one chance to probe the queenside was by 24 ♖b1, while Black cannot reply ...♕c8, whereas 24...b6 blocks the rook's defence of e6 and White can contemplate 25 ♖g1 ♖xa2 26 ♖xg7! ♖xg7 27 ♕xg7+ ♕xg7 28 ♘xe6. Even so, Black seems okay.

24...♕e8 25 ♖1g2 ♔f7

Now Korchnoi switches the defence to ♔f7 and ♕f8, White's small chance on the queenside is gone.

26 ♖g1 ♖xa2 27 ♕g2 ♕f8 28 ♖b1

Hoping for 28...b6? when White has 29 ♖g6! and if 29...♘xg6? 30 ♕xg6+ ♔e7 31 ♕xe6+ ♔d8 32 ♕xd5+ wins, or 29...♕e8 30 ♖g1 ♘xg6 31 ♕xg6+ ♔f8 32 ♘xe6+ ♔e7 33 ♘xg7 with a clear advantage.

28...♕c8! 29 ♖g1 ½-½

Game 67
Svidler-Morozevich
Frankfurt rapid 1999

---

1 e4 e6 2 d4 d5 3 ♘c3 ♘f6 4 ♗g5 ♗b4 5 e5 h6 6 ♗d2 ♗xc3 7 ♗xc3

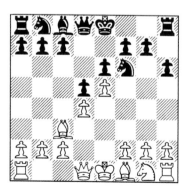

This is perhaps the most natural recapture, preserving the queenside pawn structure. However, after 7...♘e4 White still

has to do something about the bishop, giving Black time to generate counterplay against the centre with ...c7-c5.

Harding writes with apt dismissal: '7 ♗xc3!? is revived occasionally' – with the obvious implication that as soon as Black has dealt adequately any new wrinkles, the variation is put back in its box.

7...♘e4 8 ♘e2

8 ♕g4 would now be met by 8...0-0 since White does not have ♗h6. Similarly 8 ♗d3 ♘xc3 9 bxc3 c5 10 ♕g4 0-0.

8 ♗b4 looks very logical, preserving the bishop on a useful diagonal. However, Black has the tactical resource 8...c5! (Pillsbury) when 9 dxc5? is refuted by 9...♘xf2! 10 ♔xf2 ♕h4+ collecting the bishop and leaving White with a lot of weak pawns; while after 9 ♗xc5 ♘xc5 10 dxc5 White has failed in his objectives and any one of 10...♘d7, 10...♕c7 or 10...♕a5+ is fine for Black.

Fischer once tried 8 ♗a5, with the idea 8...b6 9 ♗b4 c5 10 ♗a3!, but after 8...0-0! 9 ♗d3 ♘c6 10 ♗c3 ♘xc3 11 bxc3 f6 12 f4 fxe5 13 fxe5 ♘e7 14 ♘f3 c5 15 0-0 ♕a5 Black was better in Fischer-Petrosian, Curacao 1962.

8...0-0

Black has also succeeded with:

a) 8...c5 9 dxc5 ♘xc3 (better than 9...♘c6 10 ♗d4!) 10 ♘xc3 0-0 11 ♕d2 f6! 12 exf6 ♕xf6 13 ♗b5 (or 13 0-0-0 ♕xf2 14 ♗e2 ♕f4) 13...a6 14 ♗a4 ♘d7 15 ♗xd7 ♗xd7 16 0-0 ♖ac8 17 ♘d1 ♖xc5 18 c3 ♗b5 19 ♖e1 ♖c4 20 f3 ♕g6 21 ♕e3 ♖e8 22 ♕e5 ♕f6 ½-½ Lanka-M.Gurevich, Cappelle la Grande 1999.

b) 8...♘c6!? 9 ♘f4 ♕e7 10 ♗d3 ♘xc3 11 bxc3 ♗d7 12 ♘h5 ♖g8! 13 ♗h7 ♖h8 14 ♗d3 ♖g8 – a tacit draw offer which White refused and came out worse after 15 0-0 0-0-0 16 a4 ♘a5 17 f4 c5 18 ♗b5 ♔b8 19 ♗xd7 ♕xd7 20 ♕d3 ♕c7 in Sutovsky-Psakhis, Tel Aviv 1999.

9 ♗b4

If 9 f3?! ♘xc3 10 ♘xc3 c5 11 dxc5 ♕h4+! 12 g3 ♕b4 13 ♕d3 ♘c6, as in Koch-Murey, Paris 1989.

Or 9 ♕d3!? b6 10 ♗b4 c5 11 ♗a3 and rather than 11...f6? 12 f3! ♗a6 13 ♕e3 fxe5 14 fxe4 exd4 15 ♕h3 and White won in Ostrowski-Hnyudiuk, Zakopane 2000, Black should have tried 11...♗a6 12 ♕e3 ♘c6! 13 c3 (if 13 f3 ♗xe2 14 ♗xe2 ♕h4+) 13...♖e8 when 14 f3 can be answered by 14...cxd4 15 cxd4 ♕g5.

9...c5 10 ♗a3 ♘c6!

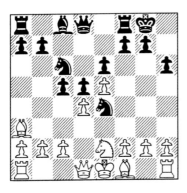

Morozevich had previously lost in this variation after 10...cxd4?! 11 ♗xf8 ♕xf8 12 f3 d3 (or 12...♕b4+ 13 c3 dxc3 14 bxc3 ♘xc3 15 ♕d2) 13 fxe4 dxe2 14 ♕xe2 ♘c6 15 exd5 exd5 16 0-0-0 and Black had no compensation for the exchange in Galkin-Morozevich, Novgorod 1997. So it was very unlikely that he would play this again, even in a rapidplay game, without an improvement in mind.

11 f3 b5!

Ignoring the threat the his knight Black targets the ♗a3 with ...b7-b5-b4. If now 12 c3 b4 13 ♗xb4 Black inserts 13...♕h4+! 14 g3 ♘xg3 15 ♘xg3 cxb4. No better was 11 c3 b5! 12 ♗xc5 ♘xc5 13 dxc5 ♘xe5.

12 fxe4 b4 13 ♗xb4

Thus White wins a pawn, but Black's lead in development ensures him of full compensation, and the break ...f7-f6 will open lines and keep the white king in the

centre. As for example, after 13 exd5 ♕xd5 14 ♗xb4 cxb4 15 c3 f6! 16 exf6 ♖xf6.

13...♘xb4 14 c3 ♘c6 15 exd5

If 15 ♕a4!? Finkel proposes 15...♕b6! 16 ♖d1 cxd4 17 exd5 exd5 18 cxd4 f6! again with excellent compensation for Black.

15...♕xd5 16 dxc5 ♕xc5 17 ♘c1

If 17 ♕d6 ♕b6! and the threat of 18...♖d8 keeps White from castling long, i.e. 18 0-0-0? ♖d8 19 ♕a3 ♕e3+ 20 ♔c2 ♗b7 with decisive threats. So Svidler gives up the e-pawn to prepare 0-0-0, but with no lessening of Black's initiative.

17...♕xe5+ 18 ♕e2

White cannot castle short since if 18 ♗e2 ♖d8 19 ♕a4 ♗b7 20 0-0 then 20...♖d2 wins material (if 21 ♖f2 ♕e3!).

18...♕c7 19 ♘d3 ♗a6 20 0-0-0 ♖fd8?!

Better was 20...♘b4!, exploiting the two pins. After 21...♘xa2+ Black may open the king up further with ...♘xc3 or first bring up more forces by ...♕a5 and ...♖ab8, when it is hard to see how White can survive.

21 ♕f2

White side-steps the pin from the bishop and thus forestalls ...♘b4.

21...♗c4

22 ♕f4!?

22 b3 (Finkel) may be technically more accurate as after 22...♗xd3 23 ♗xd3 has good chances to defend, e.g. 23...♘e5 (or 23...♘b4 24 ♗c4 ♘d5 25 ♕f3) 24 ♕c2 ♖xd3 25 ♖xd3 ♘xd3+ 26 ♕xd3 ♖c8 27

♔b2.

However, 22 ♕f4 shows nice psychology. White forces the exchange of queens, thus negating Black's hopes of winning by direct attack. True, Black gets an extra pawn for the endgame, but realising this advantage will be less easy, especially in a rapidplay game. In the end White manages to hold on for a draw.

22...♕xf4+ 23 ♘xf4 ♖xd1+ 24 ♔xd1 ♗xa2 25 ♔c2 ♖b8 26 b4 g5 27 ♘h5 ♔f8 28 ♔b2 ♗d5 29 ♘f6 ♔e7 30 ♘xd5+ exd5 31 ♗e2 a5 32 ♗f3 axb4 33 ♗xd5 ♘e5 34 cxb4

With the queenside pawns eliminated White's task becomes simpler.

34...♖xb4+ 35 ♔c3 ♖a4 36 ♖f1 h5 37 ♗b3 ♖e4 38 ♗d5 ♖e2 39 ♔d4 f6 40 ♗e4 h4 41 h3 ♘f7 42 ♖a1 ♘d6 43 ♗f3 ♖d2+ 44 ♔c3 ♖f2 45 ♔d3 f5 46 ♖a5 ♔e6 47 ♗d5+ ♔f6 48 ♗f3 ♖b2 49 ♔d4 ♖d2+ 50 ♔c3 ♖f2 51 ♔d4 ½-½

Game 68
Lanka-Morozevich
Kishinev 1998

---

1 e4 e6 2 d4 d5 3 ♘c3 ♘f6 4 ♗g5 ♗b4 5 e5 h6 6 ♗e3

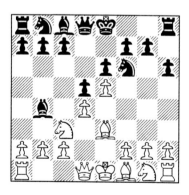

This signals a different approach by White, who wants to keep the dark-squared bishop for attacking purposes, even at the cost of a pawn at c3.

White can also sacrifice by 6 ♗c1!? ♘e4 7 ♕g4, with the added point that after 7...g6 8 ♘e2 c5 9 a3 ♕a5 (as with 6 ♗e3 below) White can simply play 10 axb4! ♕xa1 11 ♘xe4 dxe4 12 bxc5 with advantage. So Black must choose between:

a) 9...♗a5?! 10 b4! ♘xc3 (10...cxb4 11 ♘xe4) 11 ♘xc3 cxd4 (or 11...cxb4 12 ♘b5 b3+ 13 ♗d2) 12 ♘b5 ♗c7 13 f4 ♘c6 14 ♗d3 a6 15 ♘xc7+ ♕xc7 16 0-0 ♗d7 17 ♕h4 ♕d8 18 ♕f2 ♕b6 19 ♗b2 0-0-0 (Borriss-Hübner, German Bundesliga 2001) when 20 c3! is good for White.

b) 9...♗xc3+ 10 bxc3 cxd4 11 cxd4 and now 11...♕c7 12 f3 ♘c3 13 ♗d2 ♘xe2 14 ♗xe2 ♗d7 15 ♗d3 was good for White in S.Hector-Pedersen, Oxford 1998. In Rytshagov-D.Anderton, Gausdal 2000, Black improved by 11...♕a5+ 12 c3 ♗d7 13 f3 ♗b5! 14 fxe4 ♗xe2 15 ♕h3 ♗xf1 16 ♖xf1 dxe4 17 ♔f2 ♘d7 18 ♔g1 ♖h7 19 ♕e3 ♕d5 20 ♖e1 ♖c8 with an unclear position.

7...♔f8 also improves line 'a', since after 8 ♘e2 c5 9 a3 ♗a5 10 b4 ♘xc3 11 ♘xc3 cxd4 12 ♘b5?! does not threaten check at d6, giving Black time to play 12...♗b6! with advantage. White would have to play 12 ♕xd4 with an unclear position after 12...♗b6 13 ♕d3.

6...♘e4 7 ♕g4

It is noteworthy that Glek, in a rare game on the white side of the McCutcheon, chose here to play 7 ♘ge2 c5 (7...b6!?) 8 dxc5!? (8 a3 is more usual) 8...♘c6 9 a3 ♗xc3+ 10 ♘xc3 ♘xc3 11 bxc3 ♘xe5 12 ♗d4 ♕g5 13 h4 ♕f5 14 ♗e2 0-0 15 0-0 ♘c6 16 f4 ♘xd4 17 cxd4 ♗d7 18 g4 ♕f6 19 g5 ♕e7 20 ♗d3 g6 21 ♕e1 with the advantage in Glek-Hoang Thanh Trang, Budapest 1998.

7...♔f8

As White is still going to have a dark-squared bishop it seems more logical for Black to defend g7 with the king rather than weaken the dark squares by 7...g6, though the latter is played. Iordachescu-Vysochin,

Kiev 2000, continued 8 a3 ♗xc3+ (if 8...♗a5 9 ♘ge2) 9 bxc3 ♘xc3 10 ♗d3 ♘c6 11 h4 ♕e7 12 ♘h3 ♗d7 13 h5 g5 14 f4 gxf4 15 ♗f2 ♕f8 16 ♕xf4 0-0-0 (one advantage of not playing ...♔f8) 17 ♗h4 ♖e8 18 0-0 ♘e4 19 ♘f2! ♘xd4 20 ♘xe4 dxe4 21 ♕xe4 ♘f5 22 ♖ab1 ♕c5+ (not 22...♗c6? 23 ♕xc6! bxc6 24 ♗a6+ ♔d7 25 ♖fd1+ ♘d6 26 exd6 wins) 23 ♗f2 ♕d5 24 c4 ♕xe4 25 ♗xe4 b6 26 c5 ♖eg8 27 ♖fc1 ♔d8 28 ♗f3 ♖g5 29 ♖b2 ♖hg8 30 ♖d2 and White won.

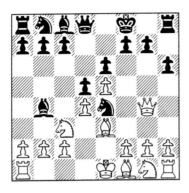

8 a3!?

The critical move. 8 ♘e2 is easily met by 8...c5 9 a3 ♕a5 10 ♖d1 ♗xc3+ 11 ♘xc3 ♘c6 12 ♗b5 ♘xc3 13 ♗xc6+ bxc6 14 ♗d2 cxd4 15 ♕xd4 ♕b5, while against 8 ♗d3 ♘xc3 9 a3 Euwe recommended 9...♘a2+! 10 ♔f1 ♗e7 11 ♖xa2 b6 12 ♘e2 ♗a6 13 h4 c5 with equality.

8...♗xc3+

The insertion of 8 a3 ♗a5 means that 9 ♘ge2! is now good for White after 9...c5 10 dxc5! ♘c6 (or 10...♘xc3 11 ♘xc3 ♗xc3+ 12 bxc3 ♘c6 13 ♗d4) 11 b4! ♘xc3 12 ♘xc3 ♘xe5 13 ♕d1 ♗c7 14 ♘b5 ♗b8 15 c4 a6 16 ♘c3 ♕f6 17 ♖c1 ♘xc4 18 ♗xc4 dxc4 19 ♘e4 ♕e7 20 ♖xc4 ♔g8 21 ♖d4 ♗a7 22 ♘d6 g6 23 0-0 with a big advantage to White in Mohrlok-Kilgour, correspondence 1992-96.

9 bxc3 c5 10 ♗d3 ♘xc3

10...h5!? was a resounding success in its first appearance: 11 ♕f3 ♘xc3 12 ♘h3

♘c6 13 ♘f4? ♔g8 14 ♘xh5 ♕h4 15 g4 ♘xd4 16 ♕f4 ♗d7 0-1 Van Mil-Murey, Amsterdam 1983. It recently appeared again in Kasparov-Korchnoi, Kopavogur rapidplay 2000, with Black making a quick draw after 11 ♕f4 ♕a5 12 ♘e2 ♘xc3 13 0-0 ♘xe2+ 14 ♗xe2 ♘c6 15 c4 cxd4 16 ♗xd4 ♘xd4 17 ♕xd4 ♗d7 18 cxd5 exd5 19 ♗f3 ♗c6 ½-½. Fressinet-Vaisser, French Team Championship 2001, saw instead 11 ♕h3 ♘xc3 12 dxc5 d4 13 ♗d2 ♕d5 14 f4 ♘c6 15 ♗xc3 dxc3 16 ♘e2 ♕xc5 17 ♗e4 ♗d7 18 ♖d1 ♗e8 19 ♕xc3+ 20 ♘xc3 when Black unravelled by 20...♘a5! 21 0-0 ♖c8 22 ♖d3 g6 23 ♗f3 ♔g7 24 ♖f2 ♖c7 25 ♘e4 ♗a4 26 ♘c3 ♖c4 27 g3 ♖hc8 and now stood quite well.

11 dxc5 ♘c6 12 ♘f3 f5 13 exf6 ♕xf6 14 ♕h5

14 ♘h4 ♔g8 15 ♘g6 ♖h7 is only a temporary inconvenience for Black as the knight cannot be maintained on g6, e.g. 16 ♕h4 (if 16 ♕h5 ♗d7 intending ...♗e8) 16...e5 17 ♗d2 ♘e4 18 ♗xe4 dxe4 19 ♕xe4 ♗f5 20 ♕d5+ ♕f7 21 ♕xf7+ ♔xf7 and the knight has to withdraw.

14...e5 15 ♗g6

If 15 ♘h4 Black can sacrifice the exchange by 15...e4 16 ♘g6+ ♔g8 17 ♘xh8 exd3 with good play. Similarly after 15 ♗g5 hxg5 16 ♕xh8+ ♔e7 17 h4 g4 18 ♘g5 e4, though here 15...♕f7 16 ♗g6 ♗g4! 17 ♗xf7 ♗xh5 18 ♗xh5 hxg5 is also acceptable.

15...♗e6!?

A new and logical move. The bishop heads for f7 to fight for the g6-square. If instead 15...♗d7 (intending ...♗e8) then 16 0-0 ♔g8 17 ♗d2! ♘e4 18 c4 ♘xd2 19 ♘xd2 d4 20 ♘e4 and White is better (Gufeld).

15...e4?! is weak as it provides White with a target: 16 ♘h4 ♔g8 17 0-0 ♗e6 18 f3! ♘e2+ 19 ♔h1 ♖f8 20 ♖ae1 ♘f4 21 ♗xf4 ♕xf4 22 g3 ♕g5 23 fxe4 ♖xf1+ 24 ♖xf1 dxe4 25 ♕d1 ♕d5 26 ♕xd5 ♗xd5 27 ♖d1

♗f7 28 ♗xe4 g5 29 ♘f5 and White won in Hall-Barnsley, correspondence 1993-95.

White is also for preference after 15...♔g8 16 0-0 ♘e2+ 17 ♔h1 ♘f4 18 ♗xf4 ♕xf4 19 h3 ♗e6 20 c3 ♗f7 21 ♖ab1 ♗xg6 22 ♕xg6 ♕f7 23 ♕xf7+ ♔xf7 24 ♖xb7+ ♔f6 25 ♖fb1 ♖hb8 (Filipenko-Volkov, Moscow 1999) and now 26 ♔g1! (Filipenko). Or if 16...♗e6 17 ♖ae1 ♖d8 18 ♗d2 ♘e4 19 c4 ♘xd2 20 ♘xd2 ♕g5 (½-½ Fressinet-Vallejo Pons, Mondariz 2000) then 21 ♕xg5 hxg5 22 cxd5 ♗xd5 23 ♗e4 or 22...♖xd5 23 ♘b3 again looks good for White.

16 0-0

The tactical justification of 15...♗e6 is seen after 16 ♗g5 ♗g4! 17 ♗xf6 ♗xh5 18 ♗xe5 ♗xg6 19 ♗xc3 ♗xc2 or 18 ♗xg7+ ♔xg7 19 ♗xh5 ♖hf8 with compensation.

16...♗f7 17 ♘h4 ♖e8 18 ♖ae1

Of course White would like to open the f-file, but 18 f4 is met by 18...e4, while if 18 ♗d2, with the idea 18...♘e4? 19 f4, Black responds 18...♘e2+! 19 ♕xe2 ♗xg6 or 19 ♔h1 ♘ed4.

18...♔g8 19 f3 ♖e6

Expelling the bishop from g6.

20 ♗xf7+ ♕xf7 21 ♕g4 ♖f6!

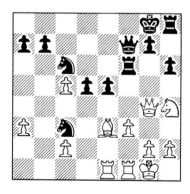

A strong consolidating move, covering f4 and c4 (with the queen). The routine 21...♔h7 would allow White to take the initiative with 22 ♗d2 ♘b5 23 c4! h5 24 ♕h3 dxc4 25 f4! White tries this in any case,

as he has to do something before Black completes development, when his strong central pawns will give him a clear advantage.

22 ♗d2 ♘b5 23 f4! e4 24 c4?!

If now 24...dxc4?! 25 a4! ♘bd4 26 ♖xe4 White gains a dangerous initiative with f4-f5, e.g. 26...♔h7?! 27 f5 ♖d8 28 ♗c3 intending ♖ff4, or 26...♕d5 27 f5 h5! (otherwise ♖e8+ wins) 28 ♕f4 (if 28 ♖e8+ ♔f7) 28...♔h7 29 ♗c3 ♖d8 with an unclear position.

However, 24 ♗c1, intending ♗b2, was better as Black can play:

24...♘xa3! 25 cxd5 ♕xd5 26 ♖e3?

White cannot play 26 ♗c3 because of 26...♕xc5+, so first he needs to close the g1-a7 diagonal. But 26 ♖e3 was a definite mistake as the rook merely invites the black knight to c4. Better was 26 ♖f2 when with 27 ♗c3 to follow White still has his chances.

26...h5 27 ♕e2 ♘c4 28 ♖d1 ♘d4!

If Black takes the exchange he still has some problems to solve after 28...♘xe3!? 29 ♗xe3 and 30 f5, as 30...♔h7 would allow 31 ♗g5! By driving the queen back Black is able to extricate his rook, counting on the strong e4-pawn to win the game.

29 ♕f1 ♔h7 30 ♖c3 ♘xd2 31 ♖xd2 ♖d8 32 f5 g5!

Forcing White to open the f-file for the black rooks.

33 fxg6+ ♔g7 34 ♕e1 ♖df8 35 ♖c1 ♔g8!

Black cannot yet play 35...♖f1+? 36 ♕xf1 ♖xf1+ 37 ♖xf1 ♕g5 due to 38 ♖xd4 ♕e3+? 39 ♔h1 ♕xd4 40 ♘f5+. Hence the preliminary king move.

36 g7

Setting the trap 36...♖f1+ 37 ♕xf1 ♖xf1+ 38 ♖xf1 ♕g5? 39 ♖xd4 ♕e3+ 40 ♔h1 ♕xd4 41 ♖f8+ wins, while 36...♔xg7? 37 ♕e3 gets a draw after 37...♕c4! 38 ♕g5+.

36...♖8f7 37 h3

Not 37 ♕e3? ♕c4! and wins.

37...♕e5 38 ♕e3 ♘c6 39 ♖e2 ♔xg7 40 ♕xe4 ♕g5!

With a semi-fork on ♖c1 and ♘h4, since ...♖f4 wins the knight.

41 ♕c4 ♕g3! 42 ♕a4

42 ♖e4 ♖f4 43 ♖xf4 ♖xf4 44 ♖f1 is equally hopeless after 44...♖xc4 45 ♘f5+ ♔g6 46 ♘xg3 ♖xc5 and the queenside pawns will win easily.

42...♖f4 43 ♕a1+ ♖7f6 44 ♖d1 ♕xh4 45 ♖d7+ ♔h6 46 ♔h2 ♖f2 47 ♕c1+ ♕f4+ 48 ♕xf4+ ♖6xf4 49 ♖e8 ♖f7 50 ♖e6+ ♔g7 0-1

Game 69
Landa-Morozevich
Samara 1998

---

1 e4 e6 2 d4 d5 3 ♘c3 ♘f6 4 ♗g5 ♗b4 5 e5 h6 6 exf6

White has two other minor possibilities:

a) 6 ♗xf6 gxf6 7 ♘f3 ♘d7 8 exf6 ♕xf6 9 a3 ♗f8 10 ♕e2 c6 11 g3 ♗g7 12 ♗g2 0-0 13 0-0 e5 and Black had no problems in Agur-Dreev, Oviedo rapidplay 1991.

b) 6 ♗h4 g5 7 ♗g3 ♘e4 8 ♘ge2 c5 9 a3 (or 9 ♕d3 ♘c6 10 a3 ♕a5) 9....♗xc3+ 10 ♘xc3 ♕a5 11 ♕d3 ♘c6 12 dxc5 ♗d7 13 0-0-0 ♘xc3 14 ♕xc3 ♕xc3 15 bxc3 ♖c8 16 h4 ♖g8 17 hxg5 hxg5 18 f3 g4 19 fxg4 ♖xg4 20 ♖h3 with a level position in Landa-Minasian, Linares 1999.

6...hxg5 7 fxg7 ♖g8

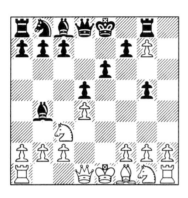

8 h4

The standard plan – after the usual 8...gxh4 White gets the h-file for the rook.

The h-pawn advance can be delayed. In Kholmov-Nikolenko, Moscow 1999, White first played 8 ♘f3 ♕f6 (or 8...♖xg7 9 ♘e5 ♘d7) 9 h4 gxh4 10 ♕d2 ♘c6 11 a3 ♗xc3 12 ♕xc3 ♗d7 13 ♖xh4 ♕xg7 14 g3 0-0-0 with a level position.

De Weerd-Glek, Korinthos 2000, saw instead 8 ♕h5 ♕f6 9 ♘f3 ♕xg7 10 a3 ♗xc3+ 11 bxc3 ♘d7 12 h4 g4 13 ♘h2 g3 14 ♘f3 gxf2+ 15 ♔d1 with a clear advantage to Black, although he lost in the first of several disasters at this tournament (c.f. 8 ♕g4 in Game 70).

8...♘c6!?

This must have come as quite a shock to his opponent. The theoretical justification of White's opening moves is that the h-pawn must be taken as otherwise it will advance further and tie Black down on the kingside. *ECO* for many years gave simply '8...♖xg7 9 h5 clear advantage to White' (though that has been revised in the new edition).

The old theory saw 8...gxh4 9 ♕g4 ♕f6 10 ♖xh4 ♕xg7 11 ♕xg7 ♖xg7 12 ♖h8+ when after 12...♔d7 13 ♘f3 ♘c6 or 12...♗f8, Black is passive, leaving White with whatever winning chances exist.

The rook recapture, 10...♖xg7, was also thought to be bad as after 11 ♖h8+ ♔e7 12 ♕h3 White has an attack. This assessment may also need to be revised following Barczay-Hoang Thanh Trang, Budapest 2001, which saw 12...♘c6 13 0-0-0 ♗xc3 14 ♕xc3 ♖xg2 15 ♕a3+ ♔d7 16 ♗xg2 ♕xh8 17 ♘f3 b5 18 ♕c5 a6 19 ♘e5+?! ♘xe5 20 ♗xd5 (20 dxd5 ♗b7) 20...♕h6+ 21 f4? (21 ♔b1 exd5 22 ♕xd5+ ♕d6 23 ♕xa8 ♘c6) 21...exd5 22 dxe5? (22 ♕xd5+) 22...♕xf4+ 23 ♔b1 ♗b7 0-1.

9 h5

Naturally, White advances his h-pawn as intended. However, he could have tried 9

♘f3!? and if 9...g4 10 ♘e5 ♘xe5 11 dxe5 ♖xg7 12 ♕d3 with the initiative (Finkel), or if 9...gxh4 10 ♖xh4 ♕f6 transposes to the known line 8...gxh4 9 ♘f3!? ♕f6 10 ♖xh4 ♘c6, with which White has not fared badly. Hodgson-Garbarino, Benidorm 1991, continued 11 ♕d2 ♗d7 12 0-0-0 0-0-0 13 ♔b1 ♕xg7 14 a3 ♗e7 15 ♖h3 ♖h8 16 g3 ♗f6 17 ♖xh8 ♖xh8 18 ♗g2 with a level position. Hodgson later won after a typically speculative sacrifice.

9...♖xg7 10 h6

If 10 ♕d3 ♕f6 11 h6 ♖g8 12 h7 ♖h8 13 0-0-0, intending 13...♗d7 14 ♘b5!? 0-0-0 15 ♕g3, Black has adequate time for 13...a6 (and if 14 ♕e3 ♗e7).

10...♖h7 11 ♗d3 ♖h8 12 ♕h5!?

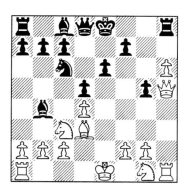

White seeks to utilise his only asset, the h-pawn, before Black gets it under control, and cannot afford the worry about the d-pawn.

12...♕f6

12...♘xd4 13 ♘h3 ♕f6 14 ♘xg5 transposes.

13 ♘f3 ♘xd4 14 ♘xg5

Continuing with his kingside play and threatening 15 ♘xf7! The greedy 14...♗xc3+ 15 bxc3 ♘xc2+!? would also create serious problems for Black after 16 ♔e2! ♘xa1 17 ♘xf7.

14...♘f5 15 h7!?

Presumably White did not care for 15 ♗xf5 ♕xf5 16 0-0-0 ♗d7, when with the

two bishops and strong centre Black is clearly for preference, e.g. 16...♗d7 17 ♖d3 (threatening ♖f3) 17...♗e7! 18 ♘f3 ♕xh5 19 ♖xh5 f6.

15...♗xc3+ 16 bxc3 ♕xc3+ 17 ♔e2 ♕e5+!

Again Black must not be too greedy: 17...♘d4+? 18 ♔d1! ♕xa1+ 19 ♔d2 and f7 cannot be defended.

18 ♔d2 ♕f4+ 19 ♔e2 ♘d6!

With f7 now protected Black is able to complete development. However, with continued pressure on f7 and a big pawn at h7 White is still able to put up a fight.

20 ♖ae1

With the idea 21 0-0-0, 22 ♘xe6, so Black quickly evacuates his king.

20...♗d7 21 ♔f1 0-0-0 22 ♕h6!

Threatening 23 ♖h4 ♕d2 24 ♘xf7!

22...♗b5

If now 23 ♖h4 ♗xd3+ 24 cxd3 ♕d2 25 ♘xf7? Black wins with 25...♕xd3+. Otherwise the exchange of bishops allows the black queen on to the kingside light squares.

23 ♗xb5 ♘xb5 24 ♖h4 ♕f5 25 ♕g7?!

The threat to f7 is not very dangerous. White could still have created trouble with 25 ♖h5!? threatening ♘xe6, while if 25...e5 26 ♘e4 ♕g6 27 ♘g5 ♕xh6 28 ♖xh6 leaves e5 and f7 in need of protection, or 25...♖de8 26 ♘e4 ♕g6 27 ♘f6 ♕xh6 28 ♖xh6 ♖d8 29 ♖e5 intending ♖g5-g7.

25...♘d6 26 g3

Not yet 26 ♖e5 ♕xc2 27 ♘xf7 due to 27...♘f5! and wins after 28 ♕f6 ♘xh4 29 ♘xh8 ♕d3+! 30 ♔g1 ♕b1+ 31 ♔h2 ♕xh7 threatening the ♘h8 and 32...♘f3+.

26...♖de8 27 c3?

A final mistake. Better was 27 ♖e5 ♕xc2 28 ♘xf7.

27...♕d3+ 28 ♔g1 ♕d2

Or 28...♘f5.

29 ♖e5 ♕xc3 30 ♖f4 ♕c2 31 ♔g2 b5 32 a3 a5 33 ♖f6

White's kingside clamp is now irrelevant

as the queenside pawns will win the game.

33...b4 34 axb4 axb4 35 ♖exe6 fxe6 36 ♖xe6 ♖xh7 37 ♖xe8+ ♘xe8 38 ♕e5 ♘d6 0-1

Game 70
Jenni-Glek
Bad Wörishofen 2001

---

1 e4 e6 2 d4 d5 3 ♘c3 ♘f6 4 ♗g5 ♗b4 5 exd5

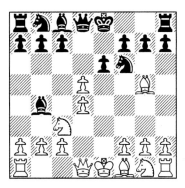

This spoiling move is surprisingly one of the very few lines assessed in *ECO* as slightly better for White (after 5...♕xd5). It was a favourite of Emanuel Lasker, and GMs Chandler and De la Villa Garcia have also scored well with 5 exd5. If Black recaptures 5...exd5 (which receives an exclamation mark in *ECO*) White has an slightly improved Exchange variation as Black's pieces are not on their best squares. If Black takes back with the queen he gives up some influence in the centre.

5...♕xd5

The usual choice of McCutcheon players.

After 5...exd5 6 ♕f3 intends to damage Black's structure by 7 ♗xf6 after which Black would be slightly worse. So Black usually replies 6...♘bd7 and then if 7 0-0-0 not 7...♗xc3?! 8 ♕e3+♕e7 9 ♕xc3 ♕d6 10 ♖e1+ ♔f8 11 f3 h6 12 ♗d2 b6 13 ♘e2 with a definite advantage in Ye Rongguang-R.Rodriguez, Cebu 1992, but 7...♗e7 8 ♖e1

0-0 9 ♗d3 ♖e8 10 ♘ge2 c6 11 ♘g3 ♘f8 12 ♘f5 ♗xf5 13 ♗xf5 ♘6d7 14 ♗xe7 ♖xe7 15 ♗h3 ♕e8 which was soon agreed drawn in Galkin-Alavkin, St Petersburg 1999.

6 ♗xf6

The only worthwhile move. Not 6 ♕d2?? ♗xc3 7 bxc3 ♘e4 winning a piece, while White has nothing after 6 ♘f3 ♘e4 7 ♗d2 ♗xc3 8 bxc3 ♘xd2 9 ♕xd2 ♘d7 or 9...b6.

6...♗xc3+!

6...gxf6 gives White the chance to protect his own structure by 7 ♘ge2! and if 7...c5 8 a3! ♗xc3+ 9 ♘xc3 ♕xd4 10 ♕xd4 cxd4 11 ♘b5 is good for White, e.g. 11...♘a6 12 ♘xd4 ♘c7 13 0-0-0 ♗d7 14 ♗d3 0-0-0 15 ♖he1 ♗c6 16 ♘xc6 bxc6 17 ♖a4 (Chandler-Carton, Blackpool Zonal 1990).

If instead 7...♘c6 8 a3 ♗xc3+ 9 ♘xc3 ♕xd4 10 ♕xd4 ♘xd4 11 0-0-0 c5 12 ♘e4 b6 13 c3 ♘f5 14 g4 ♘h4 15 ♘xf6+ ♔e7 16 g5 was also good for White in Chandler-King, Hastings 1990. However, 13...♘b3+! is better after 14 ♔c2 ♘a5 15 ♘xf6+ ♔e7 (King) or if 15 b4 ♘b7 16 ♘xf6+ ♔e7 17 ♘e4 ♗d7 and Black was not worse in Morozevich-Kovalev, Moscow rapidplay 1994.

For White, 8 ♕d2 improves this line, since after 8...♗xc3 9 ♘xc3! ♕xd4 10 ♕xd4 ♘xd4 11 0-0-0 c5 12 ♘e4 b6 13 c3 Black does not have ...♘b3+.

7 bxc3 gxf6 8 ♕g4

Probably the best try in this variation. As in the main lines with 5 e5, White tries to exploit the missing ♗f8 and come in at g7 with the queen. White also has the possibility of ♕f4 (as after 8 ♕d2).

Of the alternatives, 8 ♘f3 b6! does not trouble Black at all; nor does 8 ♕f3 ♕xf3 9 ♘xf3 b6. However, 8 ♕d2 is an important option, which Black should not take too casually.

a) 8...♘d7 9 c4 ♕e4+ 10 ♘e2 ♘b6 (10...b6) 11 f3 ♕c6 12 c5 ♘d5 13 c4 ♘e7 14 ♘c3 f5 15 ♗e2 ♖g8 16 0-0 ♗d7 17 ♕e3 b6 18 ♖fd1 bxc5 19 d5 ♕d6 20 dxe6 ♕xe6

21 ♕xc5 with an extra pawn in Capablanca-Alekhine, New York 1924, though Capablanca was unable to convert it.

b) 8...b6 9 ♗e2! (intending ♗f3) 9...♘c6 10 ♕f4 ♕a5 11 ♔d2 ♕g5 12 ♕xg5 fxg5 13 h4 gxh4 14 ♖xh4 ♘e7 15 ♗f3 ♖b8 16 ♘e2 ♘g6 17 ♖h2 ♗b7 18 ♗xb7 ♖xb7 19 ♖ah1 and the h-pawn proved a terminal weakness in Khlusevich-Glek, correspondence 1988-91.

c) 8...♕a5 has been Glek's preference, preventing ♕f4 by hitting c3. This was successful in van der Wiel-Glek, Bundesliga 2000, after 9 g3 ♗d7 10 ♗g2 ♗c6 11 ♘f3 ♘d7 12 0-0 0-0-0 13 ♖fd1 ♘b6 14 ♕h6 ♕xc3 15 ♕xf6 ♖hf8 16 ♘e1 ♗xg2 17 ♔xg2 ♘d5 18 ♕f3 ♖d6! with advantage to Black, but White did better in Lanka-Ellers, German Bundesliga 2000, with 13 ♖fb1!? ♘b6 14 a4 ♕h5 15 ♘e1 ♖d6 16 ♕d3 ♕g6 17 ♕f1 e5 18 a5 ♘d5 19 ♖b3 e4?! 20 c4 ♘e7 21 d5 ♗d7 22 ♖ab1 with a big attack.

d) 8...♘c6!? is more in keeping with the main game. Black doesn't worry about the f-pawn, intending simply ...♗d7, ...0-0-0 and to break with ...e6-e5. If 9 ♘f3 ♗d7 10 ♕f4 0-0-0 11 ♕xf6 e5 Black has obvious compensation. Or if 9 ♕f4, hitting c7 and f6, Black can defend by 9...♕a5 and 10...♔e7.

8...♗d7!?

a) 8...♕g5 9 ♕xg5 fxg5 10 h4 g4 11 ♘e2 c5 12 ♘f4 (Keres). In Verney-Hall, correspondence 1995-97, White opted for 9 ♕g3!? ♕a5 (if 9...♕xg3 10 hxg3 White gets the h-file) 10 ♘e2 ♔f8 (if 10...♔e7 11 ♘c1! and 12 ♘b3) 11 ♕e3 ♗d7 12 ♘g3 ♗c6 13 f3 ♘d7 14 ♔f2 ♖d8 15 c4 ♕g5 16 ♖e1 ♖g8 17 ♗d3 ♕xe3+ 18 ♖xe3 f5 19 ♘h5 ♘b6 20 c3 ♘a4 21 ♗e2 b6 22 ♖b1 ♖g6 23 ♘f4 ♖h6 24 ♔g1 ♖e8 (if 24...e5!? 25 dxe5 ♖d2 26 ♖a1 ♖c2 27 ♗d1!) 25 ♗d1 ♖d6 26 ♗b3 ♗d7 27 ♖be1 a5 28 ♖1e2 ♔g7 29 g3 ♔f8 30 ♔g2 ♔g7 31 g4 fxg4 32 fxg4 and Black was slowly ground down in the endgame.

b) 8...♘d7 9 ♗d3 ♔f8 is worse still after

10 ♕f4! h5 (if 10...e5 11 ♗e4!) 11 ♕xc7 ♕xg2 12 0-0-0 ♕xh1 13 ♘e2 and White is better after 14 ♖g1, winning the queen for the second rook. But this was better than 13...♘c6?? 14 ♕d8+ 1-0 Turov-Glek, Korinthos 2000, as ♖g1 now gets the king.

c) 8...♔e7!? is more enterprising, intending 9 ♕g7 (if 9 ♗d3 ♘c6 intending 10...e5) 9...♖d8 (9...♕e4+ 10 ♔d1 does not help Black) 10 ♕xh7 ♕a5 11 ♕d3 (11 ♘e2 ♖xd4!) 11...c5 12 ♕d2 ♘c6 13 ♘f3 cxd4 14 cxd4 ♕xd2+ 15 ♔xd2 ♘xd4 and Black regains the pawn, although the passed h-pawn means White still has the better chances.

d) 8...♕a5 is more accurate, since after 9 ♘e2 ♔e7! 10 ♕g7 ♖d8 Black already threatens ...♖xd4, or if 10 ♕g3 ♗d7 11 ♘c1 Black has 11...♖g8!; while 9 ♕g3 ♗d7 or 9 ♔d2 c5!? 10 ♕g7 ♖f8 11 ♕xf6 cxd4 12 ♕xd4 ♘c6 are also fine.

Glek's move, 8...♗d7, is similarly dynamic, and after a number of reverses in the 5 exd5 variation, he has clearly had enough of positional continuations.

9 ♕g7

The only consistent move after 8 ♕g4. Otherwise Black will simply play 9...♘c6 and 10...0-0-0; or if 9 ♗d3 possibly 9...♗c6!? and 10...♘d7.

9...♖f8 10 ♕xf6

If White takes the h-pawn, 10 ♕xh7, Black can choose between 10...♘c6 11 ♘f3 0-0-0 intending 12...♕a5, 13...e5; or again 10...♘c6!? planning ...♘d7, ...0-0-0. For instance, if 11 ♘f3 ♗d7 12 ♗d3 0-0-0 and the white queen is embarrassed in face of ...♖h8, or 11 ♕d3 ♘d7 12 ♘f3 0-0-0 13 ♗e2 ♕a5 14 0-0 ♘c5! 15 ♕e3 ♘e4 16 c4 ♘c3 causes problems.

10...♗a4 11 ♕f4

Similarly 11 ♔d2 ♘d7 12 ♕f3 ♕g5+! 13 ♕d2 ♕a5 and 14 ...0-0-0 with play against the king in the centre.

11...♕a5 12 ♕d2 ♘c6 13 ♗d3 0-0-0

With a lead in development and ...e6-e5

to follow Black has good compensation for the pawn.

14 f4 f6 15 ⵗf3 e5 16 fxe5?

The advance of f-pawns, if not the exchange, has helped White a little, who now had to play 16 0-0 exd4 17 cxd4 ⵗxd2 18 ⵗxd2 ⵗxd4 19 ⵗb3 and if 19...ⵗb5 20 c4! ⵗxb3 21 ⵗf5+ ⵗd7 22 ⵗxd7+ ⵗxd7 23 axb3 with an equal game.

16...fxe5 17 0-0 exd4

18 ⵗg5

Presumably White only at this point realised that if 18 cxd4? Black has 18...ⵗxf3! 19 ⵗxa5 ⵗxf1+ winning a piece. White could now have maintained material parity by taking the h-pawn, but this would further open the kingside for the black rooks. As it happens Black later forces the capture by advancing the pawn.

18...dxc3 19 ⵗe3 ⵗg8 20 ⵗe4 ⵗd4 21 ⵗf2 ⵗe5 22 ⵗaf1 ⵗc6 23 ⵗf4 ⵗg7 24 ⵗg3 h5 25 ⵗh4 ⵗg5 26 ⵗxh5 ⵗe3 27 ⵗh1 ⵗh8 28 ⵗg4+ ⵗb8 29 ⵗf4 ⵗe6 30 ⵗg5?

White should have returned the knight to e4. The players must have been short of time since both missed that 30 ⵗg5 loses immediately to 30...ⵗh3.

30...a6? 31 a3? ⵗh3!

Black spots it second time around. White has to give up a material to prevent the mate on h2.

32 ⵗxd8+ ⵗxd8 33 ⵗe4 ⵗxe4 0-1

Game 71
Zsu.Polgar-M.Gurevich
Holland 2000

1 e4 e6 2 d4 d5 3 ⵗc3 ⵗf6 4 ⵗg5 ⵗb4 5 ⵗe2

A quiet continuation which has featured in the games of all three Polgar sisters, and avoids the rigid structures of the McCutcheon main lines.

White has two lesser moves:

a) 5 f3 h6 6 ⵗxf6 ⵗxf6 7 ⵗge2 dxe4 8 fxe4 e5! and Black already stood well in Lasker-Tarrasch, Berlin match 1916.

b) 5 ⵗd3, when the simplest response is 5...dxe4 6 ⵗxe4 ⵗbd7! 7 ⵗe2 h6 8 ⵗxf6 ⵗxf6 9 ⵗf3 0-0 10 0-0 c6 (playing for ...e6-e5; 10...c5 is also fine) 11 ⵗe4 ⵗxe4 12 ⵗxe4 ⵗd6! 13 ⵗd3 f5 14 ⵗf3 e5 15 dxe5 ⵗxe5 16 ⵗc4+ ⵗh7 17 ⵗad1 ⵗf6 18 ⵗd4 ⵗd7 19 c3 ⵗae8 and Black developed an initiative, advancing all his kingside pawns ...f5-f4-f3-f2, ...g5-g4, ...h5-h4xg3 (Romanishin-Beliavsky, Belgrade 1993). This game in fact arose via 3...ⵗb4 4 ⵗd3 dxe4 5 ⵗxe4 ⵗf6 6 ⵗg5.

5 ⵗe2 is also seen in the Winawer: 3...ⵗb4 4 ⵗe2 ⵗf6!? 5 ⵗg5.

5...dxe4

5...h6!? has been castigated due to 6 ⵗxf6 ⵗxf6 7 a3 ⵗxc3+ 8 ⵗxc3 dxe4 9 ⵗxe4 when Black is slightly (and needlessly) worse. 8...c6 is better, when 9 e5 ⵗe7 reaches a classical position, 4...ⵗe7 5 e5 ⵗfd7 6 ⵗxe7 ⵗxe7 7 f4 with the king's knights removed and ...c7-c6 and ...h7-h6 vs. a2-a3 included, which clearly does not disfavour Black. Hector-Piskov, Copenhagen 1991, saw instead 9 ⵗd2 0-0 10 f4 b6 11 ⵗe2 ⵗb7 12 ⵗf3 ⵗe7 13 0-0-0 b5 14 f5 a5 15 fxe6 fxe6 16 exd5 exd5 17 ⵗde1 ⵗd6 and Black had no cause for complaint.

Piskov later came up with 7...ⵗa5!? and equalised after 8 exd5 0-0 9 ⵗd3 ⵗd8 10 dxe6 ⵗxe6 11 0-0-0 ⵗxf2 12 ⵗe4 ⵗf5 13

♘c5 ♕xd3 14 ♖xd3 ♗c8 15 g3 ♘d7 16 b4 ♗b6 17 ♗g2 c6 18 ♘f4 a5 19 ♔b2 ♘f6 in Unzicker-Piskov, German Bundesliga 1992. Subsequent games have not managed to show anything for White either, e.g. M.Kuijf-Rogulj, German Bundesliga 1999, saw 8 b4 ♗b6 9 e5 ♕e7 10 ♘a4 0-0 11 ♘f4 ♗d7 12 c3 ♗xa4 13 ♕xa4 ♘d7 14 ♗d3 a5 15 b5 ♖fc8 16 0-0 c5 17 bxc6 ♖xc6 18 ♘e2 ♗d8 19 ♕d1 ♘b6 20 a4 ♘c4 and Black was fine.

6 a3 ♗e7

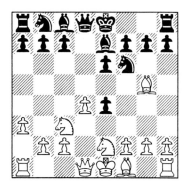

Taking the game into a sort of Burn variation, where the white knight is misplaced on e2. This allows Black to equalise without too much trouble. Instead 6...♗xc3+ 7 ♘xc3 ♘c6 8 ♗b5 is good for White, while 6...♗a5 7 b4 ♗b6 8 ♘xe4 makes a poor comparison with 5...h6 above.

7 ♗xf6 ♗xf6!

The most appropriate recapture – playing against the central dark squares which the ♘e2 does not control. As in the Burn, Black can also take back with the g-pawn, but here ♘e2 has some point (even if it is not best) – it might probe with ♘g3-h5 or ♘f4 or sacrifice itself on f5. For instance, 8 ♘xe4 b6 (8...f5 9 ♘4c3 b6 10 d5) 9 ♘2c3 ♗b7 10 ♕f3 (threatening ♘xf6+) 10...c6 (10...♔f8!?) 11 0-0-0 f5 (11...♘d7) 12 ♘g3 ♘d7 13 ♗c4! ♕c7 14 ♖he1 ♘f8? 15 ♘xf5! exf5 16 ♕xf5 ♘e6 17 ♗xe6 fxe6 18 ♖xe6 is strong (Grzeskowiak-Herrmann, Germany 1954),

or if 14...♘f6 15 ♗xe6!? (15 ♕e2) 15...fxe6 16 ♖xe6 0-0 with an unclear position (Unzicker-Keller, Bad Pyrmont 1963).

8 ♘xe4 0-0

Black has two possible pawn breaks against the white centre: either ...c7-c5 or ...e6-e5. By castling Black postpones making a decision for a move or two.

In an earlier game Gurevich inserted 8...♘c6 9 c3 before 9...0-0 10 f4 ♗e7 (Hutters-M.Gurevich, Tastrup 1992), but now instead of the time-consuming 11 ♘g1?! ♘b8 12 ♘f3 ♘d7 13 ♗d3 allowing Black to break with ...c7-c5, Gurevich suggested 11 g3 ♘b8 12 ♗g2 ♘d7 13 b4! with a slight advantage. If instead 9...e5!? 10 d5 ♘b8 11 ♘xf6+ ♕xf6 12 c4 intends ♘c3, ♗e2, 0-0 and again White is slightly better.

Black could play 8...e5 immediately, since if 9 ♕d3, rather than play 9...exd4 10 ♘xf6+ ♕xf6 11 ♕xd4 ♕xd4?! (11...♘d7) 12 ♘xd4 ♗d7 13 0-0-0 (or 13 ♘b5) 13...0-0 14 ♘b5 ♗xb5 15 ♗xb5 when White has the superior minor piece in the endgame, simply 9...0-0 returns to the game.

9 ♕d3

Preparing 0-0-0 followed by f2-f4 and/or g2-g4 with kingside attacking possibilities. 9 f4 prevents the immediate ...e6-e5, but Black is not committed to this. J.Polgar-De la Villa Garcia, Salamanca 1989, continued 9...♘d7 10 g3 c5 11 ♕d2 cxd4 12 0-0-0 e5! (after all) 13 fxe5 ♗xe5 14 ♘xd4 ♘f6 15 ♘c3 ♕b6 and Black was better.

9...e5

A consequence of the knight being missing from f3 is that Black is more easily able to achieve this freeing advance.

10 ♕f3!?

A new move. White clears the d-file for the rook, attacks f6 and creates possibilities on the long light-squared diagonal. Previously there had been 10 0-0-0 exd4 11 ♘xf6+ ♕xf6 12 ♕xd4 ♘d7 13 ♘c3 c6 14 ♗e2 ♖e8 15 ♗f3 ½-½ Unzicker-Glek, Moscow 1991.

10...♘d7 11 0-0-0

In this game White always seems to be thinking a move behind. Here 11 ♘xf6+ is preferable with a structural advantage after 11...♕xf6 12 ♕xf6 gxf6 13 0-0-0. Gurevich was considering 11...♘xf6!? 12 dxe5 ♘g4, e.g. 13 ♕e4 c6! 14 f4 (not 14 h3 ♕a5+ 15 ♘c3 ♘xe5) 14...♕b6 15 ♕d4 ♖d8 16 ♕xb6 axb6 with compensation as White is a long way from co-ordinating her forces. 13 ♕c3 intending 14 f4 seems better, and if 13...f6 (Gurevich) 14 exf6 with some advantage however Black recaptures: 14...♕xf6 15 ♕xf6 ♖xf6 16 f3 ♘e3 17 ♔d2 ♘c4+ 18 ♔c3, or 14...♖xf6 15 f3 ♘h6 16 ♘g3 or 14...♘xf6 15 ♕d4.

11...exd4 12 ♘xf6+

This now aids Black's development. Instead 12 ♘xd4 ♗xd4 13 ♖xd4 ♕e7 intending ...♘e5 concedes equality.

12...♘xf6 13 ♖xd4

Now if 13 ♘xd4? ♗g4.

13...♕e7 14 h3

Since if 14 ♘c3 ♗g4! 15 ♖xg4 ♕e1+ 16 ♘d1 ♘xg4 17 ♕xg4 ♖ad8 threatens ...♕d2+ and wins, or if 18 ♕e2 ♖fe8.

14...♗d7!

If 14...c5 15 ♖d3! ♗e6 16 ♘f4 and Black has to attend to the positional threat of 17 ♖e3, allowing White to develop her pieces.

15 ♘g3 ♗c6 16 ♕d1?!

Rather than retreat the queen White could have come forward with 16 ♘f5! ♕e5 17 ♕f4 ♕xf4+ 18 ♖xf4 ♖fe8 and then 19 ♗d3 and 20 f3 is level, since 19...♗xg2? loses to 20 ♖g1. This was the only opportunity for ♘f5 as Black now takes the square away.

16...g6! 17 ♖g1 b5!? 18 ♗e2 ♕e5 19 ♕d2 ♖fe8 20 ♕f4 a5!? 21 ♕xe5 ♖xe5 22 ♖d3 ♖ae8 23 ♗f3 ♗xf3 24 ♖xf3 ♔g7 25 ♖d1 h5 26 h4 ♖8e7 27 a4!?

Seeking either to block the queenside or give her pieces something to attack.

27...bxa4 28 ♖f4 ♘g4 29 f3 ♘e3 30 ♖d2 ♖d5 31 ♖xa4

If 31 ♖xd5 ♘xd5 32 ♖xa4 ♖e1+ 33 ♔d2 ♖g1 with a clear advantage.

31...♖xd2 32 ♔xd2 ♘xg2 33 ♘e2 ♖d7+ 34 ♔c3 ♖d6 35 ♖c4

If 35 ♖xa5 ♘xh4 36 ♘d4 ♖f6 picks up the f3-pawn with a winning kingside pawn majority.

35...♘e3 36 ♖c5

36...♘f5?!

Black has slowly built up a powerful position, but now time trouble intervenes. 36...a4! (Gurevich) was better, intending 37...♘d1+ 38 ♔b4 ♘xb2 or 38...♖d2 and 39...♖d4+ after the ♘e2 moves.

37 ♖xc7 ♘xh4 38 ♘d4 ♘g2

Similarly to the previous note, 38...♖d5 39 ♔c4 ♖e5 keeps hold of the a-pawn.

39 ♖c5 ♘f4?

And now 39...♖a6.

40 ♖xa5 h4 41 ♔c4!

White prepares to advance her pawns 41 ♔c4 was accurate, since if first 41 ♖a1 ♘d5+ then 42 ♔c4 now fails to 42...♘e3+ 43 ♔c3 ♖xd4! 44 ♖xd4 ♘xc2+ and wins.

41...h3 42 ♖a1 ♔h6 43 b4 ♔h5 44 b5 ♔h4 45 c3!

Accurate play. If 45 ♔c5 ♖d5+! 46 ♔c4 ♖d7 47 b6 ♘d5 threatens to take the b-pawn, thus gaining time for Black.

45...h2 46 ♔c5 ♖d8 47 b6 ♔g3 48 b7 ♔g2 49 ♘c6 ♖h8 50 ♔d6 h1♕ 51 ♖xh1 ♔xh1 52 c4 ♔g2 53 ♔e7 ♘e6 54 b8♕ ♖xb8 55 ♘xb8 ♔xf3 56 ♔xf7 ♘c5 ½-½

Summary

Since its inventor first brought out 4...♗b4 in one of Steinitz's simultaneous displays, the McCutcheon has resisted White's attempts to prove even a slight advantage. This appears still to be true today, with the defence showing its resilience in all variations, so that Black need fear nothing in particular. However, there is still plenty of territory to be explored after 4...♗b4, and White does hold one trump in being able to choose the nature of the game: whether to play quietly with 5 ♘e2 or 5 exd5, to initiate complications perhaps with 6 ♗e3, or to take on the main lines after 6 ♗d2.

1 e4 e6 2 d4 d5 3 ♘c3 ♘f6 4 ♗g5 ♗b4 *(D)*

5 e5
   5 exd5 – *Game 70*; 5 ♘e2 – *Game 71*
5...h6 *(D)* **6 ♗d2**
   6 ♗e3 – *Game 68*; 6 exf6 – *Game 69*
6...♗xc3 7 bxc3
   7 ♗xc3 – *Game 67*
7...♘e4 8 ♕g4 g6
   8...♔f8 – *Game 66*
9 ♗d3 ♘xd2 10 ♔xd2 c5 11 ♘f3 *(D)* **11...♘c6**
   11...♗d7 – *Game 65*
12 ♕f4 – *Game 64*

   4...♗b4   *5...h6*   *11 ♘f3*

CHAPTER NINE

Odds and Ends

1 e4 e6 2 d4 d5 3 ♘c3 ♘f6

This chapter fills in the odds and ends of the Classical French – where either White or Black chooses not to enter the Classical main lines following 4 ♗g5 ♗e7 5 e5 ♘fd7 or 4 e5 ♘fd7 5 f4. For White this means eschewing either e4-e5 or f2-f4. The most noteworthy alternative, 4 e5 ♘fd7 5 ♘f3, is the subject of Games 72 and 73, while White's fourth move alternatives are covered in Game 78. For Black to deviate requires putting the f6-knight on a different square to d7 after e4-e5 with 4 e5 ♘e4 (Games 74 and 75), or 4 ♗g5 ♗e7 5 e5 and 5...♘e4 (Game 76) or 5...♘g8 (Game 77). 4...♘g8 is rare after 4 e5 and appears only as a note to Game 74.

Game 72
Zakharov-Bashkov
Perm 1997

---

1 e4 e6 2 d4 d5 3 ♘c3 ♘f6 4 e5 ♘fd7 5 ♘f3

With 5 ♘f3 White plans a slightly different strategy to 5 f4. Rather than defend the pawn centre White intends immediately to scuttle it, i.e. if ...c7-c5 then d4xc5, and if ...f7-f6 then e5xf6. By concentrating his pieces in the centre (♘f3,

♗f4, ♕e2 and ♖e1) White hopes to restrain the Black's central pawns and occupy the e5-square with his pieces. However, without the f4-pawn supporting e5, White is less able to contest the d4-square, which lies under Black's control with ...♘c6, ...♗c5 and sometimes ...♕b6.

This position often arises via the Two Knights: 1 e4 e6 2 ♘f3 d5 3 ♘c3 ♘f6 4 e5 ♘fd7 5 d4 (the current game did in fact take this route) and occasionally via Alekhine's Defence 1 e4 ♘f6 2 ♘c3 d5 3 e5 ♘fd7 4 d4 e6 5 ♘f3.

White has one more option in the old-fashioned Gledhill variation, 5 ♕g4, pressurising the g7-pawn to keep the f8-bishops at home. This was long ago neutralised and now does not even rate a note in *ECO*. For instance, 6 ♘b5 (or 6 ♘f3 ♘c6 7 ♗b5 cxd4 8 ♘xd4 ♘dxe5 9 ♕g3 a6!) 6...cxd4 7 ♘f3 ♘c6 8 ♘d6+ ♗xd6 9 ♕xg7 ♗xe5 10 ♘xe5 ♕f6 11 ♕xf6 ♘xf6 and Black was better in Bogolyubov-Réti, Maehrisch Ostrau 1923.

5...c5 6 dxc5

Sometimes White attempts to fight for the central dark squares by 6 ♗b5. This causes Black few problems after 6...♘c6 7 0-0 cxd4!? (or 7...♗e7) 8 ♘xd4 ♕c7 9 ♖e1 a6 10 ♗xc6 bxc6 11 ♗f4 ♘b6 12 ♕g4 c5

13 ♘b3 h6 14 a4 ♗b7 15 ♘a5 ♘c8 16 ♘xb7 ♕xb7 17 ♖ad1 ♘e7 (not 17...♕xb2? 18 ♘xd5!) 18 a5? ♕xb2 and Black won in Martorelli-Baburin, St Vincent 2000. However, 8...♘xe5?! is risky after 9 ♖e1 a6 10 ♗a4 b5 11 ♗b3 ♗e7 12 ♘xc6 ♘xc6 13 ♘xd5! ♗d6 (if 13...exd5 14 ♗xd5 ♗b7 15 ♕f3) 14 ♕f3 ♗b7 15 ♕g4 ♘f8 16 ♗g5 h5 17 ♕h4 ♕a5 18 ♘f4 with a clear advantage in Gysi-Siviero, correspondence 1995.

6...♘c6 7 ♗f4

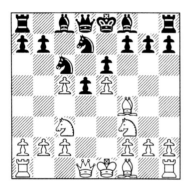

7...♗xc5

7...♘xc5 is also okay, though it is played less often. From c5 the black knight may later move on to e4 or exchange off the white bishop if it comes to d3. White should decide what to do quickly as Black has more waiting moves. For instance, 8 a3 a6 9 h4 b5 10 h5 h6 11 ♘e2 ♗b7 12 ♘ed4 ♘a4 13 ♖b1 ♘a5 14 c3 ♘c4 15 ♕c2 ♖c8 16 ♗xc4 dxc4 17 ♘xe6 ♕d5 18 ♘xf8 ♕e4+ 19 ♕xe4 ♗xe4 20 ♖d1 ♘xb2 with a clear advantage to Black in Bielczyk-Apicella, Cappelle la Grande 1995.

Instead 8 ♗d3 ♗e7 9 h4 was gloriously successful in Rogers-Delay, Martigny 1985, after 9...b6 10 ♗b5 ♗d7 11 h5 ♘e4? 12 ♘xd5! ♗c5 13 h6 gxh6 14 ♖xh6 ♗xf2+ 15 ♔f1 ♘b8 16 ♘d4! ♗xd4 17 ♖xe6+ fxe6 18 ♕h5+ ♔f8 19 ♗h6+ ♔g8 20 ♗xd7 ♘xd7 21 ♕g4+ ♔f7 22 ♕g7+ ♔e8 23 ♕xh8+ ♘f8 24 ♕xf8+ ♔d7 25 ♕f7+ ♔c6 26 ♕xe6+ ♔b7 27 ♕f7+ ♔c6 28 ♘e7+ 1-0. Black has

done better since then with mutual chances after 9...f6!? 10 exf6 gxf6 11 ♗h6 ♕b6 12 0-0 ♗d7 13 a3 ♘xd3 14 cxd3 ♔f7 (Giaccio-Jacimovic, Istanbul Olympiad 2000) and 9...d4!? 10 ♘e4 ♘xd3+ 11 cxd3 ♕a5+ 12 ♔f1 b6 13 ♕b3 ♗a6 14 ♖h3 ♕b5 15 ♕xb5 ♗xb5 16 ♔e2 (Kosteniuk-Romero Holmes, Wijk aan Zee 2000).

Black can also delay ...♘c5, awaiting ♗f1-d3, e.g. 7...a6 (or 7...♗e7) 8 ♗d3 ♘xc5 9 0-0 ♗e7 10 ♖e1 0-0 11 a3 (11 ♗f1!?) 11...f5 12 exf6 ♗xf6 13 ♘e5 ♘xe5 14 ♗xe5 ♗xe5 15 ♖xe5 ♕b6 with threats against b2 and f2. After 16 ♖e3 ♘xd3 17 ♕xd3 ♕xb2 18 ♖ae1 ♕xa3 19 ♖h3 g6 20 ♖g3 ♖f5 Black consolidated his extra pawns in A.Ledger-Kruppa, Ubeda 1998.

8 ♗d3 h6!?

8...h6 is a useful move, preparing a possible ...0-0 by pre-empting the ♗xh7 sacrifice, or a kingside advance with ...g7-g5.

Several others are worth mentioning:

a) 8...f6! 9 exf6 is the main line and is covered in Game 73.

b) 8...♕b6?! sets Black up for a trap after 9 0-0! – the b-pawn is untouchable due to 9...♕xb2? 10 ♘b5 when White threatens ♘c7+ and ♗d2-c3.

c) 8...a6 9 0-0 ♕c7 sets a counter-trap: if 10 ♖e1? ♕b6! 11 ♗g3 ♕xb2 is safe since White does not have 12 ♘b5. However, White can safely leave the e5-pawn en prise with 10 ♗g3! since if 10...♘dxe5? 11 ♘xe5 ♘xe5 12 ♕h5 ♗d6 13 ♘xd5! exd5 14 ♖fe1 recoups the material with a clear advantage.

d) 8...♗e7!? threatens 9...g5 and clears the way for ...♘c5. After 9 h4 a6 10 h5 b5 11 ♕e2 0-0 12 0-0 h6 13 ♘e4 ♘b4 14 ♘g3 ♗b7 15 ♘d4 ♗g5 16 ♗xg5 ♕xg5 17 ♖fe1 ♖ac8 an unclear position was reached in Becerra Rivero-Thorhallsson, Bermuda 2001. If 9 ♗g3 ♘c5!? 10 0-0 ♘xd3 11 cxd3 Black has wasted a tempo on ...♗c5-e7, but White only has ♗g3 as an extra move (Arizmendi Martinez-Karatorossian, Ubeda 2000).

e) 8...0-0!? may not be the catastrophic blunder that was previously thought. After 9 ♗xh7+ ♔xh7 10 ♘g5+ ♔g6 11 ♕d3+ (if 11 ♕g4 ♘dxe5 or 11 h4 ♘dxe5 12 h5+ ♔f6) 11...f5 12 ♘xe6 (or 12 ♕g3 ♘dxe5! or 12 exf6+ ♔xf6) 12...♘dxe5! 13 ♕g3+ ♘g4 14 ♘xd8 ♗xf2+ or 14 ♘xc5 ♕e7+ Black is okay.

9 ♗g3

A useful prophylactic move. White removes the bishop from possible attack by ...g7-g5 and defends f2 in case of a later ...♕b6. 9 h4 a6 10 ♗g3 also reaches the game. Note that the two h-pawn moves have not improved 9...♕b6? 10 0-0 ♕xb2 11 ♘b5 for Black, as White again threatens ♘c7+ or ♗d2-c3.

9...a6

9...g5 is supposed to be bad after 10 h3. However, Black might try 10...♗b4!? (threatening 11...d4) and if 11 0-0 h5!? with a messy position (c.f. 10 0-0 g5!? in the next note). If White doesn't like this then 9 h4! a6 10 ♗g3 should be preferred.

10 h4

Gufeld-Spassky, USSR Championship 1960, saw instead 10 0-0 b5 11 ♖e1 0-0 12 ♘e2 b4 13 c3 bxc3 14 bxc3 a5 15 ♘f4 ♗a6 16 ♗c2 ♖c8 17 ♕d2 ♖e8 18 ♘h5 ♗f8 19 ♖ac1 ♘e7 20 ♘d4 ♘c5 21 ♗h4 ♕d7 22 ♗xe7 ♕xe7 23 ♖e3 ♖ed8 24 ♖g3 ♔h8 25 ♕f4 ♘d7 26 ♗a4 when, for no apparent reason, Black gave a piece away: 26...♘xe5? 27 ♕xe5 ♕c7 28 ♕e3 e5 29 ♘f3 e4 30 ♕d4 exf3 31 ♖xg7 ♕c5 32 ♕g4 ♖d6 33 ♖g8+ ♔h7 34 ♗c2+ 1-0.

Apart from move 26, Black can perhaps improve earlier by, for example, 12...♘b4!? 13 ♘f4 ♘xd3 14 ♘xd3 ♗b6 15 c3 ♗b7 16 ♗f4 ♖c8 17 ♗e3 ♖c4 18 ♕d2 ♖e4 19 ♗xb6 ♕xb6 20 ♘d4 with mutual chances in Drozdov-Danielian, Moscow 1996. Or even 10...g5!? 11 h3 h5 12 ♖e1 g4 13 hxg4 hxg4 14 ♘h2 ♕g5 15 ♕xg4 ♕xg4 16 ♘xg4 ♖g8 17 ♗e2 ♘d4 18 ♗d1 ♘xc2 19 ♗xc2 ♖xg4 and Black was okay in Buchenau-

Putzbach, German Bundesliga 1991.

10...b5

10...♕c7 11 0-0 ♘dxe5 fails again to 12 ♘xe5 ♘xe5 13 ♘xd5! etc.

11 ♕d2 ♗b7 12 h5

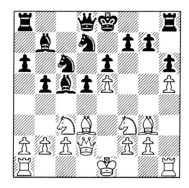

Another useful and typical move. White gains space on the kingside and the h4-square for his pieces. The use of h4 can be seen in the next note.

12...♘b6 13 ♕f4 ♘c4

Black has to be careful about castling short. If 13...0-0? 14 ♗h4 ♕c7 15 ♗f6! followed by ♖h3-g3 gives White a decisive attack.

14 ♗xc4 dxc4?!

Black opens up the diagonal for his bishop and gains an outpost on d5. On the downside White gets an complimentary outpost on e4 and the d-file for his rook. Safer is 14...bxc4 intending queenside probing with ...♕b6 or ...♕a5.

15 ♖d1 ♕b6 16 ♘e4 ♘b4

The knight is very strong on e4, threatening to come in on d6, or f6 should Black castle short. Therefore Black prepares to remove it from the board as soon as possible.

White could move in without waiting with 17 ♘d6+, but after 17...♗xd6 18 ♖xd6 ♕a5 19 0-0 0-0 20 ♗h4 ♗xf3! 21 ♕xf3 ♕xa2, this time 22 ♗f6 is only good enough for a draw: 22...gxf6 23 exf6 ♔h8 24 ♕f4 ♔h7 25 ♕e4+ ♔h8 26 ♕f4 etc., and

White lacks the ammunition for anything better. So, instead, White removes his king from the centre.

17 0-0 ♗xe4

The greedy 17...♘xc2? is a mistake due to 18 ♖d6! (Bangiev) and if 18...♕c7 19 ♖fd1 ♗xd5 (or 19...♗xd6 20 exd6) 20 ♘6xd5 exd5 21 ♖xd5 with a dominating position, or if 18...♕a7!? 19 ♖fd1 ♗d5 20 ♘6xd5 exd5 21 ♖xd5 ♗e7 22 ♘d6+ ♗xd6 23 exd6 0-0 24 ♕d2 surprisingly traps the knight on c2.

18 ♕xe4 0-0 19 ♗h4!

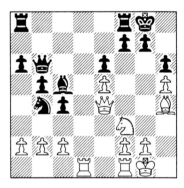

Once again the bishop manoeuvres into the attack, controlling d8 and preparing the ♗f6 sacrifice with such ideas as 20 ♗f6 gxf6 21 exf6 ♖fd8 22 ♕g4+ ♔f8 23 ♘e5 ♖a7 24 ♕g7+ ♔e8 25 ♕g8+ ♔f8 26 ♘g6!, or 21...♔h8 22 ♕f4 ♔h7 23 ♘e5! threatening 24 ♖d7 or 24 ♕g4 ♖g8 25 ♕e4+ ♔h7 26 ♘xf7 mate. Black next prevents ♗f6 but White's crude attack is still strong.

19...♘d5! 20 g4 ♖ae8 21 g5 hxg5?

Black wants to clear the ranks to allow lateral defence by his heavy pieces, but this also grants the enemy pieces more access into his position. 21...♔h8 seems better when 22 gxh6 gxh6 23 ♗f6+ ♘xf6 24 exf6 ♕c7 25 ♘e5 fails to 25...♖g8+ and 26...♖g5. The exchange sacrifice 23 ♖xd5 is no good since the black queen then covers f6 and h6, while if ♔h1 simply ...♖g8 prepares the

defence.

22 ♘xg5 f5 23 exf6 ♘xf6 24 ♕g6

Threatening 25 ♖d7! and wins.

24...♕c7 25 ♔g2

Breaking the pin on the f-pawn so that the bishop can re-route again via g3. The straightforward 25 h6!? was possible, intending 26 ♖fe1 e5 27 ♖d5. Black's only defence is 25...♖e7 preparing 26 ♖fe1 ♕f4! 27 ♖e4 ♕f5, though after 28 ♕xf5 exf5 29 ♖xe7 ♗xe7 30 hxg7 and White is better in the endgame.

25...♖e7 26 ♗g3 ♕c6+ 27 f3 ♕e8 28 ♖fe1 ♕xg6 29 hxg6

By exchanging queens Black averts the danger of being mated. Nevertheless, White remains with a clear advantage due to Black's weak e-pawn and his own g6-pawn which pins the black king to the back rank.

29...♖fe8 30 ♗d6

30 ♘e4 was also strong since if the ♗c5 moves White has either ♖d6 or ♗h4, while after 30...♘xe4 31 ♖xe4 White threatens to mate by ♖h4, ♖dh1 etc. or otherwise to win the e-pawn or infiltrate starting ♖e5.

30...♗xd6 31 ♖xd6 ♘d5 32 ♔g3

Of course not 32 ♘xe6?? ♖xe6! with ...♘f4+ to follow.

32...c3 33 bxc3 a5 34 ♘f7!

With ideas of 35 ♖h1 and 36 ♖h8 mate. Another good choice was 34 ♖exe6 ♖xe6 35 ♘xe6 ♘xc3 36 ♖d7 rendering Black helpless in the endgame.

34...♔f8

So that the king can escape after ...♖c7.

35 ♘d8! ♘xc3?!

35...♘f6 was necessary.

36 ♖h1 ♔g8 37 ♘f7??

Presumably time pressure prevented White from finding his win: 37 ♖d2! and there is no defence to ♖dh2 and ♖h8. If 37...♖c7 38 ♘xe6! keeps the king in the trap, since 38...♖xe6 39 ♖d8+ would mate immediately.

37...♖xf7! 38 gxf7+ ♔xf7 39 ♖c6 ♘xa2 40 ♖a1 ♘b4 41 ♖c5 a4 42 ♖xb5 ♘xc2

43 ℤxa4 ♘e3

With the queenside pawns eliminated Black has better chances to hold the game, which he in fact managed to do.

44 ♔f4 ♘d5+ 45 ♔e5 ℤe7 46 ℤba5 ♘e3 47 ℤa6 g5 48 ℤe4 ♘f5 49 ℤc4 ℤb7 50 ℤac6 ℤb3 51 ℤc3 ℤb5+ 52 ℤ6c5 ℤb6 53 ℤc7+ ♔g6 54 ℤ7c6 ℤb5+ 55 ℤ3c5 ℤxc5+ 56 ℤxc5 ♘h4 57 ℤc3 ♔f7 58 ℤc7+ ♔g6 59 ℤc3 ♔f7 60 ℤa3 ♘g6+ 61 ♔d6 ♔f6 62 ℤe3 ♔f5 63 ℤxe6 ♘h4 64 ♔d5 ♘xf3 65 ℤe8 ♔f4 66 ℤf8+ ♔g3 67 ♔e4 g4 68 ℤd8 ♘h4 69 ♔e3 ♘f3 70 ℤa8 ♘g5 71 ℤa5 ♘h3 72 ℤa2 ♘g5 73 ℤa1 ♘h3 74 ℤb1 ♔h2 75 ℤb2+ ♔g3 76 ℤb4 ♘g5 77 ♔e2 ♘f3 78 ♔f1 ♘h2+ 79 ♔e2 ♘f3 80 ℤa4 ♘h2 81 ♔e3 ♘f3 82 ℤa2 ♘g5 ½-½

Game 73
Benjamin-J.Sarkar
New York Open 2000

---

1 e4 e6 2 d4 d5 3 ♘c3 ♘f6 4 e5 ♘fd7 5 ♘f3 c5 6 dxc5 ♘c6 7 ♗f4 ♗xc5 8 ♗d3 f6!

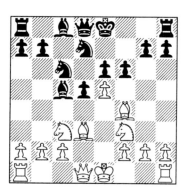

8...f5 9 exf6 is equivalent.

9 exf6 ♘xf6

The normal recapture. Not 9...gxf6?! 10 ♘h4 and 11 ♕h5+ (if 10...♕e7 11 ♕h5+ ♕f7? 12 ♗g6 wins), but 9...♕xf6 is reasonable. If 10 ♗g5 ♕f7 11 0-0 0-0 12 ♗h4 ♕h5 (12...h6!?) 13 ♗g3 is 9...♘xf6 10

0-0 0-0 11 ♗g3 with the impossible double move 11...♕d8-e8-h5!? which cannot be too bad for Black. Morozevich-Bareev, Sarajevo 1999, saw instead 11 ♕e2 0-0 12 0-0-0 h6 13 ♗h4 (13 ♗d2) 13...a6 (13...♗b4!?) 14 ♗g3 ♘b6 15 ♔b1 ♗d7 16 ℤhf1 ♕h5 17 a3 ℤac8 18 ℤde1 ℤf6 19 ♕d2 ♕f7 with a balanced game. 10 ♗g3 0-0 11 0-0 ♘d4! (not 11...♘de5? 12 ♘xe5 ♘xe5 13 ♗xh7+ ♔xh7 14 ♕h5+ etc.) 12 ♘xd4 ♗xd4 is also okay for Black, e.g. 13 ♕d2 a6 14 ℤae1 ♘c5 15 ♘d1 ♘xd3 16 cxd3 ♗d7 17 ♕b4 ♗b5 18 ♗d6 ℤf7 and Black took over the initiative in Dittmar-Yu, Gyula 2000.

10 0-0 0-0

The critical *tabiya* for 5 ♘f3. White's main strategy is to keep control of the e5-square and see what turns up.

11 ♘e5

White has nothing better than to occupy the outpost at once. If 11 ♕e2 ♗d7 12 ℤae1 ♕e7 13 ♘e5 returns to the game in any case, but also allows Black to try 11...♘h5!? 12 ♗g5 ♘f4, as in Pozin-Volkov, Ekaterinburg 1996: 13 ♕d2 ♕c7 14 ℤae1 ♘xd3 15 ♕xd3 h6 16 ♘xd5 ♕d6 17 ♘f4 hxg5 18 ♘xg5 ♕xd3 19 ♘xd3 ♗b6 20 ♘xe6 ♗xe6 21 ℤxe6 ♘d4 22 ℤe7 ♘xc2 23 ℤxb7? ℤad8 24 ♘e5 ℤxf2 0-1.

Similarly if 11 ♗g3 Black can choose between 11...♗d7, 11...♘h5 or even 11...♘g4!? 12 h3 ♘h6 intending ...♘f5.

11...♗d7

This is the most obvious and flexible move, enabling Black to develop smoothly.

Black must be wary of 11...♘e4? 12 ♗xe4 ℤxf4 13 ♘d3! and after 13...♗xf2+ 14 ℤxf2 ℤxf2 15 ♗xh7+ ♔xh7 16 ♕h5+ ♔g8 17 ♘xf2 e5 18 ℤd1 d4 19 ♘fe4! ♕e8 20 ℤf1! dxc3 21 ♘g5 White won in Ljubojevic-Bednarski, Skopje Olympiad 1972; or 13...ℤxe4!? 14 ♘xe4 ♗b6 15 ♘g3 e5 and the centre gave insufficient compensation for the exchange in Vogelmann-Glek, Eupen 1994.

As an alternative Watson has suggested

11...♕e8!? intending ...♘h5. Then 12 ♘b5 doesn't achieve anything after 12...♗b6 13 ♘d6 ♕e7 14 ♘xc8 ♖axc8 (*NCO*), or 12...♕e7 or 12...♘h5!? 13 ♘c7 ♖b8 14 ♘xc6 (not 14 ♘xd5? ♕xd1 15 ♖axd1 ♘xd5 16 ♘xc6 ♖a8!) 14...bxc6 15 ♘xd5 ♕xd1 16 ♖axd1 ♖xb2, or even 14...♘g4!? (Watson). So White should try 12 ♘xc6! bxc6 13 ♘a4! ♗e7 (or 13 ...e5 14 ♘xc5 exf4 15 ♖e1) 14 ♗e5 (or 14 c4 ♗a6 15 ♕e2! – Baker) 14...♘d7 15 ♗g3 e5 16 c4 ♕f7 17 cxd5 cxd5 18 ♖c1 with an advantage (Zhelnin-Kiseleva, Krasnodar 1997). If Black plays 12...♕xc6 13 ♗e5 ♗d7 (or 13...♗d6 14 ♖e1) 14 ♕f3 ♖ae8 15 ♕h3 ♖e7 16 ♖ae1 ♗e8 17 a3 ♕b6? (A.Ledger-Harley, 4NCL 1997) and now White had 18 b4! ♗d6 19 ♗xf6 since the planned 19...gxf6 loses to 20 ♘xd5!, otherwise 19...♖xf6 20 ♕xh7+ with the advantage; while 18...♗d4 19 ♗xf6 ♖xf6 20 ♘xd5! is even worse.

In Drozdov-Morozevich, Krasnodar 1997, Black prepared ...♘h5 by 11...g6!? and gained a clear advantage after 12 ♕d2 ♘h5 13 ♗g5 ♗e7 14 ♗xe7 ♕xe7 15 ♖ae1 ♘f4 16 ♕e3 ♕g5 17 ♕g3 ♘xe5! 18 ♕xg5 ♘f3+ 19 gxf3 ♘h3+ 20 ♔g2 ♘xg5. This idea has not received any further tests though.

12 ♕e2

12 ♘xc6 ♗xc6 13 ♕e2 ♕e7 14 ♖ae1 ♖ae8 would return to the game (see 15 ♘xc6 in the notes), but the immediate exchange allows Black to play more strongly with 13...♘e4! and then: 14 g3 ♘xf2! 15 ♖xf2 ♗xf2+ 16 ♔xf2 ♕b6+ is very good for Black (Vogt-Farago, Kecskemet 1979), similarly 14 ♗e3 ♗xe3 15 ♕xe3 (15 fxe3 ♘xc3) 15...d4 16 ♕e2 dxc3 17 ♗xe4 cxb2 18 ♖xb1 ♕f6 (Bellon Lopez-Speelman, Amsterdam 1978), while if 14 ♗g3 ♘xg3 15 ♕xe6+ ♔h8 16 hxg3 ♖xf2! (Watson).

12...♕e7

Still not 12...♘e4?? 13 ♘xe4 dxe4 14 ♕xe4, or 13...♖xf4 14 ♘xc5, or 13...♘xe5 14 ♘xc5 ♘xd3 15 ♘xd3 and White wins.

12...♘d4?! looks tempting but after 13 ♕d2! Black has merely put his knight on a more vulnerable and less influential square. 12...♘xe5 13 ♗xe5 ♕e7 is acceptable, but there is no need to capture on e5 so soon. Black would prefer to see his opponent waste a tempo on ♗g3 first.

13 ♖ae1 ♖ae8

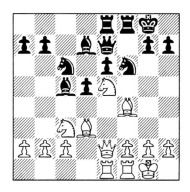

14 a3

A semi-useful waiting move, preventing anything arriving at b4, and preparing a possible b2-b4(-b5) to drive away Black's dark square defenders. GM Ian Rogers has preferred to spend the tempo on 14 ♔h1, breaking the pin on the f-pawn so that it may later advance to f4 after all. Black can continue to wait with 14...a6, and after 15 ♗g3, choose between 15...♗d4 as in the game, 15...♘xe5 16 ♗xe5 ♘c6 17 a3 (at which point a draw was agreed in I.Rogers-Psakhis, Wijk aan Zee 1997), while I.Rogers-C.Morris, 4NCL 2000, saw 15...g6!? 16 f4 ♘xe5 17 ♕xe5 ♗d6 18 ♕e3 ♘h5 19 ♘e2 e5 20 fxe5 ♖xf1+ 21 ♖xf1 ♘xg3+ 22 hxg3 ♕xe5 23 ♕xe5 ♖xe5 24 ♘f4 when 24...♗g4! keeps Black totally in control.

14..a6

Black, too, can wait and in turn prevents anything (including a pawn) arriving at b5.

15 ♗g3

Another semi-useful move, retreating the bishop from any tricks on the f-file. Instead

15 ♘xc6 ♗xc6 16 ♗g3 transposes to Spassky-Petrosian, World Championship 1966, which continued 16...♕f7 17 b4 ♗d4 18 ♗e5 ♗xe5 19 ♕xe5 ♘d7 20 ♕g3 e5 and Black should have had no problems as the centre can easily be defended. I.Rogers-Glek, German Bundesliga 1996, saw instead 15 ♔h1 ♗d4 16 ♘d1 (if 16 ♘xd7 ♕xd7 17 ♗d2 e5) 16...♘xe5 17 ♗xe5 ♗xe5 18 ♕xe5 ♘g4 19 ♕h5 ♘f6 20 ♕e5 ♘g4 21 ♕h5 with a draw by repetition.

15...♗d4!

Having completed his development, Black begins to fight for the e5-square.

16 ♘d1 ♘xe5

Black plays a simple improvement on Drozdov-Kastanieda, Briansk 1995, which saw 16...♘e4? 17 ♗xe4 ♘xe5 18 ♗xe5 ♗xe5 19 ♗xh7+ ♔xh7 20 ♕h5+ ♔g8 21 ♖xe5 and with an extra pawn, control of e5, and a good knight, White went on to win.

17 ♗xe5 ♗xe5 18 ♕xe5 ♗c6

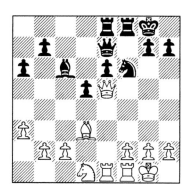

Vacating d7 for the knight and defending the d5-pawn in preparation for ...e6-e5. If Black achieves this advance with impunity it is a clear sign that White's strategy has failed. The logical 19 f4 does not prevent ...e6-e5 after ...♘d7 or ...♘g4, e.g. 19...♘d7 20 ♕c3 e5 21 ♗xa6!? ♕c5+ 22 ♕xc5 ♘xc5 and the f-pawn drops.

19 ♘e3?!

Threatening ♘f5 and adding pressure to the centre in readiness for c2-c4. However,

the threat is easily answered and the position of the ♘e3 means that after c2-c4 Black gains a tempo with ...d5-d4. It was better to play 19 c4 immediately, or possibly 19 b4!? ♘d7 20 ♕h5 g6 21 ♕h3 e5 22 c4 d4 23 f3 intending ♘f2 to blockade e4. However, this is a holding strategy with little hope of more than a draw – in the third round of an open against an opponent rated 275 points below, White is understandably reluctant to play for a draw.

19...♘d7 20 ♕g3 e5 21 c4 d4! 22 ♘g4 ♕g5 23 h4 ♕f4 24 ♕xf4 ♖xf4 25 f3 ♘c5 26 ♗c2 e4! 27 b4 ♘a4 28 g3

Hoping for 28...♖xf3? 29 ♖xf3 exf3 30 ♖xe8+ ♗xe8 31 ♘e5 when White will regain the pawn.

28...♖xg4!

This is only nominally a sacrifice as the passed pawns will recoup the material with interest.

29 fxg4 ♘c3 30 ♗b3 e3 31 b5

31 c5+ ♗d5 does not achieve anything for White either.

31...axb5 32 cxb5+ ♗d5 33 ♗xd5+ ♘xd5 34 ♖d1!?

White can't yet bring himself to resign.

34...e2 35 ♖xd4 exf1♕+ 36 ♔xf1 ♘b6 37 ♔f2 ♖a8 38 ♖d3 ♘c4 39 a4 ♘b6 40 a5 ♖xa5 41 ♖d8+ ♔f7 42 ♖b8 ♖a7 43 ♔e3 ♘d7 44 ♖d8 b6 45 g5 ♘c5 46 ♖d6 ♖e7+ 47 ♔d4 ♖d7 48 ♖xd7+ ♘xd7 49 ♔d5 ♘c5 50 ♔d6 ♘a4 51 g4 ♘c3 52 ♔c6 ♔e6 53 ♔xb6 ♔e5 0-1

Intending 54...♘xb5 and 55...♔f4 with a trivial win. A big grandmaster scalp for the young FM with his favourite French Defence.

Game 74

M.Johnson-Ha.Olafsson

correspondence 1994

1 e4 e6 2 d4 d5 3 ♘c3 ♘f6 4 e5 ♘e4!?

Just as White might have been gearing up for a heavyweight contest after 4...♘fd7 5 f4, Black suddenly changes the nature of the game, sharpening the play considerably. 4...♘e4!? had a burst of popularity in the early 1990s, following an article in *New in Chess Yearbook 17* by the Polish players Jan Przewoznik and Damian Konca, appropriately entitled 'Jumping somewhat differently'.

Black can also choose to jump backwards: 4...♘g8!? This is equivalent to the Winawer variation 3...♗b4 4 e5 ♗f8!?, though there it is better to wait for prompting (i.e. a2-a3 or ♕g4) before retreating the bishop. Nevertheless, with the centre closed Black's position is solid enough to stand a few indiscretions. White has a free hand to do more or less anything. So here are two examples of deployments for Black:

a) 5 ♗e3 ♘e7 6 f4 ♘f5 7 ♗f2 h5 8 ♘f3 b6 9 g3 ♗a6 10 ♗xa6 ♘xa6 11 ♘e2 ♕d7 12 0-0 c5 13 c3 c4 14 h3 b5 15 ♔g2 b4 16 g4 hxg4 17 hxg4 ♘h6 18 ♖h1 ♖g8 19 g5 ♘f5 with an unclear position in Berg-Bronstein, Gausdal 1990.

b) 5 f4 b6 6 ♘f3 ♕d7 7 ♗e3 c6 8 h3 h5 9 ♖g1 ♗a6 10 ♗xa6 ♘xa6 11 ♕e2 ♘c7 12 g4 0-0-0 13 0-0-0 ♔b7 14 ♔b1 ♖c8 15 ♘g5 ♘h6 16 ♕f3? f6 17 ♘xe6 ♕xe6 18 f5 hxg4 19 hxg4 ♕e8 20 ♖h1 fxe5 21 dxe5 ♕xe5 and Black went on to win in Macieja-Gonzalez Rodriguez, Dos Hermanas Internet Qualifier 2000.

5 ♘xe4

5 ♗d3 ♘xc3 6 bxc3 just damages White's pawns. The only alternative worth considering is 5 ♘ce2!? threatening to win the knight by 6 f3 ♘g5 7 h4. Black replies 5...f6! striking at the centre and giving the knight a retreat square at f7. After 6 f3 ♘g5 Black stands okay after 7 ♗xg5 fxg5 8 ♕d2 c5 9 h4 gxh4 10 f4 c4 11 ♘f3 ♗e7 12 c3 ♘c6 (Nijboer-M.Kuijf, Wijk aan Zee 1991) or 7 exf6 ♕xf6 8 ♗e3 ♘c6 9 ♕d2 ♘f7 10 0-0-0 ♗d7 11 ♘g3 0-0-0 12 f4 h5 (Lau-Kersten, German Championship 1994).

While if 6 ♘f4!? Black can choose between 6...g6 7 ♘f3 ♗g7 and 6...fxe5!? 7 ♕h5+ ♔d7 f3 ♘g5.

5...dxe4

The altered pawn structure, with Black's d5-pawn now on e4, is the crux of the variation. Of course Black's pawn is more vulnerable on e4, and White can gang up on it with moves like ♕e2, ♘e2-g3 and ♗b3-c2. But Black hopes to gain counterplay with the added pressure against d4 down the half-open d-file.

White has two main choices: either to support the central dark squares with 6 ♗e3 (as in this game) or to work around the centre on the light-squares with 6 ♗c4 (Game 75).

6 ♗e3 c5!

Black gets straight to business attacking the centre. Anything else is too passive as White quickly targets e4, e.g. 6...b6 7 ♘e2 ♗b7 8 ♘g3 c5 9 dxc5 ♕xd1+ 10 ♖xd1 ♗xc5 11 ♗xc5 bxc5 12 ♗b5+ ♔e7 13 0-0 ♗c6 14 ♗xc6 ♘xc6 15 ♘xe4 ♘xe5 16 ♘xc5 with an extra pawn in Kasparov-Galle, World U-16 Championship 1976.

7 dxc5

White shifts the target from d4 to c5. If instead 7 c3 cxd4 8 ♕xd4 ♕xd4 9 ♗xd4 ♘c6 White is tied to defence. The exchange of bishops does not help: 7 ♗b5+ ♗d7 8 ♗xd7+ ♘xd7 9 c3 cxd4 10 cxd4 ♗b4+ 11 ♔f1 0-0.

7...♘d7

Blocking the d-file and attacking the c5- and e5-pawns.

8 ♕g4

The critical move. White puts pressure on e4 and g7. Instead 8 ♕d4 ♗xc5 9 ♕xe4 ♗xe3 10 ♕xe3 ♕a5+ 11 c3 ♕xe5 is totally equal; similarly 8 f4 exf3 9 ♘xf3 ♗xc5 or 8 ♘e2 ♗xc5 9 ♗xc5 ♘xc5 10 ♕xd8+ ♔xd8 11 0-0-0+ ♔e7; while 8 b4?! b6! or 8 c6?! bxc6 are just worse for White.

8...♘xc5

This is the thematic capture in the 4...♘e4!? variation. Nevertheless 8...♕a5+ 9 c3 ♗xc5 is possible and can arise via 4 ♗g5 ♗e7 5 e5 ♘e4!? 6 ♘xe4 dxe4 7 ♗e3 c5 8 dxc5 ♘d7 9 ♕g4 ♕a5+ 10 c3 ♗xc5 where both sides have used an extra tempo with their bishops. Then 10 ♕xe4 ♗xe3 11 ♕xe3 ♕xe5 12 ♕xe5 ♘xe5 is again equal (A.Viaud-Ha.Olafsson, correspondence 1992-95), while 11 ♕xg7 ♖f8 12 ♗xc5 ♕xc5 13 0-0-0 ♕xe5 14 ♕h6 ♘f6 15 ♖d8+ ♔xd8 16 ♕xf8+ ♔c7 17 ♘h3 e3 18 ♗c4 rather than 18...b5? 19 ♕xf7+ ♗d7 20 f4! ♕e4 21 ♕xf6 bxc4 22 ♘g5 e2? 23 ♘xe4 1-0 Iordachescu-Popescu, Tusnad 1997, Black should have played 18...exf2 19 ♕xf7+ ♗d7 with an unclear position.

9 ♗b5+

9 ♗xc5 ♗xc5 is similar to the previous note, but even more promising for Black. If 10 ♕xg7 ♕a5+ 11 c3 ♖f8 12 ♘e2 the

missing ...♘d7 enables Black to develop more swiftly, with a dangerous attack after 12...♗d7 13 ♕xh7 ♗c6 14 ♕h4 ♖d8 or if 13 ♕f6 ♗c6 or 13...♗a4. If instead 10 ♕xe4 there is no bishop on e3 to take, but Black is again perfectly fine after 10...♕d4 or 10...♕b6!? (attacking f2) 11 0-0-0 ♗d7 12 ♘f3 ♗c6 13 ♕g4 0-0 14 ♗d3 ♗xf2 15 ♔b1 h6, as in Bologan-Rahman, Calcutta 1992.

9...♘d7!

A key retreat. Black is clearly worse after 9...♗d7 10 0-0-0 ♘d3+ 11 ♗xd3 exd3 12 ♖xd3 ♕a5 13 ♔b1 (Matulovic-Maksimovic, Nis 1977) and if 13...♕xe5 14 ♘f3 ♕a5 15 ♖hd1.

10 ♘e2 ♕a5+ 11 ♘c3

A critical position in the variation. Konca and Przewoznik write that 'Black has the pleasant choice between 11...a6 and 11...♗b4.' The latter looks very risky after 12 ♕xg7 ♗xc3+ 13 bxc3 ♖f8 14 ♗xd7+ ♗xd7 15 0-0 and if 15...♕xc3 (or 15...0-0-0 16 ♖ab1) 16 ♖ab1 0-0-0 (16...♗c6 17 ♖fd1) 17 ♗xa7 ♖g8 18 ♕xf7 ♖df8 19 ♕b3 (not 19 ♕e7 ♖xg2+!) 19...♕xe5 20 ♕e7.

11...a6! 12 ♗xd7+ ♗xd7 13 ♗d4

If 13 ♕xe4 ♗c6 14 ♕f4 Black plays 14...♗a3! 15 ♗c1 ♗xg2 16 ♖g1 ♗c6 17 ♖xg7 0-0-0 18 ♖g3 ♗c5 still with plenty of compensation in Tolnai-Samovojska, Makarska 1994, which continued 19 ♗e3 ♗a3 20 ♗c1 ♗c5 21 ♖d3 ♖hg8 22 ♖g3 ♗d4 23 ♕xd4 ♖xg3 24 ♕xd8+ ♔xd8 25 hxg3 ♕xe5+ 26 ♗e3 ♗f3 and Black won.

13...♗c6 14 0-0-0 0-0-0 15 ♔b1

Having defended a2, White is at last ready to capture on e4. Since this pawn cannot be defended it seems as if Black has finally come out worse. However, GM Malaniuk has found a way to rejuvenate Black's prospects.

15...♖xd4!

Black gets the two bishops and a strong kingside majority for the exchange.

16 ♖xd4 ♕xe5

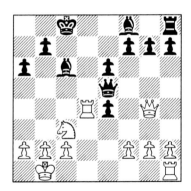

17 ♖hd1

A. Ivanov-Malaniuk, USSR 1981, saw 17 ♖c4!? f5 18 ♕e2 ♔c7 19 f3?!, when instead of 19...♗c5? 20 fxe4 b5 21 ♘d5+! ♔d6 22 ♖xc5 ♔xc5 23 ♕e3+ winning, Black should have played straightaway 19...b5! and White has to give back the exchange. Instead 19 ♕e3 offers White better prospects, or if 18...♗c5 19 f4! ♕d6 20 ♖d1 ♕e7 21 ♘a4 ♗a7 22 ♖xc6+ bxc6 23 ♕xa6+ ♕b7 24 ♕c4.

17...♗c5 18 ♖4d2

18 ♖c4 is worse now as the rook lacks squares after 18...f5 19 ♕e2 ♖d8 20 b4 ♖xd1+ 21 ♘xd1 ♖b6 22 a4 ♔b8 23 a5 ♗d8 24 ♕d2 ♗f6 25 c3 ♗d5 26 ♖c5 ♗e7 27 ♖xd5 exd5 28 ♘e3 ♗g5 29 ♕xd5 ♕xc3 30 ♘xf5 ♕c1+ 31 ♔a2 ♕c2+ 0-1 Kholmov-Malaniuk, USSR 1981.

Fritz's suggestion 18 ♖d5!? ♗xd5 19 ♖xd5 ♕c7 20 ♕xg7 ♖f8 21 ♖h5 also seems okay for Black after 21...f5! 22 ♕xc7+ ♔xc7 23 ♖xh7+ ♔c6 24 ♘d1 f4 etc.

18...h5

Konca and Przewoznik suggest that either 18...f5 or 18...♗b4 'gives Black excellent compensation for the exchange.' However, after 18...♗b4 White has the trick 19 f4! ♕f6 20 ♘d5! removing one of the bishops with advantage; White is also better after 19...h5 20 ♕g3 ♕f6 21 ♘xe4 ♗xe4 22 ♖d4 or 19...f5 20 ♕g3 ♕f6 21 ♖d4. The former is more acceptable since if 18...f5 19

♕g5 (or 19 ♕h4) 19...♔b8! answers the threat of 20 ♖d8+ (if necessary the king can hide on a7) and then Black can advance the kingside pawns.

With 18...h5 Black tries to improve on this further, with the idea 19 ♕h4 g5, so the white queen goes instead to the queenside.

19 ♕e2 f5 20 ♕c4 b5!?

The potential pin on the c-file is annoying to Black, so he breaks it with tempo and accelerates his initiative – albeit at the cost of weakening his queenside defences. It was also possible simply to remove the king from the c-file by 20...♔b8, and only then to advance the kingside pawns. 20...♔b8 also avoids a trick with 21 ♘d5!?, which would now lose to 21...♗xd5 22 ♕xc5? ♗xa2+, or if 21 ♘a4 e3! 22 fxe3 ♗xe3 23 ♖d6?! ♗d5! 24 ♕b4 ♔c7 traps the rook.

21 ♕b3 f4 22 ♖e1 e3 23 fxe3 fxe3 24 ♖de2 ♖f8?

Black intends to defend the e6-pawn from f6 and free his queen, but this is too slow, allowing White to start an attack with a2-a4. 24...♖d8! was better, controlling d3, so that if 25 a4? b4 26 ♘d1 ♗d5! 27 ♕d3 loses to 27...♗a2+, so White would have to play 27 ♖xe3 ♗xe3 (27...♕f4!?) 28 ♕xe3 ♕xe3 29 ♘xe3 ♗b7 with a level endgame. If White tries to prepare by 25 ♔a1 then 25...♖d6! parries by defending the rook, so that after 26 a4 b4 27 ♘d1 ♗d5 28 ♕d3? Black can play 28...♗xg2 and 29...♗f3 with advantage.

25 a4!

The e3-pawn is under control and White attacks the weakness created on move 20. If now 25...b4 26 ♘d1 ♗d5 does not do anything after 27 ♕d3.

25...♖f6 26 axb5 axb5 27 ♘xb5 ♕b8

27...♕xh2? loses a piece to 28 ♕c3 or 28 ♕c4.

28 c4 ♕xh2?!

Since the c-pawn closes off ♕c3 or ♕c4 Black is able to take on h2, but now White's attack is strong enough to win. Instead 28...♗xb5 29 cxb5 merely opens lines further. Relatively best was 28...♗e4+ 29 ♔a2 ♕a8+ (if 29...♗xg2 30 ♖xg2 ♕a8+ 31 ♘a7+! and White keeps the exchange) 30 ♘a3 ♕a5, but after 31 g3! and 32 ♖xe3 Black has no compensation for the pawn and should lose, if not so quickly.

29 ♕a4!

Threatening variously 30 ♘a7+ or 30 b4 or 30 ♖d1.

29...♗xg2 30 b4 ♗f8 31 ♖d1!

Shutting the door to the kingside and threatening 32 ♘a7+, e.g. 32...♔b7 33 ♕b5+ ♔xa7 34 ♖a2 mate.

31...♗e4+ 32 ♔c1 1-0

Game 75
Onischuk-Hertneck
Biel 1997

---

1 e4 e6 2 d4 d5 3 ♘d2 ♘f6 4 e5 ♘e4

One advantage of 4...♘e4 for Black is that it can also be played against the Tarrasch: 3 ♘d2 ♘f6 4 e5 ♘e4 when 5 ♘xe4 dxe4 is the same position as the Classical, thus cutting down on learning. Note however, that in the Tarrasch move order White can also play 5 ♗d3 with a slight advantage.

5 ♘xe4 dxe4 6 ♗c4

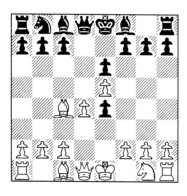

Rather than try to deter ...c7-c5 White makes ready for it, intending to answer

6...c5 with 7 d5!

6...c5!?

Black accepts the challenge. Otherwise 6...a6 is usual, intending ...b7-b5 (or if 7 a4 b6) and to defend the e4-pawn with ...♗b7.

White must not be too eager in this line. For instance, if 7 a4 b6 8 d5?! fails to 8...♗b7! 9 dxe6 ♕xd1+ 10 ♔xd1 fxe6 11 ♗xe6 ♘c6 12 ♗e3 ♘xe5 and Black was better in Imanaliev-Malaniuk, Frunze 1987.

If instead 8 ♘h3 (or 8 ♘e2) 8...♗b7 9 ♘f4, preparing to answer 9...c5 again with 10 d5, Black has found counterplay with the manoeuvre ...♘c6-e7-f5. Aseev-Lputian, USSR Championship 1984, continued 10 ♗e3 ♘e7 11 0-0 g6 12 ♕e2 ♘f5 13 ♖fd1 ♗h6 14 a5 0-0 with an unclear position.

Probably White should forget about d4-d5 and leave the knight on e2, with a slight advantage after 8 ♘e2 ♗b7 9 0-0 c5 10 c3 ♘c6 11 ♗e3 ♖c8 12 ♗b3 cxd4 13 cxd4. However, in this case it seems preferable not to play 7 a4 either, as this weakens the queenside slightly. White has done better supporting the centre by 7 ♘e2, planning c2-c3 and ♗e3, when the e4-pawn can be targeted by ♗c2, etc. White has also started with 7 c3 and 7 ♗b3 – the actual choice makes little difference.

After 7 ♘e2 b5 (or 7...c5 8 c3 ♘c6 9 ♗b3) 8 ♗b3 c5 9 c3 ♗b7 10 0-0 ♘c6 11 ♗e3 ♗e7 12 ♘g3 h5!? 13 ♘xh5 (13 ♗c2 is also good) 13...g6 was Korneev-Lima, Elgoibar 1997, and now 14 ♘g3 was simplest with a clear advantage after 14...cxd4 15 cxd4 ♘a5 16 ♗c2 ♘c4 17 ♗c1 ♖h4 18 ♖e1. In the earlier game Mortensen-Binham, Helsinki 1983, Black had tried 11...♕h4!? 12 f4 ♖d8 (better 12...exf3 13 ♖xf3 cxd4 14 cxd4 ♘a5 15 ♖f4 ♕d8) 13 ♕e1 ♕xe1 14 ♖axe1 cxd4 15 ♘xd4 ♘a5 16 ♗c2 ♘c4 17 ♗c1 e3 18 f5! (18 b3? ♘d2!) 18...exf5 19 b3 ♘xe5 (now if 19...♘d2 20 ♖xf5) 20 ♗xe3 ♗e4 21 ♗f4 f6 22 ♗xe4 fxe4 23 ♖xe4 ♖d5 24 ♖fe1 ♗d6 25 ♘f3 and White regained the extra pawn.

Exchanging dark-squared bishops does not help Black: 9...cxd4 10 cxd4 ♗b4+ 11 ♗d2 ♗xd2+ 12 ♕xd2 ♗b7 13 ♘c2 f5 14 exf6 gxf6 15 0-0 ♘d7 16 ♘f4 ♘f8 (or 16...♕e7 17 d5) 17 ♕e3 f5 18 f3 exf3 (Kuporosov-Przewoznik, Karvina 1992) with a clear advantage after 19 ♗xf5! ♕g5 20 ♗xe6.

In general Black is slightly worse after 6...a6, being unable to drum up sufficient counterplay to compensate for the weakness on e4.

7 d5!

If now 7...exd5?! 8 ♕xd5 ♕xd5 9 ♗xd5 ♘c6 (or 9...♘d7 10 ♗f4 f5 11 f3!) 10 ♗xe4 ♘xe5 11 ♗f4 ♘c6 12 ♘f3 and White has a useful lead in development.

7...♕b6!?

This was a novelty; theory had concentrated on 7...♘d7 8 dxe6 fxe6

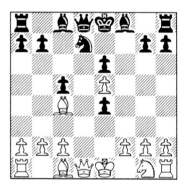

when Black's ideas are seen after 9 ♗xe6 ♕e7! 10 ♗xd7+ ♗xd7 11 f4 0-0-0 12 ♕e2 g5! 13 ♕xe4 ♖g8 14 ♕e2 gxf4 15 ♗xf4 ♗h6 16 ♗xh6 ♕h4+ 17 ♕f2 ♕xh6 18 ♘f3 ♗b5 19 a4? (but if 19 ♕xc5+ ♔b8 20 ♕xb5? ♖xg2, or 20 ♖g1 ♖d5!, or 20 ♖d1 ♖xd1+ 21 ♔xd1 ♖d8+ 22 ♔e1 ♖d5! is strong) 19...♖xg2 20 ♕xc5+ ♗c6 21 ♖d1 ♖xd1+ 22 ♔xd1 ♔b8 0-1 Rüfenacht-Konca, correspondence 1986-87.

White's play has since been improved: in particular 9 ♘h3! (intending ♘g5) 9...♘xe5 (9...♕c7 10 ♗f4) 10 ♕h5+ ♘f7 (if 10...♘g6

11 ♘g5 ♕f6 12 ♗b5+) 11 ♘g5 g6 12 ♕g4! with a clear advantage to White in all lines:

a) 12...♘xg5 13 ♗xg5 ♕d4? 14 ♗b5+! ♔f7 15 ♕f4+ ♔g8 16 ♗e8! wins.

b) 12...♘e5 13 ♗b5+ ♔e7 (13...♗d7 14 ♕xe6+) 14 ♕h4! ♕a5+ 15 ♗d2 ♕xb5 16 ♗c3 ♗g7 17 ♘xe4+ ♔f8 18 0-0-0 ♘f7 19 ♗xg7+ ♔xg7 20 ♕f6+ ♔g8 21 ♘g5 1-0 Kindermann-Dobosz, Bern 1995.

c) 12...h5 13 ♗b5+ ♔e7 14 ♕f4 ♘d6 15 ♕e5 (or 15 ♘xf7! ♔xf7? 16 ♕h4+) 15...♗h6 16 ♘xe4 ♘xe4 17 ♗xh6 1-0 Dvoirys-Florath, Berlin 1996.

d) 12...♗g7 13 ♗xe6 ♘e5 (if 13...0-0 14 ♕h3) 14 ♕xe4 ♕e7 15 ♗xc8 ♖xc8 16 0-0 0-0 17 ♗f4 and White was a pawn up for nothing in Kveinys-Crouch, Katowice 1992.

9 ♗f4 is also good for White, as is 9 f4 (for which see the note to Black's 8th below).

8 c3

Preventing 8...♕b4+. White can also play 8 ♕e2 and if 8...exd5 9 ♗xd5 ♗f5 10 ♕c4.

8...♘d7

Black is playing a 7...♘d7 variation with the extra moves c2-c3 and ...♕b6. This would appear to favour him, since if 9 dxe6 fxe6 10 ♘h3 ♘xe5 11 ♕h5+ ♘f7 12 ♘g5 g6 13 ♕g4 then 13...♘xg5! 14 ♗xg5 ♗g7 defends. 10 ♗xe6 is not possible since the queen defends the pawn, while if 10 ♗f4 Black can capture 10...♕xb2.

In turn 10 ♕a4!? makes use of White's extra move, e.g. 10...♗e7 (or 10...g6 11 ♘h3 ♗g7 12 ♘g5) 11 ♗b3! 0-0 (11...♕c7 12 ♗f4) 12 ♕xe4 with advantage, and if 12...c4!? 13 ♗e3 (not 13 ♗xc4? ♕xf2+) 13...♗c5 14 ♗c2 g6 15 0-0-0.

Alternatively if 9...♘xe5 10 exf7+♘xf7, as 11 ♗xf7+ no longer wins the queen, 11 ♕a4+! ♔e7 12 ♗d5 is good for White.

9 f4

In the line 7...♘d7 8 fxe6 dxe6 9 f4 Black answers 9...exf3 10 ♘xf3 ♘b6!, though White is still better after 11 ♕xd8+ ♔xd8 12 ♗d3 c4 13 ♗e4 ♔c7 14 ♘g5 ♗c5

(Kunsztowicz-Konca, correspondence 1983) and now 15 ♖f1! intending ♖f7. In the current game Black cannot play this way since his queen is on b6.

9...exd5?!

Black should probably play 9...exf3 in any case, though after 10 ♘xf3 exd5 11 ♕xd5 ♕e6 White is better following either 12 ♕xe6+ fxe6 13 0-0 ♘b6 14 ♗d3 or 12 ♗f4! ♕xd5 13 ♗xd5 ♘b6 14 ♗e4.

10 ♕xd5 ♕g6 11 ♘e2!

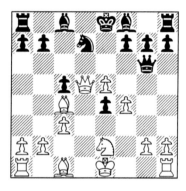

The knight heads to g3 to attack the e4-pawn.

11...♗e7

Black has nothing better. 11...♕xg2 is unplayable due to 12 ♕xf7+ ♔d8 13 ♖g1 ♕xh2 14 ♗e3 and Black cannot hope to survive after 15 0-0-0. If 11...♘b6 12 ♗b5+ ♗d7 13 ♗xd7+ ♘xd7 14 ♘g3 and the e4-pawn drops. 11...a6 12 ♘g3? ♘b6 works for Black, but 12 0-0! ♘b6 13 f5! wins.

12 ♘g3

12 0-0 is also strong, when both 12...0-0 and 12...♘b6 are answered by 13 f5!

12...♗h4

If 12...f5 then either 13 exf6 ♘xf6 14 ♕e5 or 13 ♗b5 a6 14 ♗a4 ♖a7 15 e6 b5 16 ♗c2 ♘b8 17 ♕xf5 is good for White.

13 0-0 ♗xg3 14 hxg3 0-0 15 f5 ♕xg3?

Losing quickly, but 15...♕c6 16 e6 ♕xd5 17 ♗xd5 ♘f6 18 exf7+ ♔h8 19 ♗e6 b6 20 ♗f4 offers little hope for Black in the long run.

16 ♗f4 ♕g4 17 e6!

If 17...♘b6 18 exf7+ ♔h8 19 ♕xc5 ♗xf5 20 ♗d6 wins easily. Instead Black allows the pretty finish:

17...fxe6 18 fxe6 ♘b6 19 e7+! ♘xd5 20 exf8♕+ ♔xf8 21 ♗d6+ ♔e8 22 ♗b5+ ♗d7 23 ♖f8 mate 1-0

Game 76
Carleton-Ha.Olafsson
correspondence 1992-95

1 e4 e6 2 d4 d5 3 ♘c3 ♘f6 4 ♗g5 ♗e7

Not even Alekhine could make 4...h6?! work after 5 ♗xf6 ♕xf6 (5...gxf6 6 exd5 exd5 leaves terrible a terrible structure) 6 exd5 ♗b4 7 ♗b5+ c6 8 dxc6 ♘xc6 (or 8...bxc6 9 ♗c4) 9 ♘ge2 0-0 10 0-0 with a clear extra pawn in Capablanca-Alekhine, St Petersburg 1914.

5 e5

White has a few lesser lines to dispose of:

a) 5 ♗d3?! drops a pawn after either 5...♘xe4 6 ♗xe7 ♘xc3 or 5...dxe4 6 ♘xe4 ♘xe4 7 ♗xe7 ♕xe7 8 ♗xe4 ♕b4+ and 9...♕xb2 (Gunsberg-Noa, Hamburg 1885).

b) 5 exd5 exd5 is covered in Game 78 below, unless Black wants to try 5...♘xd5!? 6 ♗xe7 ♕xe7, e.g. 7 ♕d2 ♕b4 8 ♘xd5 ♕xd2+ 9 ♔xd2 exd5 10 ♖e1+ ♔f8 11 ♗d3 ♘c6 12 c3 ♗d7 13 ♘f3 (or 13 ♘e2 ♖e8) 13...f6 14 ♗e3 ♖e8 15 ♖he1 ♖xe3 16 ♖xe3 ♔f7 17 ♗b5 ♖e8 ½-½ Kmoch-Spielmann, Budapest 1928.

c) 5 ♗xf6 is the only significant other, but Black is fine after 5...♗xf6 and then: 6 e5 ♗e7 7 ♕g4 0-0 8 0-0-0 (or 8 ♗d3 c5 9 dxc5 ♘c6 10 f4 f5) 8...c5 9 dxc5 ♘d7 10 ♘f3 ♘xc5 11 h4 f5 12 ♕g3 ♗d7 13 ♘g5 ♖c8 14 f4 ♕c7 15 ♖xd5? ♘e4 16 ♖xd7 ♘xg3 17 ♖xc7 ♖xc7 18 ♘b5 ♖xg5 19 hxg5 ♖c5 0-1 Kenworthy-Baker, 4NCL 1999. Or if 6 ♘f3 c5! 7 exd5 exd5 8 ♗b5+ ♘c6 9 0-0 0-0 10 dxc5 ♕a5 11 ♖b1 ♗xc3 12 bxc3 ♕xc3 13 ♕xd5 ♗e6 14 ♕d3 ♕xc5 15 ♗xc6 bxc6 16 ♖b2 ♖fb8 17 ♖fb1 ♖b6 with a slight advantage to Black in Matkovic-Dizdar, Solin 1994.

5...♘e4!?

Tartakower was fond of this move, which he used with success (a draw) against Capablanca and Marshall, and it sometimes bears his name.

6 ♗xe7

6 ♘xe4 dxe4 7 ♗xe7 ♕xe7 is another route to the game, but both sides have a chance to deviate. White can try 7 ♗e3!? when 7...c5 8 dxc6 ♘d7 9 ♕g4 ♕a5+ 10 c3 ♗xc5 transposes to 4 e5 ♘e4 5 ♘xe4 dxe4 6 ♗e3 c5 7 dxc5 ♘d7 8 ♕g4 ♕a5+ 9 c3 ♗xc5 as seen in Game 74 (note to 8...♘xc5); or if 8...♕c7 9 ♕d4!

For his part Black has 6...♗xg5 6...♗xg5 7 ♘xg5 ♕xg5 8 ♘f3 ♕e7 with a fairly level position after 9 c3 c5 10 dxc5 ♕xc5 11 ♗d3 ♗d7 12 ♕e2 ♘c6 13 0-0 0-0 14 ♖ad1 f5 15 exf6 ♖xf6 16 ♘e5 ♘xe5 17 ♕xe5 ½-½ Ivkov-Geller, Leningrad 1957.

6...♕xe7

If 6...♘xc3!? White has no need to enter the complications after 7 ♕g4!? ♕xe7 8 ♕xg7 ♕b4 9 ♕xh8+ ♔d7, e.g. 10 ♖d1 ♕xb2!? 11 ♕xh7 ♘xd1 12 ♕xf7+ ♔c6 13 ♔xd1 ♕b1+ 14 ♔e2 ♕b5+ etc., but can play for a slight advantage by 7 ♗xd8! ♘xd1 8 ♗xc7 ♘xb2 9 ♖b1 ♘c4 10 ♗xc4 dxc4 11 ♘f3 ♘c6 12 ♗d6 b6. In Spassky-R.Byrne, Moscow 1975, Black was slowly ground down after 13 ♔d2 ♗b7 14 ♔c3 ♖c8 15

♘d2 f5 16 f3 ♔f7 17 g4, although Black should not necessarily expect to lose.

7 ♘xe4 dxe4 8 ♕e2

The alternative 8 c3 has long been disregarded because of Capablanca-Tartakower, Budapest 1929, which continued 8...0-0 9 ♕g4 f5! 10 exf6 ♕xf6 11 0-0-0 ♕h6+ 12 ♔b1 e5 when White had to work for a draw. If instead 9 ♕e2 f5 10 f3 b6! 11 0-0-0 ♗b7 12 h4?! c5! and Black seized the initiative in Golmayo-Tartakower, Barcelona 1929.

8...b6

After 9 0-0-0 White will be ready to take on e4 so Black hurries to defend the pawn. 8...♗d7 9 0-0-0 ♗c6 is less good since after 10 g3 Black lacks counterplay with the c-pawn and hence must play 10...♘d7 11 ♗g2 f5 12 exf6 ♘xf6 with a poor structure.

9 0-0-0 ♗b7 10 g3 c5 11 ♗g2 ♘c6 12 dxc5 ♕g5+

In Tseshkovsky-Lputian, Kropotkin 1995, Black tried 12...0-0!? 13 ♗xe4 (not 13 ♕xe4? ♘a5) 13...♘xe5 14 f4 ♗xe4 15 ♕xe4 ♘g4 16 ♕f3 ♘f6 17 c6!? (or 17 cxb6 axb6 18 ♔b1 b5 19 ♘e2 ♘d5 20 ♘d4 intending f4-f5) 17...♖ac8 18 ♘e2 ♕c5 19 ♘d4 ♘d5 20 ♖he1 ♖fd8 (20...♘b4!) 21 f5 exf5 22 ♖e5 g6 23 ♘xf5 ♕xc6 24 c3 gxf5 25 ♖exd5 and White was clearly better.

13 ♔b1 ♕xe5 14 ♗xe4 ♕xc5 15 ♘f3

This was given as good for White by Keres, although it is not clear that White has much after 15...♖d8!, e.g. 16 ♖xd8+ ♘xd8 17 ♗xb7 ♘xb7 or 16 ♗xc6+ ♗xc6 17 ♖xd8+ ♔xd8 18 ♖d1+ ♔e7 19 ♘e5 ♖c8 20 ♘xc6+ ♕xc6 21 ♕d3 h6 ½-½ Pavicic-Samovojska, Caorle 1982.

Olafsson, however, had a more interesting idea:

15...♖b8!?

Black prepares kingside castling. If immediately 15...0-0 White plays 16 ♖d7 ♖ab8 17 ♖hd1. By defending the bishop in advance Black prepares 16...0-0 so that if 17 ♖d7 f5! 18 ♗xc6 ♕xc6 forks rook and knight.

16 ♕d3!

The critical response. White prevents 16...0-0 by attacking h7 and also threatens 17 ♕d7+.

16...♖d8!?

The only way to justify his previous move, even though it allows White to gain a material advantage of rook, bishop and knight for the queen.

17 ♗xc6+! ♔e7 18 ♗xb7

Better than 18 ♕xd8+ ♖xd8 19 ♗xb7 ♕xf2.

18...♖xd3 19 ♖xd3 ♖b8

Now if 19...♕xf2? 20 ♖hd1 Black has no initiative and no useful square for his rook.

20 ♗a6

Not 20 ♗e4? f5 21 ♖c3 ♕xf2 22 ♘e5 fxe4! 23 ♘c6+ ♔f6 24 ♘xb8 e3 and the e-pawn will cost White a rook.

20...b5

This is the point of Black's play – he hopes to trap the bishop. If now 21 ♖hd1 ♕c6! 22 ♖d7+ ♔e8 (not 22...♔f6? 23 ♖xf7+! and 24 ♘e5+) or 22 ♖a3 ♖d8 23 ♖xd8 ♔xd8 (threatening ...b4) 24 b4 ♕c4 creates difficulties.

21 ♘d4!

Now if 21...♖b6 22 ♗xb5! ♖xb5 23 ♘xb5 ♕xb5 24 ♖hd1 and the rooks together with the passed c-pawn will win the game for White. Faced with this it seems that Black's imaginative opening is

unsound and all he can do is try to create problems for White.

21...e5!? 22 ♘f5+ ♔f6 23 ♘e3 ♕c6 24 ♖hd1 ♔e6 25 ♘d5 ♕c5 26 f4

26 ♖1d2 threatening 27 ♖c3 ♕f8 28 ♖c7 seems fairly decisive.

26...exf4 27 ♘xf4+ ♔e7 28 a3 ♔f8 29 ♖d5 ♕c6 30 ♖d6 ♕c5 31 b4 ♕f2 32 ♖1d2

Here 32 ♘d3 also looks good, e.g. 32...♕xh2 33 ♘c5 or 32...♕e3 33 ♗xb5! ♖xb5 34 ♖e1 or 32...♕f3 33 ♘e5.

32...♕e1+ 33 ♔a2 g6 34 ♖6d5 ♖b6 35 ♖e2 ♕c3 36 ♖c5 ♕d4 37 c3 ♕d7 38 ♗c8 ♕d1 39 ♗g4 ♔g7 40 c4!?

Was this deep calculation or simply a loss of patience? By clearing the queenside White may win, but it seems a little premature.

40...bxc4 41 ♖xc4 a5 42 ♖e5 ♕d2+

Not 42...♕xg4? 43 ♘h5+! and White liquidates to a trivial rook endgame.

43 ♔b3 axb4 44 axb4 ♕xh2 45 ♘e2 ♕h1 46 ♘c3 ♕g1 47 ♗e2 ♕xg3 48 ♖e7 ♕d6 49 ♖a7 ♕e6 50 ♗g4 ♕e3 51 ♖d7 ♖f6 52 b5

Having surrounded his king with bodyguards, White now manages to advance his pawn.

52...h5 53 ♗e2 ♖f2 54 ♖e4 ♕h3 55 ♖d3 ♕f5 56 ♖d5 ♕c8 57 b6

And again.

57...♕b7 58 ♖b5 ♖f6 59 ♖e7! ♕xe7 60 b7 ♕d8

Or 60...♖e6 61 b8♕ ♖xe2 62 ♘xe2 ♕xe2 63 ♕e5+! ♕xe5 64 ♖xe5 and the rook wins against the pawns as the white king comes hurrying across.

61 b8♕ ♕xb8 62 ♖xb8

Now with two pieces against the pawns White brings his king over and consolidates to victory.

62...♖f2 63 ♔c4 h4 64 ♔d3 f5 65 ♔e3 ♖h2 66 ♘d5 ♖h1 67 ♖b7+ ♔h6 68 ♔f4 ♖a1 69 ♘e7 ♖a4+ 70 ♔f3 h3 71 ♖b6 ♔g7 72 ♖b7 ♔f6 73 ♘d5+ ♔e5 74 ♘b4

g5 75 ♔g3 g4 76 ♘d3+ ♔f6 77 ♘f4
♖e4 78 ♖b6+ ♔f7 79 ♖c6 ♖e5 80
♗c4+ ♔g7 81 ♗d5 ♖e1 82 ♘h5+ ♔h7
83 ♔f4 ♖d1 84 ♔g5 1-0

Game 77
Pfrommer-M.Heidenfeld
German Bundesliga 1992

**1 e4 e6 2 d4 d5 3 ♘c3 ♘f6 4 ♗g5 ♗e7
5 e5 ♘g8!?**

The French is full of such strange
manoeuvres. The closed nature of many
French positions enables both sides to
indulge in esoteric moves for no other
reason, it seems, than because they can.
Then comes the enjoyable attempt to prove
the moves viable – and for 5...♘g8!? this
was the work of Wolfgang Heidenfeld, and
hence the variation now bears his name.

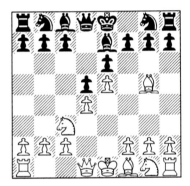

6 ♗e3

White retreats the bishop to its most
natural square and deters ...c7-c5. Playing in
Albin-Chatard style by 6 h4 is less good,
since after 6...♗xg5 7 hxg5 ♕xg5, the black
knight is usefully placed on g8, preventing
White's ♖h6 in the event of ...g7-g6, e.g. 8
♘h3 ♕e7 9 ♕g4 f5 (not 9...g6? 10 ♘xd5)
10 ♕g3 ♘d7 11 ♘f4 ♘f8 12 0-0-0 c6 13
♘a4 ½-½ Spassky-Bischoff, German Bundesliga 1988.

6 ♗xe7 ♘xe7 7 f4 creates a pseudo-
Classical (5...♘fd7 6 ♗xe7 ♕xe7) position

with ♘e7/♕d8 as opposed to ♘d7/♕e7.
Theoretically White might therefore claim
an advantage, but in practice Black has had
few problems, e.g. 7...b6 8 ♘f3 ♕d7 9 ♕d2
♗a6 10 ♗xa6 ♘xa6 11 0-0-0 0-0-0 12 ♕e2
♘b4 13 ♔b1 ♗b7 14 g4 ♖c8 15 ♖hf1 g6 16
♘g5 h6 17 ♘f3 a6 18 ♖d2 ♔a7 19 a3 ♘bc6
20 ♘d1 ♘a5 21 ♘e3 c5 with mutual
chances (Walsh-M.Heidenfeld, Irish
Championship 2000) or 11 0-0 c5 12 ♘e2
♘c7 13 c3 a5 14 ♖ab1 0-0 15 ♔h1 f5 16
♖g1 c4 17 h3 b5 18 a3 ♖fb8 19 g4 b4 with
advantage to Black (Moutousis-Gonzales,
Novi Sad Olympiad 1990).

6...b6

Having invested some time encouraging
White to play e4-e5, Black trusts to the
closed centre for protection while carrying
out the positionally desirable exchange of
light-squared bishops with ...♗a6. This is
more akin to the Modern Winawer (3...♗b4
4 e5 b6) than the Classical, and is a
favourable version for White. Compared
with 3...♗b4 4 e5 b6 5 a3 ♗f8, in the
Heidenfeld 6 ♗e3 is clearly more useful for
White than a2-a3, while Black's extra move
...♗e7 is rather unhelpful as it obstructs the
knight from emerging at e7.

7 h4

With 7 h4 White threatens 8 ♕g4 g6 9
h5! with a clear advantage, or similarly after
7...♗a6 8 ♗xa6 ♘xa6 9 ♕g4 g6 10 h5.
Therefore Black has generally felt obliged to
play 7...h5 (as in the game). However, in
Campora-J.Gonzales, Seville 1990, Black
ignored the threat, playing instead 7...♕d7!?
8 h5 ♗a6 9 ♕g4 ♗f8! when the game took
the form of a Modern Winawer: 10 ♘ge2
♘c6 11 g3 ♘a5 12 ♘c1 ♗xf1 13 ♔xf1
0-0-0 14 ♘d3 ♔b8 15 ♖h3 ♖c8 16 ♔g1
♘e7 17 ♘e2 ♘f5 18 ♗d2 ♘c4 and Black
was fine.

7...h5 8 ♗e2

With ♕d1-g4 forestalled White instead
targets the h-pawn to encourage another
weakness. Again Black has to oblige with

8...g6, since if 8...♗a6 9 ♗xh5 g6 10 ♗g4 (or 10 ♗e2) 10...♖xh4 11 ♖xh4 ♗xh4 12 ♘f3 and White gets first to the h-file following ♕d2, 0-0-0 and ♖h1.

The brutal approach 8 g4 does not achieve much, unless Black falls for 8...g6 9 gxh5 ♖xh5 10 ♘f3 ♗xh4?? 11 ♖xh4 ♖xh4 12 ♗g5 1-0 Velimirovic-Ree, Amsterdam 1994. Of course 10...♗a6 is perfectly okay.

8...g6 9 ♕d2 ♗a6 10 ♗xa6

Mostly White has allowed Black to exchange the bishops on e2, playing 10 ♘f3 ♗xe2 11 ♘xe2 ♘c6, when the critical line is 12 ♘g5! ♕d7 13 f3 intending g2-g4. Haubt-Engel, German Bundesliga 1987, continued 13...0-0-0?! (not 13...♘h6? 14 ♘xe6!) 14 ♘xf7 ♗xh4+ 15 ♖xh4 ♕xf7 16 ♗g5 ♖f8 17 0-0-0 ♘ce7 18 ♔b1 ♘f5 19 ♖h3 ♖h7 20 ♖dh1 c5? 21 dxc5 bxc5 22 g4 and White won.

10...♗xa6 11 ♘f3 ♕d7 12 0-0 ♔f8

The point of this side-step is to move on ...♔g7 and enable the knight to be developed at h6. Another idea might be to re-route the queen's knight as in the Winawer by 12...♘b8!? intending ...♘c6-a5.

13 ♘e2 ♔g7 14 ♖ac1 ♘h6 15 ♘g3

15...c5?

Opening the position only assists White, who is more ready to make use of the open files. 15...c6 16 c4 ♘c7 would have been more stubborn, or else 15...♘g4 freeing the king's rook from the knight's defence.

16 c4! dxc4 17 ♖xc4 ♖ac8 18 ♗g5 ♗xg5 19 ♕xg5

Threatening 20 ♘xh5+, so the ...♘h6 has to retreat again.

19...♘g8 20 ♘e4 ♖c7 21 ♖fc1 cxd4 22 ♖xd4

White gets pressure down the d-file. 22 ♘f6! is also very strong: if 22...♕c8? 23 ♖xc7 ♘xc7 24 ♖xc7 ♕xc7 25 ♘e8+ wins, so Black has to capture 22...♘xf6 23 exf6+ and after 23...♔f8 (if 23...♔g8 24 ♘e5 and ♘xg6) 24 ♖xd4 ♕e8 (or 24...♖xc1+ 25 ♕xc1 ♕e8 26 ♕d1 and 27 ♖d8) 25 ♖cd1 ♖c8 26 ♖d7 White wins by 27 ♖e7, ♖xf7+ etc.

22...♖xc1+ 23 ♕xc1 ♕e7 24 ♕d2 ♘b8

24...♘c5 25 ♘xc5 ♕xc5 offers little hope either after 26 b4 followed by ♕f4.

25 ♖d8 ♘c6 26 ♖d7 ♕e8 27 ♘d6

Winning the queen, but the crowd might have liked 27 ♘fg5! creating a pretty mate after 27...♘h6 28 ♘f6 ♕c8 29 ♘xe6, while if 27...♘ge7 28 ♕f4 or 27...♘xe5 28 ♖xa7 intending ♕f4 wins.

27...♕xd7 28 ♘f5+ gxf5 29 ♕xd7 ♘ge7 30 ♕d2 ♘g6 31 ♕g5 ♖d8 32 ♕xh5 ♖d1+ 33 ♔h2 ♖d5 34 ♕g5

Black can put up no resistance to the advancing h-pawn.

34...♔f8 35 h5 ♘gxe5 36 h6 ♘g4+ 37 ♔g3 ♘e7 38 h7 ♘g6 39 ♕xg6 1-0

Game 78
Mueller-Luther
German Championship 1998

1 e4 e6 2 d4 d5 3 ♘c3 ♘f6 4 ♗d3

An old-fashioned and harmless variation which Lasker used on occasion.

4 exd5 is similarly tame – 4...exd5! is just equal, e.g. 5 ♗f4 (5 ♗g5 ♗e7 6 ♗d3 ♘c6 7 ♘ge2 ♘b4 8 ♘g3 ♘e4 9 ♗xe7 ♘xc3 10 ♗xd8 ♘xd1 11 ♖xd1 ♔xd8 and was soon drawn, Short-Morozevich, Sarajevo 2000) 5...♗e7 6 ♗d3 0-0 7 ♕f3 ♘c6 8 ♘ge2 ♘b4 9 h3 ♘xd3+ 10 ♕xd3 ♘h5, again soon

draw, Landa-Morozevich, Tomsk 1998
4...c5

4...♗b4 is not good due to 5 e5 ♘e4 6 ♕g4 (Schlechter) and if 6...♘xc3 7 ♕xg7 ♖f8 8 a3 ♗a5 9 ♗d2 with a decisive advantage.

5 exd5

Returning to a tedious Exchange variation. Instead 5 ♘f3 cxd4! (5...♘c6 6 exd5 ♘xd5 is the note to Black's 6th) 6 ♘xd4 ♘c6 7 ♗b5 ♗d7 8 exd5 exd5 9 0-0 ♗e7 10 ♗e3 0-0 11 ♘b3 a6 12 ♗xc6 bxc6 13 ♗c5 ♖e8 was equal in Lasker-Bogolyubov, Zurich 1934.

5...♘xd5!?

Black feels like fighting. This time 5...exd5 is not so dull, since after 6 dxc5 ♗xc5 7 ♘f3 0-0 8 0-0 h6 the isolated queen's pawn livens things up a bit – enough for Black to outplay his opponent in Sayber-Kacheishvili, Istanbul Olympiad 2000: 9 h3 ♘c6 10 ♗f4 ♗e6 11 a3 ♘h5 12 ♗h2 ♕f6 13 ♘a4 ♗e7 14 b4 ♘f4 15 ♘c5 a5, though the position is still objectively equal.

6 ♘f3 cxd4 7 ♗b5+

White initiates more exchanges and apparently is happy to make a draw.

If 7 ♘b5 ♘c6 8 ♘bxd4 ♘xd4 9 ♘xd4 ♘b4 (or 9...♗b4+) 10 0-0 ♘xd3 11 ♕xd3 ♗e7 12 ♗f4 0-0 and Black was fine in Ljubojevic-Bednarski, Bath 1973.

7...♗d7 8 ♗xd7+ ♘xd7 9 ♘xd5 ♕a5+ 10 c3 ♕xd5 11 ♕xd4 ♕xd4 12 ♘xd4

With an extremely equal position. Black, however, wants to play on.

12...♗c5 13 ♘b3 ♗b6 14 ♗f4 0-0-0 15 ♔e2 e5 16 ♗g3 h5 17 ♗h4 f6 18 f3 g5 19 ♗f2 ♗xf2 20 ♔xf2 ♘b6 21 ♖he1 ♘c4

Black has managed to achieve a little: his knight is more active and he controls the d-file and has gained some space with his kingside majority.

22 ♖e2 ♖d5 23 ♖b1 h4 24 h3 ♖hd8 25 ♖be1 ♖b5 26 ♖b1 ♔c7

Better was 26...f5 to take control of e4 and prevent White's next.

27 ♖e4

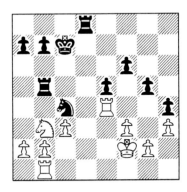

27...♘d2?!

Black decides to pack it in. He had the better knight so exchanging must be incorrect. Better 27...♘d6 intending ...♘f5 to gaze at new outposts on the kingside, or similarly if 28 ♖a4 ♘c8 (not 28...a6? 29 c4) planning ...♖bd5, ...a7-a6 and ...♘e7-g6.

28 ♘xd2 ♖xd2+ 29 ♖e2 ♖d7 30 ♔e3 ♖bd5 31 ♔e4 ♔d8 32 ♖be1

White does not need to contest the d-file since Black can do nothing with it.

32...♔e7 33 ♔f5 ♔f7 34 ♖e4 ♖d2 35 ♖1e2 ♖d1 36 ♖f2 ♖1d5 37 ♖fe2 ♖5d6 38 ♖c4 ♖d5 39 ♖ce4 ♖d1 40 ♖f2 ♖c7 41 ♖b4 ♖d5 42 ♖e2 ♖e7

Black threatens mate by 43...e4+ 44 ♔g4 ♔g6 45 fxe4 ♖d3 and ...♖g3.

43 ♖be4 ♖ed7 ½-½

Since 44 ♖e1 returns to the position at move 34.

Summary

None of the variations in this chapter is as reliable as the main lines. On the other hand, none requires as much study as the main lines. If a surprise system is desired for one, two or ten games, this chapter is the place to look. For White, 4 e5 ♘fd7 5 ♘f3 seems to score well for its regular practitioners, for no apparent reason since Black equalises fairly easily with 8...f6! For Black, 4 e5 ♘e4 offers the best winning chances, albeit at greater risk; it has an added advantage in being equally applicable against 3 ♘d2. The other lines 4 ♗g5 ♗e7 5 e5 ♘e4 and 5...♘g8 are unlikely to reap more than a draw at best.

1 e4 e6 2 d4 d5 3 ♘c3 ♘f6 *(D)*

4 e5

> 4 ♗g5 ♗e7 5 e5
>> 5...♘e4 – *Game 76*; 5...♘g8 – *Game 77*
> 4 ♗d3 – *Game 78*

4...♘fd7

> 4...♘e4 5 ♘xe4 dxe4 *(D)*
>> 6 ♗e3 – *Game 74*; 6 ♗c4 – *Game 75*

5 ♘f3 c5 6 dxc5 ♘c6 7 ♗f4 ♗xc5 8 ♗d3 *(D)* **8...h6**

> 8...f6 – *Game 73*

9 ♗g3 – *Game 72*

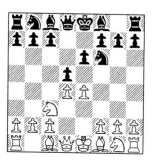 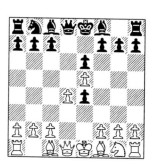 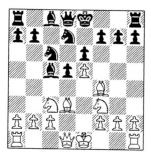

3...♘f6   *5...dxe4*   *8 ♗d3*

INDEX OF COMPLETE GAMES